BEING JEWISH AND DOII

Parkes-Wiener Series on Jewish Studies
Series Editors: David Cesarani and Tony Kushner
ISSN 1368-5449

The field of Jewish Studies is one of the youngest, but fastest growing and most exciting areas of scholarship in the academic world today. Named after James Parkes and Alfred Wiener, this series aims to publish new research in the field and student materials for use in the seminar room, to disseminate the latest work of established scholars and to re-issue classic studies which are currently out of print.

The selection of publications reflects the international character and diversity of Jewish Studies; it ranges over Jewish history from Abraham to modern Zionism, and Jewish culture from Moses to post-modernism. The series also reflects the inter-disciplinary approach inherent in Jewish Studies and at the cutting edge of contemporary scholarship, and provides an outlet for innovative work on the interface between Judaism and ethnicity, popular culture, gender, class, space and memory.

Other Books in the Series include

Holocaust Literature: Schulz, Levi, Spiegelman and the Memory of Offence
Gillian Banner

Remembering Cable Street: Fascism and Anti-Fascism in British Society
Edited by Tony Kushner and Nadia Valman

Sir Sidney Hamburger and Manchester Jewry: Religion, City and Community
Bill Williams

Anglo-Jewry in Changing Times: Studies in Diversity 1840–1914
Israel Finestein

Double Jeopardy: Gender and the Holocaust
Judith Tyler Baumel

Cultures of Ambivalence and Contempt: Studies in Jewish–Non-Jewish Relations
Edited by Sian Jones, Tony Kushner and Sarah Pearce

Alfred Wiener and the Making of the Wiener Library
Ben Barkow

The Berlin Haskalah and German Religious Thought: Orphans of Knowledge
David Sorkin

Myths in Israeli Culture: Captives of a Dream
Nurith Gertz

The Jewish Immigrant in England 1870–1914, Third Edition
Lloyd P. Gartner

State and Society in Roman Galilee, A.D. 132–212, Second Edition
Martin Goodman

Disraeli's Jewishness
Edited by Todd M. Endelman and Tony Kushner

Claude Montefiore: His Life and Thought
Daniel R. Langton

Port Jews: Jewish Communities in Cosmopolitan Maritime Trading Centres, 1550–1950
Edited by David Cesarani

Being Jewish and Doing Justice

Bringing Argument to Life

BRIAN KLUG

VALLENTINE MITCHELL
LONDON • PORTLAND, OR

First published in 2011 by Vallentine Mitchell

Middlesex House,	920 NE 58th Avenue, Suite 300
29/45 High Street, Edgware,	Portland, Oregon,
Middlesex HA8 7UU, UK	97213-3786 USA

www.vmbooks.com

British Library Cataloguing in Publication Data
An entry can be found on request

ISBN 978 0 85303 973 0 (cloth)
ISBN 978 0 85303 993 8 (paper)

Library of Congress Cataloging-in-Publication Data
An entry can be found on request

Printed by Good News Digital Books, Ongar, Essex

For Reva, my companion,

and for Den,

whose companionship I miss.

If morality has meaning, as Kant pointed out, it must be universal; concern for another must be concern for all others.

Rabbi (Dayan) Berel Berkovits (Orthodox), 1949–2005

Almost every national liberation movement in Europe, America and Africa has invoked the Exodus, drawn inspiration from it, and used its slogans, as in the spiritual, 'Let My people go'.

Rabbi Dr John D. Rayner (Liberal), 1924–2005

What is most important is not the story of the ten plagues, or the defeat of Egypt. What is so moving, what so much matters, is that the Torah should have chosen to locate our origins as a people here, in the struggle of the persecuted slave, in the anguish of the stranger and the disenfranchised, in order that we should know and remember for ever after the importance of justice, liberty and equality. Henceforth this memory of slavery and suffering is the moral touchstone of all Jewish values.

Rabbi Jonathan Wittenberg (Masorti), 1957–

Contents

Foreword

BYRON L. SHERWIN

The first question in the Bible is: 'Where are you?' In this volume, Brian Klug leaves little doubt as to where he's at. And where he's at will inevitably unnerve those who are elsewhere. Indeed, Klug is the first to admit that this is a 'troubling book'. It raises questions that some think should not be asked. It examines issues that will disturb those who otherwise ignore them. It will provide new perspectives for those who have been engaged with these issues.

Though written over more than three decades, and though they explore a plethora of diverse issues, the topics dealt with in this book remain topical. Put another way, besides its other merits, this work is strikingly and disturbingly relevant.

One suspects that this book was compiled primarily for those who do not embrace many of the views it presents. Brian Klug, after all, is not one who preaches only to the choir. After reading these pages, those who disagree with certain views, as I do, might surprisingly find themselves grateful, as I am, that Klug possesses the courage, forbearance, and analytical skills to have composed this work from his many essays, articles and lectures.

Klug is one of the few contemporary Jewish philosophers to apply his enviable professional skills to an examination of social and moral issues that either are, or should be, of particular interest to Jews. That he poses and probes questions that others avoid, but which preoccupy his own thinking, is consistent with his task as a philosopher. That he stimulates his readers to think about things in a manner they might not find comfortable demonstrates that he is an effective teacher of philosophy, following a tradition initiated by Socrates. That he draws deeply from his own conscience and consciousness as a Jew, from his personal experiences as a Jew, as well as from Jewish historical experience, demonstrates the intimate nexus between his philosophical bent and his Jewish identity. These two elements both coalesce and collide in the crucible of his erudite exposition, reasoned analysis and passionate argumentation. His is an enviable intellect, but moreover it is a *yiddische kop* (a Jewish intellect).

Though Klug eminently succeeds in his goal of 'bringing argument to life', he also brings *his* life to a variety of arguments. As Klug readily admits, the coherence of this book does not lie in its being a systematic, comprehensive treatise, but in its being linked to a particular life: his own.

Three major threads run through the tapestry of this wide-ranging work: identity, argumentation, and justice. The identity of Jews, children, and animals is prominently addressed, explored and discussed. Various methods of argumentation, largely drawn from philosophical discourse, are the tools employed to implement Klug's invitation to his reader: 'Come now, let us reason together.' Indeed, Klug describes argumentation as one of the 'staple ingredients of Judaism', and he further claims that taking self-criticism out of Judaism would be like taking 'heat out of a flame'. For Klug, this book is a series of explorations of a single idea: 'the proposition that doing justice lies at the heart of being Jewish'. 'Judaism means nothing', writes Klug, 'if it does not mean social justice.' For Klug, being Jewish, doing justice and argumentation are inseparable. Hence the title and subtitle, *Being Jewish and Doing Justice: Bringing Argument to Life*. So says the writer. But what says the reader, particularly *this* reader?

For this reader, an alternative title might be more accurate: 'Being Compassionate and Pursuing Justice: Bringing a Life to Argument'. Klug brings his life experiences and his personal convictions to bear as he argues his case regarding the issues that characterize his most visceral concerns. In so doing, it seems to me, the author's deep sense of compassion is revealed. Klug speaks much about justice, but what his reader often hears is a sustained plea for compassion. This is because (as he explains in the introduction) he is speaking of justice in the broadest sense of 'doing what is right'; and sometimes it is right to be compassionate or merciful. However, the distinction between justice (in a narrower sense) and compassion, which Klug does not discuss, is vital in Jewish thought and Jewish ethics. Not coincidentally, the old Hebrew proverb that characterizes 'being Jewish' depicts Jews as '*rahmaniyim b'nai rahmaniyim*', 'merciful people, the descendants of merciful people'. *Being* Jewish and *being* compassionate are meant to be synonymous, a redundancy. In this view, being compassionate is not something Jews *do*, but something they *are*. It is an ontological rather than a moral category. Perhaps, to put a different spin on a verse that Klug quotes in the prologue and again in the epilogue, this is why 'justice' in Deuteronomy 16:20 is described as something to be pursued, rather than as something necessarily attained. Put another way, Klug is a passionate and a compassionate Jew, pursuing justice for those for whom he has compassion because of the undesirable nature of the treatment they have received.

Precisely because the distinction between compassion and the narrower sense of justice does not come into Klug's discussion, it is worth emphasizing from the outset. According to an old rabbinic legend, God tried to create a world of justice alone, but it could not endure, for justice can easily deteriorate into harshness, retribution and cruelty. So, God destroyed that world. Then, God created a world of compassion, but it could not endure because unrestrained mercy and compassion can give license to wickedness and cruelty. So, God destroyed that world as well. Finally, God created a world with both justice and compassion, but God made compassion a little stronger because God feared the excesses of justice more than those of compassion. This world is our world. Klug, I am sure, would want us to keep this legend in mind when, using the word 'justice' in its broad and inclusive sense, he calls for 'an unconditional commitment to justice'.

'Justice' has suffered much verbal abuse in our times, especially the liberal, universalistic view of justice, which often, following the 'law of unintended consequences', can lead to catastrophic results. History tragically demonstrates that the application of universal virtues such as love, justice and compassion, have often engendered hatred, injustice and cruelty. In our pursuit of justice, we often find it to be elusive, evading crisp definitions and effective applications; hence the need to explore its ramifications, as Klug does in these pages.

Though I disagree with Klug on various issues, I welcome his determination to examine them and to reach his own conclusions. For example, as a thoughtful Jew, as a philosopher (and philosophy as Plato reminds us, begins with wonder), he wonders about the wisdom of Israeli policy. Because many fellow Jews find this threatening, reasoned argument degenerates into brutal ad hominem attacks, depicting Klug and those who share his views as 'self-hating', or as Jews who do not consider themselves Jewish, or as Jews who have excommunicated themselves from the Jewish community. This is indeed singularly ironic, for the same people who make these allegations often reject Zionist and Israeli policies when they find it convenient to do so. Indeed, some of the very Jewish organizations – religious and secular

– that today seek to stifle such discussion on Zionistic and Israeli policies were, less than a century ago, among the loudest denunciators of
Zionism. It is further ironic that Jews who defame those who question
such policies reject, by their very presence in the Jewish diaspora, the
policy that has been at the foundation of Zionist ideology since its
beginnings and that has been affirmed by Israeli prime ministers from
Ben Gurion to Olmert: the claim that every Jew should live in Israel.
Furthermore, there is a glaring inconsistency on the part of some Jewish
groups in the diaspora: while resisting discussion in the Jewish community of issues such as the Israeli treatment of the Palestinian citizens
of Israel, they are consistently vocal when Israeli policy rejects their
own, often liberal, convictions regarding Jewish identity and Jewish
religious practice. Is not the treatment and the status of Israeli Palestinian citizens at least as worthy of discussion as the treatment and the
status of liberal Jews and liberal Judaism by the Israeli government?
Are the political rights of Israeli Palestinians no less worthy of discussion
than the rights of Jews to freely practice their religion in the Jewish state?

   One may disagree with Klug's views here and there, but one should
nonetheless remain grateful to Brian Klug for raising questions that
need to be raised, for cajoling us to think about the provocative and
sometimes embarrassing questions that we often tend to avoid, for
applying his fertile mind and potent intellect to thinking these issues
through, and for sharing his insights and arguments with us in this
most compelling book.

Preface

Each of the chapters in this book was written as a freestanding piece. A version of most chapters has been published in English previously, either once (Chapters 5, 9, 10, 12, 14, 15, 19, 22 and Epilogue) or twice or more (Chapters 1, 2, 3, 13, 16 and 18). A few have appeared in another language (Chapters 8, 10 and 18). But several (Prologue, Chapters 4, 6, 7, 8, 11, 17, 20 and 21) appear here for the first time in print and in my native tongue. Even the pieces that are reproduced are not simply reproductions: in every case – more in some than in others – I have reworked the text, either in the interests of felicity or to avoid repetition and to make a better fit with the rest of the book. Several titles are different from the original. But, basically, I have let each chapter belong to the time and place of its initial occasion. That is to say, the underlying argument is left intact – even where the facts or my mind (or both) have changed. (In no case have I changed my mind fundamentally.) Where the version I use takes the form of a talk rather than an essay (Prologue and Epilogue, Chapters 4, 6, 7, 11, 12, 14 and 20), I have edited the chattiness but kept the form. In some cases, with an eye to saving space, I have reduced the quantity and length of endnotes.

The text is sprinkled with Yiddishisms and the occasional Hebraism: see the Glossary at the end for translations. In transliterating from Hebrew into English, I normally use standard spellings but at times I prefer to reflect old-style Ashkenazi pronunciation (see Chapter 7 for why). Translations from the bible are almost always from the *JPS Hebrew–English Tanakh* (1999) produced by the Jewish Publication Society. Abbreviations are not explained if it is obvious what they mean (e.g. 'UK').

The three epigraphs at the front of the book dovetail with each other, even though the rabbis in question – each of whom I have known personally – are from three different denominations. Divided by a common religion, they are connected by an uncommon *Menschlichkeit*.

Over the years, I have discussed the topics in this book with many people – different topics with different people – who have left their mark on my mind and consequently on the book. As each piece appeared, I took the opportunity to express my appreciation for their influence and help. But I have not been able to do this, of course, with those pieces that have not been published before. Moreover, I am placed in a dilemma by the sheer number of acknowledgements that are due. If I name everyone who stands out, the list would be so long that no one on it would stand out at all; this would defeat the purpose. But, if I single out some, this will rightly cause offence to others to whom I owe an equal debt of gratitude. The solution is to mention no one, thus offending everyone – a time-honoured Jewish custom.

I make three exceptions. The sudden death of Dennis Shields in December 2008, a shock to his colleagues as well as his family and friends, is a bitter personal blow. Even though Den was a lifelong shulgoer (whereas I attend in fits and starts), we shared a similar frame of thinking about Judaism. We were, so to speak, wrapped in the same *tallis*, from our teens to our 50s, right up to our very last cliff top walk on a summer's day in Sussex shortly before he died. How I wish I could have Den's reaction to this book! But how blessed I am to have Reva's! It is no coincidence that I wrote 'A Time to Speak Out', the opening chapter, just when Reva Klein and I met and opened a new – joint – chapter in our lives (2002). I am happy to report that there is no lack of argument (in the better sense, of course, of the word). But there is something of even greater value that Reva brings to my life: daily and hourly *oneg* (joy). To her and to Den this book is dedicated. My third exception, a person who makes Job seem like a model of impatience, is the man who believed in this book long before it was a twinkle in its author's eye: Tony Kushner. As well as being an intellectual collaborator he has acted as a kind of custodian of my writings. It is primarily due to Tony, calming my qualms, overriding my resistance and tolerating my ever-changing mind about the project, that this book has come into being.

I very much appreciate the collegial support and encouragement I have received from my colleagues, former and present, at St Benet's Hall, Oxford. The Parkes Institute for the Study of Jewish/non-Jewish Relations, University of Southampton, has been, at times, a second academic home. Several chapters began life as oral presentations at Saint Xavier University, Chicago, where former colleagues and students were always generous in their constructive criticism.

Finally, I am grateful to Byron Sherwin for writing the foreword, to Sybill Lunn for the index, and to a number of people for their expertise and help in the process of producing this book, especially Jodie

Abrahams, my research assistant, who quietly made an invaluable contribution; the imperturbable Heather Marchant at Vallentine Mitchell, who consistently quelled my anxious queries; and the in-house designers who created the ingenious image that graces the front cover and, lucidly and vividly, brings the argument of the book to mind – and to life.

Brian Klug
Hackney, London
April 2010

Acknowledgements

Versions of some of the essays in this collection have previously appeared elsewhere. Every effort and all possible care has been made to obtain permission to reprint material from the copyright owners, where this lies with the publishers. Any errors or omissions are unintentional and will be corrected in any future editions upon notification to the publishers.

'A Time to Speak Out' is adapted from the version published in *The Jewish Quarterly* (Winter 2002/2003), and appears here by kind permission of the publishers.

'The Collective Jew' is adapted from 'The Collective Jew: Israel and the New Antisemitism', *Patterns of Prejudice*, 37, 2 (2003), Taylor & Francis Group, www.informaworld.com.

'A Plea for Distinctions' is adapted from 'A Plea for Distinctions: Disentangling Anti-Americanism from Anti-Semitism', in Ivan Krastev and Alan McPherson (eds), *The Anti-American Century* (Budapest: Central European University Press, 2007).

'Tricks of Memory' is adapted from 'Tricks of Memory: Auschwitz and the Question of Palestinian Terrorism', in Stephen Law (ed.), *Israel, Palestine and Terror* (London: Continuum International Publishing Group, 2008), and is republished here by kind permission of Continuum International Publishing Group.

'The State of Zionism' is adapted from an earlier version published in *The Nation*, 18 June 2007, and appears here by kind permission of *The Nation* and Agence Global.

'A Time to Move On' is adapted from a version published in Anne Karpf, Brian Klug, Jacqueline Rose and Barbara Rosenbaum (eds), *A Time to Speak Out: Independent Jewish Voices on Israel, Zionism and Jewish Identity* (London: Verso Books, 2008), and is republished in this edition only by kind permission of Verso Books.

'The Language of Race' is adapted from the version that appeared in *Patterns of Prejudice*, 33, 3 (1999).

'The Other Arthur Balfour' is adapted from 'The Other Balfour: Recalling the 1905 Aliens Act', in Stephen W. Massil (ed.), *The Jewish*

Year Book 2005 (London: Vallentine Mitchell in association with the *Jewish Chronicle*, 2005).

'Old Ghosts in the New World' is adapted from the version in *Patterns of Prejudice*, 29, 2–3 (1995).

'Spring Fever in Chicago' is adapted from 'Springtime in Chicago: A Pattern of Politics and Prejudice', *Patterns of Prejudice*, 22, 3 (1988).

'Ritual Murmur in Britain' is adapted from 'Ritual Murmur: The Undercurrent of Protest Against Religious Slaughter of Animals in Britain in the 1980s', *Patterns of Prejudice*, 23, 2 (1989).

'Salomon's House on the Island of Bensalem' is adapted from 'Lab Animals, Francis Bacon and the Culture of Science', which appeared in *Listening – Journal of Religion and Culture*, 18, 1 (Winter 1983) and is republished here by kind permission of the editor.

'In the Shadow of Dr. Moreau' is adapted from 'Can We See a Moral Question about Animals?', which appeared in Andrew Linzey and Dorothy Yamamoto (eds), *Animals on the Agenda* (London: © SCM Press, an imprint of Hymns Ancient & Modern Ltd., 1998). Used by permission.

'Next Year in Neverland' is adapted from a version in Kathleen Alaimo and Brian Klug (eds), *Children as Equals* (Lanham, MD: University Press of America, 2002), and appears here by kind permission of the publishers.

The Epilogue, 'Being Jewish and Doing Justice', is adapted from the essay 'Jewish Identity and Human Rights', which appeared in Alan Brown and Mary Hayward (eds), *World Religions in Education, Vol. 27: Human Rights and Responsibilities* (London: 2006–2007), and is republished here by kind permission of the Shap Working Party.

At the time of preparing the manuscript, all website addresses in the endnotes were functional and correct.

Introduction:
Bringing Argument to Life

The chapters in this book are, in a way, chapters from my life. They were written over a period of more than twenty-five years (1983 to 2009), although the order in which they appear here does not correspond to the order in which they were composed. Almost all of Part 2, 'Angles on Identity', dates back to a long sojourn in Chicago that began in 1980. Most of Part 1, 'Approaches to Zion', was written later – after returning to England, a few years into the new millennium.

The scope of the book is almost as broad as the period of its writing was long, ranging from antisemitism, Zionism and terrorism to the language of race, the status of animals, the rights of the child and related topics. All of the topics in the book have something in common: they are troubling. To put it another way, none of them would have exercised Eve and Adam as they strolled hand in hand in their peaceable garden. Nothing would have troubled them because everything was a given – until the surreptitious serpent insinuated its question and the happy couple swallowed the bait. 'Then the eyes of both of them were opened' (Gen. 3:7). They became, in an instant, aware of themselves and cognizant of the distinction between right and wrong, the distinction that plays havoc with happiness. Henceforth, 'thorns and thistles' would be the ground of their existence (Gen. 3:18). That is, they traded a dream-world for trouble. In one sense it was their loss, for no longer were they blissfully oblivious. Looked at another way, they stumbled on the world. (The text says they were banished from paradise. It is perhaps more accurate to say that the film of paradise vanished from their eyes.) It was the moment that brought them to life. Troubling over justice, over right versus wrong: this is the stuff of *human* life and the province (as well as provenance) of this book.

A reader who scans the table of contents is liable to wonder what unity, if any, the book possesses. The consecutive chapters are not a series of steps in an overall argument. Nor do they interlock with one another, like the pieces of a jigsaw, so as to produce a complete picture. But, over the years, I have come to see them as explorations of a single idea: the proposition that doing justice lies at the heart of being Jewish. This idea is what the title of the book is intended to signal. It is, so to speak, the premise from which I set out.

Some ideas are as solid as rock and you can build on them. But the 'premise' of this book is not of that ilk. It is heuristic: it points a direction rather than laying a foundation. It is a gesture; and the wager of the author is that the gesture is not empty. I can imagine someone writing a book that developed this idea – that doing justice is at the heart of being Jewish – systematically and comprehensively. I would admire such a book and want to read it, but I could not write it. At any rate, this is not that book; it does not possess that kind of coherence. Rather, it has the coherence (or lack thereof) of a life.

To say that the contents of this book are chapters from my *life* is to say, in part, that they are not despatches from the front line of research. I try to be mindful of the canons of scholarship but, by and large, the writing is not academic. In several chapters I adapt ideas and methods from philosophy and apply them (although philosophers might think it a stretch). I also call on the resources of my Jewish education – from age 5 to 18 – at the (Orthodox) Hasmonean schools in London. I am no *tal-mud chacham*, and it is a long time since I studiously observed the Halacha. But this does not mean I have turned my back on Judaism: it just means that I help swell the ranks of the sinners of this world.

Being chapters from *my* life, the book, though concerned with matters that prey on other people's minds as much as on mine, is ineluctably personal. The topics that engage me in argument and embroil me in controversy have lain across my path where I could not ignore them. They have, as it were, forced themselves on my attention. Were it not for this, these pieces would never have come to be written, let alone collected under the aegis of a single idea. For the same reason, not only do I use the first person singular liberally, I also intrude facts from my autobiography into the text. As far as I can see, there is nothing of particular interest in these facts except to the author – except to the extent that they help *situate* the discussion for the reader, preserving a sense of occasion and bringing the argument to life.

In another sense, bringing argument to life – entering the fray and applying the mind to the thorniest questions – is the watchword of this book. Part 1, 'Approaches to Zion', focuses on the subject that causes the most heartache to Jews, as Jews, today: Zionism and the State of Israel. What does 'solidarity with Israel' mean and is this something that I, because I am Jewish, ought to feel (Chapter 1)? Is anti-Zionism essentially a form of antisemitism (Chapter 2)? Are anti-Americanism and antisemitism inextricably entangled (Chapter 3)? What sympathies draw America to Israel (Chapter 4)? What bearing does Auschwitz have on the question of Palestinian terrorism (Chapter 5)? Who were Herzl's Jewish opponents in London's East End and were they so wrong (Chapter 6)? Can the climate of debate about Israel among Jews today be improved (Chapter 7)? What does it mean to say that Israel has a 'right to exist' (Chapter 8) or that it is 'the Jewish state' (Chapter 9)? Who are the Jewish people and whither the Jewish future (Chapters 10 and 11)? These questions (roughly articulated here and allocated approximately to different chapters) concern many people. But they pertain especially to those of us who identify as Jewish; and no one is likely to agonize over them as much as we Jews.

Doing justice, however, applies across the board, not only in our own Jewish corner: hence the broad scope of the book. Part 2, 'Angles on Identity', enters different territory – different regions of life – and brings in clusters of other questions. This is certainly a departure from Part 1 and its focus on Zionism and the State of Israel. But Jewishness or Judaism is not left behind. It is conspicuous in the first sequence of chapters in Part 2: the 'ethnic question' on the UK census form (Chapter 12), Arthur Balfour's take on 'the Jewish race' (Chapter 13), ethnicity in America (Chapter 14), Black–Jewish relations in Chicago (Chapter 15) and popular attitudes in Britain towards the 'ritual' slaughter of animals for food (Chapter 16). Jewish topics surface from time to time (or lie just under the surface) in the remaining chapters: one about abattoirs in general (Chapter 17), two about the use of animals in the lab (Chapters 18 and 19), and a series of reflections on three – distinct but not unrelated – identities: being an animal (Chapter 20), being human (Chapter 21) and being a child (Chapter 22).

Because of this change of scene, there is a brief, separate introduction to Part 2 that maps the route that it takes. But, ultimately, the two halves of the book are joined at the spine. For Judaism is *this*-worldly. As the Prologue asserts, being Jewish *means* being in the world: immersed in its joys, involved in its troubles. Part 2 is in this spirit. It follows the cue that is given in the title of Chapter 10, the penultimate piece in Part 1, 'A Time to Move On'. To repeat: the 'premise' of the book is that doing justice lies at the heart of being Jewish. The whole sense of this would be different – would be lost – if the book ended with Chapter 11 and not with Chapter 22.

When I speak of justice in our dealings with each other I do not have a definition in mind – which does not mean I have nothing in mind at all. I certainly do not mean justice merely in the narrow, legal sense. Nor do I mean justice as opposed to mercy or compassion. Doing justice, says Socrates in Plato's Republic, means attending to matters that are, or ought to be, our concern. He calls this ironically 'minding your own business' (433a–b), a recipe for selfishness or apathy – unless it turns out that the general good or the welfare of others *is* our business. In any event, for Socrates justice means doing what, in the broadest sense, is right. Roughly, this is what I mean too. Justice, as I understand it, also includes a dispensation in which human rights – basic rights that accrue to each and every one of us purely and simply in virtue of being human – are a fundamental element. But I do not want to pin down the word further. Apart from the fact that I think of the realm of justice as wider than the sphere of human relations, the word has a life of its own. I prefer to allow its meaning, like the thing itself, to 'well up like water', in the phrase of Amos (Am. 5:24), and to draw on the well when faced with questions of right and wrong.

Often, with such questions, the thistles and thorns are as much in the asking as in the answering; in other words, it can be difficult to know how to go about thinking about them at all. Such are the topics in this book: they are as complex as they are contentious. Bringing argument to bear upon them means confronting heated opinion and seeking to disperse the smoke; it involves peering into the mist (especially the fog in your own mind), making distinctions where there is confusion, and seeing connections where the links are broken. It requires attentiveness to the very words in which the argument is conducted. (A previous title for this collection was 'Minding Our Language'.) It means picking up the trail of a living thought and following it to its destination. In short, and in another sense, it means doing (or seeking to do) justice to the issues.

'But', someone might say, 'doing justice – in *any* sense – is *everyone's* business. Your own reading of Genesis, chapter 3, confirms this, for Eve and Adam are not specifically Jewish: they are generically human. So, why not be inclusive? Why not say that doing justice lies at the heart of being *human*? Why *Jewish*?' Well, because Jewish is what I am. 'But are you not *both* – Jewish *and* human?' There is no 'both' about it – not if this means adding one to the other, nor if it means regarding the first as *part* of the second. Nor does 'Jewish' trump 'human': it would be as gross a mistake to imagine that this book subordinates 'human' to 'Jewish' as to think of it as a pilgrim's progress from the narrowly particular (Jewish) to the broadly universal (human)

– a familiar point of view on Judaism that I repudiate in the Prologue. It is a mistake because there is more to being Jewish than being Jewish. There I must leave it for now.

As the titles of its two parts imply, the book is a collection of approaches and angles, each of which can stand alone. And yet the order in which the chapters are placed is not arbitrary. This gives you, the reader, two viable alternatives: either to follow your nose, dipping into the book at will, or to follow the logic, such as it is, of the table of contents – which I, as the fastidious author, recommend. Either way, various lines of thought, like threads, sew the pieces together – if not into a unified theory then at least into a fabric with patterns of argument running through it; they give the book its cut.

What of its thrust? Where, at the end of the day, does the discussion lead? In the end, as in a life, there is no resolution. The Epilogue takes its name from the title theme of the book – being Jewish and doing justice – but contains no denouement. Neither a summing up nor a conclusion, it re-enters the initial fray, getting back to the context of Israel and its current conflicts, recalling the urgent business at hand, returning argument to the here and now, bringing it back to life.

Prologue: The People of God – The Very Idea
(Or, The Miracle of the Mirror)

Revised version of a talk given to members of the congregation of Westminster Synagogue, London, erev Shavuoth 2009.

> 'Ah, the scandal of the Jews as the chosen people!'
> (Emmanuel Levinas, *Beyond the Verse*)

There is a familiar view about Judaism – and specifically its difference from Christianity – that is expressed in the contrast between particularism and universalism. On this view, Christianity is *in*clusive, embracing all people everywhere regardless of their national or ethnic identity. Judaism, in contrast, is *ex*clusive, a private club for the chosen few. There are Jews as well as Christians who subscribe to this view; some do so apologetically or with regret, others assertively and with pride. But, as I see it, there is a fatal flaw, a tiny ingredient that is missing from this characterization of the Jewish people: its Jewishness. Let me explain.

First, let me thank you for inviting me to give the annual *erev* Shavuoth talk.[1] On my last visit to Westminster Synagogue, I was intrigued by the fact that the sermon was given by an Anglican priest. At Kinloss Gardens, the Orthodox shul in Finchley where, as a boy, I went with my family, week in, week out, such a thing would have been unthinkable (though not quite as unthinkable as a sermon from a rabbi of the Reform or Liberal persuasion).

Speaking of ecumenism, I am reminded of an experience in Michaelmas Term 1998, my first term at St Benet's Hall. As well as being part of Oxford University, St Benet's is a monastic house of studies founded by the Benedictine monks of Ampleforth Abbey. After Vespers one evening, about ten minutes prior to the ringing of the dinner bell, there was a gentle knock on my door. It was Fr Henry Wansbrough, the

Master. He explained that he was dining out that evening, as was the chaplain, and he wondered: Would I be so kind as to preside at dinner in the Hall in his absence? One does not turn down a request from one's Master. However, I hesitated, since the role includes saying grace before and after the meal. I explained to Fr Henry that, as a Jew, I could not bring myself to make the customary reference to the Father, Son and Holy Spirit. 'Why not say the Jewish form of Grace?' he suggested. So, I did. Picture the scene: the long table extending the length of the refectory, the (predominantly) Catholic members of the Hall lining both sides, each standing behind his chair, listening respectfully while I recited *Hamotzi*, first in Hebrew and then in English. When I finished the blessing, they all said 'Amen' – and promptly crossed themselves.

Feeling like Woody Allen caught in the glare of the spotlights, I froze. A panic took hold and I thought with alarm: 'What have I done?' The ghosts of rabbis past seemed to be looking grimly over my shoulder, as if reproaching me for betraying my roots and accusing me of having wasted their time all those years ago when they patiently tried to teach me the rudiments of Judaism. Didn't I understand *anything*? I have a sneaking feeling that my talk this evening will provoke their collective ire again, though this is not at all what I intend. I even like to think that there are some sagacious spectres who, looking down benignly from on high, will nod their ageless heads in silent approval.

Tonight I wish to present the Jewish people in a certain light. In this light, the people do not dissolve into a sea of humanity; they retain their particularity. But this particularity turns out not to be an opaque ethnicity; it is more like a reflective surface. Seen in this light, the Jewish people are like a magic mirror in which the image that floats into view is the face of the whole of humankind.

To recover this light, I shall revisit the precise spot in the Hebrew scripture where the children of Israel become the people of God. Shavuoth is a propitious time for returning to this spot, since in the liturgy the festival is called *zemun matan torosaynu*, the season of the giving of our Torah. But what does this mean? First, *whose* Torah? Who are the 'we' whose Torah it is? Second, what makes it ours? It's being *given* to us or it's being *received* by us? What, in this extraordinary case, is the relationship between giving and receiving? Third, where does the people of God, vis-à-vis other peoples, stand? What is its place in the world?

I cannot possibly do justice to these questions this evening, nor offer anything more than a meagre reading of a few scattered passages in *Tanakh* (principally from Exodus and Deuteronomy). What emerges from this reading is more like a starting point than a conclusion: a point from which to begin to approach these questions and also to embark on a different account of Judaism's difference from Christianity, one that isn't based on the contrast between particularism and universalism. It is also a vantage point from which to see why 'Jewish' is the Houdini among identities: always escaping the boxes in which it is put. If, at the end, anyone is moved to say 'Amen', I shall not object. However, I am addressing you as members of a synagogue congregation: please – unless you wish to give me cardiac arrest – don't cross yourselves.

Let us take our bearings from the place where the children of Israel, after a three-month schlep in the wilderness, find themselves (pun intended): Mt Sinai. They find themselves, to be precise, presented with an offer from someone even grander than the master of an Oxford college: the master of the universe. Now, God was an astute operator: he knew how to drive a hard bargain. First, he lures a destitute people out into the wilds and then, on a bare mountain in the middle of nowhere, amid the razzmatazz of fire and smoke and the fanfare of the shofar, he talks up a storm. He makes them an offer which they had to be mad to accept but which they could not refuse: one does not turn down an offer from one's master. Besides, they were in no position to say no. True, they had probably stashed away some unleavened dough. But, to paraphrase Deuteronomy 8:3, man cannot live by matzo alone. As for the manna that had sustained them thus far, God had a worldwide monopoly on its production. It was made in heaven: if he wished to turn off the supply, all he had to do was say the word (in a manner of speaking). So, it seems he had the children of Israel over a barrel. Be that as it may, Moses presents them with a choice – not once but twice: first at Sinai, shortly after their departure from Egypt, and again forty years later, in the land of Moab, when they are perched on the verge of Canaan and he says to them as follows: 'I have put before you life and death, blessing and curse. Choose life' (Deut. 30:19).[2] So, they choose. 'We'll take life and blessing, thank you very much', they say. (I paraphrase.) Who wouldn't, if the choice is put this way? But in choosing life they get more than they bargained for: they get a brand new identity as the chosen people. 'Hear, O Israel!' exclaims Moses, addressing the entire congregation. 'Today you have become the people of the Lord your God' (Deut. 27:9).[3]

Some blessing! If irony – especially at our own expense – is the soul of Jewish wit, then this punchline is the first Jewish joke, and not only is Moses the prophet beyond compare (Deut. 34:10), he is also the stand-up comedian nonpareil, the Woody Allen of the ancient Near

East. Had he been alive to see it, Jacob the patriarch and consummate trickster would have applauded the prank that Moses played on his guileless descendants. 'The people of God': the very idea is outrageous. Not only is it the ultimate chutzpah, it carries a double dose of mortal danger. For a chosen people is a proud people, the envy of the nations. Pride and envy: the one begets arrogance and chauvinism, the other breeds hatred and contempt. None of which is conducive to happiness and all of which sounds depressingly familiar in the chequered career of 'the people of God' from that day forth. Now, if *you* were God, would *you* have wished these things on *your* favourite people? Then why does God gull the children of Israel with an offer that is a poisoned chalice? And why on earth does he announce to the nations that the Israelites are the apple of his eye (Deut. 32:10)? If he really loves them, why not do his favourite people a favour – and stay shtum?

Unless there is more to Moses's irony – and God's partiality – than meets the eye. At first sight, it does seem as if, with the whimsicality of the divine, God reaches down onto the plane of the nations and picks out one – the people of Israel – that catches his fancy, promising them the earth (or at least a portion of it somewhere in the vicinity of the River Jordan).[4] But, on second thoughts, there is something wrong with this picture of events, something missing from this depiction of God: God. God, the master of the universe, is not just another petty despotic nepotistic totemistic Mesopotamian deity, some tinpot stone idol, a god or goddess whose dominion is purely local. 'For the Lord your God', explains Moses to the Israelites encamped in the land of Moab on the outskirts of the Promised Land, is *elohei hoelohim va'adonai hoadonim*, the God of gods and the Lord of lords, 'the great, the mighty, and the awesome God, who shows no favour and takes no bribes' (Deut. 10:17). Really? Shows no favour? Yet, only two verses earlier, Moses reminds the people of Israel: 'He chose you ... from among all peoples' (Deut. 10:15). Can a God who shows no favour have favourites? Moreover, in the previous verse, Moses points out God this way: 'Mark, the heavens to their uttermost reaches belong to the Lord your God, the earth and all that is on it!' (Deut. 10:14). Or, in the words of the psalmist: 'The earth is the Lord's and all that it holds, the world and all its inhabitants' (Ps. 24:1). The dominion of God, who shows no favour, extends to the whole of creation. So, if there is anything to which he is partial it must be the whole; it cannot be one part over and above the rest. God is God of all peoples. Yet Israel is 'the people of God'? Go figure!

I figure it this way. When God enters the frame, the whole of the frame shudders. If he singles something out, the thing in question, whatever it might be, is not granted a special privilege over and against everything else. Rather, it is raised to a higher power. The part, while *remaining* a part, is not *merely* a part: it comes to signify or stand for the whole (which is not the same as the sum). So, on the one hand, when Moses says 'Today you have become the people of the Lord your God', he does not add 'and you have ceased to be what you were yesterday.' Their brand new identity does not erase the old. Nor does 'raised to a higher power' mean elevated to a superior rank. They are still the humble house of Jacob, the ragtag mob that staggered out of slavery in Egypt. On the other hand, today this mob has taken on a meaning. Becoming the people of God, they become a signifier, signifying what it means to *be* a people, in the full sense of the word, where being a people means meeting the standard God builds into the word. This makes them *representative*, rather than *exceptional*, representing the *idea* of a people, a people that is *wholly* a people. *As such*, they are the apple of God's eye. As such, they are the people *of* God. Of *God*, that is to say (recalling and continuing Moses' description), 'God, who shows no favour and takes no bribe, but upholds the cause of the fatherless and the widow, and befriends the stranger' (Deut. 10:18). Being *of* such a God means partaking of these selfsame qualities. It means being, like God, partial to the utmost impartiality: partial, in a word, to justice.[5] 'Justice, justice shall you pursue' (Deut. 16:20): thus Moses directs the Israelites, calling them out of Egypt, calling them to go from being slaves of the master of an empire to being servants of the master of the universe. Raised to a higher power, they are called to a higher standard. Called 'the people of the Lord your God', they are called to book. The blast of the shofar, the summons 'Hear, O Israel', calls them to the bar of justice. God is a calling; doing justice is the hearing that Israel, being his people, owes the Lord their God.

But not theirs *exclusively*, any more than they are *his* exclusively; for then he would not be himself and they would be the people of *a* god, not *God*.[6] As it is, the choice of Israel is thoroughly *in*clusive, for they are chosen as an epitome and not as a pet. But why Israel?[7] What makes Israel greater than any other nation? Nothing; that is the point. Not only not greater, but least of all.[8] Consider: God is seeking a people whose peoplehood is exemplary. As his gaze passes over the mighty empire of Egypt, his eye is caught by a miserable band of wretches who have been downtrodden for generations and have no prior experience of exercising sovereignty as a nation: the obvious choice for the people of God! For God, oddly, it is. Being the lowest of the low makes them attractive to

God, who has a penchant for the humble and oppressed: we have seen this in the way Moses emphasizes his concern for the orphan, widow and stranger, and we see it again in the assertion of the psalmist that 'the lowly shall inherit the land' (Ps. 37:11).

Could it be that their innocence – their virginity as a nation, their lack of familiarity with self-government – commended them too? Did God regard them as a tabula rasa, a blank political slate, primed to receive the indelible imprint of his two tablets of stone? Absolutely not! Not for one moment does God harbour the slightest illusion about his chosen people. As he sees it, and as he tells Moses near the end of the forty-year saga, it is inevitable that Israel will let him down and betray their promise: 'You are soon to lie with your fathers. This people will thereupon go astray after the alien gods in their midst, in the land that they are about to enter; they will forsake Me and break My covenant that I made with them' (Deut. 31:16). To put it mildly, this people is not distinguished by its outstanding merit, a point that Moses immortalizes in his song, written at the end of his life, a swansong, composed at God's behest, not exactly a love song, sung 'in the hearing of the whole congregation of Israel' (Deut. 31:30), whom he addresses thus: 'O dull and witless people' (Deut. 32:6). Not that the enemies of Israel get a better press. They are 'a folk void of sense, Lacking in all discernment' (Deut. 32:28). It comes to this: neither better nor worse, par for the course: this is Israel. Fundamentally, they are no different from the rest of their kind: humankind: a typical bad lot. And God knows it.

And yet he chooses them, making the offer of a covenant, calling on them to become 'a kingdom of priests and a holy nation' (Ex. 19:6).[9] It is a beautiful idea. But no actual people is – nor conceivably can be – a thing of beauty; not *as* a people, not as *such*. A *priesthood* of priests is one thing, but a *kingdom*? A holy woman or man perhaps; but a *nation*? How can an entire *people* be of God? How can it not end (as grandma used to say about almost everything) in tears? Perhaps the Israelites needed the services of a business advisor when they were made the offer in the wilderness 'Yes', this astute advisor might have cautioned, 'You are being showered with promises, promises that are practically irresistible, a land of milk and honey, and so on, and certainly they come with a cast iron guarantee from an impeccable source – but on conditions that you cannot meet and with a penalty clause that will strip you of all your assets. Beware!' But they *did* have an astute advisor – in the person of Moses. (Moses thus represents both parties: is this the first case of a professional conflict of interests?) For not only is Moses completely upfront about the penalties – God disdains small print – but he forewarns them of their fate. He lays out the future before them and it's grim: they will break the terms of the covenant and lose the whole caboodle (although there is light at the end of the tunnel of history). He couldn't be clearer about the disastrous consequences of the offer they have received from God:

> I call heaven and earth this day to witness against you that you shall soon perish from the land that you are crossing the Jordan to possess; you shall not long endure in it, but shall be utterly wiped out. The Lord will scatter you among the peoples, and only a scant few of you shall be left among the nations to which the Lord will drive you. (Deut. 4:26–7.)[10]

So, what the devil is God up to? What the heck is going on in the drama enacted with the children of Israel in the wilderness?

There is something vaguely reminiscent about this drama, an echo of events that took place long, long ago, when the dust had barely settled on a newly-created world. God, who had brought every kind of being into existence after its kind, singled out one, which he made in his own likeness: *b'tzelem elohim*, in the image of God (Gen. 1:27). As such, humankind, his chosen creature, is raised to a higher power vis-à-vis creation as a whole. At this point, the whole of creation is a garden in Eden, a kind of promised land. Being *like* God, Eve and Adam are called to a higher standard. A beautiful idea! But being all too human, they fall short of their billing (which is their very being) and, unable to avoid going astray, do not long endure in their paradise (or their paradise does not long endure: it comes to the same thing), but are utterly expelled, their progeny scattered to the ends of the earth, where they can be found to this day. Hearing these echoes, it is tempting to say that, in the crucible of Sinai, amid the razzmatazz of fire and smoke, a bit of humankind is *remade* in the image of God – with the same instantaneous fall from grace as first time round. How *human* are the people of God! They are *just* like the rest of their kind! So much so, that in their story every people – even every person – can recognize themselves; they are less a light, more an illuminated mirror, to the nations. Sinai, which might have been a reprieve (whether for one people or ultimately for all), turns out to be a reprise of an old, universal story.[11]

Be that as it may, the outcome of the torrid affair at Sinai is never in doubt for any of the participants. God knows it from the outset, Moses too, and the people are told it in the most forthright fashion.

Each party in advance knows fully what lies in store. Yet God (who loves his people) asks of them the impossible; Moses (who faithfully leads them out of the intolerable) urges them to choose it; and the hapless people, eyes wide open, do. They choose to be what they cannot be. Go figure! This time, however, I won't, for this intimate three-way relationship, with its intricate paradoxical plot, is a riddle too far for one evening. (It is a riddle made for eternity.) For the purposes of this talk, suffice to say that becoming 'the people of God' seals the fate of the Israelites; the rest, as they say, is, so to speak, history.

But whose? One answer lies *inside* the text, where the story is handed on from book to book, from Moses to Joshua to the judges to the prophets and duly recorded in the annals of Kings and Chronicles. These are chapters in the career of a people inscribed in a book, a book forever closed: a complete testament. But *outside*, in the world, beyond the pale of the book, where the future is open: whose history and whose fate?

Enter the Jews, whom I have not mentioned by name since the preamble, since they are a kind of twist to the Hebrew tale. Who are the Jewish people? They are the people who, peering over the lip of the book, espy the children of Israel and exclaim: 'Look! That's us: We're them. See?' But no one on the page looks back at them to confirm their view. There is no mutual embrace. It is a one-sided relationship. We Jews might identify with the Israelites, but the Israelites don't identify with us. *They* interest *us* but *we* don't concern *them*. They are too occupied with being themselves, the people in the book. The point is this: Read as holy writ, the book is whole: it is complete unto itself and set apart in a manner unlike any other text. Here is God's word, there God's world, and between them – a gap, a little like the chasm that separates heaven from earth.[12] In the beginning, God divides the one from the other; which does not mean that there cannot be passage to and fro – think of the traffic on Jacob's ladder – but it does mean that every rung is a reach. Likewise, passing from *Tanakh* to terra firma, every step is a trek that is longer than the distance between Egypt and Canaan – even via the route that the Israelites took; it is infinitely longer. (Imagine the Torah suspended one tantalizing inch above the tips of your outstretched fingers: this shows how short infinity can be.)

We take Israel's story to be ours; but it *is* a *take*. We take it as given; but many a slip 'twixt give and take. What is given is the Torah; but how we take it is down to us. Seeing it as given specifically to *us*, seeing ourselves in the part of the people who receive it in the text, is already a take – for which we bear full responsibility. We have to see it as our choice; if we don't, then we are certainly *not* the people of Israel, who become the people of God through choosing. Let us by all means identify with the Israelites, but let us see this for what it is: an act of identification: an *act*, a doing, and a pretty audacious one at that, identifying with the people of God: a risk we run, a choice: a choice, like the choice that Ruth the Moabite makes when she declares herself to Naomi, saying (in the Megillah traditionally read on Shavuoth): 'Your people shall be my people, and your God my God' (Ruth 1:16).[13] Seeing the Torah as ours, we receive it; until we receive it, it is not ours. It is not ours till we take it upon ourselves to see it as given to us.

But we would be well advised to think twice about such an undertaking – just as the people whom we choose to regard as our ancestors, the chosen people, might have been wise to ponder what was on offer to them. For, like them, we run a risk or two. For what are we doing when we assume their mantle? We are inserting ourselves into the intimate three-way relationship at Sinai, with its intricate paradoxical plot, writing ourselves into the middle of a riddle 'made for eternity'. Its awesome complexity might be the making of an eternal people – but is liable to be the undoing of a people in time. Even as we say the Torah is given to us at this season, this is the risk we run: that in taking it we snatch at it and, thinking we get it, lose the plot. Unless we are very careful (which we are not), we end up spoiling the very thing that we say we prize, leaving our grubby paw prints all over the text as we grab it, flatten it, pocket it, plunder it, laying claim to its promises, covering ourselves in its glory – to our lasting shame. In short, we run the risk that every 'dull and witless' people runs when presented with an unfathomable gift: becoming a nation of nudniks – just like the biblical people of God.[14]

Who are we, *what* are we, we Jews, wandering from box to box, from people to nation to culture to ethnicity to religion to race (God forbid), traversing the categories, unable to settle into being one thing and not another? Why, notoriously, is our identity so volatile or elusive? Because our point of origin is a conundrum. Taking Israel's story to be ours, we appropriate the name 'the people of God'. 'The people of God': the very idea is a kind of surd: a quantity that does not add up or make sense, a logical scandal, a formula that is always liable to split apart at the seams. When it does, when it splits, its splinters become fragments that fit, more or less, one box or another. But suppose this idea, remaining in tension with itself, holds: then something choice comes into being: a chosen people: a people defined by a surd: an *absurd* people, conceived within the leaves of a book and dedicated to an untenable proposition: that they are radically apart from the world of which they are thoroughly a part. How can they possibly maintain this impossible stand? By taking the narrative of the Israelites and turning it into a stance, a posture towards existence; in a word, an attitude. (So, *that's* who the Jews are: a people with an attitude! We knew it all along!) Not just one attitude but three: *aspiration*, the continual striving to be an exemplary people; *atonement*, the sorrowful acknowledgement of repeated and abject failure; and *hope*, not just for ourselves but for the whole creation: the stubborn belief in the light at the end of the tunnel that will wipe away all the tears of history from the anguished and wrinkled face of the earth. It is not so much a stance as a step or dance: put on the spot, we shift from one position to the other, from aspiration to atonement to hope, and back again: constantly, faithfully, religiously. This, our style, our ritual, is our raison d'être.[15] Thus we take shape. Thus we loom in the dark: part light, part mirror, to the nations.[16]

Where (to return to a question raised at the outset) does this leave Judaism vis-à-vis Christianity? For Christians too, in their own way, take themselves to be heirs of the biblical Israel. So, for example, *Lumen Gentium* ('Light of the Nations'), one of the principal documents produced by the Second Vatican Council, refers to 'the new Israel': Israel constituted 'not according to the flesh but in the Spirit' and comprising all those 'who believe in Christ'. This – the *new* Israel – is 'the new people of God' (while the Jews, who are Israel 'according to the flesh', are the old). But are they *new* people or *no* people? It seems a fair question, for this 'people' lacks all the usual appurtenances of peoplehood. It is actually a union via communion, not a unity in virtue of a common ancestry or history, language or land.[17] It sounds more like a church. As it turns out, it *is* a church, 'the church of Christ'.[18] Judaism, in contrast, is no church. Nor does it know a systematic distinction between 'flesh' and 'spirit'.

It comes to this: On the view I am putting forward tonight, Judaism and Christianity are two alternative ways of inheriting the same universal moment in the story of our common ancestor: the Hebrews or Israelites. Parsing a human being into 'spirit' and 'flesh' and substituting the one for the other, Christianity resolves the logical scandal posed by the very idea of 'the people of God', converting this idea into a worldwide church. In effect, it replaces the particular (people) with the universal (church), throwing the doors open to all who wish to enter. Judaism resolves nothing. It is not so civilized.[19] Embracing the scandal at its heart, it insists on the flesh-and-blood particularity of the people – but aglow in the supernal light that pervades the whole creation. Seen in this light, the Jewish people are to the rest of humanity what an instance is to a universal: an example. Yet, seen in this same light, they are (or ought to be) forever scratching their collective *kop*. A people: but how so exactly? Particularity: but what precisely? These questions are as perennial as the people; and as unsettled; and as unsettling.

When I began this talk I compared the Jewish people to a magic mirror in which the face of the whole of humankind appears. But there is no such face. Each people have their own face and no face is shared by all. So, only one face – the face of this particular people (and, let's face it, no people are more particular than the Jews) – can actually show up in the frame of the mirror. Yet this singular face has the look of the whole: its *particular* features are stamped with the mark of the *universal*. This is the magic – I prefer to call it a miracle – of the mirror. Remarkably, however, this miracle happens if and only if we *choose* it to happen. Which, in conclusion, brings me round to the three questions I posed at the start about what it means to call Shavuoth 'the season of the giving of our Torah'. I realize that I have not answered any of them – certainly not adequately – this evening. But the third answers itself. Question: What is the place of the people of God in the world? Answer: *In the world*, wherever they find themselves. The rest, as Rabbi Hillel said in a different context, is commentary.[20] Now go choose.

NOTES

1. The date was 28 May 2009 (5 Sivan 5769). While I have retained the frame of this talk, the text here is significantly reworked in several places and substantial portions of the argument are completely new. The first draft was given as a talk to the monks' colloquium, St Benet's Hall, Oxford, on 16 May 2005.
2. In the argument that follows, I consciously conflate these two episodes, as though they were two moments of one event: Israel's becoming the people of God.
3. But God has already referred to them as *his* people when he appeared to Moses in the burning bush (Ex. 3:7) and, through Moses, addressed Pharaoh with the refrain 'Let My people go' (Ex. 5:1 and passim). However, in the very next chapter, the relationship is projected into the future: 'And I will take you to be My people, and I will be your God' (Ex. 5:6–7), as though they were not *yet* his people. Perhaps the way to look at it is this: At first, as the children of *Israel* (Israel being the same as Jacob), they are 'his' purely on account of the covenant he made with their ancestors (Ex. 6:3–4); later it is by virtue of the covenant they enter into in their own right. The argument I am making is focused on the latter. The bearing of the former on the latter is a complex topic, but I am bracketing it off for now, treating it as though it were just the backstory – even though manifestly it is more than this. What counts, for the present purpose, is that the second covenant cannot be reduced to the first or folded into it; for, if it could, then it would be redundant. Nothing is less redundant in the entire scripture than the covenant between God and his people.

4. The Torah (on the face of it) is neither clear nor consistent as to the area covered by the Promised Land.

5. Throughout I am using 'justice' in the broadest sense to mean (roughly) 'doing what is right', and not in a narrow sense in contrast with mercy or compassion.

6. The main principle of the argument I am making could be stated thus: Since the *subject* who chooses the people is God, the *object*, qua object of that choosing, must be such-and-such. Or: 'If God is X, then the people of God is Y.'

7. Why not? After all, the same question ('Why X?') would pop up automatically no matter which people God chooses. So, why *this* people and not *that*? More fundamentally, why single out any people at all? It's a fair question, but what is a drama without characters and plot? And what is left of the Hebrew scripture if you deprive it of its drama?
To work out the answer to the question 'Why Israel', we need to work in 'the backstory' in Genesis: see note 3. This is not part of my remit here. But a point from which to begin would be this: Why – on account of what behaviour or qualities of character, or both – does God call Abraham 'My friend' (Is. 41:8)?

8. Even numerically they are insignificant: Moses describes them as 'the smallest of peoples' (Deut. 7:7).

9. The complete sentence is this: 'Indeed, all the earth is Mine, but you shall be to Me a kingdom of priests and a holy nation' (Ex. 19:5–6). In this translation, which is from the Jewish Publication Society (JPS), 'but' translates the *vav* (the initial letter) in *v'atem*: 'but you'. This might seem to suggest that the second thought in the sentence is at odds with the first, or that there is a tension between them, as if God were saying: *Despite* the fact that all the earth is mine, I choose *you*. But, if you ask me, there is no 'but' about it. I hear the *vav* as 'and', which is commonly how it functions. This means that God is saying: 'Indeed, all the earth is Mine, *and* you shall be to Me a kingdom of priests and a holy nation', where the second thought complements the first.

10. The JPS translation in the previous verse suggests that this outcome is conditional on the conduct of the people after they enter the land: 'should you act wickedly' (Deut. 4:25). Once again (see note 9), they are putting a particular spin on the *vav* at the beginning of a word (*v'hishchatem*), whereas the face meaning, it seems to me is 'and': 'and [when] you act wickedly'. However, it comes to the same thing. In one sense, the outcome is hypothetical, for it is predicated on how the people might behave; in another sense, it is categorical, for God knows full well what their conduct will be. They *will* 'act wickedly': it is a given.

11. This is how the Torah, over and again, works: it tells a universal story through a particular case: one couple (Eve and Adam), one individual (Abraham), one people (the children of Israel). Furthermore, like God himself, the stories are many but oddly add up to one. (God, remember, is Elohim: an odd number, at once singular and plural.) In each case, moreover, the flesh-and-blood characters in the story seem to transcend themselves – but never by becoming abstractions. A creation is the opposite of an abstraction; and the Torah is the book of creation.

12. I remember being taught by the rabbis at school that everyone in the Torah is on a higher *madreigah* or level than we are – even Korach who rebels against Moses is on a higher plane – for the simple reason that they – and not we – are inside the book, part of the sacred text. This idea lies behind what I am saying in this paragraph.

13. In the story, she does not undergo a process of 'conversion', as Halacha prescribes. Her great-grandson is David, the future king of Israel. So, arguably, King David wasn't Jewish.

14. Like them, we lack 'a mind to understand or eyes to see or ears to hear' (Deut. 29:3).

15. This stance or dance is the inner sense of all the detailed observances prescribed in traditional Judaism: they are all ways of holding the pose or performing the dance. Of course, the performance of these ritual observances can be empty; they can also be full.

16. This, to clarify, is the Jewish people qua 'people of God', which is not necessarily the way in which people who identify as Jews think of the people to which they see themselves as belonging – if they see themselves as belonging, as Jews, to a *people* at all.

17. Not that any of these elements are, in a straightforward way, features of the peoplehood of the Jewish people. Each and every one is deeply problematic. But, in principle, in concept, they are all part and parcel of the identity of the people.

18. See Chapter 2, 'On the People of God'. Available in English translation on the Vatican website: http://www.vatican.va/archive/hist_councils/ii_vatican_council/documents/vat-ii_const_19641121_lumen-gentium_en.html. Not all Christians, of course, are Catholics. But this is a Catholic version of a broad Christian theme.

19. Supplanting Esau so as to receive their father's blessing, Jacob (who both *becomes* Israel and *begets* Israel) acquired the indelible traces of his twin brother's wildness. (For the story on which this comment is a gloss, see Genesis, chapters 25 and 27.)
20. Hillel said, 'What is hateful to you, do not do to others. This is the whole of the Torah. The rest is commentary. Now go learn.' (Bab. Tal, *Shabbat* 31a).

Part 1
Approaches to Zion

CHAPTER ONE

A Time to Speak Out

WHERE CAN I GO?

There is a song – and a question – that haunts me from childhood: 'Vi Ahin Soll Ich Geh'n?' (Where Can I Go?).[1] Some time in the 1940s (probably around 1948 when the State of Israel came into existence), Leo Fuld, the 'King of Yiddish Music', recorded the song in Yiddish and English. We frequently played the record, an old 78 rpm, at our North London home. My mother would sing it with feeling, as if its questions were hers and its answer an answer to her prayers. To the best of my (and her) recollection, the English version of the first verse was as follows:

> Tell me, Where can I go?
> There's no place I can see.
> Where to go, where to go?
> Every door is closed to me.
> To the left, to the right,
> It's the same in every land.
> There is nowhere to go
> And it's me who should know,
> Won't you please understand?

Even without the soulful melody, these despairing words ring in my ears; when sung they go straight to the heart. As a young child, the first verse seemed to me as melancholy as Kol Nidre – the solemn supplication that opens the evening service on Yom Kippur, the Day of Atonement – but less obscure. Here was a person in a nightmare: lost, shut out, cut off, set apart, a voice crying in the wilderness. I was a child and I understood crying. I understood lost as well. 'Won't you please understand?' Oh, but I did, to the core. But where to go, where to go? The song itself supplies the answer, expressed in the jubilant second verse:

> Now I know where to go,
> Where my folk proudly stand.

Let me go, let me go
To that precious promised land.
No more left no more right.
Lift your head and see the light.
I am proud, can't you see,
For at last I am free:
No more wandering for me.

No more wandering, no more questions. Unless it's the question 'Can't you see?' But I could see. I saw a nightmare ending. I saw the person in the song approaching a light at the end of the tunnel. This was my first glimpse of Israel. I was a child and so was the state. However, fifty years later we have both lost our innocence; I have learned that light can be deceptive and that it can also be blinding. The song comes back to haunt me, but I see a different nightmare now, one that has the whole of 'that precious promised land' and all its inhabitants, Jewish and other, in its grip. And the question I hear, subtly altered, is a cry of bewilderment rather than despair: 'Tell me, now that I'm here, where am I going?'

It is difficult to make this question audible, let alone offer an answer, given the ethos of solidarity with the State of Israel that is so strong among Jews these days. Calls for solidarity rain down from the pulpit. While this varies from congregation to congregation, and although there are notable exceptions, rabbis of every stripe (including the Chief Rabbi) tell their congregations to rally round in support of the Jewish state. Leaders of community organizations proclaim the same message. Some hasten to add that Israel is not beyond reproach. They acknowledge that Jews of goodwill may hold views about Israel that depart from the mainstream. But God forbid if anyone does. And if they do, this is taken to indicate that they are clearly *not* Jews of goodwill. They are branded as either naive or ignorant or cowards or self-hating traitors or some strange behemoth that is a hybrid of all these things. Now is not the time, we are told, for Jews in the diaspora to criticize the government of Israel. Loyalty is what is expected of us now. But why now, especially? And why of me, exactly? And what is loyalty, anyway? Or is it disloyal to ask?

The fact of the matter is that, above the din of sermons and admonitions, I hear the question the song puts to me in the here and now: 'Where am I going?' ('Am I going wrong? Where am I going wrong?') So, of one thing I am positive: now, *especially* now, is not the time for closing ranks and keeping quiet, nor for vociferous expressions of blind support for Israel in the name of unity. It is a time for clarity rather than unity: for making distinctions, for questioning certitudes, for thinking through; a time, ultimately, to speak out.

Clarity begins at home. Accordingly, I shall try to clarify why the song haunts me. What chord in me does it strike? To put it another way, what does Israel have to do with me? Well, when I am asked (or expected) to show solidarity, at least two separate claims are made, though they are so fused together that it is hard to pick them apart. There is the claim based on the idea that Israel, being a Jewish state, is *my* state, and that its people, the Jewish people, are *my* people. This is the point of view of Zionism, the movement to establish a home for the Jewish people in the land of Israel on the model of a nation state. Zionism, a modern political idea, draws heavily on Judaism, an ancient religious and ethical tradition whose roots lie in the Torah and the Talmud. The fact that Zionism uses the vocabulary of Judaism, but adapts it to the idiom of modern political theory, goes a long way towards explaining why this subject – Israel and Jewish identity – is so confusing. For at the heart of Judaism there is also the notion of the Jewish people, but it is a significantly different notion. This notion – the religious and ethical notion of the Jewish people – is the other basis on which I am asked to show solidarity with the State of Israel. I shall discuss this basis first, and then turn to the claim that derives from Zionism.

Zion, in the Bible, refers to Jerusalem. But it is not a city merely. In the biblical and religious context, Zion is the place of which Isaiah speaks when he proclaims his vision of 'the last days', saying, 'out of Zion shall go forth the Torah, and the word of the Lord from Jerusalem' (Is. 2:2–3). Isaiah speaks as a prophet and 'Zion' is a term of his art. Now, if this is the Zion in whose name I am being asked to show solidarity with Israel, then surely it is appropriate to apply the religious ethic to which this idea of Zion belongs and judge Israel accordingly; for this is the standard I am being asked to affirm. It is the standard I do affirm if I am in shul on Shabbos for the opening of the Ark at the beginning of *Krias Hatorah* (the Reading of the Torah) and join the congregation in the singing of the very verse from Isaiah that I have just quoted. To appeal to my Jewish identity, and at the same time tell me not to apply to Israel those standards of truth and justice which, along with peace, Judaism itself insists upon as fundamental: this strikes me as inconsistent. It is certainly incongruous when, week in, week out, in the Torah readings that are the focus of the Shabbos service, the children or people of Israel are constantly being chastised and criticized for their failings. To take self-criticism out of Judaism would be like taking the light out of a candle or the heat out of a flame:

it would mean taking the 'Jewish' out of the Jewish people. The whole point of this people, in the context of the Torah, is that they are not just another nation or ethnic group. They are the people of God, 'a kingdom of priests and a holy nation' (Ex. 19:6). They become this people at Sinai by entering into a covenant in which they choose to live according to a certain ethic: a standard of behaviour and a set of principles and values. This is the concept of *am Yisroel*, the people of Israel, the Jewish people, in the Torah: a people constituted by their commitment to an ethic. This commitment constitutes a way of life, not a modern state. It cannot be the basis for unconditional solidarity with a state – any state, especially one called Israel. For the whole idea of Israel in the Torah is conditional – conditional upon the people keeping their side of the bargain, living up to their billing as a 'light of nations' (Is. 49:6).

If, however, I am expected to show solidarity on the basis that Israel, being a Jewish state, is *my* state, then my response is this. I do feel a tie to Israel insofar as Israel came into existence to provide a home for Jews fleeing persecution and seeking a place where they could live in peace and security. After the Second World War and the Holocaust, Israel was a state for the stateless, for Jews who had lost everything and had nowhere to go because, in the words of the song that still haunts me, every door was closed to them. It was the same in every land. Then suddenly, miraculously as it seems, there was one door that opened and they stepped through it into what they believed would be the safe haven of Israel. At last they were free. It was the end of a nightmare – or so they believed. But now their dream is shattered. They live in fear of their lives every day. Even when they go to the market, or eat at a pizzeria, or sit down to a Seder with family and friends to celebrate freedom: they are not free. At every turn their lives are at risk – just as it was before they came to this land. What can they do? Where can they go? I see their plight and my heart goes out to them. It goes out to them as fellow human beings. But on top of that I know that there but for the proverbial grace of God go I, for they are Jewish, and I am Jewish, and being Jewish is what brought them to these straits. This makes their predicament more poignant for me – not greater than the predicament of other human beings in similar circumstances but more pointed.

This is the tie that I feel, these are the chords that are struck by the song. They resonate with me deeply. But the tie is a tie of sentiment, not loyalty or allegiance. Israel is not my country and I am not its citizen. To put it another way, 'the people of Israel', in the modern political sense of that phrase, is not synonymous with 'the people of Israel' of which the Torah speaks. Many Jewish Israelis feel no affiliation whatsoever to Judaism and even repudiate it totally. They are *Jewish people* but they do not see themselves as part of 'the Jewish people', *am Yisroel*, the People of the Book. Moreover, about 1.5 million Israeli citizens – approximately one fifth of the total population – are not Jewish: they are ethnically Arab or Palestinian and profess either Islam or Christianity or feel as secular as some of their Jewish co-citizens. They also are part of the (modern) people of Israel. *They* are, *I'm* not. There are other minority groups within Israel too. In short, while in terms of the public culture Israel is a Jewish state, the people of Israel, like the people of Britain, are a motley crew.

Moreover, if Israel *were* my country, I would not consider it my patriotic duty to support it right or wrong. If I thought its policies were foolish or shameful, unwise or unjust, I hope I would not hesitate to speak out, even in a time of crisis – especially in a time of crisis – because this is the part of a conscientious citizen. More to the point, it is what Israelis do. Israel is not a monolith and Jewish Israelis do not form a single bloc. They are at odds over the issues of the day and are hardly shy about saying what they think. On the subject of the future of the Occupied Territories, the question of land for peace, the 'two-state solution' and the treatment of Palestinians under occupation, there are diametrically opposed camps. The divisions pit Israeli Jew against Israeli Jew. Consequently, not only do I not feel under an obligation, as a Jew, to show solidarity with Israel, but *there is no such thing* as 'solidarity with Israel': it is a sentimental illusion.

THE ISRAEL SOLIDARITY RALLY

Some readers who have got this far will, I expect, be itching to tell me that I have completely missed the point about solidarity with Israel. In particular, they will want to put me right about the rally that took place in Trafalgar Square on Bank Holiday Monday, 6 May 2002, in which tens of thousands of people took part, and to which I now turn. I imagine them giving me a little lecture, speaking, as it were, on behalf of the Jewish community. To draw on published sources, I would hear something like this:

> *Of course there are diametrically opposed camps in Israel. What do you expect: it's a Jewish state. But there is something that transcends party politics: survival and the right to live in peace and security.*

> *This is why Jews were urged to attend the Israel Solidarity Rally:*
> *to stand shoulder to shoulder with the people of Israel and to say*
> *in one clear voice: 'We are with you. Yes to peace. No to terror.' Is*
> *this so wrong?'*

Yes. Given the spin being put on it, it is *so* wrong that it is hard to
know where to start. The lecture makes the claim that the Israel Solidarity Rally transcended party politics. I take it that this claim refers
to domestic politics in Israel, and I assume for the sake of argument
that the rally was genuinely intended to be non-partisan. No doubt,
many people who took part saw it that way. The fact that there was
some diversity of view on the speakers' platform might have seemed to
give substance to that perception. However, what the *onlooker* saw
was something else: a high-profile public statement of support by
British Jewry for the policies of Prime Minister Ariel Sharon.

Consider the message proclaimed by the main official banner (and
cited in the lecture): 'Yes to peace. No to terror.' What does this really
mean? Saying 'yes to peace', in itself, means nothing. Who says *no* to
peace? Everyone, unless they are insane, ultimately wants peace. The
real issue is not peace per se but peace *on whose terms* and peace
by what means. Here, for example, is Sharon on the subject of Israel's
intentions: 'Israel will act, and with might. Israel will fight anyone who
tries to wage fear [*sic*] through suicide terrorism. Israel will fight.
Israel will triumph. And when victory comes, Israel will make peace.'[2]
So, if peace means triumph, Sharon is 'a man of peace', to use President
Bush's sobriquet.[3] But who isn't? 'Yes to peace' is an empty platitude, a
well-meaning but meaningless gesture. 'No to terror', on the other hand,
is telling. It determines the political sense of the rally – because of what
it does *not* say. It does not say 'No to settlements'. Nor does it say no to
curfews, closures, collective punishment, deportations, demolition of
homes, destruction of vineyards, uprooting of olive groves, and all the
other apparatus of Israel's occupation of the West Bank and Gaza Strip.

Thus, far from being apolitical, the rally could hardly have been
more partisan. Within the Israeli political spectrum it came down,
broadly speaking, on one side (say, Likud) over another (say, Meretz).
This was compounded by the way the limelight fell on Benjamin
Netanyahu, the former Prime Minister, whose hard-line hawkish views
are similar to Sharon's. When I told an Israeli friend that Netanyahu
was going to be one of the main speakers, she emailed me emphatically:
'I'd agree that it would be far more supportive to stay away from such
a rally!'[4] So, when the demonstrators waved their banners saying 'Israel,

we're with you', who were they with exactly? Not with my friend, and not with those Israelis who feel as she does: who oppose the appropriation of Palestinian land and the spread of Jewish settlements in the Occupied Territories; who stand up against their own government's repeated violations of the international human rights conventions to which Israel is a signatory; who promote Jewish–Palestinian cooperation; and who seek a resolution of the conflict that will enable two long-suffering populations to have a future side by side. These far-seeing Israelis want and need solidarity. They and their cause – which includes the peace and security of Israel – were betrayed by the Israel Solidarity Rally on 6 May 2002.

Of course, there are those who attended the rally who take a different view of the conflict with the Palestinians and of Israel's long-term interests. In their opinion, the Israelis I am calling far-seeing are at best short-sighted. The last thing they would want is to give succour to Israelis like my friend. Some of these people think the Palestinians must be bludgeoned into submission; some believe in a 'Greater Israel' that incorporates the Occupied Territories; some went on the rally in the spirit of ethnic bonding, pure and simple. (As one letter to the *Jewish Chronicle* put it, 'We cannot abandon our kith and kin.'[5]) All such people are entitled to express their views. However, on the one hand, they should stand up and be recognized for who they are, rather than hide behind the fuzzy veil of a vague 'solidarity with Israel'. On the other hand, for some Jews who took part in the rally, nothing could have been further from their minds than the policy of brute force or the cause of expansionism or the values of ethnic bonding. These people went in a spirit of peace, a peace based on negotiation, not subjugation; on sharing the land, not appropriating the whole of it; on universal principles of justice and human rights, not on the racial or ethnic interest of one of the parties to the conflict. But a public rally makes a public statement. And the statement it *actually* makes is not necessarily the same as the one in the minds and hearts of people who take part.

What did the world see on 6 May? It saw a mass expression of jingoism in which Jews, as Jews, were siding with an established state occupying the land of a stateless people. True, the banners said 'Yes to peace'. But again: by what means and on whose terms? If this had genuinely been a peace rally, rather than a blatantly nationalistic one, then Trafalgar Square would not have been awash with blue-and-white Israeli flags (plus the odd Union Jack). As it is, irrespective of intentions, and even without any overtly anti-Arab placards, the slogan 'Israel, we're with you' conveyed to the onlooker the message 'Palestinians, we're against you', as surely as tails is the opposite of heads. This is not the attitude of peace – unless for 'peace' read 'triumph'. Those people who took part in the rally and whose sympathies lie with the peace movement in Israel were either duped or self-deceived.

Yet, given the way the State of Israel and its institutions are written into Judaism and Jewish identity, it is almost impossible to keep one's head. For example, the new edition of the widely-used Singer's siddur includes the following prayer as part of the liturgy for the Shabbos morning service: 'Heavenly Father: Remember the Israel Defence Forces, the guardians of our Holy Land. Protect them from all distress and anguish, and send blessing and prosperity upon all the work of their hands.'[6] *All* the work? Including the destruction and havoc caused in Jenin and Ramallah and Nablus, the humiliation and indignities visited daily on Palestinians at checkpoints in the Occupied Territories, not to mention the violence sometimes meted out to Israeli Jews who protest against their government's violations of human rights? Note the poetic, biblical language – 'all the work of their hands' – and the sacred epithet, 'the guardians of our Holy Land'. This makes Israel's military an institution of Judaism itself. The rabbi or *chazan* recites this prayer in front of the open Ark, holding a Sefer Torah, with the whole congregation standing united. United as what? As *Am Yisoel* before God? Or as the local weekly Israel Solidarity Rally? There is no room, in such a climate, to stop and think about the nature of your tie as a Jew to the State of Israel. How can you *think*, when your very identity is *soldered* to the state?

So, where do you go if, as a Jew, you do not identify yourself in terms of Israel, but no longer feel you can ignore the community's definition? Or if you are alienated by a prayer that implicates you in military actions that you abhor? Where do you go if you wish to go to shul, whether regularly or for festivals and special occasions? More and more individuals are liable to feel that the doors of the synagogues are closed to Jews who either do not define themselves in terms of Israel or who repudiate the Israeli government of the day. Increasingly, they will feel excluded. Reform or orthodox, to the left to the right: there is nowhere to go.

And yet, even as I protest, I myself feel a longing to believe the very thing I am repudiating. There is something in me that wants it to be true – that wants the modern State of Israel to be the salve that heals all the wounds of Jewish history. Those wounds go deep. Even if there were no external pressures brought to bear by the community to show 'solidarity with Israel', there would be those exerted from within: experiences, memories, stories stored at the back of the mind that seep into the heart, a song from childhood that resonates down to the present day. Unless I am mistaken, when Jews turned up in their tens of thousands to support Israel, they were simultaneously showing solidarity with the past, with all those Jewish communities, long gone, that came under attack and did not – could not – defend themselves. It feels like a debt to the dead: to stand up and fight for the living. It also seems like a duty to posterity: not to let history repeat itself, the history of discrimination, inquisition, expulsion, pogrom, and finally mass extermination. But who will discharge this debt and perform this duty? For many Jews, Israel came into the world for this very purpose. 'Never again' is the state's unofficial motto.

This gets to the crux of the relationship between Jews in (what is called) 'the diaspora' and Israel. It is something I grew up with: the sense that Jews must come to the defence of Israel so that Israel can come to the defence of Jews. Hence the prayer for the Israel *Defence* Forces; it is as if they defend not only Israel but Jews everywhere. Hence also Sharon, Prime Minister of Israel, calling himself in an interview with CNN (on 16 April 2002) 'the prime minister of the Jewish people'.[7] And when he says, 'Israel is the only place in the world where Jews have the right and capability to defend themselves, by themselves', he hits a nerve with Jews around the globe.[8] Significantly, he said this at Yad Vashem, Israel's memorial to the Holocaust, on 18 April 2001, the eve of Holocaust Remembrance Day. Speaking, as it were, in his dual capacity of (elected) Prime Minister of Israel and (self-appointed) Prime Minister of the Jewish people, Sharon has described the conflict with the Palestinians in epic terms: 'This is a battle for the survival of the Jewish people, for survival of the state of Israel.'[9] The leaflet advertising the rally used the same word: survival. 'Survival', for Jews, is a buzzword. Once the conflict with the Palestinians is put in terms of survival, the floodgates of collective memory open and Jews are moved to rally round. To invert what I said earlier, it is as if a massive congregation assembled in the open-air synagogue of Trafalgar Square in order to affirm with one voice: 'We will survive.' All distinction between religious and secular, Orthodox and Reform, was dropped for the purposes of this non-denominational 'service' so as to make it as inclusive as possible. Seen this way, the rally was less a demo than a love-in, a coming together for its own sake: which is why those words 'Yes to peace' seemed to signify something, even though they didn't. In the spirit of this love-in, the slogan 'Israel, we're with you' was not meant badly; it wasn't intended to imply 'Palestinians, we're against you.' It wasn't really aimed at them at all but at 'the world', a world that has always been against 'us', that has denied 'us' peace, and, in the words of a London Jewish lawyer 'does not like to see Israel strong'.[10]

I understand – from the inside – these perceptions and emotions and why they seem so compelling. Nonetheless, in fact the Jewish people do *not* have a Prime Minister. Israel is *not* the only place in the world where Jews have the right – or the capability – to defend themselves. Israel's conflict with the Palestinians is *not* a battle for the survival of the Jewish people. And 'the world' is not a unified body that wants to see Israel weak. These ideas are not just false, they are crazy. Even to say that the survival of the state is at risk is to distort both reality and history. One correspondent to the *Jewish Chronicle* put it succinctly: 'The suggestion that it is Israel, rather than the Palestinians, whose survival is currently threatened is not only nonsense, it also diminishes the very real dangers that the Israeli nation – and the Jewish people – have faced in the past.'[11]

Nonsense and craziness are all that can come from a state of mind that cannot distinguish fantasy from fact, Arafat from Hitler, the intifada from the Inquisition.

NOWHERE ELSE TO GO

'Vi Ahin Soll Ich Geh'n?' 'Where Can I Go?' There were two echoes of this song in the reportage that followed the intense ten-day battle fought between the Israel Defence Forces and Palestinians in the Jenin refugee camp in April 2002. One was a message left on a wall of a house that the Israeli army had occupied and used as a base. A soldier had written 'in neat blue ink' the simple sentence, 'I don't have another land.'[12] The other was a remark attributed to an elderly Palestinian who refused to leave his home when soldiers were about to demolish it. This 'stubborn old man' is reported to have said: 'Fifty years ago you expelled me from Haifa. Now I have nowhere to go.'[13] In a way, these two statements sum up the whole conflict. However, the appearance of parity is misleading. For, when the dust settled on the battle, where did each of them go? The soldier to his barracks – and ultimately to his home in Israel. But the 'stubborn old man' was left in the dust. There is no equality between this Israeli and this Palestinian. The one has a state, the other is stateless. He has nowhere to go – and it's we who should know.

Jews should know, partly from their own historical experience, and partly because of the impact this had on Palestinians. The old man alluded to this when he said, 'Fifty years ago you expelled me from

Haifa.' Like many Jews, I grew up believing that the Palestinian 'refugee problem' was not caused by Israel; that it was an artificial problem created by surrounding Arab nations who, promising to crush the new Jewish state, urged Palestinians to flee their homes temporarily. The whole truth of this story, however, is more complex and less comfortable, as Israeli historians such as Simha Flappan, Benny Morris and Avi Shlaim have shown.[14] What cannot be denied is that, tragically, solving one refugee problem led to another. Jews who survived the Holocaust found a haven in Israel, while the creation of the state displaced around 700,000 Palestinians.[15] This is why Palestinians call 15 May, the day after Israel declared its existence, Nakba Day, the day of the catastrophe. It is not because they are antisemites who think that anything good that happens to Jews is ipso facto catastrophic. They are not Nazis actuated by hatred. They are people who suffered a great loss: their homes, their land, their livelihoods. The creation of the State of Israel was, for them, a catastrophe: this is fact, not anti-Israel propaganda.

It is time to face this fact and to stop insisting on the exclusive righteousness of Israel's cause. While Israel, despite the way it is sometimes portrayed, is not the wicked witch of the Middle East, nor is it a paragon of virtue, with the Arabs as the villain of the piece. The conflict between Israel, its Arab neighbours and the Palestinians is political. It is not a battle between good (Us) and evil (Them); thinking this way can only lead to moral blindness. It is time to see the Palestinians in the light of the Jewish experience of statelessness; to recognize their predicament; to say 'Never again' and refuse to subjugate them or force them out – as if they had somewhere to go. The truth is that neither Israelis nor Palestinians have anywhere else to go. Any solution to the conflict that is not based on this truth is either doomed to fail or, if it were to succeed, would be abominable.

The ethos of solidarity, which led to thousands of British Jews rallying round Israel in Trafalgar Square on 6 May 2002, is part of the problem. Israel and Jewry are locked in an embrace that is distorting life for both parties. There needs to be a new understanding. Israel needs to be taken off its mythic pedestal and relieved of its impossible millennial role as the defender and saviour of the Jewish people. Jews outside Israel must allow Israel to be its own state, not theirs, so that it can concentrate on its own vital interest in the here and now – making its peace with the region of which it is a part – rather than carrying the whole burden of Jewish history on its shoulders. By the same token, Jewish communities in the so-called diaspora need to live in *their* here and now. This double need implies the reverse of blind solidarity.

Instead of lumping everything together, it is time to make distinctions
– between Judaism and Zionism, Israeli and Jew, the biblical and the
political. Making distinctions does not mean abandoning connections.
It allows those Jews who care about Israel to offer something better
than blind, unconditional support: cool, careful, measured, qualified,
sustained, candid criticism. (This is solidarity worth its salt – the kind
you cannot give unless you are at one remove, keeping a critical
distance.) At the same time, it means making room within Jewry for *all*
Jews, including those who feel no tie to Israel whatsoever.

For my part, my tie with Israel goes back to the song that haunts me
from childhood and the question it puts in the here and now: 'Tell me,
Where am I going?' ('Am I going wrong? Where am I going wrong?')
Hearing this question, holding to the standards Judaism affirms,
and believing as I do that Israel has gone off the rails: how can I not
speak out?

NOTES

1. This chapter is adapted from the essay with the same title that appeared in *Jewish Quarterly*, 49, 4 (Winter 2002–03), pp.35–41.
2. *Ha'aretz*, 8 May 2002. Available at Canadian Institute for Jewish Research: http://www.is-ranet.org/isranetbriefings/Permanent2002/Permanent-May-02.htm.
3. Peter Slevin and Mike Allen, 'Bush: Sharon A "Man of Peace" ', *Washington Post*, 19 April 2002, http://www.washingtonpost.com/ac2/wp-dyn/A12206-2002Apr18?language=printer.
4. Private email correspondence, 3 May 2002.
5. *Jewish Chronicle*, 3 May 2002, p.26.
6. Revd S. Singer (ed.), *The Authorised Daily Prayer Book of the United Hebrew Congregations of the Commonwealth* (London: Kuperard, 1998), p.384.
7. Joseph Algazy, 'Children are Subject to the Law but not Protected by It', *Ha'aretz*, 10 June 2002, http://news.haaretz.co.il/hasen/pages/ShArt.jhtml?itemNo=174655. Compare calling the government of Israel 'the government of the Jewish people' (Israel Harel, 'Democracy (is not) above Existence', *Ha'aretz*, 11 July 2002, http://www.haaretz.com/hasen/pages/ShArt.jhtml?itemNo=185461.)
8. 'Address by Prime Minister Ariel Sharon at Yad Vashem on the eve of Holocaust Remembrance Day – 18-Apr-2001'. Available at Israel Ministry of Foreign Affairs: http://www.mfa.gov.il/mfa/government/speeches+by+israeli+leaders/2001/address+by+prime+minister+ariel+sharon+at+yad+vash.htm.
9. In an address on Israeli television: see Serge Schmemann and Joel Brinkley, 'Attack Follows Ambush that Killed 13 Israeli Troops', *New York Times*, 10 April 2002, http://www.nytimes.com/2002/04/10/international/middleeast/10MIDE.html.
10. Quoted in Ann Treneman, 'In Defence of Israel', *The Times*, 11 April 2002, T2, p.2.
11. *Jewish Chronicle*, 3 May 2002, p.26.
12. Suzanne Goldenberg, 'The Lunar Landscape that was the Jenin Refugee Camp', *Guardian*, 16 April 2002, http://www.guardian.co.uk/world/2002/apr/16/israel.readersyear. 'Ein li eretz akheret', 'I don't have another land', is the opening line – and title – of a popular Israeli song written by Ehud Manor and Korin Al-al.
13. Amira Hass, 'What Kind of War is This?', *Ha'aretz*, 19 April 2002. Available at Z Net: http://www.zmag.org/znet/viewArticle/12182.
14. Simha Flappan, *The Birth of Israel: Myths and Realities* (New York: Pantheon Books, 1987); Benny Morris, *The Birth of the Palestinian Refugee Problem, 1947–1949* (Cambridge: Cambridge University Press, 1987); Avi Shlaim, *Collusion Across the Jordan: King Abdullah, the Zionist Movement, and the Partition of Palestine* (Oxford: Clarendon Press, 1988).
15. Avi Shlaim, *The Iron Wall: Israel and the Arab World* (New York: W.W. Norton & Company, 2001), p.31.

CHAPTER TWO

The Collective Jew

NEW ANTISEMITISM

In the Preface to his pamphlet *The Jewish State* (1896), one of the founding documents of political Zionism, Theodor Herzl declared: 'The world resounds with outcries against the Jews.'[1] Chapter 2, 'The Jewish Question', opens with this description:

> No one can deny the gravity of the situation of the Jews. Wherever they live in perceptible numbers, they are more or less persecuted. Their equality before the law, granted by statute, has become practically a dead letter. They are debarred from filling even moderately high positions, either in the army, or in any public or private capacity. And attempts are made to thrust them out of business also: 'Don't buy of Jews!'[2]

In short: 'The nations in whose midst Jews live are all, either covertly or openly, Anti-Semitic.'[3] For Herzl, Zionism, in the sense of a political movement to establish a sovereign Jewish state, offered the solution – the only workable solution – to the problem of antisemitism. He recognized that 'the Jews will always have sufficient enemies, much as every other nation has'. But he thought that, if they had a state of their own, their situation would be fundamentally changed for the better in two ways. First, 'once fixed in their own land, it will no longer be possible for them to scatter all over the world. The diaspora cannot take place again, unless the civilization of the whole earth should collapse.' Second, 'if we only begin to carry out the plan, anti-Semitism would stop at once and for ever'. As Herzl saw it, the conditions of life for Jews would be normalized once their *status* was normalized. No longer perpetual 'strangers' in other people's countries, they would be at home in their own land, possessing their own constitution, language, laws, army and flag, 'much as every other nation has'. In short, a Jewish state would provide 'the solution of the Jewish Question after eighteen centuries of Jewish suffering'.[4]

A century later, fifty years or so after the creation of the State of

Israel in 1948, there are those who see the rise of a 'new antisemitism' in the world, with the Jewish state itself as the focus of hostility towards Jews.[5] According to proponents of this view, contemporary antisemitism is new in two respects. First, on their account, a new *wave* or *outbreak* of hostility towards Jews began with the start of the second Palestinian intifada in September 2000 and is continuing at the present time. They see this expressed in an increase in attacks against Jews and Jewish institutions. They perceive a change in the public climate of western European societies whereby anti-Jewish sentiment has become more socially acceptable among 'the chattering classes' and on the activist left. And they cite the growth of an antisemitic discourse in Muslim circles. Some commentators, such as Avi Becker, believe the current wave of antisemitism 'is unprecedented since the end of World War II'.[6]

Second, and more fundamentally, the 'new antisemitism' is said to involve a new *form* or *type* of hostility towards Jews: hostility towards Israel. 'New' here does not necessarily mean within the last few years; it could be as old as the state itself or even older. However, those who hold this view tend to think that the new form of antisemitism has intensified with the recent intifada. They point to a persistent anti-Israel bias in western media, especially on the part of journalists of a 'liberal-left' persuasion. They refer to the animus with which certain prominent non-Jewish intellectuals have attacked Israel. They accuse the UN of being unfair to Israel, singling out the Jewish state for criticism and applying double standards when judging its behaviour. They quote the vitriolic language in which Israel is sometimes condemned, citing in this connection the UN World Conference against Racism held in Durban, South Africa, in September 2001. Noting that the polemic against Israel at this conference originated at the Asian regional meeting in Tehran, they tend to see Arab and Muslim anti-Israel propaganda as the locus classicus of the new form of antisemitism.

Proponents of this view see an equivalence between (a) the individual Jew in the old or classical version of antisemitism and (b) the State of Israel in the new or modern variety. Jonathan Sacks, Chief Rabbi of Britain and the Commonwealth, explains: 'At times it [antisemitism] has been directed against Jews as individuals. Today it is directed against Jews as a sovereign people.'[7] In classical antisemitism, the Jew was frequently associated with the Antichrist and the Devil. Likewise, according to Rabbi Michael Melchior, former Deputy Foreign Minister of Israel, the Jewish state today is portrayed as 'the new anti-Christ of the international community, or the devil of the international community'.[8] Per Ahlmark, former Deputy Prime Minister of Sweden, has put the equivalence this way: 'We certainly could say that in the past the most dangerous anti-Semites were those who wanted to make the world *Judenrein* [free of Jews]. Today the most dangerous anti-Semites might be those who want to make the world *Judenstaatsrein* [free of a Jewish state].'[9] Irwin Cotler sums it up when he says, in a striking phrase, that Israel has emerged as 'the collective Jew among the nations'; hence the title of this chapter.[10]

One way to flesh out this concept is to take Herzl's words quoted above and to substitute 'Israel' or 'the Jewish state' for 'Jews'. The result, mutatis mutandis, should give us a description of Israel as 'the collective Jew'. It goes something like this: 'The world resounds with outcries against the Jewish state.' Like Jews in Herzl's time, Israel today is 'more or less persecuted' in the world. Just as 'equality before the law' was 'practically a dead letter' for individual Jews, so it is for the Jewish state in international forums: it does not get a fair hearing. At one time, Jews were 'debarred' from public office; now Israel is 'debarred' from permanent membership of a regional group in the UN. 'Don't buy of Jews!' has become 'Don't buy of Israel!' And so on. Ultimately, just as individual Jews in the past were denied the most basic right of all, the right to live, so the very existence of the State of Israel is being questioned today. In short, adapting Herzl again: 'The community of nations in whose midst Israel exists is, either covertly or openly, antisemitic.' Such, more or less, is the view I am examining in this chapter.

Although the State of Israel, on this account, is the *object* of a 'new antisemitism', the *effects* are felt by Jews and Jewish communities everywhere. Ahlmark explains how this works. 'So they [anti-Zionists] now focus on the *collective Jew* – the State of Israel. Such attacks spark a chain reaction of assaults on *individual* Jews and Jewish institutions.'[11] In other words, on this account, the new *wave* of antisemitism is due, in part at least, to the new *form* that antisemitism takes today: antagonism towards the State of Israel.

The concept of Israel as 'the collective Jew' is thus both a thesis in its own right and a hypothesis for explaining hostility towards Jews around the world. I believe that the concept is confused and that the use to which it is put gives a distorted picture of the facts it purports to explain. This is not to deny that the facts give cause for concern. On the contrary, there are good reasons for the insecurity and discomfort that many Jews say they feel. It appears, for one thing, that there has been a sharp rise in attacks, physical and verbal, directed at Jews in several parts of the world since the second intifada began.[12] Moreover, given the political situation in the Middle East, there is reason to think that this trend will continue – unless Israel is integrated into the region and its conflict with the Palestinians is peacefully resolved. There is, furthermore, an unmistakable vein of antisemitism in public discourse on Israel, whether in the salon, on 'the street', in the mosque, in the UN or in the media.[13] It is in the air and, as some say, you can smell it. But, in the first place, you cannot always trust your sense of smell. And, in the second place, I see nothing radically 'new' about contemporary antisemitism. Exaggerating its extent, or confusing it with other forms of hostility towards Jews, only exacerbates the situation.

I shall neither attempt to make the whole of the argument for these claims nor to explore all their ramifications. My focus is on the concept of Israel as 'the collective Jew'. I begin by recalling classical antisemitism: the familiar, common-or-garden, old-fashioned variety, the kind that led to the persecution of European Jewry to which Herzl's Zionism was a reaction. On this basis, I briefly reformulate the question of whether and when hostility towards Israel is antisemitic, and then discuss the so-called new form of antisemitism, especially the equation of anti-Zionism with antisemitism. I shall first take a historical approach and then consider some objections to my argument. I conclude by revisiting Herzl's optimistic vision, and consider how he might react if he heard there was a 'new antisemitism' in the world.

OLD ANTISEMITISM

A good, simple working definition of antisemitism, according to a broad consensus of scholars, is this: hostility towards Jews *as* Jews.[14] This definition has the virtue of ruling out such cases as the London bus conductor (let us call her Lucy) who, in a hypothetical scenario, angrily throws Rabbi Cohen off the 73 bus for smoking.[15] Even if smoking is something Rabbi Cohen does religiously, even if he is wearing a *kipah* identifying him as Jewish: even so, his situation is no different from that of Jane Smith or Ahmed Khan or Bhupinda Singh or any of the other smoking passengers that Lucy evicts that morning from her bus for smoking.[16] His crime is that he is a smoker, not that he is a Jew.

It is a little more complicated if Lucy's hostility to Rabbi Cohen is based on the fact that he is singing *zemiros* (hymns) on the upper deck at the top of his voice. But is it because he is singing *zemiros* or is it because he is singing, full stop? Suppose he would have been singing

'Oh I do like to be beside the seaside': would Lucy have taken the same action? In other words, which is he guilty of being: loutish or Jewish? Let us give Lucy the benefit of the doubt: let us say that she is a liberal, tolerant, broad-minded woman, but rules are rules and she throws him off the bus because he is creating a nuisance. The fact that he is Jewish is neither here nor there – for Lucy. But for Rabbi Cohen it matters. I mean specifically that it is the reason why he is singing *zemiros*. Rabbi Cohen is not merely a person who happens to be Jewish and happens to be singing. He is singing *as* a Jew. But she evicts him *as* a lout. This is the second scenario. Mrs Goldstein, who is watching this scene from the back of the bus, smells antisemitism. She is wrong.

But now let us *not* give Lucy the benefit of the doubt. Let us assume the worst and suppose she is bigoted. But about what or whom, exactly? What does she know from 'Jewish'? Rabbi Cohen is singing in Hebrew. Does *she* know it is Hebrew? It could be any foreign lingo. She looks at Rabbi Cohen, with his foreign appearance and foreign ways, and she sees a figure that she recognizes vaguely from the pages of the *Sun* or *Daily Mail*: an asylum seeker. And under the guise of enforcing the rules against creating a nuisance, she deports him from her bus. Even if she is aware of the fact that he is Jewish, it is not his Jewishness per se that bothers her, but what she sees as his alienness. We might call this 'xenophobia', hatred of strangers or of anyone 'different'; but it is not antisemitism. This is the third scenario.

However (fourth scenario), perhaps Lucy's prejudice is more specific. She is not an ignorant woman. One look at Rabbi Cohen's black garb and long flowing beard and Lucy knows precisely what he is: one of them mullahs. 'Clear off, Abdul' she shouts in his ear as she shoves him on to the pavement. As Rabbi Cohen picks himself up off Stoke Newington High Street, he reflects philosophically that he is the victim of Islamophobia. But Mrs Goldstein is convinced that all London bus conductors hate Jews.

But suppose now that Mrs Goldstein is right, not about London bus conductors in general but about Lucy. Suppose, in other words, that Lucy knows Rabbi Cohen is Jewish and that this is why she ejects him from her bus. This is the fifth scenario: she knows he is Jewish and she feels contempt or hatred for him *because* he is Jewish. What does this mean? Knowing he is Jewish, what exactly does Lucy think she knows? She is antisemitic: she despises him because he is a Jew. And what, pray, is a Jew?

In his essay 'The Freedom of Self-Definition', Imre Kertész, the Hungarian-Jewish writer who survived a Nazi concentration camp, reflects on Jewish identity in the light of his wartime experience. 'In 1944', he writes, 'they put a yellow star on me, which in a symbolic sense is still there; to this day I have not been able to remove it.' What he is unable to remove is the meaning of the word 'Jew' that the Nazis invested in the badge. Kertész recalls Montesquieu's dictum, 'First I am a human being, and then a Frenchman', and comments: 'The racist ... wants me to be first a Jew and then not to be a human being any more.' In a brilliant dialectical riff, he works through the implications for the victim: 'After a while, it's not ourselves we're thinking about but somebody else.' That is to say, the self that we think about is not our own: I am not my own person. 'In a racist environment', he concludes, 'a Jew cannot be human, but he cannot be a Jew either. For "Jew" is an unambiguous designation only in the eyes of anti-Semites.'[17]

This is how I understand Kertész: he is saying that the yellow star was not just a form of identification, *picking him out* as a Jew, but a whole identity, *projected onto him* as a Jew. Pinning the star to his breast, they were pinning down the word 'Jew' or 'Jewish', determining what it means. This meaning or identity – this 'unambiguous designation' – belonged to the Nazis, not to the Jews, not to him.

Kertész observes that 'no one whose Jewish identity is based primarily, perhaps exclusively, on Auschwitz, can really be called a Jew'. What he means is that they cannot call *themselves* a Jew – they cannot define themselves as Jewish – because the word is not theirs to use: it is someone else's brand stamped on them and they are stuck with it: 'Jew'. This appears to be how Kertész sees his own condition. Recall his words: 'to this day I have not been able to remove it'. But (to get back to the 73 bus), Rabbi Cohen, singing *zemiros* at the top of his voice on the upper deck, is Jewish on his own terms: he 'can really be called a Jew'. So, Lucy knows Rabbi Cohen is Jewish. Rabbi Cohen knows Rabbi Cohen is Jewish. But do they know the same thing? They do not. For he is not the 'Jew' – the figment – that Lucy perceives and despises.

This suggests that our working definition of antisemitism, hostility towards Jews as Jews, is flawed. It should be amended to read: hostility towards Jews as 'Jews'. Adding the scare quotes around 'Jews' might seem like a detail, but it transforms the meaning of our definition. That is to say, our working definition is not merely imprecise, it is positively misleading. It would be more accurate (if cumbersome) to define the word along these lines: a form of hostility towards Jews as Jews, in which Jews are perceived as something other than what they are. Or more succinctly: hostility towards Jews as *not* Jews. For the 'Jew' towards whom the antisemite feels hostile is not a *real* Jew at all (even if some real Jews fit the stereotype). Thinking that Jews are really 'Jews' is precisely the core of antisemitism.

Antisemitism is best defined not by an attitude to Jews but by a definition of 'Jew'. Defining the word in terms of the attitude – hostility – rather than the object – Jew – puts the cart before the horse. Indeed, hostility is not the only 'cart' that the horse can 'pull' behind it. Envy and admiration can also attach to the figure of the 'Jew'. Wilhelm Marr, who founded the Antisemiten-Liga (League of Antisemites) in Germany in 1879, described Jews as 'flexible, tenacious, intelligent'.[18] These are not in themselves terms of contempt. However, their antisemitic bent is evident when they are read in context: 'We have among us a flexible, tenacious, intelligent, foreign tribe that knows how to bring abstract reality into play in many different ways. Not individual Jews, but the Jewish spirit and Jewish consciousness have overpowered the world.' This 'Jewish spirit' and 'Jewish consciousness' is what Marr meant by *Semitism*. It is the main element in the word he popularized: *anti*semitism (*antisemitismus*).[19] It is the horse that pulls the cart.

Who, then, are the 'Jews' that the antisemite hates – or fears or despises or envies or admires? What is the 'unambiguous designation' of the yellow star that Kertész 'to this day' is unable to remove? When they pinned the badge on him and he became a 'Jew', what did he become? He ceased to be a mere mortal and became, in a way, timeless: a cipher of 'the eternal Jew', an instance of 'the Jewish peril'.[20] Here is a thumbnail sketch of this figure:

> The Jew belongs to a sinister people set apart from all others, not merely by its customs but by a collective character: arrogant yet obsequious; legalistic yet corrupt; flamboyant yet secretive. Always looking to turn a profit, Jews are as ruthless as they are tricky. Loyal only to their own, wherever they go they form a state within a state, preying upon the societies in whose midst they dwell. Their hidden hand controls the banks, the markets and the media.[21] And when revolutions occur or nations go to war, it is the Jews – cohesive, powerful, clever and stubborn – who invariably pull the strings and reap the rewards.

Not all these themes need to be present; not all receive equal emphasis in a given case; and there are variations on each. But such, more or less, are the Semites in the antisemitic imagination – whether they are seen as a nation, an ethnic group, a religious community, a race or whatever. Wilhelm Marr conceived of Jews in biological terms: he saw them as a race. But his idea of the Semite is detachable from his racial ideology. And he did not invent it. He inherited it; for, in one form or another, it has been around a long time, long before anyone dreamed up the newfangled theory of race. The figure of the 'Jew' has been transmitted from generation to generation in popular culture. Nor is it likely to disappear overnight. This is the character whom Lucy sees when she ejects Rabbi Cohen from the 73 bus in the fifth scenario: a parasite that preys on humanity and seeks to dominate the world. It is what Kertész became when, stripped of everything except the badge they pinned on him, he was made a 'Jew' in Auschwitz.

In short, antisemitism is the process of turning Jews into 'Jews'.

ANTISEMITISM AND ANTI-ZIONISM

If this is what 'old' antisemitism is, then the decisive question concerning hostility towards Israel is (something like) this: Does it ever turn the Jewish state into a 'Jewish' state? Does it, as it were, pin a yellow star on to the State of Israel? Does it project on to the state, explicitly or otherwise, those traits that make up the classical stereotype of the 'Jew'? If and when it does, then it is a form of antisemitism. If not, it is not.

Those who hold the view I am examining see the question differently. They draw the line in a different place. They start out, however, from the same point: it is legitimate in principle to oppose and criticize Israel. Jonathan Sacks observes, 'We can too easily dismiss all criticism of the state or government of Israel as anti-semitism. It is not. No democratic state is entitled to consider itself beyond reproach, and Israel is a democratic state.'[22] Abraham Foxman, National Director of the Anti-Defamation League, agrees: 'We are always careful to say that not every criticism against the State of Israel is anti-Semitic. Yes, Israel is a state, a member of the community of nations, and it is subject to criticism as any other state. Therefore, if you criticize Israel, that doesn't make you an anti-Semite.'[23] Then what does? Where do they draw the line between legitimate and illegitimate opinion? Foxman speaks for virtually all proponents of the view under discussion in this chapter when he says, 'The harsh but undeniable truth is this: what some like to call anti-Zionism is, in reality, anti-Semitism – always, everywhere, and for all time.'[24] Hillel Harkin, writing in the *Wall Street Journal*, elaborates:

One cannot be against Israel or Zionism, as opposed to this or that Israeli policy or Zionist position, without being anti-Semitic. Israel is the state of the Jews. Zionism is the belief that the Jews should have a state. To defame Israel is to defame the Jews. To wish it never existed, or would cease to exist, is to wish to destroy the Jews.[25]

All the proponents of the view I am examining tend to draw the line in the same place. Like Harkin, they all tend to rule out, on the grounds that it is antisemitic, any criticism of Israel that 'defames' the state. Precisely what this permits and what it excludes is left somewhat open. Some commentators, for example, think it is antisemitic to describe the administration of the Occupied Territories as a form of apartheid. Others object even to describing them as 'occupied' (and not 'disputed'). Be that as it may, on one point there is a virtual consensus: anti-Zionism as such is beyond the pale.

There is an irony about this view. Antisemitism in civil service and government circles in Britain played a vital role during the early days of the Zionist movement. David Fromkin, in *A Peace to End All Peace*, tells the story in the context of the collapse of the Ottoman Empire at the end of the First World War, when the map of the modern Middle East was drawn. He says: 'The notion of committing Britain to Zionism was inspired by Gerald FitzMaurice and Mark Sykes.'[26] Both Fitzmaurice and Sykes believed in 'the existence of a cohesive world Jewish community that moved in hidden ways to control the world'.[27] FitzMaurice, based in the British embassy in Constantinople, maintained that Jews had taken control of the Ottoman Empire. Sykes, whose name is immortalized in the secret Sykes–Picot Agreement between Britain, France and Russia (1916), in which the parties agreed to divide up the Middle East into spheres of influence, 'harbored an abiding and almost obsessive fear of Jews, whose web of dangerous international intrigue he discerned in many an obscure corner'. He was convinced that 'Jews were a power in a great many places and might sabotage the Allied cause.'[28] Fromkin continues: 'But unlike the Russians, Sykes believed in attempting to win them over. He reported to the Foreign Office that he had told Picot that, while Britain had no interest in taking possession of Palestine, it was what the Zionists wanted, and that they ought to be propitiated if the Allies were to have a chance of winning the war.'

This was in 1916, a year prior to the momentous declaration by Arthur Balfour, British Foreign Secretary, that stated that 'His Majesty's Government view with favour the establishment in Palestine of a

national home for the Jewish people.'[29] Balfour shared (at least partly)
Sykes's view of Jews. A contemporary, summing up a conversation with
the Foreign Secretary, wrote that Balfour 'is inclined to believe that
nearly all Bolshevism and disorder of that sort is directly traceable to
Jews'.[30] 'Always in the background', writes the Israeli historian Tom
Segev, 'was his evaluation of Jewish power.'[31] As Prime Minister, Balfour had introduced the Aliens Bill (which became law in 1905), aimed
specifically at limiting the admission of East European Jews who
sought refuge in Britain, warning Parliament that the Jews 'remained
a people apart'.[32] This view of Jews – a people suspiciously apart –
recalls the phrase used by the German idealist philosopher Johann
Fichte, who in 1793 described the Jews as 'a state within a state'. Fichte
was against granting Jews civil rights, 'except perhaps, if one night we
chop off all of their heads and replace them with new ones, in which
there would not be one single Jewish idea'. He continued: 'And then,
I see no other way to protect ourselves from the Jews, except if we
conquer their promised land for them and send all of them there.'[33] Thus
he anticipated by more than a century the antisemitic pro-Zionist British
policy pursued by the likes of FitzMaurice, Sykes and Balfour.[34]

The irony of antisemitic support for Zionism deepens when we look
at the other side of the argument, so to speak. Balfour's letter, containing his benevolent Declaration, might have been sent to Lord Rothschild earlier than 2 November 1917 had it not run into opposition.
The opposition was not led by antisemites of a different stripe. It 'came
from leading figures in the British Jewish community', notably Edwin
Montagu, a member of the Cabinet.[35] Montagu rejected the basic
premise of Zionism: that Jews constitute a separate nation.[36] In his
memorandum 'The Anti-Semitism of the Present Government' (23
August 1917), he wrote: 'I wish to place on record my view that the
policy of His Majesty's Government is anti-Semitic in result and will
prove a rallying ground for Anti-Semites in every country in the
world.'[37] Fromkin notes wryly that Montagu was worried about his
own position and the position of his family in British society. Be that
as it may, 'The evidence suggested that in his non-Zionism, Montagu
was speaking for a majority of Jews.'[38] Certainly, his views were shared
by the Conjoint Foreign Committee of the Board of Deputies of British
Jews and the Anglo-Jewish Association. In a letter to *The Times* published on 24 May 1917, the Conjoint Committee wrote what was, in
effect, a critique of Zionist ideology. The letter registers objections to
two 'points' or planks in the Zionist programme, the first being the
'claim that the Jewish settlement in Palestine shall be recognized as

possessing a national character in a political sense'. Here is part of what they say about this claim:

> It is part and parcel of a wider Zionist theory, which regards all the Jewish communities of the world as constituting one home-less nationality, incapable of complete social and political identi-fication, with the nations among whom they dwelt, and it is argued that for this homeless nationality, a political center and an always available homeland in Palestine are necessary. Against this theory the Conjoint Committee strongly and earnestly protests.[39]

The letter goes on to warn that 'the establishment of a Jewish nation-ality in Palestine, founded on this theory of Jewish homelessness, must have the effect throughout the world of stamping the Jews as strangers in their native lands, and of undermining their hard-won position as citizens and nationals of those lands'. In effect, the thrust of the argu-ment made by the Conjoint Committee in 1917 was that Zionism, in theory and in practice, tends to endorse the classical antisemitic view of Jews as essentially alien, a people apart and a state within a state. This argument might or might not be valid. But is it plausible to describe it, in Foxman's words, as 'in reality, anti-Semitism'?

According to the view under discussion in this chapter, anti-Zion-ism is inherently or invariably antisemitic. But as this historical excur-sus has shown, anti-Zionism and antisemitism are in fact independent variables: one can exist without the other. Certainly, antisemitism can, and sometimes does, take the form of anti-Zionism; but as we have seen, it can also take the opposite form.

OBJECTIONS AND REPLIES

Someone might object:

> *This argument is all very well but it is too theoretical. It ignores two facts. First, history has overtaken the question. Israel exists, and for millions of Jews Israel is their home. They have nowhere else to go. To oppose Zionism at this point in time means nothing less than wanting to deprive them of their homeland and perhaps their very lives. Only an antisemite could want such a thing. Second, anti-Zionists single out the Jewish state unfairly. They accept the princi-ple of self-determination for everyone else – but not for Jews. Why not? They accept the right of every other state to exist – but not Israel. Why? Clearly, anti-Zionism is just a form of antisemitism.*

The first thing to say about these objections is that 'anti-Zionism' refers to several different positions concerning the existence of Israel as a Jewish state. These include the view that the State of Israel has no right to exist; that it should not have been created in the first place; that it ought not to continue to exist at all; or that it should not survive as a specifically Jewish polity. The objection lumps these positions together whereas each should be taken separately. Some people today, precisely because of the difference that history has made, reject the anti-Zionist stance that Israel should cease to exist, but still maintain the anti-Zionist view that it ought never to have been created. They might also harbour the anti-Zionist (or post-Zionist) hope that Israel one day will repeal the Law of Return and evolve into a society that ceases to define itself in ethnic terms or to see itself, in Harkin's phrase, as 'the state of the Jews'.[40]

Furthermore, there is nothing inherently or inevitably antisemitic about any of these anti-Zionist positions. To some extent, Zionism raises issues that are unique; to that extent it is legitimate to 'single out' the Jewish state. For one thing, the question of whether Jews constitute a nation in the relevant, modern sense is no less a burning issue today – not least for Jews themselves – than it was in 1917. For another, Israel is not a Jewish state in a vacuum. The special circumstances of its creation in the Middle East, where Jewish aspirations have clashed with Arab, Palestinian and Muslim aspirations, make it a special case. But to a great extent, Zionism is controversial in much the same way as other forms of nationalism are controversial. For the Zionist idea is modelled on the nineteenth-century idea of the nation state. It is not antisemitic to reject this model. Jews, as much as anyone, have suffered from nationalism in the lands where they have lived. It is by no means obvious that the solution to their suffering – or the solution to the conflict with the Palestinians – is to continue to accept Herzl's nineteenth-century idea and embrace the very ideology that has oppressed them in the past.

No doubt, there are those who single out the Jewish state unfairly. But the notion that everyone who opposes the cause of Jewish nationalism supports every other national cause on the planet is implausible. Even among people who tend to support national liberation movements in general, their attitude in a given case can depend on the cause in question and on the circumstances. Conceivably, someone who sympathizes with the Chechens in their conflict with the Russians, or the Kurds in their conflict with various states, might believe that 'the principle of self-determination' does not apply to, say, the Basques.

(And if so, this does not make them bigoted anti-Basque racists, though this might be how they appear in Bilbao.) It is equally implausible to maintain that Israel is the only state whose legitimacy has been questioned or denied in the modern world. Perhaps one of the distinguishing marks of the last century is the extent to which people questioned the legitimacy of existing states. The former Soviet Union and the former Yugoslavia are two examples that come to mind, both of which, in terms of scale and complexity, dwarf the case of Israel.

But even when Israel is singled out unfairly, even when it is 'defamed' by its detractors, it by no means follows that the hostility towards the state is antisemitic. This goes to the heart of the quarrel I have with the view under discussion in this chapter. I shall make my case via a document notorious for its hostile tone towards Israel and for its defamatory content: the resolution adopted by the UN General Assembly in 1975 that concluded 'Zionism is a form of racism and racial discrimination.'[41]

I remember it well. I recall the feeling of alienation that many other Jews at the time must have felt, regardless of their political views about Israel and its policies: the primordial sense that 'the world is against us', the hollow feeling in the pit of the stomach that it was happening again. For the UN is the world body. When it speaks, it is as if the world were speaking in unison. And the world seemed to take no cognizance whatsoever of the Jewish experience of oppression and the active struggle against it. For historically, Zionism, however misbegotten and whatever its faults, came into existence as a reaction to antisemitism. Antisemitism is a form of racism. Yet 'the world' was saying that Zionism was itself a form of the evil it fought against. No ifs and buts. No qualifications or caveats. No acknowledgment of the Jewish story. The preamble to the resolution, 'recalling' and 'taking note' of one evil and injustice after another, neither recalled nor took note of antisemitism at all. It did not so much as mention the word. It was as if there never had been the persecution of which Herzl spoke, let alone the Nazi genocide, the wholesale destruction of Jewish communities in Europe, and the massive displacement of Jewish people that gave such impetus to the Zionist movement, bringing so many Jews round to a cause they might otherwise have spurned. Worse, the preamble did not merely ignore the Jewish story; it folded it into the larger narrative of European colonialism. It described the 'racist regime' in Israel as having 'a common imperialist origin, forming a whole and having the same racist structure and being organically linked' with the white supremacist regimes in South Africa and Rhodesia. But in fact the origins of Zionism did not lie in the imperialism of European states, even if, like other national movements at the time, Zionism played the game and sought to benefit from imperial politics. Nor was Zionism based on an ideology of European or white supremacy. On the contrary, Jews had been marginalized by white European civilization. Zionism saw itself as a national movement aimed at liberating Jews from the chronic circumstances of their rejection and persecution. This entire history was obliterated by the UN resolution. It was this total blotting out of Jewish experience in the preamble, as much as the conclusion itself, that cut like a knife. The silence was deadening. In this accounting of history, Jews as Jews had no place. The feeling of rejection was chillingly familiar. You didn't have to be a Zionist to have this reaction; being Jewish was enough.

I have said this as powerfully as I can in order to make it as hard as possible to argue, as I now shall, that the animus towards Israel that informed the UN resolution was not antisemitic and that it completely misses the point to see it this way. Ironically, the clue to the true nature of the hostility to Israel in this resolution lies in the very features of the text to which I have drawn attention: on the one hand, the failure to acknowledge a Jewish point of view and, on the other hand, the dominance of an anti-European or anti-western perspective. For the resolution reflected the situation of the developing nations that predominate in the General Assembly, nations that share a common experience as former European colonies. And, as Tal Becker (former legal adviser to Israel's permanent mission to the UN) has observed, 'Palestinians are a symbol of third-world struggle for self-determination.'[42] Israel, in contrast, tends to be seen in light of its European provenance.

Historically, Zionism has seen itself as the national liberation movement of the Jewish people. But, like the Roman god Janus, it has two faces that look in opposing directions at once. That is to say, it belongs to two opposite histories at one and the same time. On the one side, Zionism is part of the history of the Jews, the 'inside outsiders' of Europe, a people whose past includes a catalogue of exclusion, oppression and persecution, for whom the movement sought self-determination. On the other side, Zionism was part of the history of colonialism. This is because, despite being a reaction to the experience of powerlessness in Europe, it was itself part of European expansion into non-European territory. For, in the Jewish case, in contrast with other self-styled national liberation movements, there was no existing national territory under occupation; the project was to 'gather in the exiles' and populate another land – Palestine – rather than expel a foreign power from the homeland where the people already dwelt. From the beginning, starting with Theodor Herzl's address to the first Zionist congress in 1897, Zionism spoke the language of 'colonization'; but it was colonization for the sake of emancipation, not empire.[43] Seen from *this* side, Zionism was a flight from Europe, not an extension of the European homeland. But seen from the *other* side, the Jews who came as settlers were Europeans by any other name. And they were. They were both. They were Jewish as distinct from European, and they were European as distinct from Arab.[44]

The UN resolution is written from a point of view that sees only one side of the double-sided phenomenon that is Zionism. From *this* side, Jews are precisely not seen as Jews as such; they are seen as Europeans or at least as the agents of Europe. Whatever we call this, patently it is not antisemitism. This does not justify the text nor does it make it any more palatable; but it does explain it. It explains why the story of Zionism is folded into the larger narrative of European imperialism and colonialism. The one-sidedness of the text reflects perceived territorial, economic and political interests, along with general principles of justice and human rights; not antisemitism.[45] (Political interests at the time were, of course, partly a function of the realpolitik of UN machinations, which in 1975 included the Cold War alignments of member nations behind the rival superpowers of the United States and the Soviet Union.)

If this hypothesis is true, if the underlying causes are (broadly) political, we would expect hostility towards Israel to fluctuate relative to the politics of the Middle East. And it does. As the Jewish Agency for Israel points out: 'Anti-Israel resolutions at the United Nations coincide with events in the Middle East.'[46] Thus, when the peace process got underway in 1991 with the convening of the Madrid Conference, Israel's star began to rise. Within weeks, the UN General Assembly revoked its 1975 resolution equating Zionism with racism.[47] Israel's standing in the UN continued to improve when, in 1993, the Israelis and Palestinians signed the Oslo Accords.[48] Moreover, bilateral relations with other states improved concomitantly. In 1994 Israel and Jordan signed a peace treaty. David Harris, Executive Director of the American Jewish Committee, has provided a helpful shortlist of other favourable developments in the 1990s. 'Several Arab countries', he notes, 'including Oman, Qatar, Morocco, and Tunisia, established formal sub-ambassadorial links with Israel, while Mauritania went the extra mile and announced full diplomatic ties with Israel.'[49] Nor was this confined to Arab countries: other nations sought out the Jewish state. 'It reached the point', says Harris, 'where, like a busy New York bakery on a Sunday morning, they had to take a number and wait on line for visits to an Israel that loomed large in the public imagination, but that was too small to handle all the interest and attention at once.'[50]

Then in 2000, says Harris, 'we got mugged'. By 'we' he means both Israel and Jewry. By 'mugged' he is referring to two things: first, the 'worldwide campaign being waged to isolate, condemn, and weaken Israel'; second, 'the wave of documented anti-Semitic incidents' in western Europe.[51] But there was no mugging. What happened was that peace talks broke down at Camp David in July, Ariel Sharon marched to the Temple Mount in September, the second intifada broke out, and the Israel Defence Forces made increasing incursions into the West Bank and Gaza Strip. In other words, the political conflict flared up. Again, the Jewish Agency states the matter plainly: 'Since the escalation of violence in the Middle East, there has been renewed movement at the UN with Israel again the target of one sided condemnations, and unfair criticism.'[52]

In short, the empirical evidence overwhelmingly supports the view that hostility towards Israel, at bottom, is not a new form of anti-semitism; it is a function of a deep and bitter political conflict. The depth and bitterness of this conflict is sufficient to explain, for the most part, the strength and intensity of the polemic against the state, especially on the part of those who are directly impinged on by Israel's presence in the Middle East and by the expansion of Jewish settlements in the territories it has retained since the June 1967 war. They see the state through the lens of their own history and their own interests. And why shouldn't they? They see it as an integral part of a conflict in which the West has sought, since at least the end of the nineteenth century, to dominate the Middle East, to colonize it and control its affairs, either directly or through its clients, and continues to do so still. True, this perception of Israel is one-sided. But there is one-sidedness on both sides. When pro-Israelis 'defame' the Palestinians, this does not make them anti-Arab racists. By the same token, when pro-Palestinians do the same to Israel, this does not make them antisemites. It cuts both ways.

As an auxiliary argument, I would like to conduct a simple thought-experiment. Imagine if Israel were the same in every essential respect as the state that exists today, including its occupation of the West Bank and Gaza Strip, except that it were not Jewish. Suppose it were Catholic, like the Crusader states that Europeans created in the Middle East in the twelfth and thirteenth centuries. Let's call this imaginary state 'Christiania' instead of 'Israel'. Would Christiania be accepted into the bosom of the region more readily than Israel has been? I doubt it. Would the animosity felt towards Christiania be qualitatively different from, or significantly less than, the hostility now directed at Israel? Again, I think not. Any differences would, I submit, be a matter of nuance. As it happens, Israel is often called a 'crusader state' in Arab and Muslim circles. In a way, this says everything about the Israeli–Arab and Israeli–Palestinian conflicts. Crusader states, like the imaginary Christiania, were Christian; the State of Israel is Jewish. But the underlying hostility towards it in the region is not hostility towards the state *as* Jewish but *as* a European interloper or *as* an American client or *as* a non-Arab and non-Muslim entity; moreover, *as* an occupying force. Whatever names we may legitimately give to these attitudes, 'anti-semitism' is not one of them.

This is not to say that antisemitism cannot and does not enter into anti-Zionism in the Arab and Muslim world. Clearly it does. Moreover, the longer Israel is at loggerheads with the rest of the region, the more likely it is that antisemitism will take on a life of its own. But this is, as it were, a secondary formation. Classical antisemitism 'did not exist in the traditional Islamic world'.[53] Primarily, anti-Zionism and anti-Israel sentiment in the Middle East is no more antisemitic than Lucy's attitude to Rabbi Cohen in the first four of the five hypothetical scenarios I sketched above. In the first two cases, in which Rabbi Cohen is either smoking or singing at the top of his voice, Lucy's hostility towards him is due to the fact that he is breaking the rules – rules that apply to everyone – or disturbing the peace of her bus. In the third, it is simply because he is 'different' or strange; while the fourth is a case of mistaken identity. So, she is hostile to him either (in the first two cases) *as* rule-breaker and *as* troublemaker or (in the third) *as* outsider or (in the fourth) *as* someone with another identity; but not (in any of these cases) *as* Jewish. She is no antisemite: not even in the second case in which Rabbi Cohen is singing *zemiros*. For, although, from *his* point of view, he is merely expressing himself as a Jew, from *hers* he is being a lout. On the analysis I have given in this chapter, Israel's situation in the Arab and Muslim Middle East is somewhat similar to Rabbi Cohen's in these four scenarios. Depending on how you view things, the parallel is closer to one of the first two cases – Israel's actions seen as violating international law or causing conflict in the region – or to the third or fourth – Israel's presence seen as alien and its Jewish population as outsiders or 'crusaders'; or it could be any permutation of the four.

There remains the fifth and final scenario: Lucy, knowing Rabbi Cohen is Jewish, is hostile towards him on that account. This is not, au fond, because of anything he does but because of what she perceives him to be: the personification of the 'Jew' that haunts her febrile imagination, a token of a type.[54]

Now, there are two possibilities here. Either she is open about it, subjecting him to an antisemitic diatribe. Or she conceals her real feelings, perhaps hiding behind company rules or pretending to be concerned for her other customers. Suppose he starts to sing *zemiros*: 'Sorry, Sir', she says disingenuously, 'but no one is permitted to make such a hullabaloo. Off you get!' In the latter case, there is no sure way of diagnosing the animus that underlies her actions. It is the same with attitudes towards Israel. There are times when Israel is attacked in explicitly antisemitic terms: the state is portrayed as 'the Jewish peril', all-powerful, capable of manipulating governments, responsible for all wars, seeking to dominate the world, and so on. But at other times any antisemitism that might be present is disguised and there might be no easy way of telling whether it is there or not. In the absence of a discourse that, so to speak, pins a yellow star onto the State of Israel, we can only make a judgement, case by case, based on the available evidence. (We might, for example, look at other literature produced by the group or person in question; their history; their political connections; and so on.) Sometimes all we can say is that we 'smell' antisemitism. And sometimes when we do, we are right. But Mrs Goldstein, who *always* sniffs it whenever anyone attacks Israel, is wrong.

HERZL'S VISION REVISITED

On the view I have been examining in this chapter, there is an equivalence between (a) the individual Jew in the old or classical version of antisemitism and (b) the State of Israel in the new or modern variety. How would Herzl react to this way of seeing Israel's position in the world?

Herzl thought that, with the creation of a Jewish state, antisemitism would 'stop at once and for ever'. Zionism was meant to provide 'the solution of the Jewish Question after eighteen centuries of Jewish suffering'. Moreover, the solution was one that Jews themselves would implement; that is to say, Zionism called on Jews to take their destiny into their own hands.[55] Herzl's idea could be put this way: 'If we Jews are not wanted by the nations in whose midst we live, then we should take ourselves off and form a state of our own where we can live in peace.' If Herzl knew about the extent to which Israel would be embroiled in conflict and controversy and if he thought that this was fundamentally due to antisemitism, he would be appalled. First, it would mean that his solution was itself encumbered with the very problem it was intended to solve. Second, if the predicament of the Jewish state today is equivalent to that of the individual Jew in the past, there is no equivalent solution. Israel cannot apply the same remedy: it cannot 'take itself off' to another corner of the globe. It has nowhere to go. Herzl's advice no longer avails.

What, in that case, can Israel do? If it is true that the community of nations is, either covertly or openly, antisemitic, what steps can it take to solve its own problem? Apparently none. If Israel is basically the victim of persecution in an antisemitic world then it bears no responsibility for the position in which it finds itself: the object of widespread condemnation. For antisemitism is a phenomenon for which Jews, neither collectively nor individually, can be held responsible. It is an a priori prejudice that revolves around a fiction, a figment of what Jews are like.[56] It is in the nature of such a prejudice that it will always find facts that seem to corroborate its fiction. Nothing that the Jewish state does or refrains from doing could produce it or prevent it. All Israel can do, if it really is 'the collective Jew among the nations', reprising the role of pariah, is fight for its survival, defying the world and keeping it at bay. In short, the view I have been examining in this chapter carries political implications. It is oddly disempowering, casting the Israeli state in the old mould of Jewish victim. More precisely, it combines the old bogey of pre-Israeli Jewish helplessness with the new mentality of Israeli Jewish aggressiveness. This combination lends itself to a particular style of politics in Israel, one that is not confined to any single party but which is nicely exemplified by the policies of its present Prime Minister.[57]

Looked at another way, the view I have been examining removes Israel from the realm of politics altogether and returns it to a mythic state of affairs in which 'the world' is to 'the Jews' what (in an antisemitic delusional fantasy) 'the Jews' are to 'the world': an eternal and implacable foe. If Herzl were alive today, I believe he would hold up his hands in horror at this perception. It would go completely against his grain, which was decidedly political and pragmatic.[58] If, however, he accepted that this was the reality, it would mean, in his eyes, that Zionism had failed. The goal of Zionism was to normalize the Jewish condition. The point of the Jewish state was to put the Jewish people on the same footing as other peoples. But if Israel is a lightning rod for worldwide antisemitism, then what Zionism has done is to reproduce, in the form of a state, the plight of the individual Jew down the centuries.

In short, I do not think that Herzl would care to hear that Israel has emerged as 'the collective Jew among the nations'.

Yet, in another inflection of this phrase, that is exactly the Zionist conception of Israel. This is why proponents of the view under discussion in this chapter are virtually unanimous in maintaining that anti-Zionism equals antisemitism and that 'to defame Israel is to defame the Jews'. These equations presuppose that Israel and the Jews are, in a profound sense, one and the same. This is how Israel itself sees the case. Israel does not regard itself as just *a* Jewish state, a state that happens to have a Jewish identity (like the medieval kingdom of the Khazars). It defines itself as *the* Jewish state. Note the definite article. It does not merely signify singularity, as if Israel were the only state that, as it happens, is Jewish. It implies that Israel is, in Harkin's phrase, 'the state of the Jews', i.e. of the Jewish nation, where the nation comprises the whole of Jewry, whether all Jews see themselves as part of it or not and whether they accept that Israel is their state or not. The State of Israel sees itself as the 'centre' of the Jewish People. This doctrine, which takes the biblical and religious themes of *am Yisrael* and *Tzion* and transposes them into the key of an ethnic nation state, lies at the heart of Zionism as an ideology. It is written into Israel's basic laws. It is a message that the state, via its public institutions and political representatives, conveys to the outside world. It is the basis for how Israel views Jews in what is called 'the diaspora'. To what extent the view is reciprocated by Jews is hard to say. At the height of Operation Defensive Shield in the Occupied Territories in Spring 2002, Jews, as Jews, gathered in large numbers in public rallies in numerous cities to affirm their solidarity with Israel.[59] Community leaders, religious and secular, have tended to reinforce this solidarity. Communal organizations, such as the current Board of Deputies of British Jews, regularly come to Israel's defence, as if defending Israel and defending the British Jewish community were one and the same. All in all, the average onlooker is liable to gain the impression that Israel is indeed 'the state of the Jews', the unique entity that represents all Jews collectively. It is as if Israel were, politically or even metaphysically, 'the collective Jew among the nations'.

In these circumstances, it is difficult to assess the extent to which the new wave of hostility towards Jews, radiating out from the Middle East, is antisemitic. If Jews as Jews align themselves with Israel, publicly and predominantly, then hostility towards Israel is liable to spill over into hostility towards Jews as such. Not that this is justifiable; it is never justifiable to lump all members of a religious or ethnic group together, dissolving the individual into the collective. The belief that all Jews are Zionists, or that all Jews identify with Israel, or that all Jews who identify with Israel support its every action, is false. But while this false belief can reflect an antisemitic canard about Jews forming a cohesive group that acts in unison, it can also be based on a rash generalization from the facts I have just rehearsed concerning the relationship between Jewry and Israel. A rash generalization is certainly reprehensible; but per se it is not antisemitic. The difference is between a belief reached by jumping to a conclusion that exceeds the evidence, and an a priori prejudice. When the State of Israel claims Jews as its own, and when Jews en masse proclaim Israel to be theirs, it is not surprising if others fail to make the distinction between Jewish state and Jewish people.[60]

The question at issue in this chapter has been one of interpretation. I have argued that, primarily and for the most part, hostility towards Israel is not based on the fact that the state is Jewish, let alone on a morbid and timeless fantasy about 'Jews'. It springs from Israel's situation in an Arab and Muslim Middle East and the direction taken by successive Israeli governments, especially in the Occupied Territories. Why does the question of interpretation matter? After all, hostility is hostility, whatever its causes or sources. Does it really make a difference whether we call it antisemitism or something else? It does. It matters because the question of how we act, and whether we are even capable of acting, is at stake. Antisemitism certainly enters the fray. But if we overstate its role, there is a price to pay. For one thing, we are liable to overlook other material factors, including ones that are under our control. For another, when we use the word too lightly and too loosely, it starts to lose its meaning. If it loses its meaning, we cannot speak out effectively against the real thing.

Furthermore, the picture becomes confused. I see it this way: The longer Israel persists in its current policies towards the Palestinians, the more it will be excoriated, not only by antisemites but by people of goodwill. Almost no one will take Israel's part except mainstream Jews. To the latter this will seem all too familiar: on the one side 'the world' and on the other side 'the Jews'. So they will dig their heels in further and become even more defensive of Israel. In their exasperation, others will accuse them of being hard-hearted and stubborn, which to Jews sounds like an old refrain. Thus, people will not know how to avoid seeming antisemitic and Jews will not know how to stop being victims.[61]

Be that as it may, and putting interpretation to one side, the fact remains that the world resounds with outcries against the Jewish state, the adverse effects of which are felt by Jews who live in other countries. If Herzl knew, he would turn in his grave.

POSTSCRIPT

Six years after writing this essay, in a lecture to the Arbeitskreis Nahost (Middle East Study Group) in Berlin, March 2009, shortly after Operation Cast Lead in Gaza, I revisited the penultimate paragraph and asked whether we have reached the point where 'people will not know how to avoid seeming antisemitic and Jews will not know how to stop being victims'. My verdict was that we have exceeded it. The situation, I argued, is worse in two ways. First, while the *problem* of antisemitism is growing, the *concept* is becoming more and more corrupted by persistent misuse and 'crying wolf'. As a result, we are in danger of losing our capacity to articulate the problem, which makes it all the more difficult to tackle it. Second, the gap between public opinion and mainstream Jewish opinion about the Israeli–Palestinian conflict is widening. This reinforces old feelings – of marginalization and exclusion – that are deeply planted in Jewish memory. This in turn tends to produce an even harder political line. Some people call this a swing to the right. I see it as a swing to the past, a swing back to a mindset that transcends the difference between left and right and is dominated by the Nazi Holocaust.[62]

NOTES

1. Theodor Herzl, *The Jewish State: An Attempt at a Modern Solution of the Jewish Question* (1896), translated from the original German by Sylvie D'Avigdor (London: Henry Pordes, 1993), p.7.
2. Ibid., p.22.
3. Ibid., p.23.
4. Ibid., pp.76, 78, 15, 30.
5. Those who see the rise of a 'new antisemitism' include: Abraham D. Foxman, *Never Again? The Threat of the New Anti-Semitism* (New York: HarperOne, 2004); Phyllis Chesler, *The New Anti-Semitism: The Current Crisis and What We Must Do About It* (San Francisco, CA: Jossey-Bass, 2003); Gabriel Schoenfeld, *The Return of Anti-Semitism* (New York: Encounter Books, 2004); Denis MacShane, *Globalising Hatred: The New Antisemitism* (London: Weidenfeld & Nicolson, 2008). This chapter is adapted from the essay with the same title that appeared in *Patterns of Prejudice*, 37, 2, (2003), pp.117–36.
6. Avi Becker, 'Anti-Semitism in the Guise of Intellectualism', *Ha'aretz*, 7 October 2002, http://www.haaretz.com/hasen/pages/ShArt.jhtml?itemNo=216763&contrassID=13.
7. Jonathan Sacks, 'The Hatred that Won't Die', *Guardian*, 28 February 2002, http://www.guardian.co.uk/world/2002/feb/28/comment.
8. 'Briefing to the Foreign Press by Deputy FM Melchior', 9 August 2001, Israel Ministry of Foreign Affairs, http://www.mfa.gov.il/mfa/government/speeches%20by%20israeli%20leaders/2001/briefing%20to%20the%20foreign%20press%20by%20dep%20fm%20melchior%20-.

9. Per Ahlmark, 'Anti-Semitism, Anti-Americanism, Anti-Zionism: Is There a Connection', 5 May 2004. Available at American Jewish Committee: http://www.ajc.org/site/apps/nlnet/con tent2.aspx?b=838459&c=ijITI2PHKoG&ct=1124913.

10. Irwin Cotler, *New Anti-Jewishness* (Jerusalem: Jewish People Policy Planning Institute, November 2002), p.5. This idea, according to Yossi Klein Halevi ('The Wall', *New Republic*, 7 July 2002), can be traced back to Jacob Talmon, who, in 1976, following the UN resolution equating Zionism with racism, referred to Israel as 'the "Jew" of the nations'.

11. Ahlmark, 'Anti-Semitism, Anti-Americanism, Anti-Zionism'.

12. See, for example, *Manifestations of Antisemitism in the EU 2002–2003* (Vienna: European Monitoring Centre on Racism and Xenophobia, March 2004) p.24.

13. The Muslim columnist Yasmin Alibhai-Brown has candidly written about 'the anti-Semitism that we all know is freely traded in mosques and other places' ('The Middle East is Destroying My Friendships', *Independent*, 24 February 2003), http://www.independent. co.uk/opinion/commentators/yasmin-alibhai-brown/the-middle-east-is-destroying-my-friendships-598637.html.

14. Tony Kushner points out some of the difficulties with this definition but regards it as 'a useful tool': *The Persistence of Prejudice: Antisemitism in British Society During the Second World War* (Manchester: Manchester University Press 1989), pp.2–8.

15. At the time of writing, the 73 bus went to Stamford Hill, an area in Hackney, North London, with a substantial Orthodox and Ultra-Orthodox Jewish population. Alas, the old double-decker Routemaster has been replaced by a single-decker bendy bus.

16. I have refined this section of the argument in accordance with a talk, 'The Concept of Anti-semitism', given at a symposium on antisemitism organized by the Oxford University Chabad Society, 7 June 2009. In the original version the bus conductor was Mary. I am not sure why, but Mary has changed her name to Lucy.

17. Imre Kertész, 'The Language of Exile', *Guardian*, 19 October 2002, http://books.guardian. co.uk/departments/generalfiction/story/0,,814806,00.html.

18. Wilhelm Marr, *Der Sieg des Judenthums ueber das Germanenthum vom nicht confessionellen Standpunkt ausbetrachtet* (1879), excerpted and translated in Paul Mendes-Flohr and Jehuda Reinharz (eds), *The Jew in the Modern World: A Documentary History* (Oxford: Oxford University Press, 1995), p.332.

19. Walter Laqueur, *The Changing Face of Antisemitism: From Ancient Times to the Present Day* (Oxford: Oxford University Press, 2006), p.21.

20. *Der Ewige Jude* (The Eternal Jew) was the title of a famous Nazi propaganda film made in 1940, based on a book with the same name published in Germany in 1937. *The Jewish Peril* was the title under which the *Protocols of the Elders of Zion* appeared in London in 1920.

21. *The Hidden Hand* was a periodical published in England by the Britons, a group on the far right, in the 1920s.

22. Sacks, 'The Hatred that Won't Die'.

23. Abraham Foxman, 'New Excuses, Old Hatred: Worldwide Anti-Semitism in Wake of 9/11', speech to Anti-Defamation League's National Executive Committee, 8 February 2002, http://ww.adl.org/anti%5Fsemitism/speech.asp.

24. Foxman, *Never Again?*, p.18.

25. Hillel Harkin, 'The Return of Anti-Semitism', *Wall Street Journal*, 5 February 2002, http://www.opinionjournal.com/forms/printThis.html?id=95001818.

26. David Fromkin, *A Peace to End All Peace: The Fall of the Ottoman Empire and the Creation of the Modern Middle East* (New York: Avon Books 1989), p.291.

27. Ibid., p.198. Compare Mark Levene, 'The Balfour Declaration: a Case of Mistaken Identity', *English Historical Review*, January 1992:

> By extension of my argument, the origins of the Balfour Declaration are to be located less in the wartime policies and strategies of Britain in the Middle East and more in the murky waters of modern anti-Semitism. At the bottom of the pool was the fear that a collective, potentially conspiratorial Jewry knew something which the rest of the world did not know, and could manipulate it accordingly for its own ends. (p.76.)

28. Fromkin, *Peace to End All Peace*, pp.41–2, 181, 197.

29. Ibid., p.297.

30. Diary entry by Colonel Edward M. House, Chief Aide to Woodrow Wilson, quoted in Tom Segev, *One Palestine, Complete: Jews and Arabs Under the British Mandate* (London: Abacus, 2001), p.119.

31. Ibid., p.45.
32. Bernard Gainer, *The Alien Invasion: The Origins of the Aliens Act of 1905* (London: Heinemann Educational Books, 1972), p.116. Gainer describes Balfour's attitude towards Jews as 'ambivalent' (pp.117, 119). I explore some of the complexity in Balfour's view of Jews in Chapter 13, 'The Other Arthur Balfour'.
33. Johann Gottlieb Fichte, 'Beitrag zur Berichtung der Urteils des Publicums ueber die Franzoesische Revolution' (1793), translated by M. Gerber, in Mendes-Flohr and Reinharz (eds.), *The Jew in the Modern World*, p.309.
34. Herzl wrote in his diary, 'The antisemites will become our most loyal friends, the antisemitic nations will become our allies'. Quoted in Segev, *One Palestine, Complete*, p.47 (note).
35. Fromkin, *Peace to End All Peace*, p.294.
36. Segev, *One Palestine, Complete*, p.47.
37. Public Record Office, London: Cab. 24/24 (British Cabinet Papers). Stuart Cohen describes this memorandum as 'the most stinging' of a series of 'rebarbative memoranda' from Montagu: see *English Zionists and British Jews: The Communal Politics of Anglo-Jewry, 1895–1920* (Princeton, NJ: Princeton University Press 1982), p.278.
38. Fromkin, *Peace to End All Peace*, p.294. He continues, 'As of 1913, the last date for which there were figures, only about one per cent of the world's Jews had signified their adherence to Zionism. British Intelligence reports indicated a surge of Zionist feeling during the war in the Pale of Russia, but there were no figures either to substantiate or to quantify it.'
39. Mendes-Flohr and Reinharz (eds), *The Jew in the Modern World*, p.580. The letter states, however, that, given 'the reorganization of the country under a new sovereign power', they 'would have no objections to urge against a local Jewish nationality establishing itself' in Palestine. At the same time, the second 'point' in the Zionist programme to which they object is 'the proposal to invest the Jewish settlers in Palestine with certain special rights in excess of those enjoyed by the rest of the population'. They caution: 'Any such action would prove a veritable calamity for the whole Jewish people' (p.581).
40. According to Israel's Law of Return (1950), every Jew, anywhere in the world, has the right to come to Israel as an *oleh* (a Jewish immigrant) and to become an Israeli citizen.
41. UN General Assembly Resolution 3379, 10 November 1975. Available at the Jewish Virtual Library: http://www.jewishvirtuallibrary.org/jsource/UN/unga3379.html. In a sense this proposition – Zionism is a form of racism – is the mirror image of the claim that anti-Zionism is a form of antisemitism. Both distort the truth and do so in the same way: by equating ideas that are independent variables.
42. Quoted in Allison Kaplan Sommer, 'The UN's Outcast: Why is Israel Treated Differently than All Other Nations?', *Reform Judaism*, 31, 2 (Winter 2002), http://www.reformjudaismmag.net/02winter/outcast.shtml.
43. Theodor Herzl, 'First Congress Address' (1897), in Arthur Hertzberg, *The Zionist Idea: A Historical Analysis and Reader* (Philadelphia, PA: Jewish Publication Society, 1997), pp.226–30.
44. The point I am making is not quite the same as the one made by Tony Klug in his writings on the Middle East, beginning with *A Tale of Two Peoples* (London: Fabian Society, 1973), but it is inspired by his approach.
45. This is not to say that antisemitism never motivates obliviousness to the Jewish historical experience of persecution and its fundamental importance for the rise of Zionism.
46. 'The Myth of Zionism = Racism after Durban', available at the Jewish Agency for Israel (Department for Jewish Zionist Education): http://www.jajz-ed.org.il/actual/zr/3.html.
47. UN General Assembly Resolution 46/86, 16 December 1991. Available at the Jewish Virtual Library: http://www.jewishvirtuallibrary.org/jsource/UN/unga46_86.html.
48. 'The Myth of Zionism = Racism after Durban'.
49. David A. Harris, 'Letter from One Jew to Another', 29 October 2002, available at the American Jewish Committee: http://www.ajc.org/site/apps/nlnet/content2.aspx?c=ijITI2PHKoG&b=838459&ct=1089661.
50. The Association Agreement between Israel and the European Union signed in November 1995, which entered into force on 1 June 2000, is another example of Israel coming in from the cold during the 'thaw' of the peace process.
51. Harris, 'Letter From One Jew to Another'. See the reply by Rabbi John D. Rayner, 'Open letter to David A. Harris, Executive Director of the American Jewish Committee', in his *Signposts to the Messianic Age* (London: Vallentine Mitchell, 2006), pp.258–62.
52. 'The Myth of Zionism = Racism after Durban'.

53. Bernard Lewis, 'The Arab World Discovers Anti-Semitism', in Sander L. Gilman and Steven T. Katz (eds), *Anti-Semitism in Times of Crisis* (New York: New York University Press, 1991), p.346.

54. This analysis of Arab and Muslim hostility to Israel bears some comparison with the analysis in Chapter 15, 'Spring Fever in Chicago', of Black hostility to Jews.

55. 'A people can be helped only by its own efforts, and if it cannot help itself it is beyond succor. But we Zionists want to rouse the people to self-help' (Herzl, quoted in Hertzberg, *Zionist Idea*, p.228).

56. When I say that it is a priori, I am referring to the status of the antisemitic stereotype of the 'Jew' once it is in place – not necessarily to its genesis or the sources on which it draws. In general, prejudice is often spun out of facts that are selective or exaggerated or taken out of context, rather than out of pure invention or sheer fantasy. Some prejudices can be corrected by counterevidence. I take antisemitism, typically, to be immune to evidence.

57. At the time of writing, this was Ariel Sharon.

58. 'I must, in the first place, guard my scheme from being treated as Utopian by superficial critics who might commit this error of judgment if I did not warn them.' 'I shall therefore clearly and emphatically state that I believe in the practical outcome of my scheme' (Herzl, *Jewish State*, pp.7, 9).

59. Well-attended solidarity rallies were held in many cities, including Washington, Paris and London. For London, see Chapter 1, 'A Time to Speak Out'.

60. 'Jewish people' is ambiguous, being both the people (plural) who are Jewish (i.e. individuals) and the people (singular) that is Jewish (i.e. the collective). This is one of several ambiguities that complicate the subject of Israel and Jewish identity. For the present purpose, however, the ambiguity is convenient.

61. People of goodwill who are conscientious can in fact go a long way to avoid seeming to be antisemitic. This remark is a starting point for analyzing some of the media coverage that is hostile to Israel and that, without necessarily being antisemitic, nonetheless feeds into an antisemitic discourse.

62. See Chapter 5, 'Tricks of Memory', and Chapter 9, 'The State of Zionism'.

CHAPTER THREE

A Plea for Distinctions

WHAT'S IN A WORD?

Leafing through the London newspaper the *Evening Standard*, as I travelled home on the tube from King's Cross to Arsenal, I learned a new word. I wish I hadn't. The word is 'Ameriphobia' and it was used in an article with the headline 'Anti-American Feelings We Must Strive to Curb'.[1] The feelings that *I* had to strive to curb, at that precise moment, were directed not at America but at Fleet Street. I suffer, you see, from neologophobia: fear of inelegant, misbegotten, bogus new words. And when I read this article I felt a bad attack coming on, hands quivering with the primal urge to rip the newspaper apart. It is a personal problem and I managed to deal with it. But 'the problem of Ameriphobia', according to the article, is rampant and out of control. 'It needs to be brought out into the open', the article explained, 'if there is to be any hope of stemming the tide, let alone reversing it.'

The prescription 'we must strive to curb' our feelings implies that the 'problem' lies with us rather than with America itself or the way the country conducts its affairs in the world.[2] The very term 'Ameriphobia' suggests a morbid condition: either an anxiety disorder, like arachnophobia (extreme fear of spiders), or a personality disorder, say, Judeophobia: irrational hostility to Jews. The latter example is not chosen at random. There is a burgeoning literature, both popular and academic, that makes the claim that anti-Americanism and antisemitism (to use terms that are more congenial to this writer) are inseparable. This claim is the subject of my chapter.

I should clarify at the outset that although several of the authors in this literature refer favourably to each other's work, they do not constitute a school of thought exactly: there are significant variations in tone, views and arguments. I shall not be dwelling on their differences. The focus of my discussion is on a common tendency that I detect in their writing: the tendency to treat attitudes that are both unlike and unconnected as though they were similar and inseparable. Moreover,

I regard this tendency as tendentious. It promotes (or expresses) a certain mindset about America, Israel and the Jewish people: a predisposition to bracket them together and to see any hostility towards one as indicating an underlying hostility to all.

There are, as I say, variations on the theme of inseparability. One writer has gone so far as to say: 'Anti-Americanism and Anti-Semitism are the Same Thing' (the title of his article). It turns out that what he means is that they have the same 'underlying causes' and that their victims share the same experience; which, even if true, is not the same thing as being the same thing.[3] According to Daniel Johnson, they have *become* the same. He refers to 'the conflation of attitudes to the United States with attitudes towards Jews' and concludes: 'Put simply: anti-Americanism has become a continuation of anti-Semitism by other means.'[4] Then there is Natan Sharansky's essay, 'On Hating the Jews', which has the subtitle 'The inextricable link between anti-Semitism and anti-Americanism'.[5] Andrei Markovits, similarly, says that since the late nineteenth century, European antisemitism and anti-Americanism have been an 'inseparable tandem' and that since the First World War they have been 'inextricably intertwined'. He refers to their 'longstanding interaction'. This way of speaking suggests that the two phenomena, even if inseparable in practice, are distinguishable in principle. (Two things cannot be said to interact with each other – even to be inextricably intertwined with each other – if ultimately they are one and the same.) However, Markovits says that 'in the course of the twentieth century it [antisemitism] has become one of anti-Americanism's most consistent conceptual companions, perhaps even one of its constitutive features'. This seems to make it *internal* to anti-Americanism, integral to what it is (or has become).[6]

That anti-Americanism and antisemitism can be – and sometimes are – connected is indisputable. They were connected, for example, by an anti-modern, anti-cosmopolitan discourse within the European intelligentsia before the Second World War. As Tony Judt explains, 'Many critics of America, in Germany, France or Russia, were all too quick to identify the shifting, unfamiliar contours of an Americanising world with the essential traits of homeless Jewry.'[7] (One such 'critic' was the German Führer.) More recently, Osama bin Laden, alluding to the presence of female soldiers on American bases in Saudi Arabia, exclaimed: 'By God, Muslim women refuse to be defended by these American and Jewish prostitutes.'[8] Not only is it possible for anti-Americanism and antisemitism to be connected, but the result, when they combine, can be toxic or worse. But equally, it can be noxious –

especially for the purposes of developing public policy – to insist they are linked when they are not.

In this chapter I seek to undo what others have knotted together: to disentangle anti-Americanism and antisemitism. I begin by contrasting the logic of the two terms, arguing that they are not, au fond, symmetrical. I then turn from the conceptual to the empirical. Focusing on two cases raised in an essay by Josef Joffe – an anti-globalization protest at Davos and a Eurobarometer poll – I shall look at the way he and others use evidence to support their point of view. A brief conclusion places the analysis in a larger context.

Bishop Joseph Butler is credited with the elegant truism 'Everything is what it is, and not another thing.'[9] In the spirit of his remark, this chapter is a plea for distinctions; but it is not a plaint against making connections.[10] It is, rather, a caution against the confusions that arise when things that are different are conflated. The point of view of this chapter can be summed up in a slogan: 'No connections without distinctions!' And distinctions, by and large, come first.

THE 'GRAMMAR' OF TERMS

'What is the meaning of a word?' This is the disarming sentence that opens the Blue Book, which Ludwig Wittgenstein dictated to students at Cambridge University in 1933–34.[11] In a way, it is the sentence that ushers in the later period of his philosophical thought, which occupied him until his death in 1951. Wittgenstein's question goes to the very idea of a word – any word – having a meaning. So, it could be glossed this way: What do we mean by the meaning of a word?

This might lead us to expect an answer in the abstract, a general theory of linguistic meaning. But this is precisely the approach to philosophy that Wittgenstein kicks against in this work and throughout his later period. The opening sentence of the Blue Book turns out to be a point of departure for a long and winding path of philosophical investigation into what – idiosyncratically – he calls the 'grammar' of words. Roughly, this means paying close attention to their actual use in the ordinary employment of language. He pursues this activity not for its own sake but with a view to 'clearing misunderstandings away'.[12] But where do the misunderstandings of which he speaks come from? They arise, paradoxically, from language itself, from certain formal properties that 'tempt' us into conceptual confusion.[13] 'Philosophy, as we use the word', says Wittgenstein, 'is a fight against the fascination which forms of expression exert upon us.'[14]

I mention this because disentangling anti-Americanism and anti-semitism begins with recognizing a difference in the 'grammar' of the two terms, a difference that we are tempted to overlook due to the fact that the two expressions share a similar form. We are subject in this case (to quote Wittgenstein again) to 'the fascination which the analogy between two similar structures in our language can exert on us'.[15] Markovits takes it for granted that anti-Americanism and antisemitism belong to the same logical category: 'Both are "isms" ', he says, 'which indicate they are institutionalized and commonly used as a modern ideology.'[16] Similarly, Joffe asks, 'What is the difference between criticism and anti-Semitism or anti-Americanism? What, indeed, are the elements of *any* "anti-ism"?'[17] Both Markovits and Joffe assume that there is a class of concepts called 'isms' or 'anti-isms', all of which are on the same logical footing. This is a natural assumption to make: the structural analogy is strong, and it is tempting to think that words with the same form perform a similar function. But in the case of 'anti-Americanism' and 'antisemitism' appearances are misleading.

One way of revealing the underlying difference is to remove the affixes 'anti' and 'ism' from both words. A little reflection will show that the bits in the middle are not logically equivalent. There is such a thing as America: it is an existing political state. The territory, government, institutions, people, culture and history: these are among the many things that the words 'America' and 'American' denote. But what – in the real world – corresponds to the words 'Semite' and 'Semitic'? Nothing. There is a black hole at the heart of the word 'antisemitism'. By this I do not mean that no Jewish person fits the antisemitic stereotype. But this stereotype is a construction, not a description; it does not *describe* what Jews *are* like but *prescribes* what they *must* be like. The 'Semite' or 'Jew' that is the object of the antisemite's animus is *essentially* unreal: the *product*, not just the *object*, of that animus or of the ideology informing it. Simply, there is no Semitism without antisemitism.[18]

But there *is* an America – and even Americanism – with or without anti-Americanism. The difference to which I am pointing is reflected in a difference in the orthography of the words 'antisemitism' and 'anti-Americanism'; or rather, in the fact that there is a question about the one but not the other. Which is the right spelling: 'anti-Semitic', 'anti-semitic' or 'antisemitic'? Opting for the third alternative, the Holocaust scholar Yehuda Bauer remarks (very much in the spirit of what I have been arguing): 'Antisemitism, especially in its hyphenated spelling, is inane nonsense, because there is no Semitism that you can be anti to.'[19] The authors of a landmark report on antisemitism in the European Union, published by the European Monitoring Centre on Racism and Xenophobia in 2004, also prefer the solid version of the word. In their view, it helps avoid 'the problem of reifying (and thus affirming) the existence of races in general and a "Semitic race" in particular'.[20] Perhaps; although this might be overestimating the power of a hyphen or the efficacy of removing one. Be that as it may, my point is this: No one would think of questioning the spelling 'anti-Americanism' on the grounds that it reifies America or that it affirms the existence of states; for there is such a thing as America, and states, as it happens, exist.

The argument I am making is open to the objection that the difference to which I am drawing attention, though real, is irrelevant. Yes, America is part of the external world. But the 'America' that is the object of anti-Americanism is every bit as imaginary as the 'Jew' who is hated by the antisemite. Such is the drift of the literature under discussion.

Or is it? There is some confusion on this point. Take, for example, Paul Hollander's introduction to the anthology *Understanding Anti-Americanism*: he says that it is a 'premise' of the book 'that a proper understanding of anti-Americanism can only be achieved by balancing two apparently incompatible perspectives or propositions'.[21] On the one hand, there is the view that anti-Americanism is 'a direct and rational response to the evident misdeeds of the United States abroad and its shortcomings and inequities at home'. On the other hand, in the opposing view, it is 'a largely groundless, irrational predisposition (similar to racism, sexism, or anti-Semitism), an expression of a deeply rooted scapegoating impulse'.[22] In the first view, the 'America' that is the object of anti-Americanism is the real thing; in the second view, it is (essentially) a fiction.

Having pointed out this duality, Hollander goes on to say, confusingly, that only those described by the *second* view 'qualify for the designation of "anti-American" '.[23] Which means that the first view of anti-Americanism is just wrong. Which obviates the need to balance the two views – which, you recall, is a premise of his book. This is the logical equivalent of slipping on your own banana skin. It is the result, I suggest, of being pulled in two opposite directions by two different considerations. One is the actual use of the word 'anti-Americanism', which, in its ordinary employment, fits positions covered by *both* of the views that Hollander outlines. The other is the a priori conviction that 'anti-ism' words *must* function in the same way; in which case only the second view *can* be right.

In practice, we use the term 'anti-American' quite differently from the way we use the term 'antisemitic'. For one thing, it is much looser, covering a multitude of views that lack a common denominator and might even conflict with each other. One person might oppose American foreign policy in the Middle East, another might reject certain values associated with the United States, and both could be called 'anti-American'; yet each might denounce the other's anti-Americanism. Furthermore, there could be good reasons for their anti-American views; or reasons which, though insufficient or poor, do not signify an underlying bigotry. Emphatically, the same cannot be said about anti-semitism, which is precisely a species of bigotry. Disentangling anti-Americanism and antisemitism begins with recognizing this 'grammatical' difference between the two terms.

WHAT'S IN A FACT?

But it does not end there. Some of the confusion in the literature under review arises on a different level altogether: it lies in the account that is given of the facts or the way that facts are interpreted.

I shall illustrate the point via Joffe's essay, 'The Demons of Europe'. The essay opens with a description of an incident in Davos, Switzerland in January 2003, involving anti-globalization protestors: 'At the World Economic Forum in Davos earlier this year, a demonstrator wearing a mask of Donald Rumsfeld and an outsized yellow Star of David (inscribed with the word "Sheriff") was accompanied by a cudgel-wielding double of Ariel Sharon; the two of them were followed by a huge rendition of the golden calf.' Joffe then gives his reading of this scene: 'The message? The United States is in thrall to the Jews/Israelis; both are the acolytes of Mammon; and both represent the avant-garde of a pernicious global capitalism.' He continues thus:

> This is the face of the new anti-Semitism. Lacking certain murderous elements of the classical type, it is nevertheless rife with some of its most ancient motifs. What is new about it is the projection of these old fantasies onto two new targets: Israel and America. Indeed, the United States is an anti-Semitic fantasy come true: the *Protocols of the Elders of Zion* in living color. Do not Jews, their first loyalty to Israel, control the Congress, the Pentagon, the banks, the universities, and the media? Having captured the 'hyperpower', do they not finally rule the world? That at least seems to be the consensus of the Europeans, who in a recent EU

poll declared Israel and the United States, in that order, to be the greatest threats to world peace.[24]

Notice that Joffe reads the same content into both cases: the scene at Davos and the EU poll. Let us look at each case in turn and assess his reading – which is shared (more or less) by several other commentators.

The description of the scene at Davos is based on a widely-disseminated picture that the photographer Fabrice Coffrini took of a performance of street theatre.[25] Like the biblical story to which the protesters' model of a golden calf refers, the Coffrini image has acquired a significance that transcends its immediate context. Yossi Klein Halevi reads it in much the same way as Joffe: 'In that photograph is a convergence of the recurring themes of European anti-Semitism and anti-Americanism.'[26] Daniel Goldhagen calls it an 'emblematic image of globalized antisemitism' which, in the form of anti-Zionism, 'has become interwoven with anti-Americanism'.[27] Markovits refers to the 'openly anti-Semitic iconography' of the scene at Davos.[28] He argues that 'antipathy towards Israel and its accompanying anti-Semitism cannot be separated from a larger enmity towards the United States and what it represents'.[29]

If you take the image out of context and consider it in isolation of any other evidence, then Joffe's reading strikes me as about right. However, if we (as it were) widen the lens, then the picture turns out to be misleading. It transpires that Rumsfeld and Sharon were just two of several world leaders impersonated by the protestors. Most of them – not 'Sharon' alone – were wielding clubs; several can be seen in another shot using them to bat a giant inflatable globe around.[30] And while the US Defense Secretary takes the lead in carrying the calf, the remaining figures (all of whom seem to be dressed in the same monkey costume) do not appear to be artfully posed.[31] In particular, 'Sharon' is caught in another picture standing apart from 'Rumsfeld', his back to the golden calf ensemble, a face in the crowd, arms lowered, no longer looking dominant as the powerful taskmaster driving the American lackey.[32]

Joffe describes the badge worn by the Rumsfeld character as 'a yellow Star of David'. It is certainly a six-pointed star and the colour is indeed yellow. As such, it immediately recalls the badge that Jewish people were required to wear during the Second World War in Nazi-occupied Europe and in concentration camps.[33] But in wild west iconography, sheriff's badges are frequently (though not always) six-pointed; they are normally made of brass (a yellow alloy); and the word 'sheriff' typically appears across the middle – all of which fits the badge in the Coffrini image. One of the people involved in the street theatre at Davos said subsequently that it had not occurred to any of the protestors at the time that the design of the sheriff's badge recalled the Nazi symbol for Jews.[34] If true, then this group is guilty of obliviousness or naivety or stupidity, but not bigotry. As (the Jewish socialist) Steve Cohen writes in his analysis of antisemitism on the left, 'Any group which claims to be against antisemitism should be ultra-vigilant in the imagery it evokes.'[35] This group's best defence is that it was ultra-negligent. Sadly, such is the state of historical awareness among some political activists today that this defence is all too believable.

In short, a scrupulous investigation or interrogation of the Coffrini image casts doubt on the reading given by Joffe et al. – or suggests that they have overreached. It is one thing to decry an image; another to ascribe bigotry to a group; a third to attribute the same bigotry to a movement; and so on. In the literature under review in this chapter, the authors do not always respect such niceties. But suppose the *Guardian* or *Le Monde* were to print a photograph of an Israeli soldier pointing a gun at a Palestinian child. And suppose someone who is sympathetic to the Palestinian cause were to seize upon this picture, interpret it to mean that the soldier was acting with murderous intent, and call it an 'emblematic image' of Israel as a state or of Zionism as a movement: these authors would spring to their feet. They would point out, quite reasonably, that while the camera cannot lie, nor does it necessarily tell the whole truth: all it can do is capture one angle at a given moment in time. Probably, they would go further. Detecting a bias, they would denounce the 'liberal press' for printing the picture. Yet they do not suspect a bias on their own part when, seizing on an image, they jump by leaps and bounds to conclusions about groups or movements, convicting them of projecting old antisemitic fantasies onto Israel and America.

Let us now take up the final sentence in the long passage I quoted from Joffe's essay. This is where he cites 'a recent EU poll' in which, he says, European citizens 'declared Israel and the United States, in that order, to be the greatest threats to world peace'; from which he infers that 'the consensus of the Europeans' seems to be that Jews 'finally rule the world'. He is referring to a survey of public opinion carried out in October 2003 for the European Commission.[36] The poll interviewed 7,515 citizens in fifteen European states over a period of nine days. In the context of the aftermath of the invasion of Iraq, they were asked a series of questions. Question 10 presented respondents with a list of fifteen countries. For each country, they were asked whether or not, in their opinion, it presents 'a threat to peace in the world'.[37] In the case of Israel, 59 per cent of respondents said yes, a higher percentage than for any other country.[38]

The poll was greeted with outrage by the Israeli Government and by many leading Jewish organizations on both sides of the Atlantic. Sharansky, who was Israel's Minister for Diaspora Affairs at the time, saw it as 'additional proof that behind the "political" criticism of Israel stands pure anti-semitism'.[39] In the United States, Rabbi Marvin Hier, dean and founder of the Simon Wiesenthal Center, described the poll as 'a racist flight of fancy that only shows that antisemitism is deeply embedded within European society, more now than in any other period since the end of World War II'.[40] Cobi Benatoff and Edgar Bronfman, presidents respectively of the European Jewish Congress and the World Jewish Congress, made an additional point: the mere fact of publishing the poll was, in their view, an expression of antisemitism on the part of the European Commission itself.[41] But Joffe's reading picks up on something else: the fact that the United States came second to Israel in the poll with a rating of 53 per cent.

These reactions overlook three points. First, the question did not ask respondents which countries were to *blame* for posing a threat to peace. This should especially be kept in mind in assessing the response to Israel, since Palestine, not being a state, was not on the list. So, anyone who thought that the Israeli–Palestinian conflict destabilizes the region, and that this instability is 'a threat to peace in the world', could have answered in the affirmative – wherever their sympathies might lie.[42] Second, respondents were not asked to *rank* the fifteen countries on the list. So, the data does not support the claim that the respondents saw Israel and America as 'the greatest threats' to world peace (let alone that this was 'the consensus of the Europeans'). In other words, it is a leap to go from 'more people saw Israel and America as a threat' to 'people saw Israel and America as more of a threat'. The question did not ask respondents to quantify the *size* of the threat, if any, and the results do not license any inference at all about this. Third, what Joffe fails to mention is that the same percentage that said yes to America (53 per cent) said yes to Iran and North Korea.[43] Does this imply that there is a European antisemitic consensus against Iran and North Korea as well? The mind begins to boggle.

Joffe does go on to say that 'the issue is more complicated than the reconditioning of an old myth'.[44] But he does not retract or qualify his reading of the Eurobarometer poll. Instead, he offers further evidence to support his view that the 'similarities' between anti-Americanism and antisemitism 'are hard to escape'.[45] He refers, for example, to a poster at an anti-Bush demonstration in Berlin in 2002 which read 'Stop Bush's Grab for Global Power!' and describes this as 'echoing a classic indictment of "World Jewry"'.[46] In a similar vein, he writes that 'Franz Alt, a German author and TV moderator, denouncing Bush as the "greatest enemy of mankind," seemed to be echoing the old Nazi slogan: *"Die Juden sind unser Unglück"* – the Jews are our misfortune.'[47] Perhaps my ear is not as finely tuned as Joffe's, but I think that the fact that he hears these examples as 'echoes' of antisemitism, and therefore thinks they support his position, supports mine. Due to his cast of mind he is, as it were, hearing things.

The results of the Eurobarometer poll are open to interpretation. One is Joffe's: that there is a consensus in Europe that is animated by antisemitic prejudice. But there are other possibilities. Perhaps the respondents, or most of them, or just some of them, were not bigots; maybe they were normal reasonable human beings who, exercising their capacity for rational judgment, believe, on the basis of evidence, that the foreign policies of America and Israel (which are closely intertwined) are inimical to the prospects for peace and security in the world. (There *are* such people, even in benighted Europe.) Or perhaps fear, rather than reason, was at play, but fear grounded in reality rather than rooted in paranoia. (Arachnophobia might be an anxiety disorder but if you aren't afraid of sharks then you had better see a shrink.) Which hypothesis is true – whether Joffe's or mine or some other – is an open question. We need to look into it. And I do not see how anyone could, without further ado, jump to Joffe's conclusion or Rabbi Hier's, or accuse the European Commission of bigotry, unless they were seeing antisemitism hidden behind the veil of data *before they even began to look.* Unless, in other words, they were in the grip of a mindset that is prone to seeing hostility to Israel as the 'familiar hatred of the Jew'. Joffe talks about the 'projection' of antisemitic 'fantasies' onto Israel and America. But this works in both directions. That is to say, there is such a thing as antisemitism in reverse: projecting the figure of the antisemite onto individuals or groups who are innocent as charged.

THE IDOLS OF THE TRIBE

The view (or set of views) that I have been examining is that anti-Americanism and antisemitism are inseparable. It is tempting to turn this thesis around and say that, in the literature under discussion, it is the *allegation* of anti-Americanism and the *allegation* of antisemitism that are inseparable. This would certainly be an exaggeration, but it makes a point: that there is a propensity, in certain quarters, to see Americans and Jews as the joint victims of a global prejudice, and that this is itself a phenomenon that calls for investigation.

The point is worth making in view of what is at stake in this discussion. In their book *America Against the World*, Andrew Kohut and Bruce Stokes discuss the data produced by a series of worldwide public opinion surveys conducted by the Pew Global Attitudes Project since its inception in 2001. The aim of the book is to make sense of one of the principal findings of the project: 'the rise of anti-Americanism around the world in the first decade of the twenty-first century'.[48] This rise comes at a time when the world is heating up politically, and one of the most incandescent spots on the planet is the Middle East, where both America and Israel, separately and (to an extent) together, are involved in conflicts that are on the boil. International peace and security: this is what is at stake. The view that I have been examining in this essay conflates different kinds of hostility and reduces them all to bigotry. It is crude and partisan. Such a simple-minded, one-sided account is likely to inflame the situation; it is not only untrue but unwise.

Kohut and Stokes warn that anti-Americanism is 'one of the principal challenges facing the United States in the years ahead'. They go on to make, in effect, a plea for distinctions: 'Dealing with it will require that Americans distinguish among the differing sources of this antagonism and address them appropriately.'[49] Much the same can be said about attitudes towards Jews collectively and towards Israel. This calls for research. It means slow, painstaking work on the part of social scientists, historians and others: work that lays a foundation for an informed public debate and enlightened public policy; work that others are better equipped and more able to pursue than I.

In his 'Epistle to the Reader', a sort of preface to *An Essay Concerning Human Understanding*, John Locke remarks: ''tis ambition enough to be employed as an under-labourer in clearing ground a little, and removing some of the rubbish that lies in the way to knowledge'.[50] Such has been my limited aim in this chapter: to subtract from the sum total of obstacles that stand in the way of the pursuit of knowledge – knowledge in the sense of understanding. Among these obstacles are certain tendencies of the human mind – 'the idols of the tribe', in Francis Bacon's phrase, and in particular the first two on his list: our propensity to oversimplify and our habit of selecting evidence that confirms a view that we have previously embraced.[51] If Bacon is right, these 'idols', being deeply rooted in our nature, are even more ancient than the golden calf to which the Israelites bowed down in the Bible. They are as old as Eve and Adam – and as current as ourselves. It might not be possible to *remove* them exactly, but we can seek to overcome them. We can check and double-check for factual complexity; spoof inelegant, misbegotten, bogus new words; fight against the fascination that forms of expression exert on us; and resist being dazzled by an image as mesmerizing as the one that Coffrini captured at Davos. We can, in short, seek to think, thinking freely, rather than be in thrall to the idols in our mind. And thinking, rather like creating in the opening chapter of Genesis, begins with the making of distinctions.

NOTES

1. Anthony Hilton, 'Anti-American Feelings We Must Strive to Curb', *Evening Standard*, 14 March 2006, p.29. This chapter is adapted from the essay with the same title that appeared in I. Krastev and A. McPherson (eds), *The Anti-American Century* (Budapest: Central European University Press, 2007), pp.127–60.
2. In this essay I use the word 'America' in the narrower sense to refer to the United States rather than to both American continents, since this reflects the use of the term 'anti-Americanism'.
3. Rabbi Shmuley Boteach, 'Anti-Americanism and Antisemitism are the Same Thing', 12 March 2004, http://www.newsbull.com/forum/more.asp?TOPIC_ID=12996. However, the same article on another website has the title 'How Bush has embarrassed Europe': http://www.wnd.com/news/article.asp?ARTICLE_ID=37551. Rabbi Boteach writes: 'Two hundred and eighty million Americans are getting a taste of what it's like to be Jewish.' He is a nationally syndicated talk show host in the United States and was the subject of the BBC documentary 'Moses of Oxford'.
4. Daniel Johnson, 'America and the America-Haters', *Commentary*, 120, 6 (June 2006), pp.30–1.
5. Natan Sharansky, 'On Hating the Jews', *Wall Street Journal*, 17 November 2003, http://www.opinionjournal.com/extra/?id=110004310.
6. Andrei Markovits, 'European Anti-Americanism (and Anti-Semitism): Ever Present Though Always Denied', Center for European Studies, Harvard University, Working Paper Series 108 (January 2004), pp.12, 14, http://www.ces.fas.harvard.edu/index.html.
7. Tony Judt, 'Goodbye to All That', *Prospect*, 105 (December 2004), p.42.
8. This was in 1998. Quoted in Tony Judt, 'America and the War', *New York Review of Books*, 15 November 2001, http://www.nybooks.com/articles/14760.
9. I am not aware that any definitive source for this exact form of words has been located. It is, however, in the spirit of his thought.
10. The title of this chapter alludes to 'A Plea for Excuses', J.L. Austin's 1956 Presidential address to the Aristotelian Society, reprinted in J.O. Ursmon and G.J. Warnock (eds), *J.L. Austin: Philosophical Papers* (Oxford: Oxford University Press, 1979), pp.175–204.
11. Ludwig Wittgenstein, 'The Blue Book', in *The Blue and Brown Books: Preliminary Studies for the 'Philosophical Investigations'* (Oxford: Blackwell, 1972), p.1.
12. Ludwig Wittgenstein, *Philosophical Investigations* (Oxford: Basil Blackwell, 1967), p.43e, par. 90.
13. Wittgenstein has various terms for the hold that language can have over us due to its formal properties, including 'tempt', 'seduce' and 'bewitch'.
14. Wittgenstein, *Blue and Brown Books*, p.27.
15. Ibid., p.26.
16. 'European Anti-Americanism and Antisemitism: Similarities and Difference', an interview with

Andrei S. Markovits, *Post-Holocaust and Antisemitism*, 1 January 2004 (Jerusalem Center for Public Affairs), http://www.jcpa.org/phas/phas-16.htm.

17. Josef Joffe, 'The Demons of Europe', *Commentary*, 117, 1 (January 2004), p.29.
18. For a fuller treatment of this point, see the discussion of Imre Kertész and 'the yellow star' in Chapter 2, 'The Collective Jew'.
19. Yehuda Bauer, 'Problems of Contemporary Antisemitism' (2003), available at the University of California Santa Cruz: http://web.archive.org/web/20030705131522/http://humanities.ucsc.edu/JewishStudies/docs/YBauerLecture.pdf. Bauer points out that spelling it 'as one word' matches the original German term '*Antisemitismus*'. The irony, however, is that Wilhelm Marr, who popularized the word (in the 1870s), did precisely think that there was such a thing as Semitism: the racialized 'Jewish spirit' and 'Jewish consciousness' to which he was opposed.
20. *Manifestations of Antisemitism in the EU 2002–2003* (Vienna: European Monitoring Centre on Racism and Xenophobia, March 2004), p.227.
21. Paul Hollander (ed.), *Understanding Anti-Americanism: Its Origins and Impact at Home and Abroad* (Chicago, IL: Ivan R. Dee, 2004), p.7.
22. Ibid., pp.7, 9.
23. Ibid., p.9.
24. Joffe, 'The Demons of Europe', p.29.
25. The image, which first appeared in the *Santa Monica Daily Press*, 27 January 2003, is available at http://en.wikipedia.org/wiki/File:Davos_Switzerland_G8_Summit.jpg. Joffe does not say explicitly that his description is based on this photograph, but the allusion is unmistakeable.
26. Yossi Klein Halevi, 'Hatreds Entwined', *Azure*, 16 (Winter 2004), p.25.
27. Daniel Jonah Goldhagen, 'The Globalization of Antisemitism', *Forward*, 2 May 2003, http://www.forward.com/issues/2003/03.05.02/oped1.html.
28. Markovits, 'European Anti-Americanism (and Anti-Semitism)', p.18.
29. Ibid., p.17.
30. Image available at http://www.nadir.org/nadir/initiativ/agp/free/wef/images/davos3266.jpg.
31. For a general account, see 'Anti-WEF Protests in Switzerland, January 2003'. Available at http://en.wikipedia.org/wiki/Anti-WEF_protests_in_Switzerland%2C_January_2003. More images available at http://www.remote.ch/search/search.dbc?WHAT=wef.
32. Image available at http://www.nadir.org/nadir/initiativ/agp/free/wef/images/wef3453.jpg. A simple moral to be drawn is that first impressions can be misleading. Compare, in this respect, the discussion in Chapter 15, 'Spring Fever in Chicago', of the misperception of the words of Revd Herbert B. Martin.
33. In some areas the identifying badge for Jews was a different colour or shape.
34. 'File talk:Davos Switzerland G8 Summit.jpg'. Available at http://en.wikipedia.org/wiki/File_talk:Davos_Switzerland_G8_Summit.jpg.
35. Steve Cohen, *That's Funny, You Don't Look Anti-Semitic: An Anti-Racist Analysis of Left Anti-Semitism* (Leeds: Beyond the Pale Collective, 1984), p.86.
36. European Commission, *Iraq and Peace in the World: Full Report*, Flash Eurobarometer 151 (November 2003). Available at http://www.mafhoum.com/press6/167P52.pdf.
37. There were two affirmative and two negative ratings: 1 = Yes, absolutely; 2 = Yes, rather; 3 = No, rather not; 4 = No, absolutely not. There was also 5 = don't know or not applicable (Ibid., Annexe: Questionnaire).
38. Ibid., p.78.
39. Chris McGreal, 'EU Poll Sees Israel as Peace Threat', *Guardian*, 3 November 2003, http://www.guardian.co.uk/world/2003/nov/03/eu.israel.
40. 'European Poll: Israel Biggest Threat to World Peace'. Available at The Jewish Federations of North America: http://www.jewishfederations.org/page.aspx?id=50080.
41. Edgar Bronfman and Cobi Benatoff, 'Europe's Moral Treachery Over Anti-Semitism', *Financial Times*, 5 January 2004, available at Canadian Institute for Jewish Research: http://www.isranet.org/isranetbriefings/Permanent2004/Permanent-January-2004.htm#786. The reply by Romano Prodi, European Commission President at the time, 6 January 2004 is available at http://www.eurunion.org/news/press/2004/2004001.htm.
42. Arguably, this observation is supported by findings in the '15-Nation Pew Global Attitudes Survey' (13 June 2006), available at http://pewglobal.org/reports/pdf/252.pdf. In a question about 'Dangers to World Peace', one of the items is the 'Israeli–Palestinian conflict' (not 'Israel'). The figures show that almost exactly the same percentage of Americans and Turks

(43 per cent and 42 per cent respectively) consider this conflict to be a 'great danger' to world peace (p.3). Yet, in terms of their sympathies with the parties to the conflict, the two populations are almost a mirror image of each other: 48 per cent of Americans sympathize with Israel, 13 per cent with the Palestinians, while the corresponding figures for Turks are 5 per cent and 63 per cent (p.23).

43. When countries share the same rating, as in this case, they are listed in alphabetical order. So, Iran and North Korea actually appear above the United States in the table. Anyone looking at the table could hardly fail to notice this.

44. Joffe, 'The Demons of Europe', p.29.

45. Ibid., p.32.

46. Ibid.

47. Ibid., p.33.

48. A. Kohut and B. Stokes, *America Against the World* (New York: Henry Holt & Company, 2006), p.xiii. More precisely: 'This book has as its principal objective to consider the difference between US opinion and world opinion so as to understand global anti-Americanism' (p.xix).

49. Ibid., p.39.

50. John Locke, *An Essay Concerning Human Understanding* [1706] (London: Penguin Books, 1997), p.11.

51. Francis Bacon, *The New Organon* [1620], L. Jardine and M. Silverthorne (eds), (Cambridge: Cambridge University Press, 2000), Book I, Aphorisms 45 and 46, pp.42–3.

CHAPTER FOUR

The New World and the Promised Land

Revised version of a talk given at Limmud Conference, December 2007.

A HIGHLY CONTROVERSIAL CLAIM

Perhaps it is because I grew up in the 1950s and 1960s and my family used to spend Pesach and other holidays in Bournemouth on the English south coast, but when I hear the phrase 'Jewish lobby' the first thing that comes to mind is not a sinister image of a Semitic cabal fresh from the pages of the *Protocols of the Elders of Zion* but the entrance foyer to the Majestic or Cumberland hotels: strictly kosher establishments presided over respectively by Mrs Schneider ('Auntie Fay') and Mrs Feld, *les grandes dames* of British Jewish catering, who greeted you emotionally as you entered their overheated domain, where the air was always tinged with the lingering odours of the last meal: a very Jewish lobby that felt like home from home. The Green Park (for those who are aficionados of the seaside Jewish hotel scene of that era) might be closer to what the phrase 'Jewish lobby' usually conjures, for this was the posh place where the Jewish toffs stayed, the people who could afford the crème de la crème (or *smetana de la smetana*): the ones who had something that, in its limited way, could be called 'power'.

When John Mearsheimer and Stephen Walt claim that 'America's support for Israel' is due to 'the unmatched power of the Israel Lobby', some people hear 'Israel lobby' as a euphemism for 'Jewish lobby' and condemn their thesis as antisemitic.[1] The two authors seek to refute this charge by various disclaimers. They stress that, in their view, the lobby is not 'a unified movement with a central leadership'; not all Jewish Americans are part of it; and it 'also includes prominent Christian evangelicals'.[2] They expressly deny that it is 'a cabal or conspiracy that "controls" US foreign policy' and they emphasize that its activities 'are legitimate forms of democratic political participation'.[3]

Be that as it may, and setting aside the allegation of antisemitism, their claim is highly controversial. Without denying the existence of a conspicuous and influential lobby for Israel, critics take issue with Mearsheimer and Walt over their central argument, which, roughly, is as follows: If (1) the extent of American support for Israel is not in the national interest, then (2) it must be the case that it serves the interest of some other party, specifically (3) Israel, whose (apparent) interests are promoted by the Israel lobby. All of these claims have been vigorously disputed. So, for example, some people challenge the premise that America's level of support for Israel is not in the US national interest. Some point to the role played by other interest groups – especially oil, arms and the military – in influencing American foreign policy in the Middle East. Noam Chomsky argues that Mearsheimer and Walt fail to explain why US policy in the region 'is so similar to its policies elsewhere'.[4] It is of course possible that Chomsky himself is a recruit to the Israel lobby; which, if true, means that the power of the lobby is awesome indeed – far greater than Mearsheimer and Walt ever dreamed.

As it happens, I tend to agree with these criticisms of Mearsheimer and Walt. But I shall not dwell on them in this chapter.[5] By and large, defenders and critics of their position share an underlying assumption: that US support for Israel can be explained purely or primarily in terms of power and self-interest. The debate among them tends to be over whose interests are being served – those of America or Israel or the energy corporations or whomever – and whose power is being expressed. These questions are important; but there is something else, something deeper, that they leave out of the reckoning: the self-perception of the American people: the idea that America has of its own identity, of what it is and what it stands for. This is the zone to which I would like to take us this evening.

There are several cultural and emotional ties that connect the US to the State of Israel. I shall look at two of these ties, both of which exist on the plane of imagination or myth; for the connection they make is between the New World of America and the Promised Land of scripture. I begin with the theme of America as Zion, revisiting the formative years of the former – both the period of the Puritan settlers who projected Zion onto the American wilderness and the era of the founding of the federal republic. I then turn to Christian Zionism, which has projected an eschatological drama onto the territory of the State of Israel, including the land that the state currently occupies, especially 'Judea and Samaria'.

These two ties are reinforced by a third: seeing Zion as America rather than the other way round: thinking of Israel as a faraway 'little

America', a state created by pioneers who left the tyranny of Europe to establish a place in the sun where, despite the hostile natives whom they have to subdue by force ('the Arabs' as 'the Indians'), they could be free. This perception is reinforced by actual cultural change that, in the view of the Israeli historian Tom Segev, amounts to 'the Americanization of Israel'.[6]

But it is the first two ties on which I shall dwell tonight, partly because they are more antique and partly because both derive from the same source: the biblical word of God. It was as if America and Israel were united by the holy bond of matrimony. At this deeper level, 'America's support for Israel' is an affair of the heart, a romantic attachment; and the potency of romance is unmatched by the mere power of a lobby.

SEEING AMERICA AS ZION

Let me begin with a verse from the theme song for the television series 'Daniel Boone', starring Fess Parker, broadcast in the 1960s. Perhaps it will jog the memories of those of you old enough to remember (unless your memory does not need jogging because, like me, you are pathetic enough to watch reruns on DVD):

> Daniel Boone was a man.
> He was a big man.
> And he fought for America
> To make all Americans free.

The real Daniel Boone lived from 1735 to 1820. He was a frontiersman who pioneered expansion into the territory now known as Kentucky, which at the time lay beyond the western borders of the Thirteen Colonies. He was a family man, husband to Rebecca with whom (at least in the TV drama) he had a son called Israel. Daniel, Rebecca, Israel: the very names of this legendary pioneer family bespeak a presence of Zion in America that, by the eighteenth century, was already well established.

The map of America reflects this presence in the frequency with which biblical names occur. There are counties, cities and towns called Adam and Eve, Cain and Abel, Abraham, Isaac and Jacob, Sarah, Moses, Saul and Solomon, and so on. There are several Sinais and Mt Sinais and over fifty Mt Zions.[7] Moshe Davis, founding head of the Institute of Contemporary Jewry at The Hebrew University and the man who established the field of America–Holy Land Studies, observes, 'Viewing the "biblical" map of America, one senses how founders with an intimate knowledge of scriptural sources instituted a spiritual folklore.' In particular, 'Zion as a place-name reflected the organic relationship between the United States and the Land of Israel.'[8] (It is a mark of the significance of Zion for American history and culture that there is such a field as America–Holy Land Studies.)

What Davis calls a 'spiritual folklore' was more like religious ideology when it entered the North American continent with the Puritan pioneers who preceded Daniel Boone by over 100 years. Davis himself, harking back to 'the earliest formulations in Colonial times', refers to 'the Puritan aspiration to a biblical commonwealth, where America itself was considered to be the embodiment of Zion'. He reminds us that one of the earliest settlements was Salem, Massachusetts, and remarks: 'In 1626–1628, when the Pilgrims received corn from the Indians, they immediately associated the event with the patriarch Abraham and Melchizedek, king of Salem.'[9]

The colonists continued to cross the Atlantic, seeing the opposite shore through their Old Testament lens. One notable event took place in April 1630 when 1,000 Puritans set sail for New England. Victoria Clark explains: 'Puritan identification with the sufferings of the Israelites during their Babylonian and Egyptian captivities was at its height. To those crossing the Atlantic in four ships in that spring of 1630, King Charles I was the tyrannical Egyptian pharaoh whose bondage they were fleeing.' She adds, 'Their flight across the ocean was a second Exodus, the Atlantic another Red Sea'.[10]

The Exodus story is a recurring trope in American culture. Referring to the period of the founding of the republic 150 years after the Puritan colonists, Davis says: 'The Fathers of the Republic ... did not cite Holy Scriptures in the past tense, but as living, contemporary reality. Their political condition was described as "Egyptian slavery": King George III was Pharaoh; the Atlantic Ocean nothing other than the Red Sea; and Washington and Adams – Moses and Joshua.' Thus, when a committee consisting of Benjamin Franklin, John Adams and Thomas Jefferson designed a seal that was meant to portray 'the underlying purpose of the Revolution', it chose to depict the exodus of the Israelites from Egypt. Here is Jefferson's description of the seal in his own words:

> Pharaoh sitting in an open chariot, a crown on his head and a sword in his hand passing thro' the divided waters of the Red Sea in pursuit of the Israelites; rays from a pillar of fire in the cloud,

expressive of the divine presence, and command, reaching to Moses who stands on the shore and, extending his hand over the sea, causes it to overwhelm Pharaoh.[11]

The inscription on the seal, a motto coined by Franklin, was this: 'Rebellion to tyrants is Obedience to God.'[12] In the next two centuries, black African-American slaves adopted the same motif – the Exodus story – in their pursuit of liberty. We tend to associate liberty with the ideas and values of the Enlightenment. However, liberty, American style, carries a strong connotation of deliverance – as in 'Let my people go.'

But back to the Puritan dawn and to that little flotilla of April 1630. John Winthrop, who led the pilgrims on their voyage and subsequently became the first governor of the Massachusetts Bay Colony, composed a sermon aboard the flagship *Arbela*. Let us imagine ourselves transported back in time, listening with rapt attention, along with Winthrop's ragged congregation, to his rousing words carried by the breeze:

> The Lord will be our God and delight to dwell among us as his owne people and will command a blessing on us in all our wayes, soe that we shall see much more of his wisdome, power, goodness and truthe than formerly wee have been acquainted with. Wee shall finde that the God of Israell is among us, when ten of us [did he mean a *minyan*?] shall be able to resist a thousand of our enemies, when hee shall make us a prayse and glory, that men shall say of succeeding plantacions: the lord make it like that of New England: for wee must Consider that wee shall be as a Citty upon a Hill, the eies of all people are uppon us ...[13]

Our preacher continues in the same vein and after a while, as usual with *drashahs*, our attention begins to wander. We are nodding off at the back. But, as Winthrop approaches the climax of his sermon, he catches our ears again and we sit up with a start. Sounding just like Moses admonishing the Children of Israel as they approached Canaan, he declares emphatically: 'Therefore lette us choose life, that wee, and our Seede, may live; by obeying his voice, and cleaving to him, for hee is our life, and our prosperity.'[14]

Winthrop's radiant image of New England as 'a city on a hill' has been seminal for America's sense of itself and its place or presence in the world. The phrase alludes directly to a passage in Jesus's Sermon on the Mount (Matt. 5:14), but indirectly it recalls Isaiah: 'I will make you a light to the nations, that my salvation may reach the ends of the earth' (Is. 49:6). And, as we have seen, although the Puritans passed into history, their identification with the Israelites survived them, shaping the national consciousness that was emerging with the revolution of 1776. We see this in the very titles of sermons. For example, 'The American States Acting Over the Part of the Children of Israel in the Wilderness and Thereby Impeding Their Entrance into Canaan's Rest': a sermon preached at New Haven, Connecticut, in April 1777 by Nicholas Street. 'The Republic of the Israelites an Example to the American States': a sermon preached at Concord, New Hampshire, in June 1788 by Samuel Langdon. In his 1799 Thanksgiving sermon, Abiel Abbott observed: 'It has often been remarked that the people of the United States come nearer to a parallel with Ancient Israel, than any other nation upon the globe. Hence *Our American Israel* is a term frequently used; and common consent allows it apt and proper.'[15]

I have referred to Jefferson, Adams and Franklin, three of the 'founding fathers'. Let me now bring in George Washington, the first US President (1789–97), the man Americans often call 'the father of our country'. In a letter to the French military officer Lafayette, explaining his policy towards the American West, Washington wrote:

> I wish to see the sons and daughters of the world in Peace and busily employed in the ... agreeable amusement of fulfilling the first and great commandment – *Increase and Multiply*: as an encouragement to which we have opened the fertile plains of the Ohio to the poor, the needy and the oppressed of the Earth; anyone therefore who is heavy laden or who wants land to cultivate, may repair thither & abound, as in the Land of promise, with milk and honey ...[16]

So, when Daniel Boone went forth into the American West, he was performing a mitzvah; he and Rebecca together. Making their home in 'the Land of promise, with milk and honey', they could not have chosen a more appropriate name when they named their son 'Israel'.

SEEING ZION AS RESTORED

The years in which the idea of America as Zion first took shape were also formative for Christian Zionism, to use the term that is current today. It is not a bad term, if we understand by 'Zionism' the idea that Herzl mentions in the very first sentence of his Preface to his 1896 pamphlet *Der Judenstaat*: 'The idea which I have developed in this pamphlet is a very old one: it is the restoration of the Jewish state.'[17] 'Restorationism' was, until quite recently, the more common term for what has come to be known as 'Christian Zionism'. Whatever we call it, its roots go back to the Puritans of the seventeenth century. And although at first it might seem to be completely separate from the idea we have been examining – the idea of America as Zion – I see it as the other side of the same coin. That is to say, for the Puritans, the New World of America and the Promised Land of Canaan were two sites where the Word of God would be fulfilled by a people of destiny: themselves in the one place, the Jews in the other.

Let us leave the New World for a moment and return to the Old, where, in 1649, the year in which King Charles I was executed, Joanna Cartwright and her son Ebenezer, two English Puritans living in Amsterdam, drew up a petition that they submitted to the English Council of State. This was the new authority governing England under their fellow Puritan, Oliver Cromwell. The petition made two requests, one being as follows: 'That this Nation of England, with the inhabitants of the Netherlands, shall be the first and the readiest to transport Izraell's [sic] sons and daughters in their ships to the Land promised to their forefathers, Abraham, Isaac and Jacob for an everlasting inheritance.'[18]

The other request, by the way, one of particular interest to us as Britons, was for the readmission of the Jews to England, 'to trade and dwell in this land, as they now do in the Netherlands'.[19] Both requests reflect biblical prophecy: the 'in-gathering of the exiles' and the scattering of God's people to 'the ends of the earth'. And what is England (at least north of Watford Gap) if not the end of the earth? But I digress.

The Cartwrights were by no means the first Puritans to propose a national restoration for the Jews in their ancient homeland.[20] The idea had been mooted in Nonconformist circles for many years.[21] When it was revived in the nineteenth century, the leading exponent in Britain was the Earl of Shaftesbury, the 'acknowledged lay leader' of the Christian Evangelical movement.[22] The same Shaftesbury who, out of Christian piety, championed the Factory Act, the Mines Act and other philanthropic initiatives, made the following entry in his diary in 1854: 'There is a country without a nation, and God now, in His wisdom and mercy, directs us to a nation without a country.'[23] He was referring to Palestine and the Jews. His remark recalls – or more precisely anticipates by several decades – the Jewish Zionist slogan (attributed to Israel Zangwill): 'A land without a people for a people without a land'. But Shaftesbury was a missionary; and, if he sought the 'restoration' of the

Jews, he also desired their conversion. As President of the London Society for Promoting Christianity among the Jews (known familiarly as The Jews' Society), he actively campaigned to bring the Jews into the Christian fold.[24] His goodwill, it seems, knew no bounds.

Staying in roughly the same era, let us now nip back across the Atlantic to America. It is 1819. The Puritans have long gone. John Adams, one of the driving forces of the 1776 revolution that led to the creation of the US, the man who had been the new republic's second President (1797–1801), writes a letter to Mordecai Manuel Noah, an American playwright, diplomat, journalist and (in case you have not guessed from the name) Jew.[25] The letter contains a surprising ingredient. 'Dear Sir', writes Adams, 'I have to thank you for another valuable publication your travels in "Europe & Africa" which though I cannot see well enough to read.' He goes on to say that his hearing, however, is fine and that he has 'heard read' (*sic*) most of Noah's magazine. He continues: 'I have been so pleased with it that I wish you had continued your travels – into Syria, Judea & Jerusalem ... If I were to let my imagination loose I should wish you had been a member of Napoleons [*sic*] Institute at Cairo.' Now comes the surprise:

> Nay farther I could find it in my heart to wish that you had been at the head of a hundred thousand Israelites indeed as well disciplined as a French army – & marching with them into Judea & making a conquest of that country & restoring your nation to the dominion of it. For I really wish the Jews again in Judea an independent nation.

But there is the usual sting in the tail: 'For I believe the most enlightened men of it ... once restored to an independent government & no longer persecuted ... would soon wear away some of the asperities & peculiarities of their character & possibly in time become liberal Unitarian Christians'.[26]

Incidentally, a year later, Noah did try to establish a Jewish homeland. But instead of 'Judea', he chose an island in the middle of the Niagara River and called it, appropriately, 'Ararat'. Ararat was intended to be 'a City of Refuge for the Jews'.[27] But again, I digress. Adams concludes his letter to Noah fraternally, saying 'for your Jehovah is our Jehovah & your God of Abraham Isaac & Jacob is our God'.[28] But fundamentally, his 'Zionism', like Shaftesbury's, was part of a Christianizing agenda, a mission to the Jews.

Generally speaking, contemporary Christian Zionism maintains a similar attitude towards Jews: a mixture of friendly sentiment and ulterior motive. Predominantly, it is not about our *realizing* our Jewish identity but about our *relinquishing* it; or (as a Christian Zionist might say) realizing it *by* relinquishing it: by seeing the light and becoming Christian. In the Christian Zionist script, the 'restoration of the Jewish state' (in Herzl's phrase) is one episode in a cosmic spectacular. The conflict between good and evil culminates, in the final act, with the triumphal return of Jesus as messiah, victory over the Antichrist, resurrection of the dead and (the coup de grâce to Satan) conversion of those Jews who survive the maelstrom. The Christian Zionist script gives a whole new meaning to 'restoration drama'.

If it were a tiny cult in the US, Christian Zionism would not warrant any place in my argument. But it is not. Precise figures are hard to come by. David Katz mentions that according to the National Survey of Religious Identification (1990), '20 per cent of the American population – fifty million people – can be called "Evangelical Protestants", that is, Fundamentalists.'[29] Anatol Lieven refers to a survey carried out by the University of Michigan in 2000 that showed that 'white evangelical Protestants (including churches defining themselves as fundamentalists) made up 23.1 percent of the U.S. population in that year'.[30] A poll conducted by the Pew Research Centre in 2004 'indicated that 40 percent of Americans believed in the literal word-for-word truth of the Bible'.[31] Not that all these people are Christian Zionists; some are, some not. In an article on Christian Zionist doctrine about the 'end time', written in 2004 and delightfully entitled 'Their Beliefs are Bonkers, but They are at the Heart of Power', George Monbiot reported the following statistics: 'American pollsters believe that 15–18% of US voters belong to churches or movements which subscribe to these teachings.'[32] I daresay that a substantial number of Americans, even if they do not exactly subscribe, have a sneaking suspicion that there is 'something in it'.

In short, there is reason to believe that a significant – and influential – section of the American public is inclined to think, on the basis of the prophetic and apocalyptic books of the Bible alone, that a God-fearing country like theirs should support the State of Israel, the 'restored' kingdom of the Jews.

AN AFFAIR OF THE HEART

Taken together, the two ties that I have discussed give rise to what in the introduction I called 'an affair of the heart'. And of the two, the more fundamental is the first: the belief that the American people and the American state, like the people and State of Israel, have a special status and a universal mission: that America, like Zion, is exceptional.

Earlier, I looked only at the formative years of this idea in the seventeenth and eighteenth centuries in order to make the point that this mark was branded into the flesh of the nation at its conception and birth. Subsequently, others picked up and developed the theme. In the process, the old Puritan idea was transformed into something new; but the theme lived on. Lieven writes:

> Underlying the nationalism not only of the American Right, but of American culture in general, is a belief that America has been specially 'chosen' and is therefore, in the words of former Secretary of State Madeleine Albright, the 'indispensable nation' – whether chosen by God, by 'Destiny', by 'History' or simply marked out for greatness and leadership by the supposed possession of the greatest, most successful, oldest and most developed form of democracy.[33]

In other words, the initial idea of chosenness, anchored firmly in a Puritan worldview, has broken free of its moorings and developed into a national idea that transcends the Christian/secular divide. Moreover, it transcends the division between Republican and Democrat. Lieven points out how close Albright's language is to that of George W. Bush, and observes that 'this illustrates the widespread and bipartisan nature of this belief in US society'. He sums up: 'This sense of America ... as a country with a national mission, is absolutely central to the American national identity and also forms the core of the nation's faith in its own "exceptionalism".'[34]

In effect, Lieven is talking about America's 'civil religion'. The religious historian Conrad Cherry observes: 'The history of the American civil religion is a history of the conviction that the American people are God's New Israel, his newly chosen people.'[35] So, Zion, inflected and transmuted, lies at the heart of America's romance with itself. Small wonder, then, if America has a romance with Zion.

It is in this light that we should view the controversial claim made by Mearsheimer and Walt. The argument that I have been making suggests that 'America's support for Israel', which *they* say is due to 'the unmatched power of the Israel Lobby', is due, in the first place, to the incomparable power of self-love. America looks into the mirror of Israel and, like Narcissus, sees its own reflection. Modelling itself on ancient Zion, and seeing in modern Israel a kindred spirit, America is disposed, lobby or no lobby, to bond with 'the Jewish state'. It is, to be sure, no more than a cultural disposition; yet strong enough to prevail over other dispositions and other considerations. Generally speaking, the power of a political lobby is in direct proportion to the susceptibility of the body politic. And any lobby that promotes, for whatever reason, American support for Israel will find that it does not have to knock hard for the door to open. Mearsheimer and Walt lean heavily on the premise that the level of American support for Israel is not in the national interest. That's as may be. But even if they are right about this, it does not follow that a group with its own agenda has hijacked American policy. They do not appear to understand that, with nations as with individuals, self-love does not always conduce to self-interest. If they *are* right about the national interest, then America's support for Israel illustrates the general truth that romantic attachments, not least to yourself, are liable to obscure your vision and skew your judgement. When the pet names of your beloved and yourself are as enchanting as in this case – 'Promised Land', 'New World' – it is even easier to lose your head.

This is not to deny that there is a set of serious political questions that call for sober analysis regarding the composition and influence of domestic lobbies, such as the one for Israel, on American foreign policy in the Middle East. It is only to say that nations are not necessarily rational beings – and that politics is not just about power.

NOTES

 1. John Mearsheimer and Stephen Walt, 'The Israel Lobby', *London Review of Books*, 23 March 2006, http://www.lrb.co.uk/v28/n06/john-mearsheimer/the-israel-lobby.
 2. Ibid.
 3. John Mearsheimer and Stephen Walt, *The Israel Lobby and US Foreign Policy* (London: Allen Lane, 2007), p.5.
 4. Noam Chomsky, 'The Israel Lobby?', ZNet, 28 March 2006. http://www.zmag.org/znet/viewArticle/4134.
 5. This chapter is adapted from a talk I gave at the Annual UK Limmud Conference, University of Warwick, December 2007.
 6. Tom Segev, *Elvis in Jerusalem: Post-Zionism and the Americanization of Israel* (New York: Metropolitan Books, 2002).
 7. 'Biblical United States County/City/Town Names'. Available at America's Christian Heritage: http://www.whateveristrue.com/heritage/biblenames.htm.
 8. Moshe Davis, *America and the Holy Land* (Westport, CT: Praeger, 1995), pp.13, 14.
 9. Ibid., pp.11, 14. Salem, a particularly popular place name in America, is, of course, a variation on 'shalom'.
10. Victoria Clark, *Allies for Armageddon: The Rise of Christian Zionism* (New Haven, CT: Yale University Press, 2007), p.39.
11. Davis, *America and the Holy Land*, p.12.
12. Ibid.
13. John Winthrop, 'A Modell of Christian Charity', in Conrad Cherry (ed.), *God's New Israel: Religious Interpretations of American Destiny* (Chapel Hill, NC: University of North Carolina Press, 1998), p.40. (Spelling as in original).
14. Ibid., p.41. Compare Deuteronomy 30:19.

15. Cherry (ed.), *God's New Israel*, pp.67, 93, v (epigraph).
16. Quoted in Henry Nash Smith, *Virgin Land: The American West as Symbol and Myth* (Cambridge, MA: Harvard University Press, 1950), p.203.
17. Theodor Herzl, *The Jewish State: An Attempt at a Modern Solution of the Jewish Question* (1896), translated from the original German by Sylvie D'Avigdor (London: Henry Pordes, 1993), p.7.
18. Barbara W. Tuchman, *Bible and Sword: England and Palestine from the Bronze Age to Balfour* (New York: Funk & Wagnalls, 1956), p.121.
19. Pamela Fletcher Jones, *The Jews of Britain: A Thousand Years of History* (Gloucestershire: Windrush Press, 1990), p.80.
20. It is tempting to speculate about a possible connection between these seventeenth-century Cartwrights and the family (Ben Adam, Hoss and Little Joe) who lived on the Ponderosa in the television series 'Bonanza'. But, despite the fact that three of the four names of the Ponderosa Cartwrights are biblical (all four if we contrive to derive 'Hoss' from 'Hosea'), it is a temptation that I shall resist.
21. Douglas J. Culver, *Albion and Ariel: British Puritanism and the Birth of Political Zionism* (New York: Peter Lang, 1995), p.7.
22. Tuchman, *Bible and Sword*, p.180.
23. Quoted in S.A. Morrison, *Middle East Survey: The Political, Social and Religious Problems* (London: SCM Press, 1954), p.25.
24. Tuchman, *Bible and Sword*, p.183.
25. 'Mordecai Manuel Noah', Wikipedia, available at http://en.wikipedia.org/wiki/Mordecai _Manuel_Noah.
26. Davis, *America and the Holy Land*, p.26. (Punctuation as in the original.)
27. 'Mordecai Manuel Noah', Wikipedia. Mount Ararat was where Noah's Ark came to rest (Gen. 8:4).
28. Davis, *America and the Holy Land*, p.26.
29. David S. Katz, *The Occult Tradition: From the Renaissance to the Present Day* (London: Jonathan Cape, 2005), p.185.
30. Anatol Lieven, *America Right or Wrong: An Anatomy of American Nationalism* (Oxford: Oxford University Press, 2004), p.140.
31. Ibid.
32. George Monbiot, 'Their Beliefs are Bonkers, but They are at the Heart of Power', *Guardian*, 20 April 2004, http://www.guardian.co.uk/world/2004/apr/20/usa.uselections2004.
33. Lieven, *America Right or Wrong*, p.32.
34. Ibid., p.33.
35. Cherry (ed.), *God's New Israel*, p.19.

CHAPTER FIVE

Tricks of Memory

THE AUSCHWITZ PICTURE

On 4 September 2003, as part of a commemoration ceremony, three Israeli Air Force F-15 fighter jets, piloted by descendants of Holocaust survivors, staged a flypast at the former Nazi concentration camp at Auschwitz, whose name is synonymous with Hitler's Final Solution of the so-called 'Jewish Question'.[1] A photograph taken from the air (which is before me as I write) features two of the warplanes flying side by side. Blue Stars of David are visible on their wings and fuselages. Below, in a landscape that is eerily green and pleasant, rows of identical oblong huts, evenly spaced and neatly laid out like graves in a well-kept cemetery, mark the site of Birkenau, the extermination camp that was part of the Auschwitz complex.

On the face of it, the Auschwitz picture is simply a snapshot of an event. But it can also be seen as an iconic representation of an idea. With this in mind, a friend of mine, a committed Zionist on whose office wall the picture hangs, has asked rhetorically: 'Get the point?'[2] He means, I think, 'Never again'. But this point is just the tip of the iceberg. What the photo captures is an entire mindset about the State of Israel and the Jewish people. In this essay I shall trace the lineaments of this mindset, finding them refracted in the way that Israel views its situation in the Middle East. I shall argue that the Auschwitz picture (or the mindset that I take it to represent) distorts the contours of the Arab–Israeli conflict in general and the Israeli–Palestinian conflict in particular. I shall conclude with some observations about breaking the hold of the picture that I have just described.

This essay originated as a response to an invitation from Stephen Law to contribute something 'broadly philosophical' to a collection of essays entitled *Israel, Palestine and Terror*.[3] In view of the title and scope of the book, I pay special attention to the subject of Palestinian terrorism.[4] Several contributions are responses to Ted Honderich, who has an essay in the book in which he argues (as he has argued elsewhere) that the Palestinians have a 'moral right' to their terrorism. My own contribution is not about this, although I do get round to discussing his position in the final section, where I explain why I reject it.[5]

I should say at the outset that, even speaking broadly, I do not think of my essay as philosophical. But what is philosophy? There is a conception of philosophy, one that I associate chiefly with Plato and (the later work of) Wittgenstein, in which philosophy is, in a sense, the province of memory. I am thinking, for example, of Plato's dialogue the *Meno*, where Socrates points the enquiry in the direction of recollection (*anamnesis*). I am thinking also of a remark of Wittgenstein's: 'The work of a philosopher consists in assembling reminders for a particular purpose.'[6] Many people will find it paradoxical to bracket these two philosophers together; they will say that the similarity between the two examples I have just given is superficial. I think it goes deep. It depends, I suppose, on how you read Plato and (the later) Wittgenstein. On my reading, both of them construe remembering, insofar as it is the activity of philosophy, as entailing more than merely calling past facts to mind. It is more like calling *the mind* to mind: acquainting the mind with itself, with its prior proclivities, where the trick (if memory can carry it off) is to overcome its own bent: to know itself and, in knowing itself, obtain its freedom.

I specify this conception of philosophy for two reasons. First, it is one to which I am drawn. Second, everything I have just said about it applies, mutatis mutandis, to the topic at the heart of this chapter: a certain fixed condition of mind and the problem it presents. Thus, while not in itself what I would call 'philosophical', the topic of this chapter evokes philosophy after a certain manner. I shall get back to philosophy, broadly and narrowly, in the concluding section.

REMEMBERING THE PAST

Along with 'Never again', the point that my friend might have been making with the Auschwitz picture is this: 'Never forget.' It is a point worth making: sometimes the only kind of justice that we can render victims, or the only gesture we can make in lieu of the justice that can never be theirs, is to honour their memory. However, it is simplistic to think in terms of a simple disjunction: either forget, which is bad, or remember, which is good. The cast of mind that I am about to describe, and which I see as posing a problem for the present and the future, results from what is, in a way, a surfeit of remembering.

A culture of memorialization has grown up around the Nazi Holocaust. 'The World Remembers': this was the headline on the front page of the *Guardian* on 28 January 2005.[7] It referred to a memorial ceremony held the previous day at Auschwitz. The ceremony, attended by political leaders from around the world, marked the sixtieth anniversary of the liberation of the camp where more than a million people perished between 1940 and 1945, the vast majority because they were Jewish.[8] Following this anniversary, the UN General Assembly passed a resolution designating 27 January as 'International Day of Commemoration in memory of the victims of the Holocaust'.[9] The resolution 'calls for a remembrance of past crimes with an eye towards preventing them in the future'.[10] In other words, 'Never forget' for the sake of 'Never again'. However, memory can play tricks; and I am referring not to the accuracy with which we recollect the past but to our perception of things in the present.

A case in point is Menachem Begin, founder of the Herut party, who, as leader of the right-wing Likud coalition, was Prime Minister of Israel from 1977 to 1984.[11] 'The Holocaust', says Tom Segev, 'shaped his entire political career.'[12] More specifically, it shaped his political mind. So, for example, explaining why Israeli warplanes bombed a nuclear reactor in Iraq in June 1981, Begin said that 'there will not be another Holocaust in history'.[13] One year later, as Israel prepared to invade Lebanon, he told his Cabinet, 'Believe me, the alternative is Treblinka, and we have decided that there will be no more Treblinkas.'[14] During the 1982 bombardment of Beirut, which destroyed the headquarters of Yasser Arafat, head of the Palestine Liberation Organization (PLO), Begin wrote to President Ronald Regan of the United States: 'I feel as a Prime Minister empowered to instruct a valiant army facing "Berlin" where amongst innocent civilians, Hitler and his henchmen hide in a bunker deep beneath the surface.'[15]

It is tempting to say that the bunker in which Hitler was hiding was deep beneath the surface of Begin's mind. But this does not mean that he was literally deluded. The term 'delusion', as J.L. Austin points out, suggests 'something totally unreal, not really there at all'.[16] Of course, the argumentative context is quite different: criticizing A.J. Ayer's theory of sensory perception, Austin is distinguishing between delusion and illusion, not delusion and mindset. Nonetheless, his observation fits. And the fact that Begin places scare quotes round 'Berlin' signals that he is aware of the difference between Berlin and Beirut – and therefore not deluded. He himself draws attention to this punctuation later in the same telegram when he declares 'that what happened from Berlin – with or without inverted comas – will never happen again'.[17] For Begin, Beirut was 'Berlin' but not Berlin, Arafat was 'Hitler' but not

Hitler, and the PLO were 'Hitler's henchmen' but not Hitler's henchmen. So, to say that the Holocaust *shaped* Begin's mind is to say that it gave his mind a certain bent: a tendency to see current events in terms of the Holocaust; specifically, to view Israel and its troubles through the lens of the catastrophic Jewish experience in Nazi-occupied Europe. This was his Auschwitz mindset.[18] It was a species of remembering: an awareness of the present that was structured by a sense of the past.

Had Begin been genuinely deluded – if he had actually believed that Hitler, in the guise of Arafat, was alive and well and living in a bunker beneath a building in Beirut – then he would merely have been insane. This would make him a nutcase rather than a case in point. Furthermore, as Austin observes, it is no use trying to reason with someone who is suffering from a delusion: such a person simply 'needs to be cured'.[19] Having delusions is a clinical condition and a problem for a psychiatrist or psychoanalyst. But, while it might colour your perceptions and hinder your ability to listen to reason, having a mindset about something is not a form of madness. It is a normal condition of everyday life that we have to negotiate with other people's pre-existing frames of mind – and they with ours. This is a crucial point since it means that the topic of this essay lies within the realm of the political, not the medical. The practical, political question is this: What kinds of argument, if any, are capable of breaking the hold of the Auschwitz picture?[20]

The mindset that Begin exemplified certainly consisted well with his brand of right-wing nationalist politics. Moreover, it is probable that his personal background – he escaped from Warsaw as German bombs were falling on the Polish capital in September 1939 – had a strong bearing on how he viewed the world.[21] However, it would be a mistake to think about his attitudes in terms that are either purely ideological or merely biographical. His was, perhaps, a more extreme case than most, but, as Colin Shindler tells us, his 'deep-seated beliefs were often widely shared by large sections of the Israeli populace'.[22] Moreover, other politicians who have held high office in Israel have shared, to a degree, a similar mindset without necessarily occupying the same position on the political spectrum or coming from a similar background. So, for example, at the time of the Eichmann trial in 1961, Prime Minister David Ben-Gurion, 'father of the nation', declared, 'We, the sovereign Jewish people in Israel, are the redeemers of the blood of six million Jews.'[23] And it was the urbane Abba Eban, 'voice of Israel', who, soon after the 1967 Six Day War, originated the idea that the pre-war 1949 Armistice borders between Israel and its neighbours ('the Green Line') were 'Auschwitz lines', implying that they were so tight that they imperilled the survival of Israel's Jewish population.[24] Both Eban and Ben-Gurion were major figures in the left-wing Mapai Party, opposed to the right-wing Likud, while Eban, in contrast with Begin, grew up in a secure environment in England. Other examples abound, from Golda Meir, the Labour Prime Minister (who once explained, 'We resolved that there would be no return to Hitler's Final Solution; there would be no second Holocaust') to Benjamin Netanyahu, the current Likud Prime Minister (who says that 'ultimately the only assurance' that there will not be another Holocaust is the 'rebirth of Israel, its development and empowerment').[25]

That the existence of the state is in constant danger; that this danger constitutes a threat to the lives of its citizens; that this threat amounts to the imminence of another Holocaust; and that only brute force – the power of the Israeli military on behalf of the Jewish people – can prevent this from happening: these ideas not only play on the minds of many Israeli Jews (and Jews in general around the world), they also profoundly affect the way the country conducts its foreign affairs. In his history of the Arab–Israeli conflict, Shlomo Ben-Ami remarks: 'Whether in times of war or during intervals of truce, Israel was unable to extricate herself from her mental ghetto or, worse, from her Holocaust complex.'[26] His book explains at length how much this has affected the way the country has conducted its foreign policy over time. Not that we should take his word for it; but I imagine that, as a former Israeli Foreign Minister as well as a distinguished historian, he knows whereof he speaks. Idith Zertal sums up the record this way: 'There has not been a war in Israel, from 1948 till the present ongoing outburst of violence which began in October 2000, that has not been perceived, defined, and conceptualized in terms of the Holocaust.'[27]

Israel, in short, is not in danger of forgetting Auschwitz.[28] Auschwitz, says Zertal, has become 'Israel's main reference in its relations with a world defined repeatedly as anti-Semitic and forever hostile'.[29] It is a reference with multiple connotations: honouring the memory of the murdered six million, protecting Jewish communities around the world, fending off Israel's imminent annihilation, even reinventing the Jewish self as bold lion rather than meek sheep that goes to the slaughter: all these associations hang in the air, like a penumbra, in the Auschwitz picture. Concomitantly, in the mindset that the image represents, every Israeli military triumph constitutes, in Zertal's phrase, a 'victory over "Auschwitz" '.[30] (Think of the quiescent camp beneath the screaming jets.)

Thus, what the camera captured at Auschwitz was not a mere moment in time but what purports to be a recurring truth. 'Never again' might be the picture's motto but its subtext is almost the opposite. 'Again and again, forever': *that* is the point. That is the trap.

FORGETTING THE PRESENT

Some readers of this chapter will have been waiting with growing impatience to make an objection along these lines:

> *This is all very well, but your argument overlooks one small thing: reality. The reality is that the Middle East is a dangerous neighbourhood; Israel has enemies who fundamentally wish it did not exist; the Palestinians would like to reclaim the whole territory west of the river Jordan for their own state; and the lives of Israeli Jews are constantly under threat from Palestinian terrorism. In short, the hostility that you attribute to a 'mindset' is not in the mind: it is in the world. This pulls the rug out from under your feet.*

The curious thing about this objection is the extent to which it manages to miss the point, for, far from pulling the rug out from under my feet, the reality it describes is itself the rug on which my argument stands. That the Middle East is a dangerous neighbourhood and that Israel is not welcome in the region are givens. Not only are these facts not in dispute (although they belie a greater complexity) but, if it were otherwise, then the mindset of which I speak would have no purchase. For I am not speaking of a mind that is unhinged from the real world but of a mind whose hinge (if I may so put it) is a set of expectations that it brings to the experience of reality. If reality were nice, if Israel were embraced by its neighbours, if the Palestinians loved their occupiers, then Begin, for example, would not have compared Arafat with Hitler; for, to repeat, he was not insane.

That said, the greater complexity that the facts possess is telling. For, while it is true (as the objection asserts) that countries in the region would like to wish Israel away, this does not entail that they will reject it unconditionally. Once upon a time all of them did. But a desideratum is not the same as a non-negotiable demand. Thirty years ago Egypt and Israel concluded a peace treaty (1979) in which each country recognized the other. A similar treaty was signed with Jordan in 1994. It is several years (March 2002) since the Saudi peace plan offered 'normal relations' with Israel on terms that have long been laid down in UN resolutions – a plan that was endorsed in 2007 by the Arab League.

These facts are, to be sure, open to interpretation; and there's the rub. Israel's leaders have a chronic tendency to put a negative spin on any peace initiative by Arab states and, as Ben-Ami bemoans, take decisions 'only on the basis of worst-case scenarios'. Hard-line pessimism is the result when foreign policy is distorted by 'the paranoiac instincts of the Israelis' and 'the Jewish atavistic fear'.[31]

In the same vein, while indubitably 'the Palestinians would like to reclaim the whole territory west of the river Jordan for their own state', the Palestine National Council effectively accepted the existence of Israel within its pre-1967 borders with the Algiers Declaration (1988).[32] (This position, moreover, has been reiterated, even more explicitly, on subsequent occasions.[33]) This too is a fact. Yet Israel is *minded* to give the second fact – the acceptance of Israel's existence – far less weight than the first. This mindedness, persistent and entrenched, is what this essay is about: it is the point that the objection misses.

In general, whenever the Auschwitz picture is projected onto the Middle East, the facts about Israel's predicaments appear differently. I do not mean that there appears to be a different set of facts (although a number of basic facts are, of course, contested); it is the *appearance* of the *same* facts that is changed.

It is, however, harder to recognize this when the question of interpretation does not affect the bottom line; which brings us to the subject of Palestinian terrorism. The bottom line is this: to enter a café crowded with people and blow them all (along with yourself) to smithereens is an abomination. Irrespective of the motive or the worthiness of the cause, it is an unutterable atrocity; anyone who is in doubt about this should read first-hand accounts of the experience by victims who somehow survived.[34] Equally, the act is horrific regardless of how it is perceived in Israel. Nonetheless, perception matters. For, if Israel (or anyone else) is going to confront this horror, the act needs to be understood for what it is. Seen with an Auschwitz mindset, the hostility that the suicide bomber feels towards Israel, rather than being resistance to an occupying power or the result of despair or revenge for the loss of friends and family at the hands of the Israel Defence Forces (IDF), appears to stem from the same ancient anti-Jewish bigotry that led to the ultimate disaster for European Jewry. In this perspective, the perpetrator is not just a political zealot or enemy of the state or avenging relative or even a callous murderer, but a rabid antisemite whose precursors include the Russian Black Hundreds and the Nazi SS and whose successors might one day plan another Auschwitz, perhaps on Palestinian soil, or throw all the Jews into the sea, as the final solution of 'the Israeli Question'. The whole complexion of the act, along with the question of how the state should confront such a dreadful deed, is drastically altered when seen through the lens of Auschwitz.

Furthermore, if the occupation of the West Bank and Gaza Strip constitutes Israeli policy, if Israeli policy is understood as representing the interests of the Jewish people as a whole, and if the Jewish people is seen as a collective victim asserting its rightful claims against all-comers, then *any* Palestinian resistance to the occupation is, prima facie, iniquitous. The moral difference between the suicide bomber who attacks civilians in a café and the stone-thrower whose target is a soldier wearing the uniform of the IDF, is diminished or blurred. At the extreme, all Palestinian resistance, whatever form it takes, howsoever legitimate in international law, is perceived as contributing to the incipient genocide of the Jewish people.[35] Thus, an Auschwitz mindset leads to a highly restrictive view of the rights of Palestinians to take steps in their own defence; it rules too much out.

In contrast, the same mindset is highly permissive – ruling too much in – when the Israeli military acts in the name of security. Double standards are thus built in to the moral calculus with which the kind of mind I am describing judges actions by each side. (Blind to its own bias, such a mind is liable to view the allegation that it is biased as *itself* biased or even 'antisemitic'.) An incursion by the IDF into a Palestinian refugee camp, destroying homes and wrecking the infrastructure of everyday life, becomes a noble blow against evil. So does any military action taken by Israel against neighbouring Arab states, which tend to be seen as implacable enemies of the Jewish people. 'We don't want the Arab Nazis to come and slaughter us', said Ben-Gurion in December 1951, less than four years into Israel's existence.[36] More than forty years later, Netanyahu referred to 'the Arab war against the Jews', a phrase that recalls the title of Lucy Dawidowicz's classic study of Nazi antisemitism *The War Against the Jews 1933–45* and which suggests that the Arabs, like the Nazis, were driven by what Netanyahu calls 'a blind obsession'.[37] In general, an Auschwitz mindset tends to elevate 'security' to a higher moral plane – the protection of the innocent Jewish people against dark Satanic forces – and to valorize actions taken by the Israeli military or, at least, airbrush their excesses.

Which brings us back to the picture that I described at the beginning of this chapter. Who can blame us if, momentarily, it goes to our heads? But it ought to be a sobering thought that those selfsame F-15 fighter jets – two defiant phoenixes soaring over the House of Hades – might themselves be harbingers of terror, say in southern Lebanon, on another day or night, delivering their messages – 'Never again', 'Never forget' – from their bellies to a non-Jewish population on the ground. It *ought* to be sobering but it isn't. 'Never forget', for a mind in the grip of this picture, turns out to be a prescription for oblivion: crammed with the there and then, such a mind overlooks the here and now. Which prompts the question: Is it not possible to remember the past without forgetting the present?

BREAKING THE HOLD

At one point in the *Philosophical Investigations*, confronting the way of thinking that dominated his own earlier work, Wittgenstein reflects as follows: 'A *picture* held us captive. And we could not get outside it, for it lay in our language and language seemed to repeat it to us inexorably.'[38] The fixed idea to which he refers is different in kind from the idée fixe that is the subject of this chapter; one is a formal concept that gives rise to philosophical confusion, while the other is a substantive view that distorts the perception of political reality. And yet, to borrow a phrase from the same author, I detect a family resemblance. Both are cases where the mind is in the grip of an idea (or picture); in both cases the effects are systematic, affecting our way of seeing things across the board; both are self-perpetuating; and each is a predicament from which the mind can escape if, and only if, it comes to recognize the predicament it is in. In a way, moreover, the difficulty of doing this is the same: we cannot 'get outside' the Auschwitz picture, for it lies in the language in which we speak about Israel, language that seems to repeat the horror of the Holocaust to us inexorably. We (or some of us, or part of us) are held captive by a picture.

But it *is* a different *kind* of picture and captivates in quite a different fashion. There is no reason to suppose that the methods that Wittgenstein employs in philosophy will work – or even make sense – in the present context. This is not to say that philosophy has no role to play, for it does: it can refrain from making matters worse. It is not easy to carry this off, as we see when we turn to the argument that Ted Honderich makes for the claim that the Palestinians have a moral right to their terrorism.[39]

Honderich bases his argument on what he calls 'the Principle of Humanity'. This is not Kant's principle: that we should treat humanity, whether in our own person or in the person of another, never simply as a means but always as an end.[40] It would, on the face of it, be hard to argue on the basis of *this* principle that someone has the right to

enter a café crowded with people and blow them all – including themselves – sky-high for the sake of a political cause. So, Honderich's
terminology is a little confusing. (This is not a small point; in a way,
as we shall see, it is the most important point of all.) We shall not be
misled, as long as we remember that Honderich is not Kant.

There are two versions of Honderich's Principle of Humanity. The
short version is that 'we must actually take rational steps to the end
of getting and keeping people out of bad lives'.[41] 'Bad lives' are con-
trasted with 'good lives'. Both are defined in terms of the six 'great
goods of our lives', the goods that, in virtue of our common human
nature, we all desire.[42] Here, roughly and in a nutshell, is Honderich's
argument:

1. The Palestinians under Israeli occupation are living bad lives.
2. Only a viable national state of their own alongside Israel will get
   them out of their bad lives.
3. Their terrorism is the only means of achieving this end.
4. The right or justified course of action for the Palestinians is that
   which will get them out of their bad lives. (Derived from the Principle of Humanity.)
5. So, the Palestinians have a moral right to their terrorism.

If I were disposed to evaluate this argument I would say that it is
shot through with holes from top to bottom. I would point out that it
is unclear who the subject of the argument is, for while the Palestinians
are a collectivity they are not a collective agent. The fact that an act of
terrorism is performed *in their name* does not make that action *theirs*.
So, 'they', the people under occupation in line 1, and 'they', the
perpetrators of the terrorism in lines 3 and 5, are not the same 'they'.[43]
Furthermore (I would say) the argument goes only to those terrorist
acts that are means to an end of a Palestinian state alongside the State
of Israel (line 2).[44] Yet, in practice, it is often unclear *what* end is in view
on the part of the people who carry out such acts; or it *is* clear and
some *other* end is intended. To put it another way, the conclusion (line
5) requires complex caveats that are liable to render it useless. I might also
query the use Honderich makes of his own Principle of Humanity, since
clearly the lives of *some* Palestinians are made *worse* by Palestinian
terrorism, and this is not factored into the argument. Most likely, I
would take issue with line 3 on the grounds that it is very doubtful that
terrorism is an effective means, let alone the *only* effective means, for
achieving the end stated in line 2. I would, in this connection, point out
that several hundred Palestinian public figures and intellectuals signed

a petition in June 2002 condemning suicide bombings for giving the Israeli government 'the excuse to continue its harsh war against our people'; that in the same year the Interior Minister of the Palestinian Authority (PA) urged all armed groups to stop suicide attacks which, he said, 'harm[ed] the Palestinian people'; and that Mahmoud Abbas, as chair of the PA, went so far as to call a suicide bombing in the Israeli town of Netanya in July 2005 'a crime against the Palestinian people'.[45] Moreover, I would argue that there is a missing premise without which it is impossible to weigh the conclusion in line 5: a statement about the consequences of terrorist acts for those, Israeli and other, who are targeted or hit, including those who are close to them and survivors whose lives are destroyed. For, if the Principle of Humanity enjoins us to get people *out of* bad lives, presumably it forbids us from getting them *into* bad lives (and depriving people of *good* lives), which, as a description of what terrorism does to victims, is a grotesque understatement. Nor, if I were disposed to evaluate the argument, would I stop there.

But I shall stop here because I am not disposed to give this argument the time of day. Let me put it this way: If I were persuaded that the argument were sound, I still would not accept its conclusion. I have too much faith in reason and too little in my powers of reasoning to do so. I cannot believe that reason could lead us to a conclusion that is foul; and the idea that someone – anyone – has a moral right to murder and maim innocent people is pretty stinky.[46] If reason appears to take us there then either we have made a mistake along the way or our very idea of reason is mistaken, that is to say, misshapen.

'Philosophers', says Wittgenstein, 'constantly see the method of science before their eyes, and are irresistibly tempted to ask and answer questions in the way science does.'[47] By 'the method of science' he means 'the method of reducing the explanation of natural phenomena to the smallest number of primitive natural laws'. He has in mind the hardcore areas of the subject: logic, metaphysics and epistemology. But the same tendency exists with ethics. There is in moral philosophy a desire to reduce the rough manifold of ordinary moral experience to a few smooth concepts and a minimal number of principles. The idea is that we can take this apparatus to any moral problem and settle it – rather like a physicist or a biologist in their respective fields. This is the shape of our very idea of what it is to reason about moral questions – or such appears to be the case in much of the philosophical literature on ethics. To this extent, moral philosophy evinces a 'craving for generality', in Wittgenstein's phrase; an appetite that betrays (to adapt his expression) a contemptuous attitude towards the particular word.[48] Words, the ordinary vocabulary of practical life, are waylaid on the public highway, seized, sized and press-ganged into sentences that seem to want to straighten them out, to regiment their meanings, rather than discover them; or that lead us to forget their reach. In the process, the meaning of a given word can flip into its opposite.

Take, for example, the word 'humanity', Honderich's name for the principle that, in his view, justifies Palestinian terrorism. Let us consider an actual case or two and see whether the word consorts with the experience. Twenty-year-old Efrat Ravid was sitting by the bar at the Café Moment in Jerusalem on 9 March 2002 when a suicide bomber struck. Here is part of her testimony:

> Suddenly I heard a tremendous explosion and immediately blacked out. I must have blacked out from the pain, because my thighbone was broken into smithereens, and a major artery was ruptured. I had a serious head injury with hemorrhaging in the brain and stayed unconscious for three days ... The friend I had been with was also injured – her intestines spilled right out. We don't talk any more. It brings up too many bad memories. The girl sitting on the other side of me – I didn't know her – she was killed. My friends don't go out any more.[49]

In the second case, a man took his 16-month-old daughter on an outing to the town of Hadera on 22 November 2000. Here is an excerpt from his account of what occurred:

> When we arrived, she started asking for pizza. She likes to eat it with ketchup – more for the fun than for the flavor. I took her to a pizza place where I know the owners ... I was sitting in the pizzeria – my daughter was in my arms. Suddenly, I found myself somewhere and the child was somewhere else. I thought a gas balloon had blown up. Everywhere was filled with dark smoke. I tasted something bad in my mouth. Thick smoke. The smell of burning flesh in my mouth ... I saw someone without legs – they were blown away. I was stunned – I forgot that my daughter had been with me. Suddenly I remembered. I went to find her. She was a ball of fire.[50]

'Humanity' isn't the word that exactly springs to mind when contemplating the acts that lay behind these devastated lives. 'But', someone might say, 'So what? What difference does it make whether a principle is called by this name or that? What's in a name?' But if nothing, then why use *this* word for this principle? And if something, then we are right to fight for the word. The man in the second case, by the way, was Hussam Abu Hussein, a Palestinian Arab citizen of Israel. He and Efrat Ravid, by their ethnic diversity (she is certainly a Jewish Israeli), call attention to the relevant thing they have in common: their humanity. Theirs and ours. Let Honderich, if he will, seek to justify the terrorist acts of which they were victims; but not with the word 'humanity'. This we cannot grant, for then we would be giving up the word that, naming us, names the ground of our horror. And if we lose such basic vocabulary for such vital moral emotions, how are we going to discuss such a thing as terrorism?

So, my quarrel with Honderich is not just over the *soundness* of his argument but its very *stance*. It is also over his conclusion which, apart from other considerations, does not conduce to breaking the hold of the Auschwitz picture; it does the opposite. Earlier I asked: Is it not possible to remember the past without forgetting the present? Not if the present keeps returning us to the past – which is what a campaign of terror against Israel does to many of us who are Jewish. For Jews, Auschwitz is precisely the symbol of the ultimate terror; this is how the picture holds us captive. Nothing is more distinctive of the Holocaust than terror as such: the terror of being torn away from ordinary life and, utterly powerless, extinguished. Every suicide bomb in a market, café or pizzeria, let alone at a Passover Seder attended by elderly Holocaust survivors, evokes that terror.[51] Every time a terrorist group targets Jewish civilians in the name of the Palestinian people, and every time their 'moral right' to carry out such acts is defended by well-wishers from afar, including moral philosophers, the hold of the Auschwitz picture is strengthened.[52] Not that all moral philosophers, plying their trade, applying their machinery of principles, come to the same conclusion as Honderich: far from it. Nevertheless, we do not need to hold our breath, waiting for the profession to tell us whether it is wrong to murder and maim innocent people.

Perhaps the question of what role, if any, philosophy has to play depends on what it takes itself to be. Much (though not all) moral philosophy is in the same cut or style as Honderich's argument. Moral philosophers come across often as assuming that they are better placed, by virtue of their training and knowledge, to settle the questions with which ordinary people grapple in their lives; as if ordinary people were laity and philosophers were experts; as if ethics were merely a higher level discussion of ordinary moral debate. For my part, I do not believe that philosophy can settle differences of moral opinion. I see no reason to think that moral philosophers are authorities on the issues they discuss; and plenty reason to think otherwise. Nor do I think that the role of moral principles is to generate moral conclusions. (This is not the role of *Kant*'s Principle of Humanity.[53]) I see philosophy as essentially reflective, not productive. 'Work on philosophy', remarks Wittgenstein, 'is ... actually more of a ... work on oneself. On one's own conception. On the way one sees things. (And what one demands of them.)'[54] The difficulty of this work is not purely intellectual. Or put it this way: one's *conception* is not purely an intellectual matter. When Socrates asks an interlocutor (say, Euthyphro) what he means by a given word (say, 'piety'), what he confronts is not just the propositional content of the answer but the conception that represents the person who answers. In taking on Euthyphro, the difficulty that Socrates faces is this: how to get Euthyphro to take on Euthyphro. What looks like conversation in Plato's dialogues is more like one person (Socrates) placing himself between someone else and their monologue, placing his finger on their lips: not to *shut* them up but to *open* them up by keeping *their* words *there*; so they might read their own lips; so that they might reflect, for example, on what they mean by the word 'humanity'. Philosophy, to repeat, cannot settle the questions that arise in the course of our lives. All it can do is strive to keep words fit for human speech, or to make them fit again when they have lost their spark. It does this by reminding us: reminding us what they mean to us. This is trivial if words are trivial, but they are not; for our souls are in them – and perhaps trapped inside.

Moral questions are questions that address the soul. Except in special cases, they are addressed to us all: they are everybody's business. Questions of right and wrong can be elusive, complex and bewildering, for which reason we need to argue with one another, urging considerations on each other and weighing them with such scales as we have. If moral philosophers are willing to leave the club and join the fray, they are most welcome. Otherwise, let them mind their own business; this is perhaps the best way to ensure that philosophy refrains from making matters worse.

This has not been a philosophical chapter – not on anyone's version of philosophy. It has posed a practical, political question to which I have still not given an answer: What kinds of argument, if any, are capable of breaking the hold of the Auschwitz picture? I am reminded of the famous passage from the beginning of Book VII of Plato's *Republic*, which is, in a way, the *ur* scene of western philosophy. Socrates imagines a cave where the inhabitants are 'fixed in the same place, with their necks and legs fettered, able to see only in front of them, because their bonds prevent them from turning their heads around'. All they can see are images on the wall in front of them: pictures that they mistake for reality. A vital element in this allegory (for the passage is an allegory of education) is that these people, whom Socrates calls 'prisoners' and says are 'like us', are unaware of their situation. It sounds hopeless, as though they – we – are condemned to be in thrall to the images on the wall for all their lives. Then, unexpectedly, one of the prisoners is 'freed and suddenly compelled to stand up, turn his head, walk, and look up toward the light' (514a to 515c).[55] But how does this come about? What could possibly cause this happy release from captivity? How does this prisoner recognize his predicament? What is it that he finds so compelling that it sets him free and turns him round? Is it an argument? What kind of argument? Or is it just a trick of the light (like a flash of memory)? Socrates does not say. I believe he does not know.[56]

NOTES

1. 'Auschwitz Anger at Israeli Fly-past', BBC News, 4 September 2003, http://news.bbc.co.uk/1/hi/world/europe/3079016.stm.
2. Private email correspondence, July 2005, to which the photograph described in the text was attached.
3. Stephen Law, *Israel, Palestine and Terror* (London: Continuum, 2008). All the authors are described in the introduction as 'professional philosophers' (p.1). My essay appears under the title 'Tricks of Memory: Auschwitz and the Question of Palestinian Terrorism', pp.202–19.
4. 'Terrorism' is notoriously difficult to define and the argument over its definition is frequently politicized. I take the word to mean, roughly, politically motivated acts (or threats) of violence aimed at civilians or non-combatants; but this is not intended as a *definition*. Typical terrorist acts include hijackings, abductions, assassinations and suicide bombings. By 'Palestinian terrorism' I mean terrorist acts carried out by Palestinians, whether individuals or groups, acting in the name of the Palestinian national cause.
5. Honderich is Grote Professor Emeritus of the Philosophy of Mind and Logic at University College London, where, for his sins, he was my ethics tutor when I was an undergraduate. I do not discuss his position in the version published in *Israel, Palestine and Terror*.
6. Ludwig Wittgenstein, *Philosophical Investigations* (Oxford: Basil Blackwell, 1967), p.50e, par. 127.
7. Ian Traynor, 'The World Remembers', *Guardian*, 28 January 2005, p.1.
8. According to Laurence Rees, the 'current estimate' of the death toll at Auschwitz is 1.1 million, of whom one million were Jews: *Auschwitz: The Nazis and the 'Final Solution'* (London: BBC Books, 2005), p.301. This is a conservative estimate. Overall, approximately six million Jews, about two-thirds of the total Jewish population of Europe and one-third of world Jewry, were murdered in the course of the Nazi Holocaust. This entailed the wholesale destruction of Jewish community life in most of Europe.
9. A/RES/60/7, 1 November 2005, http://www.un.org/holocaustremembrance/docs/res607.shtml. Several countries, including the UK, have an annual Holocaust Memorial Day.
10. UN General Assembly Press Release GA/10413, 1 November 2005, http://www.un.org/News/Press/docs/2005/ga10413.doc.htm.
11. Likud became a unitary political party in 1988 when its various factions merged. It was the party of Ariel Sharon until he formed Kadima ('Forward') in 2005 and is currently led by Benjamin Netanyahu.
12. Tom Segev, *The Seventh Million: The Israelis and the Holocaust* (New York: Henry Holt, 2000), p.396.

13. Colin Shindler, *The Land Beyond Promise: Israel, Likud and the Zionist Dream* (London: I.B. Tauris, 2002), p.148.
14. Segev, *Seventh Million*, p.399. Treblinka was a major Nazi extermination camp in occupied Poland.
15. Shindler, *Land Beyond Promise*, p.150. Amos Oz took Begin to task in an article that appeared in *Yediot Aharanot*, one of the most widely read dailies in Israel, under the headline 'Hitler is Already Dead, Mr Prime Minister'. Oz wrote dryly, 'Unfortunately or not, it is a fact: Hitler is not hiding in Nabatea, in Sidon, or in Beirut. He is dead and gone.' He continued, 'Again and again, Mr Begin, you reveal to the public eye a strange urge to resuscitate Hitler in order to kill him every day anew in the guise of terrorists' (Segev, *Seventh Million*, p.400).
16. J.L. Austin, *Sense and Sensibilia* (Oxford: Oxford University Press, 1962), p.23.
17. Shindler, *Land Beyond Promise*, p.150.
18. By an 'Auschwitz mindset' I mean a set of habits of mind, though not necessarily a set that is unchanging over time or identical from one mind to the next.
19. Austin, *Sense and Sensibilia*, p.24.
20. Sometimes a symbolic act can achieve a breakthrough. Tony Klug describes what happened when the Egyptian President Anwar Al Sadat flew to Israel, out of the blue, in November 1977 and spoke to the Knesset. His gesture, unprecedented for an Arab head of state, broke through the dominant mindset of the Israeli Jewish public and paved the way for a peace treaty between Israel and Egypt, along with Israel's complete withdrawal from the territory captured from Egypt in the 1967 Six Day War. See his *How Peace Broke Out in the Middle East: A Short History of the Future* (London: Fabian Society, 2007), pp.7–8.
21. Eric Silver, *Begin: A Biography* (London: Weidenfeld & Nicolson, 1984), p.21.
22. Shindler, *Land Beyond Promise*, p.148.
23. Idith Zertal, *Israel's Holocaust and the Politics of Nationhood* (Cambridge: Cambridge University Press, 2005), p.106.
24. Ibid., p.126, n.100. Eban was foreign minister at the time he made the remark. Zertal adds that he 'later tried to dissociate himself' from the phrase. Be that as it may, she quotes him as saying to the UN's Special Assembly after the war that, had Israel lost, '[t]here would have been two million corpses added to the six million Holocaust victims' (p.112).
25. For Meir, see Tom Segev, *1967: Israel, the War and the Year that Transformed the Middle East* (London: Little, Brown, 2007), p.545. For Netanyahu, see his preface to *A Place Among the Nations: Israel and the World* (New York: Bantam, 1993), p.xxvii.
26. Shlomo Ben-Ami, *Scars of War, Wounds of Peace: The Israeli–Arab Tragedy* (London: Weidenfeld & Nicolson, 2005), p.90. Ben-Ami was a member of Israel's delegation to the Madrid peace conference in 1991 and, as Minister of Foreign Affairs, took part in the Camp David and Taba peace talks in 2000 and 2001.
27. Zertal, *Israel's Holocaust*, p.4. Someone might object that what I refer to as a mindset is actually cold, calculated propaganda in which the Holocaust is cynically instrumentalized for political ends. In reality, there is a mix. On this question, Segev observes sagely, 'The story of Israelis and the Holocaust alternates between true emotion and manipulative argument, which are not always easily distinguished' (*1967*, p.283).
28. That there is another way of remembering is brought home by the existence of Holocaust survivors who have dissented from the use of the Holocaust to justify their country's military actions: see Segev, *Seventh Million*, pp.400–2, and Shindler, *Land Beyond Promise*, pp.150–1. The very term 'dissenter', however, implies the existence of a dominant view from which such people depart.
29. Zertal, *Israel's Holocaust*, p.4.
30. Ibid., p.126.
31. Ben-Ami, *Scars of War*, p.329.
32. 'Palestine National Council: Declaration of Independence (November 15, 1988)', in G.S. Mahler and A.R.W. Mahler (eds), *The Arab–Israeli Conflict: An Introduction and Documentary Reader* (Abingdon: Routledge, 2010), pp.185–8.
33. See, for example, the letter from Yasser Arafat to Yitzchak Rabin, 9 September 1993, in ibid., p.195.
34. See the final section of this chapter for two such testimonies.
35. Israelis and Palestinians alike are subject to standards and norms that apply to both state and non-state actors as enshrined in international humanitarian law, including the 1949 Geneva Conventions (of which the Fourth deals with the protection of civilians), the 1977

Additional Protocols thereto, and relevant parts of customary international law. They are also subject, where appropriate, to provisions set out in the treaties that comprise international human rights law.

36. Zertal, *Israel's Holocaust*, p.99. Ben-Gurion was speaking at the Mapai Central Committee.
37. Netanyahu, *Place among the Nations*, p.187. On comparing Arabs (and Jews) with Nazis, see Anne Karpf, 'The "Arab Nazi" and the "Nazi Jew" ', in A. Karpf, B. Klug, J. Rose and B. Rosenbaum (eds), *A Time to Speak Out: Independent Jewish Voices on Israel, Zionism and Jewish Identity* (London: Verso, 2008), pp.108–24.
38. Wittgenstein, *Philosophical Investigations*, p.48e, par. 115.
39. The argument in this section of the essay is revised from a lecture that I gave on two occasions: a joint seminar of the Parkes Institute and the Department of Philosophy, University of Southampton (5 February 2008) and a philosophy colloquium at Saint Xavier University, Chicago (26 March 2008).
40. Immanuel Kant, *Grounding for the Metaphysics of Morals* (Indianapolis: Hackett, 1981 [1785]), pp.36–7.
41. Ted Honderich, *Humanity, Terrorism, Terrorist War: Palestine, 9/11, Iraq, 7/7 ...* (London: Continuum, 2006), p.60 (in italics in the original). For the longer version, see p.61.
42. Ibid., p.58. For definitions of a bad and good life, see p.60. The six kinds of goods are summarized in Honderich's essay, 'Terrorisms in Palestine', in *Law, Israel, Palestine and Terror*, p.3. Honderich's Principle of Humanity is an original contribution in the tradition of consequentialism. Setting aside the precise enumeration of greatest human goods, my initial attitude to this principle was to welcome it as a helpful guideline, a useful rule of thumb. But for Honderich it is the prince of principles, the rule that overrules others when they conflict. I neither accept that there needs to be such a single higher principle, nor that there is, nor that his principle is it.
43. Honderich seems to attribute collective agency to the Palestinians, as in 'the Palestinians have been right to kill as they have' (*Humanity*, p.112).
44. By the same Principle of Humanity, Honderich upholds the existence of the State of Israel roughly within its borders prior to the June 1967 Arab–Israeli war. He thinks that 'the terrorism of Zionism' prior to 1948 as a means to the end of creating the State of Israel was justified (ibid., pp.106, 109).
45. Re both the petition (which was published in the Palestinian daily *al-Quds*) and the Interior Minister, see Human Rights Watch, *Erased in a Moment: Suicide Bombing Attacks against Israeli Civilians* (New York: Human Rights Watch, 2002), pp.40–1. Re. Abbas, see Steve Erlanger and Greg Myre, 'Suicide Bomber and 2 Women Die in Attack at Mall in Israeli Town', *New York Times*, 13 July 2005, http://www.nytimes.com/2005/07/13/international/middleeast/13mideast.html?_r=1. In August 2003, following a bus bombing, Abbas said, 'I announce my strong condemnation of this horrible act which does not serve the interest of the Palestinian people at all' ('18 Killed, over 110 Hurt in Jerusalem', *Ha'aretz*, 20 August 2003, http://www.haaretz.com/hasen/pages/ShArt.jhtml?itemNo=331242).
46. It is also pretty stinky that Honderich, on account of his views about Palestinian terrorism, was publicly accused of being antisemitic, an accusation that is as baseless as it is base.
47. Ludwig Wittgenstein, 'The Blue Book', in *The Blue and Brown Books: Preliminary Studies for the 'Philosophical Investigations'* (Oxford: Blackwell, 1972), p.18.
48. Ibid. Wittgenstein's expression is: 'a contemptuous attitude towards the particular case'.
49. Human Rights Watch, *Erased in a Moment*, p.19.
50. Ibid., pp.23–4.
51. The Seder incident was at the Park Hotel, Netanya, 27 March 2002.
52. Sometimes the echoes of the past are overwhelming. Take, for example, an incident that occurred during the hijacking of an Air France plane, en route from Tel Aviv to Paris in 1976. After forcing the plane to land in Entebbe, Uganda, the hijackers separated the Israelis from the other passengers. When I heard about this at the time, it sent shivers down my spine; it still does. Many other Jews will have felt the same shiver. Segev explains why: 'That action inevitably recalled the "selection" at Auschwitz.' (*Seventh Million*, p.395). The 'selection' was a routine procedure that followed the arrival of every cattle train carrying its load of Jews. On leaving the train, prisoners were screened and told to go in one of two directions: to the right meant forced labour and life, to the left meant the gas chamber and death. When the Entebbe hijacking was reported, I did not need Begin to make the connection: for me too, the 'selection' at Entebbe resuscitated Hitler 'in the guise of terrorists'. That the Palestinian

hijackers were led by a German did not exactly help to counteract this unfortunate association of ideas.

53. I am conscious of the fact that this discussion raises a number of meta-ethical issues – the status of moral principles, their relationship to the cases they cover, their relationship to each other – without addressing them. The thoughts about moral philosophy expressed here are prompted (or provoked) by Honderich's argument; they are starting points only.

54. 'Philosophy', in Ludwig Wittgenstein, *Philosophical Occasions: 1912–1951*, edited by James Klagge and Alfred Nordmann (Indianapolis, IN: Hackett Publishing, 1993), pp.161, 163. The second set of continuation dots in the quote do not indicate a gap in Wittgenstein's sentence but a variant draft in which he substituted *eine* for *die* before *Arbeit*. The alternative reading given in the translation is 'a kind of work' rather than 'a work'.

55. Plato, *Republic*, trans. G.M.A. Grube (Indianapolis, IN: Hackett, 1992), pp.186–7.

56. On one standard reading, the *Republic* is the chief source in the western philosophical canon for the view of moral philosophy that I have been criticizing, depicting the philosopher as someone who, grasping the supreme form (or principle) of 'the good', makes magisterial pronouncements on questions of conduct: the 'philosopher-king'. This is not how I read the *Republic*, although I think that the fact that it *invites* this reading is no accident: it is how Socrates lures Glaucon and Adeimantus away from the compelling figure that Thrasymcachus extols: the 'tyrant-king', as it were. Philosophers, even radical left-wing philosophers, continue to be spellbound by the magnificent figment of Socrates's creation, the wise ruler, whether they are aware of this or not. But the prospect (that begins in the mouth of the cave) of clambering up 'the rough, steep path' (515e), reaching the summit, seizing the prize – knowledge of the *summum bonum* – and ruling with a golden wand is a philosopher's dream, the dream that is the stuff of Plato's *Republic*.

CHAPTER SIX

Anti-Zionism in London's Jewish East End, 1890–1948

Originally a lecture given at a seminar on 'The Jewish East End and the Rise of Zionism', Toynbee Hall, London, May 2009.

MOISHE THE PEDLAR

I wish my talk could be light-hearted, but Zionism and anti-Zionism always give rise to strong feelings and heated argument among Jews.[1] This is partly because political Zionism was largely a response to anti-semitism; and antisemitism is no laughing matter.

Which reminds me of a Jewish joke. That's not quite as paradoxical as it sounds, when you remember that irony, and especially self-mockery, is a staple of Jewish humour. Why, I am not sure. But I know it is true, not just because I grew up in a Jewish household but because Freud says so; and he took humour *very* seriously. In his 1905 treatise, *Jokes and Their Relation to the Unconscious*, he said this about the Jews: 'I do not know whether there are many other instances of a people making fun to such a degree of its own character.'[2] It seems perverse: to mock ourselves when everyone else is laughing at our expense. Perhaps it is the Jewish yearning to be normal: The rest of the world pokes fun at us, why should *we* miss out on the joke?

Be that as it may, the joke of which I am reminded is about Moishe the pedlar. Moishe was pushing his cart down an alley in Vitebsk, minding his own business, when he was stopped by an antisemite. 'Hey, Jew!' yelled the antisemite, jabbing Moishe's tattered gaberdine with his finger. 'Who gave *you* the right to control the world?' Moishe looked puzzled. 'You mean *me*, personally?' he asked. 'Don't be a wise guy', retorted the antisemite, jabbing him again. 'I mean *you*, the Jews.' Moishe was amazed. 'You know something *I* don't know?' 'You know perfectly well what I mean', said the antisemite gruffly. 'I'm talking about your cousins, the Rothschilds.' Suddenly Moishe's face lit up with pleasure. 'The Rothschilds!' he exclaimed. 'I had no idea they were *mishpochoh*!'

Moishe stands for Jews in general who, down the centuries, did not possess any real power. Yes, there were families like the Rothschilds. But they certainly were not *my mishpochoh*, any more than they were really Moishe's. To my grandparents, all of whom were from Eastern Europe (including one from Vitebsk), the very idea of Jewish power would have sounded like a Jewish joke. The vast majority of Jews in Europe were like Moishe: barely able to run their own lives, never mind control the world. Such power as they had was limited, contingent and temporary. But, to the antisemite in the joke, Moishe, though a pedlar, is not a *mere* pedlar. He is a *Jewish* pedlar, which makes him part of a worldwide web, a cousinhood whose hidden hand controls the banks, the markets, the media and even governments. Ultimately, he is a pedlar of power. If Moishe could see himself through the eyes of the antisemite he would not know whether to laugh – or give a *shrei*.

My four grandparents were in the same boat (so to speak) as Moishe. So were nearly all the 150,000 Jews who migrated to England from the European mainland between 1880 and 1914, most of them making their home in London's East End.[3] They were leaving antisemitism behind them in the Old Country; which did not mean that they would not run into it again here. Indeed, according to Theodor Herzl, they were not so much leaving it behind as importing it: 'The unfortunate Jews', he wrote in his 1896 pamphlet *The Jewish State*, 'are now carrying Anti-Semitism into England', adding: 'they have already introduced it into America'.[4] This is an odd way of looking at it. To me, it sounds like another Jewish joke: the one about the antisemite who lists all the problems caused by the Jews. 'If it weren't for the Jews', he thunders, 'there would be no evils in the world: no poverty, no corruption, no war, no disease, no floods and no antisemitism.' But Herzl was not joking. He was laying the foundation for a seriously serious argument and a bold, new political movement: Zionism.

ENTER HERZL

Zionism entered the Jewish East End as a harbinger of hope for people who came off the boat with little or nothing. It said to Moishe and people like him: 'Here is how to leave antisemitism behind you once and for all.' It offered them a ticket to normality – not by sharing the joke about Jews but by joining the family of nations. Now, Jews know something about families. True, 'the family of nations' is not the kind of close-knit unit that stays at home every Friday night and gathers round the table to eat a meal together under the warm glow of the Shabbos candles. On the other hand, it is just as dysfunctional. For this reason alone, Herzl might have expected that Jews would flock to Zionism.

And flock they did to hear him speak, one Sunday morning, 12 July 1896, when, like Elijah descending in his winged chariot, Herzl landed in the midst of Whitechapel, at the Jewish Working Men's Club on Great Alie Street, his first public appearance in London.[5] These were early days for Zionism as a political movement: it was not until the following year that the first Zionist Congress was held (in Basel, Switzerland) and the Zionist Organization founded. However, Herzl's reputation preceded him – his 'A Solution to the Jewish Problem' had been published in the influential *Jewish Chronicle* in January – and he was a star attraction.[6]

Paul Goodman, who was to become a leading light in the British Zionist movement, was there on the day.[7] His eyewitness account, published over thirty years later, describes how 'Herzl met face to face those who were henceforth to become his devoted followers.' Who were they, these 'devoted followers'? Goodman describes them as 'recent immigrants ... who were eagerly awaiting a "deliverer," national, political or economic'. The hall 'was filled far beyond its capacity, and left thousands in the street outside clamouring for admission'. Inside, the speaker had 'a Messianic glamour in the eyes of the multitude'. Goodman remarks: 'To the observer with a historic sense, the acclamation of the Man recalled the raptures which greeted the expectations aroused by the Sabbethaian movement in the seventeenth century.' This is a reference to Sabbatai Zevi, the most notorious of the 'false messiahs' who down the centuries have pressed their claim to be the saviour and redeemer foretold by the biblical prophets. Goodman, however, does not mean to cast aspersions. He too was won over by this man, Herzl, whose 'presence', he says was 'that of an Oriental monarch of majestic stature'.[8] Monarch or Messiah, clearly he regarded Herzl as the man of the hour.

As Goodman tells, it, the enthusiasm in the hall spread throughout the whole area. 'The public appearance of Dr Herzl in the East End of London', he writes, 'set the teeming Jewish population in a state of ferment.' But not all the Jews in England were part of this 'teeming population'. There were also those who were established in the land, whose antecedents had come to England decades – even centuries – earlier. In particular, there were the *West* End Jews (so to speak): families that had acquired material wealth and achieved status in English society. Goodman's account rather suggests that the story of *Zionism in England* (the title of his book) is largely the story of a clash of interests between these two groups: 'the immigrants, with their nationalist instincts, and the Anglicised natives'.[9] In other words, the penniless, downtrodden Zionist masses versus the prosperous, privileged, assimilated few. And the good guys won.

This is 'history written by the victor'.[10] Not only does it give a tendentious picture of the past but, as the dominant narrative, it prejudices the current debate about Israel and Zionism. Which brings me to the point of view from which I have written this talk. The subject that I have been allotted for this seminar is too vast to cover in a single lecture. A whole Megillah could be written on it; and I am not the person to write it. I have neither first-hand knowledge of the facts (since I am not an East Ender and did not even exist until 1949), nor am I a historian of the period. Nor am I a historian, period. Facts are not my forte (which is why I ended up in philosophy). So, I shall be dipping my pen deep in the pots of other people's scholarly research and memoirs, drawing portraits of selected events and places, sometimes painting in brushstrokes that I know are too broad. I take an interest in the *old* controversy for the light it sheds on the *new* – on the current debate going on in the Jewish world about Israel. I am interested, that is to say, as a participant in that world and in that debate. As we shall see (paraphrasing *Koheles*), there is not much new under the sun. Yesterday's arguments are not altogether dissimilar to today's. Even the polemics are much the same: then as now, for example, anti-Zionists were accused of 'treason' against the Jewish people.[11]

In short, as the grandchild of grandparents who emigrated to the East End from Eastern Europe, I am interested not only in *recollecting* the debate in the Jewish East End but in *reconnecting* to it. Such is the point of view from which I have written this talk.

OPPOSING ZIONISM AS THE SOLUTION TO 'THE JEWISH PROBLEM'

From this point of view, it is important to know how much the debate mattered at the time and to whom. To what extent *was* it a *debate* and not a clash of interests among different groups? Was the Jewish East End greatly divided over the question of Zionism or was the principal fault line in this country the one that separated the haves from the have-nots, the Anglo-Jewish gentry from the *Ostjuden* grassroots? In particular, was the anti-Zionism of the former mainly motivated by a selfish regard for their own welfare (a prominent element of the story in the 'history written by the victor')? Or are the Anglo-Jewish gentry irrelevant in a talk that focuses on the East End?

As to the last of these questions, the answer is: No, they are not irrelevant. The distinction between wealthy West and destitute East is not precise, nor were the classes cleanly separated from each other by their allegiances or views. Contrary to Kipling's famous line, the twain did meet. They met on both sides of the argument. On the Zionist side, the leaders of the English Zionist Federation were from the 'West End' and were 'associated with the mainstream of Anglo-Jewry's political elite'.[12] The historian David Feldman tells us: 'The conflict between East End and West End Jewry, native and immigrant, was reproduced within the Zionist movement.'[13] On the anti-Zionist side, two figures from two different generations come to mind. One is Sir Samuel Montagu (later Lord Swaythling), whose address was 12 Kensington Palace Gardens (*very* West End), but who was instrumental in creating the Jewish Working Men's Club in 1874 and was elected Liberal MP for Whitechapel in 1885.[14] The other is Sir Basil Henriques who, despite his Oxford education and aristocratic pedigree, made his home in the East End. (At one time he lived in this building, Toynbee Hall.[15] Later he lived on the premises of Oxford and St George's, the Jewish youth club that he founded in Stepney, 'the largest and most ambitious of the Jewish Settlements'.[16]) We shall look later at the opinions of these two gentlemen concerning Zionism. For the time being, suffice to say that the question of what motivated their opinions *is* relevant to this talk.

It is, however, secondary in my treatment of the subject. In talking about the Jewish East End, I prefer to focus more on the proletarian than the patrician. Not that I am uninterested in the ideas of the likes of Montagu and Henriques. But, apart from making an immense subject a bit more manageable, I think that this focus on 'the street' will give a better reflection of the place of anti-Zionism in the life of the district. And I would like, to the extent that it is possible in a short talk, to bring the district to life, the better to reconnect to it. With this in view, I shall be singling out certain faces in the crowd, individuals who have caught my eye or ear. They shall not be the great and the good; but this does not diminish them in the least.

Let us, then, get back to Goodman's claim that the 'teeming Jewish population' of London's East End was set in 'a state of ferment' by Herzl's debut appearance at the Jewish Working Men's Club on 12 July 1896. I see no reason to doubt Goodman's first-hand account of the meeting. However, there is a question mark about his assessment of its impact on the immigrant community. The historian Stuart Cohen says that Herzl 'did not take the community by storm'. He cites a letter written by Israel Zangwill in September 1896 in which Zangwill says that Herzl's ideas had initially 'startled' the community but that things had 'rather simmered down now'.[17] This turned out to be the pattern whenever Herzl addressed the people of Whitechapel, which he did almost annually until his death in 1904. His visits occasioned 'bursts of enthusiasm'. But in the intervening periods, there was 'Jewish working class apathy and even opposition'. Nor did fresh boatloads of immigrants from the Pale alter the situation. According to Cohen, 'the bulk of the new arrivals were not more forthcoming in support of Zionism'.[18] So much for the 'state of ferment' in the 'teeming Jewish population'.

The fact is that this was a population with other – more immediate and mundane – things on its plate. (Writing this, I seem to hear a voice floating through a window of one of the crowded tenements, echoing in the narrow alley: 'Zionism Schmionism!' Rivka exclaims. 'Eat up your *lockshen* pudding, Isy, and then do the dishes.') There is an episode in *Jacob's Gift*, Jonathan Freedland's memoir of three of his close relatives, which perfectly captures the down-to-earth worries and aspirations of many of the East Enders. Young Mick Mindel had made his name as a trade union organizer, becoming President of the United Ladies Tailors, 'the most successful Jewish garment union in the East End'.[19] It was 1939. Mick, who was 29 years old, was invited to meet a visitor to Whitechapel: David Ben-Gurion, chair of the Jewish Agency for Palestine, the man who was to become the first Prime Minister of the State of Israel. They met on a Sunday at Circle House, in the offices of the Workers' Circle (a friendly society that Mick's father, Morris, a well-known Bundist, had co-founded).[20] They shook hands and then Ben-Gurion got down to brass tacks. With just a hint of flattery, he said (in Yiddish): 'I wanted to see you because you are the leader of the Jewish proletariat of this country.' Then he made his pitch: 'I am calling on Jewish leaders throughout Europe and delivering the same message: there is no future here. You must tell those who follow you, Jewish workers, that their destiny is in Palestine.' He added: 'You are the man to do it. You are a young man and you can lead the young. Go from here and urge them to sell up, sell whatever they have, and take the next ship to Palestine.'[21] But what did Mick's members *have* that they could *sell*? Freedland imagines Mick's thoughts as he pondered his reply:

> He knew what his members wanted: a roof over their heads, a kitchen they could keep clean and walls that did not slither with bugs. They wanted a decent school for their children, so they at least might have a shot at something better than stitching a fur collar or pushing a punishingly heavy iron. They did not dream

of the cool stones of Jerusalem or the birthplace of the prophets; they dreamed of getting out of Stepney, of having a house with a small patch of garden, perhaps in Essex or a north London suburb somewhere, of a son trained to be a doctor. Their heads were full of this land of promise, not the Promised Land.[22]

So, Mick, politely but decidedly, turned down Ben-Gurion. He earned himself a name, in Freedman's words, as 'the man who had dared say no to the king of Israel'.[23]

But it was not only the trade unionist in Mick that said no; it was also the communist, for Mick was a member of the party. If Zionism entered the East End as a 'harbinger of hope', its claim did not go uncontested. Communism, likewise, offered a vision of a better future for the huddled masses. That better way went via class rather than nation. It substituted working-class solidarity for Jewish ethnic bonding, a revolution against oppression for a movement to create a nation state. It said, in effect: There is a better way of belonging to the human family than by seeking to join 'the family of nations'.

Actually, on the radical Jewish left there were several variations on this theme, each rivalling Zionism as well as each other. There were also combinations, with some Zionists being socialists. Proponents of one ideology or another rubbed fraternal shoulders and crossed swords at various venues in the district. Quoting the anarchist Millie Sabel, Bill Fishman, 'the chronicler of London's East End', gives us a glimpse inside the Workers' Friend Club on Jubilee Street: 'Over countless glasses of tea, "discussion would go on far into the night between Bundists, Zionists, Anarchists and Social Democrats, who argued excitedly together".'[24] Joe Jacobs, a central figure in the Stepney Communist Party in the mid-1930s, recalls similarly lively scenes at Circle House. There were 'former "Bundists" from Poland, Anarchists and Libertarians from all parts, Socialists and Freethinkers. Every shade of Russian and European Labour thought and action was represented here. In addition there were Zionists and other purely Jewish organisations.' He adds that there was 'a very good bar' but no alcohol.[25] Who needs alcohol when you can get drunk on argument? Presumably tea, once again, acted as a lubricant: *Russian* tea, no doubt.

Would it not be nice to be able to travel back in time to the 1930s and eavesdrop on two Jews, say a communist and a Zionist, ventilating their differences? Thanks to the novelist Simon Blumenfeld, himself an East End Marxist, we can do the next best thing and read a fictionalized account of the kind of exchange that undoubtedly took place in these clubs. The scene, from his novel *Jew Boy* (published in 1935), is Circle House. One Saturday evening, Alec, a young tailor who is drawn to communism, is sitting at a table in the corner, sipping his lemon tea, when the door opens and three people, roughly his own age, enter the room. All three have Zionist sympathies. One of them, John Caplan, takes Alec to task:

> 'I ask you, as a Jew, have you never felt the urge, the desire, to go to Palestine, the home of our fathers?'
>
> Alec shook his head, 'No!'
>
> 'But really, haven't you ever felt that Palestine was part of you, and that you'd like to live there, and help build the new Jewish culture?'
>
> 'Never,' said Alec, 'I've never had the least interest of that sort in Palestine!'
>
> John was thunderstruck. He couldn't believe Alec meant it. He leaned still closer to him, a red flush glowing under his skin, looking like a feverish invalid.
>
> 'I put it to you', he said weightily, like an amateur debating society's star orator, 'all the nations of the world have homes, countries, they can claim as their own, why should the Jew be the pariah amongst nations?'
>
> Alec shook his head. He had heard all those arguments years ago, he had even used them himself while still at school, but the workshops and factories had taught him how much his nationalism was worth. He had scrapped that childishness for good, that part of his life was also way back, in the gone and forgotten.
>
> 'Look here', he said. 'Whether the Jew is a pariah or not, I believe this nationalism talk is all bunk, whoever it comes from. I haven't the faintest desire to claim Palestine as my own. I believe that wherever a man lives, and does useful work, and brings up his children, is his country. As a worker, I won't be better off in Palestine, maybe worse. I don't see why I should change one set of exploiters for another because they happen to be Jewish.'[26]

The novel concludes with an image of 'the red banner' fluttering in the wind.[27] But did communism fare any better than Zionism with the 'teeming Jewish population' of London's East End? Somehow I seem to hear the same dismissive voice that I heard earlier, only now Rivka is saying, 'Communism, Schmommunism! Finish your strudel so we can all *bentsh* and go to bed!'

Except that this time, perhaps, the voice carries less conviction. For communism came closer than Zionism to meeting the everyday concerns of the ordinary people of the Jewish East End. As historian Geoffrey Alderman remarks: 'Communists were seen as people who evinced a genuine concern for Jewish needs, and who matched words with deeds.'[28] For one thing, there were those Jewish comrades who, like Mick Mindel, were active in the unions, campaigning for higher wages and better working conditions. But this is not all; it is not even the half of it. Beyond the shop floor were the streets of Stepney, where the black-shirts of the British Union of Fascists were throwing their weight around; and the communists were in the vanguard of the fight against fascism.

For 'fascism' read 'antisemitism'; which brings us to the centre of the arena in the contest between Zionism and anti-Zionism in the Jewish East End. As I said at the outset, political Zionism was largely a response to antisemitism. Thus, in leading the anti-fascist charge, the communists beat the Zionists on their own turf; so much so that, as Alderman remarks wryly, 'even East End Jewish businessmen gave money to the Communist Party to help combat the Fascist menace'.[29] The party put itself forward as the Jewish people's champion, a bold David smiting the fascist Goliath; and their actions spoke louder than Zionist words. David Cesarani, who has studied the inter-war period extensively, concludes that during the 1930s 'Zionism was in a state of collapse in the East End.'[30] Communism, on the other hand, was in the pink. Alderman quotes a correspondent to the *Young Zionist* in December 1932, who wrote that Zionism 'has made no headway' among young working-class Jews. The writer continued: 'The tendency in the best part of our Jewish working class ... is to join the Communist party.'[31]

This is reminiscent of a similar tendency earlier in the twentieth century. 'Some of the most prominent left-wing groups', says Stuart Cohen, writing about the decade before the First World War, 'do seem to have attracted many of the more vibrant, sensitive, and politically active inhabitants' of the immigrant Jewish quarters.[32] These left-wing groups were ideologically diverse; and communism in the 1930s was, to an extent, their beneficiary. Joe Jacobs writes: 'Our opposition to Zionism was made much easier by the fact that so much of the working-class movement, as far as the Jews in East London was [sic] concerned, had a long tradition based on the original immigrants, who were supporters of the Bund in Poland and East Europe.'[33]

Oddly, Bundism and Zionism came into existence together: the Jewish Labour Bund was founded in 1897, the year of the inaugural Zionist congress. It is as if twins were born facing opposite directions. For, from the start, the Bundists rejected the Zionist solution to the problem of antisemitism; as did the anarchists. Zionism was attacked in the pages of the radical Yiddish paper the *Arbayter Fraynd* (Worker's Friend), which around the turn of the century came under the editorship of the remarkable Rudolf Rocker, the most improbable figure you could imagine on the 'Jewish' left. I put 'Jewish' in quotes because Rocker (to reverse a phrase of Isaac Deutscher) was a 'Jewish non-Jew': a man with a German Catholic past, he enjoyed an 'extraordinary rapport' with Jewish workers and became 'the unique mentor of East End Jewish anarchism'.[34] Just before his paper was closed (by court order in 1916), its readers were reminded of the anarchist position on Zionism: 'The solution to the Jewish question is not to be found in an antediluvian formula of nationalism, but in the struggle for the unity of Jewish and gentile forces in the fight against exploitation.' The article continues: 'Anti-Semitism will cease to exist in a society in which the oppressed are united against the oppressors.'[35]

Rocker and other libertarians were critical of the Marxian theory of historical change. Yet, you could almost lift this passage word for word, carry it forward twenty years, and deposit it in a communist rag.[36] In any case, it was the question of antisemitism that weighed most heavily with Mick Mindel when he and Ben-Gurion were face to face in Circle House on that Sunday in 1939. Mick, you recall, turned Ben-Gurion down for various reasons. 'But', says his great-nephew Jonathan Freedland, 'the argument that struck Mick with greatest force was that Zion would not solve the Jews' largest problem. "A Jewish homeland will not be a cure for the disease of anti-Semitism", communist speakers would say ... "Those Jews who live there will be fleeing from the problem – but the problem will remain, in the world outside." '[37] On this view, Zionism was not a *solution* – not even an inferior one – but an *escape*.

Or was it even that? Israel (Issie) Panner, a member of the Workers' Circle, and a specialist on Jewish affairs for the Communist Party of Great Britain, took a less sanguine view of the position of Jews who moved to Palestine.[38] In *Anti-Semitism and the Jewish Question* (published in 1942 and dedicated 'To the Hackney Study Group'), he wrote that Zionism 'has not even solved the Jewish problem for the Jews in Palestine, let alone for the 15½ million Jews outside Palestine. *It has merely extended the Jewish problem to Palestine, where hitherto it had scarcely existed.*' He goes on to say, 'What Zionism has done ... is to bring the age-long curse of our people into Palestine.'[39] He means the 'curse' of being caught in the middle: in this case being a 'buffer' between the British and the Arabs. If his remark seems vaguely familiar, it might be because of something I quoted at the beginning of my talk:

'The unfortunate Jews are now carrying Anti-Semitism into England;
they have already introduced it into America.' This, you recall, is from
Herzl's *The Jewish State*. In effect, Panner is taking Herzl's words and
turning them against political Zionism; as much as to say: 'This unfortunate movement is now carrying antisemitism into Palestine.'

I imagine one of Panner's Jewish readers thinking: 'We need this
solution *vi a loch in kop*! If this is the solution, better to have the
problem!' It sounds like a Jewish joke. But Panner wasn't joking. He was
pulling the rug out from under a staple argument for the bold, new movement that Herzl founded: Zionism. But there was more than one rug.

OPPOSING ZIONISM AS A THEORY OF JEWISH IDENTITY

Political Zionism was not only a response to antisemitism; it was also
a movement for national renewal. In other words, the project of joining 'the family of nations' as a Jewish nation state was not merely a
device to solve the problem of persecution. It was also based on a
theory of Jewish identity: that Jews everywhere and of every stripe
constitute a nation in the modern sense of the word: a single corporate
or collective entity that is the bearer of political rights, especially rights
of autonomy and self-determination. Furthermore, according to the
dominant or mainstream view within the movement, there is one place
on earth that is, as it were, this nation's natural home: Zion or Palestine.
Such was the texture of the *other* rug under Zionism's feet; and
opponents tugged away at that too.

For Jewish communists (and for Jews on the radical left in general),
the question of identity lay at the heart of their quarrel with Zionism.
Look at it this way: Zionism is a form of nationalism; nationalism puts
nation before class; this divides the working class against itself; a divided
working class cannot wage the workers' revolution; therefore, Zionism
is an enemy of the revolution. In a nutshell: Zionism, by uniting the
nation, divides the class. Not that the radicals accepted that there *was*, so
to speak, a Jewish nation-in-waiting. They regarded such a notion as a
will-o'-the-wisp; which made Zionism doubly delusive and diversionary.

In this regard, the Bundist case is somewhat complex, since Bundists
did assert a *kind* of Jewish nationality, a *cultural* one, for which they
sought a form of autonomy. But first, this applied only to Ashkenazi Jews
to the extent that they *in fact* shared a culture of *Yiddishkeit*; it did not
involve projecting a new Palestine-based identity onto the whole of world
Jewry. Second, the original context for the Bundist idea was Russia, the
aim being to carve out a place for Jews in a socialist and democratic

multicultural state. Though some former Bundists might have strayed into the Zionist camp, Bundism itself remained emphatically outside. Like the rest of their comrades on the Jewish radical left, the Bundists rejected the Zionist theory of Jewish identity.

But now a down-to-earth voice in my head is making itself heard again. With a shrug of invisible shoulders it says: 'What do I know from Bundism? Bundism, Buddhism, all I know is this: I left the Old Country to get away from a lot of *tsuris*. What do I find when I get here? More *tsuris*. Still, it could be worse. Okay, it's not the *goldene medina*. But I'm here. My *kinder* are here. Why should we leave? Enough with all your isms!' Somehow I think this voice belongs to our friend, Moishe the pedlar. It's the voice of the plain Jew. Remember what Alec said to John Caplan in their conversation at Circle House: 'I believe that wherever a man lives, and does useful work, and brings up his children, is his country.' It's a commonsensical point of view. It's what I think Joe Jacobs means when he says that the majority of Jews in the East End in the 1930s 'saw themselves as British Jews'.[40]

Maybe that is what it meant to them to be *British*, but what did it mean to them to be *Jews*? Let us consider an example, a typical *Yidl*, someone representative of the East End Jewish masses. I am thinking again of our friend. I am not sure why, but I do not think of Moishe as a card-carrying member of the Communist Party. Nor do I see him as an anarchist at one of the Yom Kippur balls, cramming ham sandwiches down his throat, mocking his pious relatives in the synagogue. To the contrary, I envisage him inside, a member of the congregation, *davaning*. Bill Fishman observes: 'Religion was ingrained in the cultural experience of the *stetl*, and an inalienable part of [the immigrant's] identity as a Jew.'[41] I think he was talking about Moishe.

In the *shtiebels* and shuls of the East End shtetl, Zionists were on the back foot on the issue of Jewish identity – just as much as they were at the Workers' Circle or the Workers' Friend Club. Yes, Jews turned towards Zion when they prayed. And they longed for the end of the exile when the scattered remnants of the people would be gathered and returned to *Eretz Yisroel*. Down the centuries they identified with the psalmist, who exclaimed: 'If I forget you, O Jerusalem, let my right hand forget its cunning' (Ps. 137). But there is remembering and there is remembering. The rabbis had a take on what it meant for the Jewish people to be a people and for their hopes to be centred on Zion; and, generally speaking, their take wasn't Zionist. A person who wanted the people to be a nation like any other nation: such a person was an *apikoros*, a non-believer or heretic.[42] As for hastening the longed-for return, there was 'a stream of traditional thought that was at odds with the activism of the Zionists'.[43] To many rabbis, political Zionism smacked of trying to force God's hand; and unless you are Abraham or Moses, that's even worse than a sin: it's a chutzpah.

When I speak of rabbis I am (for the moment) thinking only of those of the Orthodox persuasion; for even if Moishe did not go to shul much, I am sure that the shul he did not go to was not Reform or Liberal. Probably it was part of the Federation of Synagogues. What would Moishe have learned from his rabbi at such a shul? The Federation was a group of immigrant Orthodox communities united in 1887 under the patronage of Sir Samuel Montagu.[44] His was a simple, straightforward, unreflective Judaism.[45] My impression of him is this: As an Orthodox Jew, he loved Zion. As a British citizen, he was attached to his country. The one thing should be kept separate from the other, like milk from meat. (He kept a strictly kosher mansion.[46]) Zionism confused the two. Chaim Bermant, alluding to the fact that Montagu was a member of the Liberal Party, remarks dryly that he 'prayed for the Messiah, but until the Messiah came along he was prepared to make do with Gladstone'.[47] Is this what Moishe would have learned from his rabbi: to make do with Gladstone?

The answer depends partly on which rebbe his rabbi learned from. The rabbi himself would have been an immigrant. Many immigrant rabbis looked over their shoulder to the great teachers in the lands from whence they came, seeking guidance on the Halacha and interpretation of the Talmud.[48] On Zionism they got advice without seeking it: there was a 'barrage of anti-Zionist polemic emanating from the "sages" of Eastern Europe'.[49] There were, however, some respected rabbis who, with reservations, supported the Zionist movement.[50] On this question, as on all others, different authorities authoritatively gave their different opinions. Moishe's rabbi might well have been openly hostile to Zionism; he might have felt ambivalent; possibly he thought that the better part of *chochmoh* was to stay shtum.[51] But the odds are he would not have been an advocate.

If not all Orthodox rabbis were anti-Zionist, not all anti-Zionist rabbis were Orthodox. When, in May 1897, German Jewry heard that Herzl was planning to hold the first Zionist Congress in Munich, Reform and Orthodox rabbis joined hands in protest. (Think of it: normally they would not even shake hands with each other on Shabbos.) The so-called *Protestrabbiner* published open letters, one of which said: 'The efforts of so-called Zionists to create a Jewish National State in Palestine are antagonistic to the messianic promises of Judaism, as contained in Holy

Writ and in later religious sources.' So vigorous was the protest – to which Jewish groups in Munich added their voice – that Herzl relented and changed the venue; and that is how it came to pass that the first Zionist Congress was held in Basel rather than Bavaria.[52]

Had Herzl planned to hold the event in London he might well have run into a similar alliance barring his way. It was, above all, in their view on the question of Jewish nationality that leading religious authorities on both sides of the denominational divide converged in rejecting Zionism. 'The Jews', wrote Claude Montefiore, the pioneering Progressive thinker, 'are not a nation but a religious community.'[53] This was a theme, says Cohen, 'with which most Orthodox clergy (immigrant as well as native) entirely sympathized'.[54] Their sympathy with Montefiore's variation on this theme – that Judaism should aim at 'spiritual univeralism' – would have been less than entire.[55] But based on an old universalist idea in Judaism – that the Jewish people as the people of God are a light to the nations of the world – they might have felt some affinity with his views.

The East End was not exactly a bastion of Progressive Judaism, but the St George's Settlement Synagogue at 26a Betts Street followed Montefiore's lead. It was founded by Basil Henriques, the well-off Oxonian who chose to live in the East End and to devote his life to social work with immigrant Jewish youth.[56] A disciple of Montefiore, Henriques was the driving force behind the Jewish Fellowship, an anti-Zionist group, formed in 1944.[57] Looking back at evidence that the Fellowship gave to the Anglo-American Committee of Inquiry in 1946, Henriques remarked: 'No one else stood up and said that our nationality is British, that there is no such thing as a Jewish nation, that we are Jews by the faith which we possess and that we are not political exiles awaiting repatriation to a Jewish state.'[58] It is a clear and succinct summation of a position with which Montagu, had he still been alive, would have agreed. To religious anti-Zionists, whatever their denomination, *Jewish* identity and *national* identity were two different things. Zionism confused the picture.

Moreover (the argument went), in confusing the picture, Zionism put Jews at risk. In 1900, Montagu told the executive of the Federation of Synagogues that, in his opinion, 'for a Jew to espouse political Zionism made him unfit to be a member of the British parliament ... and [would] bring trouble upon the loyal and patriotic Jews of England'.[59] In *The Dangers of Zionism*, Montefiore took this argument further. He wrote: 'Is it not ... a suspicious fact that those who have no love for the Jews, and those who are pronounced anti-Semites, all seem to welcome the Zionist proposals and aspirations? Whence this welcome, if it were not that Zionism fits in with anti-Semitic presuppositions and with anti-Semitic aims?' He went on to argue that if Zionism succeeds in its goal, then in 'every country ... the position of the Jews will tend to become worse instead of better'.[60]

You did not have to be devout in order to see these dangers, nor did you need to be well born. This argument was a commonplace across the anti-Zionist spectrum: it was a point where religious met secular and East met West. And it was the ultimate indictment of Zionism. Israel Panner was merely taking Herzl's view – that wherever Jews go they carry antisemitism with them – one step further and extending it to Palestine. But *this* argument is both wider and deeper. It is wider because it claims that Zionism promotes antisemitism *in the countries where it already exists*; deeper because it holds the Zionist theory of Jewish identity – that being Jewish involves a separate political nationality – responsible. If the argument is sound, then the two halves of Zionism – the solution to the problem of antisemitism and the movement for national renewal – come apart at the seams: the second undermines the first. It is as if Zionism itself pulls the rug out from under its own feet.

Be that as it may, on 14 May 1948, Ben-Gurion declared that the State of Israel, the Jewish nation state, was born, Jews danced the hora on the streets of Tel Aviv, and Herzl's *neshumah* was in seventh heaven, where he was the star turn at the Jewish Working Angels' Club. A few months later, in November, the short-lived anti-Zionist Jewish Fellowship was dissolved.[61] Zionism had won the day.

MOISHE IN WILLESDEN

But did it win the argument? If winning the argument means convincing the masses, then neither side won. Stuart Cohen, writing about the period up to 1918, says that the immigrant community was largely ambivalent about Zionism.[62] My guess is that most minds were not made up until catastrophe struck in the 1940s, when Europe seemed like a Jewish graveyard and Palestine the place of rebirth. Even communists changed their minds, especially when Moscow changed its line. In Spring 1947, comrade Gromyko announced that the Soviet Union accepted the principle of partition of Palestine, and when the United Nations debated the question on 29 November, their representative voted *da*.[63] But it was not this *da* that caused Mick Mindel, the party man who turned Ben-Gurion down in 1939, to become 'a reluctant Zionist' after the war; it was the slaughter and abandonment of European Jewry.[64] Understandably, minds were changed in the crucible of the moment. But this does not mean that the argument was won and lost. These are twists at the end of the tale. They reflect the impact of extraordinary events, not the outcome of in-depth analysis.

To win an argument you have to engage it. But many Zionists preferred to sidestep the case against Zionism and attack their opponents instead, sneering at them and calling them names. They argued ad hominem: denigrating the person rather than engaging the argument. Basil Henriques, for example, was called 'the Jewish anti-semite', 'the man who stabbed Zionism in the back', 'the traitor', 'the cold-hearted snob indifferent to the sufferings of foreign Jews'.[65] (So indifferent was he, that he devoted his life to their welfare in the East End.) In a different vein, Herzl called Claude Montefiore 'a stupid ass who affects English correctness'.[66] This was a man who, at one time or another in his life, was President of the Jewish Historical Society of England, President of the Anglo-Jewish Association, President of the World Union for Progressive Judaism, co-editor of the *Jewish Quarterly Review*, and recipient of the British Academy Medal for Biblical Studies (along with several honorary degrees). Some ass!

These were not random allegations against isolated individuals. They were part of a systematic rhetorical strategy. Stuart Cohen writes that the 'ideological and theological objections' to Zionism by people like Montefiore were dismissed out of hand as a 'camouflage' for self-interest.[67] Anti-Zionists in general were accused of not giving a hoot either for Judaism or the Jewish masses. The eminent Zionist Nahum Sokolow wrote in 1919 that Jews who oppose the movement are 'impelled by a desire to destroy the distinctive characteristics which recalled their origin'.[68] In other words, they seek to efface their own Jewishness, whether because they are ashamed of it or for some other reason. How did he know this? What special faculty did he possess for seeing through the 'camouflage' into the souls of the people who did not agree with him? Sokolow's contention was not a one-off; it was, says Cohen, a 'standard Zionist taunt'.[69]

It still is. A similar 'taunt' was made in a letter to the *Jewish Chronicle* in October 2008, shortly after the publication of *A Time to Speak Out*, a volume of essays by twenty-seven Jewish contributors, all of whom are sharply critical of either Israel or Zionism. The letter-writer stated: 'The harsh truth is that here is a group of people whose Jewish identity is defined by their dislike of Israel.'[70] How on earth does she know this? What mysterious power enables her to see so clearly into twenty-seven different *neshumahs* – including a rabbi's? Including mine. And how odd that all of us should define our Jewishness in exactly the same wretched way! I am tempted to say that the harsh truth is that here is someone whose Jewish identity is defined by her *defence* of Israel. But since I do not approve of ad hominem arguments, it is a point I shall not make.

It is impossible to say who won the argument at the end of the day, for the day has not ended. The debate continues; and for good reason: so much is at stake for so many people, Jew and non-Jew, Palestinian and Israeli, the living and the yet-to-be-born. The main lines of argument on both sides of the question were laid down in the pre-State debate, not least in the halls and shuls of the Jewish East End, as were the terms of abuse. Though Jews have largely moved out of the district, they took it all with them: the fair and the foul, the vigour and the vitriol. If Moishe is following the controversy today, I imagine him saying: What's new?

What's new for Moishe (as I picture him now) is that he is living in a nice little flat in Willesden, north-west London. His children come to see him from time to time. On the mantelpiece in the living room, hemmed in by snapshots of grandchildren and great-grandchildren at various stages of life, one photo stands out: a picture of a dignified man wearing a black top hat: Walter Rothschild: *Lord* Rothschild: the one to whom Arthur Balfour addressed his letter, dated 2 November 1917, containing the famous Declaration. 'So, you believe in Zionism?' asks the *Jewish Chronicle* reporter who has come to interview Moishe for a feature on Vitebsk. Moishe waves a hand through the air as if he were swatting a fly. 'Enough with all your isms!', he exclaims. (This is one of his trademark phrases.) Then, with a twinkle in his eye that could either signify a pedlar's simplicity or a people's self-mocking irony, he says: 'I shouldn't be proud of my cousin?'

NOTES

1. This chapter reflects a lecture given at a seminar at Toynbee Hall, London, on 'The Jewish East End and the Rise of Zionism', organized by the Jewish East End Celebration Society, 17 May 2009.
2. Sigmund Freud, *Jokes and Their Relation to the Unconscious* (Harmondsworth: Penguin, 1976), p.157.
3. Stuart A. Cohen, *English Zionists and British Jews: The Communal Politics of Anglo-Jewry, 1895–1920* (Princeton, NJ: Princeton University Press, 1982), p.18.
4. Theodor Herzl, *The Jewish State: An Attempt at a Modern Solution of the Jewish Question* (1896), translated from the original German by Sylvie D'Avigdor (London: Henry Pordes, 1993), p.15. Herzl reiterated this point in his inaugural address to the Fourth Zionist Congress in London in 1900: 'He would be a poor friend of the Jews in England, as well as of the Jews who reside in other countries, who would advise the persecuted to flee hither ... For the latter, with their miserable bundles, would bring with them that from which they flee – I

mean anti-Semitism' (quoted in Nahum Sokolow, *History of Zionism, 1600–1918* (New York: Ktav, 1969), vol. 2, p.xliv).

5. Cohen, *English Zionists*, facing p.32, beneath a photograph of a handbill advertising the meeting. Both Cohen and Paul Goodman (see below) give the date of the meeting as 13 July. But the handbill says clearly 'Sunday July 12th'. A check of the calendar for 1896 verifies that Sunday that week fell on the 12th, not the 13th.

6. Stuart A. Cohen, 'Religious Motives and Motifs in Anglo-Jewish Opposition to Political Zionism, 1895–1920', in Shmuel Almog et al. (eds), *Zionism and Religion* (Hanover, NH: University Press of New England, 1998), p.169, n.3. One month later *The Jewish State* was published.

7. Israel Cohen (ed.), *The Rebirth of Israel: A Memorial Tribute to Paul Goodman* (London: Edward Goldston & Son, 1952), pp.12–13.

8. Paul Goodman, *Zionism in England 1899–1949: A Jubilee Record* (London: Zionist Federation of Great Britain & Ireland, 1949), pp.14–15.

9. Ibid., p.15. Though the West End is an actual district, it is best to think of 'West End Jews' as referring figuratively to the established, comfortable Anglo-Jewish population, whether living in the West End or elsewhere in London or Britain. Not all Jews in the (actual) West End were wealthy. Tailoring was 'the dominant Jewish occupation' in both East End and West End, and wages 'were similar in both districts': see Gerry Black, *Living Up West: Jewish Life in London's West End* (London: London Museum of Jewish Life, 1994), p.24.

10. Stuart Cohen complains of 'a conscious or unconscious type of Whig history', written by Zionists or under Zionist influence, that tends to efface the Jewish anti-Zionist tradition (*English Zionists*, p.15).

11. Ibid., p.15.

12. Ibid., pp, 251, 320. See also pp.64–5, 127.

13. David Feldman, *Englishmen and Jews: Social Relations and Political Culture, 1840–1914* (New Haven, CT: Yale University Press, 1994), p.346.

14. Chaim Bermant, *The Cousinhood: The Anglo-Jewish Gentry* (London: Eyre & Spottiswoode, 1971), p.201; Mordechai Rozin, *The Rich and the Poor: Jewish Philanthropy and Social Control in Nineteenth-Century London* (Eastbourne: Sussex Academic Press, 1999), p.189. Montagu was MP from 1885 to 1900.

15. L.L. Loewe, *Basil Henriques: A Portrait Based on His Diaries, Letters and Speeches as Collated by His Widow, Rose Henriques* (London: Routledge & Kegan Paul), 1976, p.20.

16. Bermant, *Cousinhood*, p.377.

17. Cohen, *English Zionists*, p.27.

18. Ibid., p.56, 57.

19. Sharman Kadish, *Bolsheviks and British Jews The Anglo-Jewish Community, Britain and the Russian Revolution* (London: Routledge, 1992), p.270, n.37.

20. Jonathan Freedland, *Jacob's Gift* (London: Penguin, 2005), p.97.

21. Ibid., pp.185, 186.

22. Ibid., p.186.

23. Ibid., p.189.

24. William J. Fishman, *East End Jewish Radials,1875–1914* (Nottingham: Five Leaves Publications, 2004), p.267. The epithet 'the chronicler of London's East End' is from the blurb on the back cover.

25. Joe Jacobs, *Out of the Ghetto: My Youth in the East End, Communism and Fascism, 1913–1939* (London: Janet Simon, 1978), p.38.

26. Simon Blumenthal, *Jew Boy* (London: Lawrence & Wishart, 1986), pp.166–7. I am grateful to Dave Rosenberg for this reference and for suggesting several other sources, all of which proved to be useful.

27. Ibid., p.348.

28. Geoffrey Alderman, *London Jewry and London Politics, 1889–1986* (London: Routledge, 1989), p.96.

29. Ibid.

30. David Cesarani, 'East End Jewry Between the Wars' (lecture given to the Jewish East End Project, 1986), pp.1–2, quoted by Alderman in *London Jewry*, p.96.

31. Alderman, *London Jewry*, pp.96–7.

32. Cohen, *English Zionists*, p.125.

33. Jacobs, *Out of the Ghetto*, pp.208–9.

34. Fishman, *East End Jewish Radicals*, p.240; Cohen, *English Zionists*, p.125. Deutscher's phrase is 'non-Jewish Jew'.
35. Ibid., p.252.
36. Compare: 'For us the matter was simply a class question in which the Jewish workers had to identify themselves with workers everywhere to organise for the overthrow of the capitalist system. This, we said, was the only way that anti-semitism and racialism could be ended' (Jacobs, *Out of the Ghetto*, p.208).
37. Freedman, *Jacob's Gift*, pp.187–8.
38. Worker's Circle: see Jacobs, *Out of the Ghetto*, p.229; specialist on Jewish affairs: see Paul Kelemen, 'British Communists and the Palestine Conflict, 1929–1948', *Holy Land Studies*, 5, 2 (2006), p.139.
39. I. Rennap, *Anti-Semitism and the Jewish Question* (London: Lawrence & Wishart, 1942), p.85 (emphasis in original). 'Rennap' was a pseudonym formed by reversing the spelling of the author's name.
40. Jacobs, *Out of the Ghetto*, p.208.
41. Fishman, *East End Jewish Radicals*, p.211.
42. Lit. 'Epicurean', meaning a Greek philosopher: what could be worse?
43. Cohen, *English Zionists*, p.210.
44. Feldman, *Englishmen and Jews*, p.322.
45. Bermant, *Cousinhood*, p.208.
46. Ibid., pp.201, 241.
47. Ibid., p.247.
48. Cohen, *English Zionists*, p.209.
49. Cohen, 'Religious Motives', p.166.
50. Cohen, *English Zionists*, p.200.
51. On feeling equivocal or ambivalent: ibid., p.199; also Cohen, 'Religious Motives', pp.165–6.
52. See Paul Mendes-Flohr and Jehuda Reinharz (eds), *The Jew in the Modern World: A Documentary History* (Oxford: Oxford University Press, 1995), pp.538–40.
53. Claude Goldsmid Montefiore, *Liberal Judaism: An Essay* (London: Macmillan & Co., 1903), p.177.
54. Cohen, 'Religious Motives', p.167.
55. 'The Centres of Judaism', in Edward Kessler (ed.), *A Reader of Early Liberal Judaism: The Writings of Israel Abrahams, Claude Montefiore, Lily Montagu and Israel Mattuck* (London: Vallentine Mitchell, 2004), p.143.
56. Rory Miller, *Divided Against Zion: Anti-Zionist Opposition in Britain to a Jewish State in Palestine, 1945–1948* (London: Frank Cass, 2000), p.89.
57. Daniel R. Langton, *Claude Montefiore: His Life and Thought* (London: Vallentine Mitchell, 2002), p.29; also Miller, *Divided Against Zion*, p.89.
58. Loewe, *Basil Henriques*, p.119. The Inquiry was set up to recommend policy on admitting displaced Jewish refugees into Palestine.
59. Feldman, *Englishmen and Jews*, p.345.
60. 'Zionism and Anti-Semitism', in Edward Kessler (ed.), *An English Jew: The Life and Writings of Claude Montefiore* (London: Vallentine Mitchell, 2002), pp.146, 147.
61. Loewe, *Basil Henriques*, p.119.
62. Stuart Cohen, ' "How Shall We Sing of Zion in a Strange Land?": East European Immigrants and the Challenge of Zionism, 1897–1918', *Jewish Social Studies*, new series, 1, 2 (1995), p.117.
63. Kelemen, 'British Communists and the Palestine Conflict', p.149.
64. Freedland, *Jacob's Gift*, pp.248, 249.
65. Loewe, *Basil Henriques*, p.118.
66. Langton, *Claude Montefiore*, p.8.
67. Cohen, *English Zionists*, p.49.
68. Sokolow, *History of Zionism*, vol. 1, p.194. Sokolow was general secretary of the Zionist Organization for three years from 1906.
69. Cohen, *English Zionists*, p.163.
70. 'Israel critics' "fury" ', *Jewish Chronicle*, 3 October 2008, p.26.

CHAPTER SEVEN

The Climate of Debate about Israel in the Jewish World

Revised version of a talk given at a meeting organized by Jewish Voice for a Just Peace, Zurich, June 2009.

INSIDE THE HOTHOUSE

Rabbi Yitzchak and Rabbi Yehudah were both *talmudai chachomim* and respected leaders of their community. Like the House of Hillel and the House of Shammai, they seemed to take opposite sides on every issue. One day, Naphtali the humble cabinetmaker came to Rabbi Yitzchak and said: 'Rabbi, our community is small but our *tsuris* are great. We are faced with difficult choices and we need our elders to give us guidance and advice. Forgive me, but couldn't you and Rabbi Yehudah, just occasionally, not disagree?' Rabbi Yitzchak was deeply offended. 'You ask *me* this question?' he said sharply. 'Ask Rabbi Yehudah: he's the one who's always disagreeing!'

Ever since Abraham and Moses disputed with God, Jews have loved the give and take of argument. 'Come now, and let us reason together' (Is. 1:18) could be the epigraph of the Talmud. But 'reasoning together' does not exactly describe the way we discuss Israel or Zionism. Denounce the 'security wall' or accuse the Israeli army of brutality and the temperature immediately shoots up. It is as if we were inside a hothouse. Global warming is nothing compared to the climate of debate about Israel in the Jewish world. Not that you will necessarily be prevented from speaking your mind. But if you cross an invisible line in the sand – if you take your dissidence too far – then you are liable to become a pariah or traitor in the eyes of many fellow Jews, especially those in the Jewish mainstream.

I call the line 'invisible' because where it is drawn is not always clear; it is shifting sand and the line moves over time. Consequently, you can never be sure when you cross it. But it exists; and if you *do* cross it, you *can* be sure of this: jeers and sneers, vitriol and vilification, will replace the give and take of argument.

Now, people are obnoxious about other subjects as well and some people are rude about everything. Moreover, even the nicest people can be irritable and bad-tempered in certain circumstances: for example, if they are depressed or if they have eaten too much *lockshen* pudding. Indigestion is certainly a common Jewish complaint and we ought to take it seriously. But it is not my subject tonight.[1] Furthermore, the issue that I wish to address is not merely about incivility; it is about identity.

A couple of examples will illustrate what I mean. (Both are taken from the UK, though similar examples could be found almost anywhere in the world where Jews live.) On 2 September 2005, the *Jewish Chronicle* (the foremost Jewish newspaper in the UK) had the following front-page banner headline: 'Rabbi: Amos Oz is a Jew-hating Jew'. The Israeli novelist had written an article opposing religious settlers in Gaza and the West Bank, who dream of a 'Greater Israel'. The article, though it first appeared in Israel, was reprinted in the British newspaper *The Times* and broadcast on BBC radio. Speaking from the pulpit in his synagogue at a Sabbath morning service, Rabbi Dr Jeffrey Cohen, 'one of Britain's most senior Orthodox rabbis', said: 'There can be no more pathetic sight than that of a Jew-hating Jew, or to be a little more charitable, a Jew embarrassed by his own people and their historic aspirations.' He added, 'Even worse, that of a Jewish novelist courting the acclaim, adulation and royalties of a left-wing, anti-Israel gentile world and seeking an international platform to revile his own people.'[2] Notice how this goes beyond mere disagreement with Oz's views. It is an ad hominem attack: an attack on the man and his motives. In particular, it accuses him of treachery, of turning on 'his own people'. Thus, in crossing the invisible line in the sand, Oz had crossed the identity line, the line that divides Jews into two kinds: the true from the false, the faithful from the perfidious, *chaverim* from *oyevim*.

Two years later, in February 2007, a number of us in Britain crossed the same line when we launched Independent Jewish Voices (IJV). We published a statement which, focusing mainly on the Middle East conflict, affirms such principles as these: putting human rights and social justice first, rejecting all forms of racism and antisemitism, and giving equal priority to Palestinians and Israelis in their quest for a peaceful and secure future. 'These principles', the statement continues, 'are contradicted when those who claim to speak on behalf of Jews in

Britain and other countries consistently put support for the policies of an occupying power above the human rights of an occupied people.' As the preamble says, the 'official' view does not reflect 'the broad spectrum of opinion' among Jews in Britain. Wishing to put the record straight, and believing that these issues are urgent, we called our statement: 'A Time to Speak Out' and invited fellow Jews to sign it.[3] The statement was published in the same week in three newspapers: the print editions of the *Jewish Chronicle* and *The Times*, and the website of the *Guardian*. The launch of IJV was front-page headline news in the *Jewish Chronicle*, which included a number of articles on the initiative, including one by Rabbi Dr Sidney Brichto. Rabbi Brichto, head of Liberal Judaism in the UK for many years, was at the opposite end of the religious spectrum from Rabbi Cohen; but in writing his piece about IJV he seemed to dip his pen in the same inkwell. He wrote: 'These Jews ... reveal themselves as enemies of the Jewish people.' Not content to question our views, he said 'I doubt the motives of these Jews.' And he concluded thus: 'My conscience does not permit me to fraternise with those who undermine the future of my people.'[4] As if *we* did not belong to 'his people'; or did so as the worst kind of enemy: the enemy within.

Even as I prepare this talk, a hate message has arrived in my email inbox. The writer, who gives his name but whom I do not know, describes himself as 'the son of an Auschwitz survivor who served in the Israel Defence Forces', as though these facts were his credentials. He cites my articles on Israel in the *Guardian* and writes: 'I must agree with those Jews who call you and your ilk "Kapos" ', equating us with prisoners in Nazi concentration camps who were seen as collaborators in crimes against fellow Jews. He continues: 'There were many Jews like you in Germany who ... looked down on their fellow Jews, who didn't even consider themselves Jewish'. Detecting the note of scorn in his voice, I have to wonder who is looking down on whom. But as to not considering myself Jewish: he is right in a way – not because I consider myself *not* to be Jewish, but because it is not anything that I *consider*. I no more 'consider' myself Jewish than I 'consider' myself human. I *am* human, I *am* Jewish. I am formed from the dust of the earth, like anyone, but when I took my first breath of life it tasted like kiddush wine. It still does. (This suggests a definition of a Jew: someone who, from birth to death, is always a *bissel shikker.*)

This is my point of departure for the subject under discussion tonight. I talk about the climate of debate *from the inside*. Doubly so: not only am I part of the debate, but the debate is part of me. So, on the one hand, I speak about it as a participant, as someone with a definite point of view on Zionism and on the Israeli–Palestinian conflict. This might affect my perception of the debate. It could lead me to overemphasize certain features and understate others. If so, then it needs others to put me right, to rectify any bias in my presentation. I am confident that there will be no shortage of volunteers. On the other hand, I bring to the debate about Israel a sensibility that I believe I share with many of the people with whom I disagree: people, moreover, who place people like me on the wrong side of the identity line. And if I do not 'consider' myself Jewish, I do stop to consider – *because* I am Jewish – what being Jewish means.

My talk falls into four parts. Having provided a glimpse, in this opening section, of the climate of debate inside the Jewish hothouse, I shall try, in the next section, to shed light on the heat. Why do we get so aerated about Israel and Zionism? What is the complex sensibility that causes the temperature – and our blood pressure – to rise? In the third section I propose a different line in the sand from the current one. Keeping the figure of the discomforting Hebrew prophet before my mind's eye, and drawing on three principles that I regard as staple ingredients of Judaism – rejection of idolatry, respect for human dignity and commitment to argument – I shall outline a Jewish case for outspokenness. Finally, in the fourth part of the talk, I look briefly at the prospects for lowering the temperature of the debate.

A COMPLEX SENSIBILITY

Not everyone who identifies as Jewish is sensitive about Israel, but many of us are. We bring to the subject a complex sensibility, one that we have acquired through upbringing, education, experience, family stories, *bubbemeises* and so on. I would be surprised if, in this room tonight, there are not a large number of people who share this sensibility. Without understanding it – without understanding ourselves – we shall not be able to make sense of the climate of the debate about Israel, let alone change it. So, let us begin by trying to get inside our (collective) skin.[5]

I call this Jewish sensibility 'complex' for several reasons. First, it is Jewish. Second, even the *definition* of 'Jewish' is not a simple matter. What is Judaism? It is tempting to say 'God knows!', but I am not sure that he does. God is wise enough to know what it is *impossible* to know; and it is impossible to pin down Judaism. Moses would not have known – for the simple reason that there was no word for 'Judaism' in classical Hebrew. Is it, like Christianity, a religion? Neither the Hebrew scripture nor the Talmud has a word for 'religion'.[6] Paradoxically, the category 'religious' had no purchase in the world of the ancient Israelites and the nations around them bowing down to their many gods. You do not call something X except to mark a difference from Y. Where there is no Y, there is no X. Where there was no 'secular', there was no 'religious'. True, hovering over the biblical text is a character called God who creates heaven and earth. And yes, the Children of Israel become 'a kingdom of priests' by entering into a covenant with this character (Ex. 19:6). And, certainly, today we would call this narrative 'religious'. But it *is* a *narrative*; and stories can be taken in various ways, with pinches of salt, grades of literalness, shades of irony. If Judaism were a religion tout court, then 'secular rabbis' would not be ordained in seminaries in Israel and America, but they are. And 'a secular Jew' would be a contradiction in terms, which it is not. Which is not to say that it is *not* a religion: for *some* Jews it is. Others make a religion out of *rejecting* the religion. I once heard of a person who never ate pork – except on Yom Kippur: in his own way he was devout. Be that as it may, the distinction between 'secular' and 'religious' does not always apply. Even when it does, there can be depths of feeling and association that the distinction is unable to reach. So, what is Judaism? When I use the word, I mean, broadly, the cultures of the Jews, whether we parse those cultures as religious or secular, neither or both – but this is not a *definition*.

In his recent essay 'Zion', the writer George Steiner observes: 'The relations of a Jew to his or her identity can be so opaque, so stressful and replete with historical, social and psychological ambiguities, that these define, if definition is allowed to include undecidability, the very condition of Jewishness.'[7] This is the place from which to start if we want to get a handle on the sensibilities that many of us, as Jews, bring to the debate about the Middle East. Zion by any other name ('Jerusalem', 'Israel') is as ubiquitous in the Jewish imagination as it is ambiguous. Its multiple meanings might not be altogether separable. And yet, it is worth trying to disambiguate the concept; for, unless we can distinguish between its various strands, we shall not be able to understand the magic it weaves.

On 10 February 2009 I was driving home, with the car radio tuned to BBC Radio 4. It was 6 o'clock in the evening, time for the news. I was only half listening, but one of the headlines caught my ear: 'The people of Israel are voting for a new government.' 'The people of Israel': the phrase rang a bell. Actually, it rings *three* bells. The first is for that ragtag collection of tribes that congregate in the Hebrew scripture and who come together at Sinai, becoming 'the people of God'. This is *am Yisroel*, 'the people of Israel' *inside* the text: the people *in* the book. The second is for Jews who have carried that scripture to the corners of the earth and who, every time they peer into it, identify with *am Yisroel*. This is 'the people of Israel' *outside* the text: the people *of* the book. The third bell is for a motley population of Jews, Muslims, Christians and others who inhabit a territory along the east coast of the Mediterranean. This is 'the people' of 'Israel': the citizens of a country.

The third bell is the one that rings the changes: a shift of register from book to state, from the textual to the political. But this is not a shift that registers on the ear, not when your head is humming with the simultaneous peal of all three bells. Even when we know what is intended (for obviously the reference in the news headline is to the Israeli electorate), the inward ear cannot help but hear the overtones of the phrase. 'The people of Israel' strikes a deep chord; and this harmonic contains the key to a complex sensibility.

There is an entire vocabulary like this: words and phrases associated with Zionism that reverberate in the corridors of the Jewish imagination. 'The very name of the movement', observes Arthur Hertzberg in *The Zionist Idea*, 'evoked the dream of an end of days, of an ultimate release from the exile and a coming to rest in the land of Jewry's heroic age.'[8] In other words, it evoked the utopian vision of the Hebrew prophets. Similar associations arise with 'the very name of the nation', as Jacqueline Rose points out in *The Question of Zion*.[9] Imagine if Israel were not called Israel but, say, Western Palestine or The Theodor Herzl Republic or Balfouria: if this were its name, sublime (and subliminal) resonances – of the eternal hope of an eternal people – would not resound. Yet, for most of its career Zionism has been predominantly – even aggressively – a secular movement. Hertzberg points out that 'modern Zionist ideology' set out to give a 'radically new meaning' to the old messianic concept.[10] No doubt; but the language has a life of its own. Never mind the ideology, feel the poetry.

The poetry is in the prose. The music of Zionism is fusion: sounds from traditional liturgy melded together with the jargon of a secular political terminology. The 'goal of our revolution', said David Ben-Gurion in 1944, '*is the complete ingathering of the exiles into a socialist Jewish state*'.[11] It is a perfect example of the genre; you could almost hear 'revelation' for 'revolution'. Four years later, the Proclamation establishing the State of Israel, teeming with biblical allusions (without ever quite mentioning God), writes Ben-Gurion's script (sans his socialism) into the state's certificate of birth. The effect is to solemnize: to elevate the status of the new Jewish state into something higher than a civil institution but a little lower than the angels. Thus, in Zionist parlance (which has become so common among Jews that they hardly know what they are saying), Jewish immigrants to Israel do not merely acquire citizenship: they 'make aliyah', the Hebrew word for 'ascent', a term that implies being summoned or called, as when called to the *bimah* when the Torah is read in shul. It is as if becoming an Israeli (if you are Jewish) were entering a higher state or climbing a rung on Jacob's ladder.

But it is not just the language of politics; it is the language per se that is packed with more meaning than its words can contain. Until it was revamped or reinvented in the late nineteenth century in the context of the project of 'national revival' (or revisal), Hebrew was primarily a sacred tongue. In a letter to Franz Rosenzweig, dated 26 December 1926, Gershom Scholem asks: 'What will be the result of updating the Hebrew language?' Here is part of his answer:

> Is not the holy language, which we have planted among our children, an abyss that must open up? People here do not know the meaning of what they have done. They think that they have turned Hebrew into a secular language and that they have removed its apocalyptic sting, but it is not so. The secularization of the language is merely empty words, a rhetorical turn of phrase. In reality it is impossible to empty the words which are filled to bursting with meaning, save at the expense of the language itself.[12]

I take this to mean not that the older layers of meaning *supplant* the newer but that they *suffuse* them. The old words are time capsules. They are semantic bombs. Scholem remarks: 'All those words which were not created arbitrarily and out of nothing, but were taken from the good old lexicon, are filled to the brim with explosive meaning', meaning that they explode the categories that separate the holy and the profane.[13] As a result, the ancient sacred tongue is no longer purely sacred and its modern secular version is not simply secular.[14]

There are, of course, regions of Modern Hebrew where the words are not taken from 'the good old lexicon'. This, it might seem, weakens Scholem's argument. However, in the first place, no region of a language is an island. In the second place, the old system of pronouncing Classical Hebrew with which Ashkenazi Jews (like me) grew up has been largely replaced by the Modern. (For example, *natan* [who has given] for *nosun*; shalom [peace] for *sholome*.) This means that 'the sacred tongue', used in the sanctuary of the synagogue, now *sounds* like the language spoken in a Tel Aviv shop or on an Egged bus. The similarity of sound tends to blur two lines of demarcation: one between the secular and the religious, the other between the groups that I distinguished earlier: 'the people of Israel' (Israelites and Jews) and 'the people' of 'Israel' (Israelis).

Where the ear hears little difference, it is harder for either the heart or mind to make distinctions. This does not mean that the different identities are obliterated. But they are leaky; they bleed into each other; they blend or fuse. They become, in Steiner's word, undecidable.

And underneath it all: the bedrock of historical experience, the collective memory of marginalization, exclusion and persecution in Europe. It is the persistence of this history into modern times that has determined the disposition of many Jews today. Expulsions in the Middle Ages are one thing, but pogroms in Russia in the late nineteenth century are another. The Dreyfus Affair in France, the rise of antisemitic parties in Germany and Austria, the growth of anti-Jewish legislation in Eastern Europe, the ascendancy of the Nazis to power and the implementation of the Final Solution (which did not distinguish between religious and secular Jew): all of this has forged a hard-core distrust of 'the world' and a feeling of betrayal after the bright promise of the Enlightenment, the sense of a broken promise of a secure and normal existence for Jews. Concomitantly, it has inspired a deeply ambiguous ambition for a place to be Jewish; a Jewish place; a place that is both within 'the world' and without it; a miraculous place, a place where the real is the magical and the magical is the real.

This is the place of Israel: not on the planet but on the plane of imagination; not for *all* of us who are Jewish but for enough of us to create a climate of debate in which, as with a *chamsin*, the temperature can suddenly soar. It is impossible to understand this climate without appreciating the *eminence* of Zion in the Jewish imagination. Zion stands out like a city on a hill (if it is permissible to compare a thing to itself). It is too massive to miss, too ethereal to grasp. Bursting with meaning, it fills the air with nuances, as thick as dandelion seeds, so that the debate about Israel is about more than Israel the state. For Israel is more than the state. It is more than itself. It is more like *your* self; hence that 'identity line' in the sand. It is as if any Jew who crosses it – anyone who takes their criticism of Zionism or the State of Israel too far – is taking the very *neshumah* out of their fellow Jews.

Thus it is that Amos Oz is labelled a 'Jew-hating Jew', and dissident Jewish groups like IJV are derided as '*kapos*' and 'enemies of the people'. But I ask you: in reality, who is taking whose *neshumah* out of whom?

A CASE FOR OUTSPOKENNESS

Which puts me in mind of a family simcha. What is a simcha? A celebration: a joyous occasion when relatives and friends get together in order to be reminded why they never want to get together. I once invented a board game about a simcha. It was called *Broyges*. Each player invites guests to a wedding feast and places them on a table plan. When the table plan is filled, the game is over. The rules were based on two premises. First, every guest is offended for no reason. Second, some are offended more than others, depending who they sit next to and whether they feel that they ought to be on the top table with the *chasan* and *kallah* instead of a table at the back for people who matter even less than the people who are not invited at all. (Unfortunately, the game no longer exists and I cannot recall whether the winner was the player who caused the *least* number of *broygeses* or the *most*. But the reality lives on.)

Now, I did say that indigestion is not my subject tonight. But there is a profound lesson that simchas teach us: The point of Judaism is not to avoid heartburn at all costs. It was not to settle their stomachs that Moses made the Children of Israel schlep across the wilderness for forty years with nothing to eat except some kind of frost from the sky. True, when he came down from the summit of Mount Sinai, he brought two tablets. But they were meant to *give* the people a headache, not *cure* them of one. In other words (and in all seriousness), Moses led the people out of misery, but he did not set out to make them feel comfortable about themselves or their lives: far from it. And the later prophets followed in his footsteps. King Ahab knew this from first-hand experience. When Elijah took him to task for worshipping Baal, he scolded the prophet, calling him 'you troubler of Israel'. Elijah, being a prophet, was not lost for words: 'It is not I who has brought trouble on Israel', he retorted, 'but you' (1 Kings, 18:17–18). Nonetheless, Ahab had a point – and not only about Elijah. As a breed, the Hebrew prophets were 'troublers of Israel': trouble was their trade. Speaking out, they caused discomfort to ruler and people alike.

With their ancient example in mind, I wish to make a Jewish case for outspokenness. I do not mean the right to free speech. Not that I am against free speech; people should be entitled to speak their minds, even if they have nothing to say, provided they do not harm anyone else. But

that is not what I am talking about. When I say 'outspokenness' I do not
mean the licence to spout nonsense. I mean the duty – the mitzvah –
of using speech to give people a headache. But not just *any* headache;
it has to be a headache of the right sort. By the same token, it must not
be the *wrong* sort. (Perhaps to a medical doctor there is no such distinction, but in ethics there is.)

The case that I wish to make is, in effect, for a different line in the
sand from the one currently drawn in much of the Jewish world when
Israel is the subject of debate. By way of preamble, I shall describe a
vivid example, one that I know at first hand, of what can happen when
you cross the current line, the identity line that (supposedly) separates
'true' Jew from 'false'.

On Sunday 11 January 2009, while Operation Cast Lead was still in
full swing in Gaza, a rally in support of the Israeli government,
organized jointly by the Board of Deputies of British Jews and the Jewish
Leadership Council, was held in London's Trafalgar Square. Under the
auspices of IJV, a number of us gathered on the fringe of the square for
a counter rally, calling on Israel to cease the bombing and to talk to
Hamas. To get to our site outside Canada House we had to run a
gauntlet of jeers. 'Traitors!' 'Cowards!' 'Scum!': these and other
epithets were hurled in our direction. Thanks to police protection, we
did not feel at risk, but we were conscious of a menacing wrath
simmering under the surface. When the rally was over, some of us were
spat at and called by the familiar slur, '*kapos*'. The contempt and
hatred for us, as Jews, was palpable. But it did not come from fanatical
Jihadists, nor from fascists in the British National Party. It came from
fellow Jews. A ritual was being enacted in which we were being sym-
bolically 'othered'.

Now, there are always individuals who bring their venom to a
political rally. But this is not just a matter of a few isolated fanatics.
When Jewish leadership, both secular and religious, lines up almost
solidly behind the Israeli government; when synagogues act as con-
duits for Israeli propaganda from Zionist groups; and when no distinction is made between supporting Israel's wars and fighting
antisemitism: then a climate is created that breeds the abuse dished out
to us in Trafalgar Square.

In a way, I am glad of it. Being 'othered' reminds me that I am a Jew,
especially when I consider what provoked this behaviour: open opposition to the behaviour of the State of Israel. For what does this mean?
What does it mean when, week after week, many of the very people who
cannot bear to hear Jews condemn Israel attend services in shul where

they open the Hebrew scripture and read about Moses castigating the people, Elijah admonishing the king, Isaiah berating 'a sinful nation' (Is. 1:4) and Jeremiah declaiming 'against Judah's kings and officers, and against its priests and citizens' (Jer. 1:18)? No one can claim the mantle of the prophet today; no one can speak with that kind of authority. But we can all follow their lead in treating the state – any state but especially a state that calls itself Jewish – as a legitimate target for open criticism and, if necessary, denunciation.

What does it mean when every time the State of Israel speaks, the congregation of diaspora Jewry says 'Amen'? What does it mean when to approach the state is to ascend, as if it were resting on a pedestal – which is precisely where this state has been put? It is not the state as such but its *status* that is the issue; it is this, more than anything else, that heats up the climate of debate in the Jewish world. In the minds and hearts of many Jews, Israel is not just a political reality. It is the magic focus of hopes and fears, a kind of fetish. The state has been made into a statue. You can call it a cause or ideal. But it is an idol by any other name.

Which is no idle thing. In fact nothing is weightier in the Hebrew scripture than the matter of idolatry. What, in heaven's name, does it mean to be Jewish if not to knock statues off their pedestals? If, whatever our political opinions about Israel, we cannot rise above the state and put it in its place; if we do not reduce its status to that of a mere thing among things; then we are not Jews, or we are Jews in name only. But *things* can be criticized, challenged, opposed, rejected, replaced: there is not a line that you may not cross when approaching a *thing* – not in the iconoclastic Judaism to which I lay claim.

Fellow human beings, however, are another matter. They are fellow members of the largest Jewish family in the world: the *human* family, sharing the same *bubbe* and *zeyda*, grandma Eve and grandpa Adam, through whom (in the Genesis story) they inherit the image of God, from which the Talmud derives the principle of *kevod habriyos*, literally 'honour of the created', or, as we might say today, 'human dignity'. 'The dignity of every person is sacred', writes Rabbi Chaim Shmulevitz, who for fifteen years was *Rosh* of the famous Mirrer Yeshiva in Jerusalem.[15] Attaching 'overriding importance' to the concept, he explains: '*Rabbinic enactments and various scriptural prohibitions are set aside when they conflict with human respect and dignity.*'[16] He emphasizes that the concept 'does not ... stop at refraining from insulting or degrading one's fellow human being. One is also obligated to enhance and magnify the prestige and honor of one's fellow.'[17]

So, you cross any line in order to speak out about the degradation of others: this is a rule in the Judaism to which I lay claim – where 'others' encompasses 'the other'. 'When a stranger resides with you in your land', says God through Moses, 'you shall not wrong him. The stranger who resides with you shall be to you as one of your citizens; you shall love him as yourself' (Lev. 19: 33–4). Not just the stranger. 'When you encounter your enemy's ox or ass wandering, you must take it back to him' (Ex. 23:4). Justice extends to your enemy too; for your enemy also has the stamp 'human'. These are the directives that Moses gives the people of Israel in the wilderness; this is the direction that he points out. And, starting with the Hebrew prophets, there is a long straggling line of Judeans and Jews, ancient Israelites and modern Israelis, rabbis and writers and activists, who have followed suit. Some call themselves secular, others religious, others just plain Jewish.

Between them, these two principles, the one positive (respect for human dignity), the other negative (rejection of idolatry), lay the substantive basis for a Jewish case for outspokenness. On the one hand, they motivate; on the other hand, they limit, free expression of opinion about anything whatsoever. To which we can add a third – essentially procedural – principle: commitment to argument.

'Argument for the sake of heaven': this is how the Mishna puts it when argument is conducted not for its own sake or for the sake of winning but with a view to a higher purpose.[18] Even God enters the arena when, for example, Abraham engages him in moral reasoning over the fate of Sodom (Gen. 18: 22–33). God cannot resist argument, any more than Abraham, when justice is at stake. And, according to a remarkable tale in the Talmud, not even God can *settle* the argument. Once (goes the story) there was a dispute between two rabbis, Rabbi Eliezer and Rabbi Joshua, when a heavenly voice intervened to say that Rabbi Eliezer was right. To which Rabbi Joshua retorted, in effect, that God has no standing. 'For the Torah has already been given from Mount Sinai and we pay no attention to a heavenly voice.' God 'smiled in that hour' and said, 'My children have defeated me. My children have defeated me.'[19] After quoting this passage, Rabbi Joseph Soloveitchik comments: 'It is as if the Creator of the World Himself abides by man's decisions and instruction.'[20] Earth looks to heaven for guidance but heaven, in this story, looks back to earth. '*You* decide. Argue it out': argument for the sake of the world. (Argument for the sake of the world is argument for the sake of heaven: this, in a way, sums up Judaism.)

In the argument over Israel, there are no 'no-go' areas except as determined by the first two principles applied via the third. Anything goes, even discussion of the most sensitive issues, even its existence as 'the Jewish state'. And if this causes offence, tough: no political entity, no state, no object: nothing is above and beyond the reach of argument for the sake of what matters most: the three things by which, according to Rabbi Shimon ben Gamliel in the Mishna, the world endures, the pillars on which it rests: truth, justice and peace.[21]

I rest my case – which I acknowledge is more full of holes than a piece of matzo (and for some of you just as indigestible). I shall stand accused of being selective in the Jewish sources on which I have drawn, to which I plead guilty. But I would like to know what it feels like to be innocent as charged, since I do not think this is possible. Certainly, there are other sources, far less congenial to my whole approach, which I have ignored. But, starting with the Torah itself, we are faced with a hundred conundrums. What Moses gives is ours to receive; but how do you receive the vast, complex, paradoxical book of creation? You cannot stand there passively with begging bowl in hand, waiting for your cup to be filled with truth. You have to come forward as a mensch and, like Jacob 'left alone' with the angel, wrestle with it (Gen. 32:25). (This is the making of Jacob; it is precisely on account of his 'striving with God' that he becomes 'Israel': Gen. 32:29.[22]) You have to have a *take* on what is *given*. And in making my case for outspokenness I take the three principles on which it rests – rejection of idolatry, respect for human dignity and commitment to argument – as elementary: the *aleph bais gimmel* (the ABG) of Judaism.

LOWERING THE TEMPERATURE

I have a feeling that more than one person in the room is bursting to make an objection along these lines:

> *It is all very well, but your entire lecture has been unbalanced. You speak as if only one side in the debate about Israel is responsible for the unhealthy climate. What about the other side – the dissidents whom you present in such a favourable light? Don't they also overreact at times and smear their opponents? Why do you let them off the hook? You are like Rabbi Yitzchak in the joke: you blame one side for always disagreeing!*

It is a fair point – as far as it goes. But I do not think it goes very far. I agree that there is discourteousness and misrepresentation on the other side too. (I experienced it myself earlier this year.[23]) But if the problem with the climate of debate about Israel were merely a matter of manners, there would not be much to discuss and I would not be here tonight giving this lecture.

Insofar as incivility is the issue, there are certain steps that we could agree to take in order to lower the temperature of the debate. Following the example set by Moses, we could devise a code of conduct that requires us to behave with *derech eretz* or common decency; for example, 'Thou shalt not demonize thy opponent in argument' or 'Thou shalt not direct thy spittle in his or her general direction.' But would we keep it? *Can* we keep it, and for how long? For, if I am right, there is something disruptive that lurks in the depths.

This is the bottom line; the identity line; the line that divides Jews into the true and the false, the faithful and the perfidious, *chaverim* and *oyevim*; the line in the sand that is drawn and redrawn in relation to the State of Israel. In the final analysis, prospects for improving the atmosphere in the Jewish world depend on whether we can examine the place that Israel occupies in the economy of our emotions. Beneath the surface of the (very) public question of Israel's relations with the Palestinians, there is the (intensely) private matter of its relationship to us. This is not the business of a day. But it is the crisis of the hour and cries out for our collective attention.

The matter is urgent. 'Come *now*, and let us reason together.' Not that we are likely to achieve a consensus. I am not even sure that we should seek one. Except at Sinai, when 'all the people answered with one voice' (Ex. 24:3), consensus has not been a particularly Jewish value. But argument is. Who knows? Perhaps, unlike Rabbi Yitzchak and Rabbi Yehudah, occasionally we might not disagree.

NOTES

1. This chapter is adapted from a talk I gave at a meeting at the Haus der jüdischen Jugend, Zurich, organized by Jewish Voice for a Just Peace between Israel and Palestine, 22 June 2009. The audience consisted mainly of a cross-section of the Zurich Jewish population.
2. Simon Rocker, 'Rabbi: Amos Oz is a Jew-hating Jew', *Jewish Chronicle*, 2 September 2005, p.1.
3. The full text of the IJV statement is available at http://jewishvoices.squarespace.com.
4. Sidney Brichto, 'You Are Undermining Us', *Jewish Chronicle*, 9 February 2007, p.37.
5. Most of this section and the next are adapted from the first and (especially) third chapters of my *Offence: The Jewish Case* (London: Seagull Books, 2009).
6. Louis Jacobs, *The Jewish Religion: A Companion* (Oxford: Oxford University Press, 1995), p.418.
7. George Steiner, *My Unwritten Books* (London: Phoenix, 2008), p.86.
8. Arthur Hertzberg, *The Zionist Idea: A Historical Analysis and Reader* (Philadelphia, PA: Jewish Publication Society, 1997), p.16.
9. Jacqueline Rose, *The Question of Zion* (Princeton, NJ: Princeton University Press, 2007), p.34.
10. Hertzberg, *Zionist Idea*, p.17.

11. David Ben-Gurion, 'The Imperatives of the Jewish Revolution' in Hertzberg, *Zionist Idea*, p.618 (emphasis in original).
12. Gershom Scholem, 'Thoughts About Our Language (1926)', in Gershom Scholem, *On the Possibility of Jewish Mysticism in Our Time and Other Essays* (Philadelphia, PA: Jewish Publication Society, 1997), p.27.
13. Ibid., p.28.
14. The linguistics of this is explored in Azzan Yadin and Ghil'ad Zuckermann, '*Blorit*: Pagans' Mohawk or Sabras' Forelock? Ideological Secularization of Hebrew Terms in Socialist Zionist Israeli', in Tope Omoniyi (ed.), *Sociology of Language and Religion* (London: Palgrave Macmillan, 2010).
15. Chaim Shmulevitz, *Reb Chaim's Discourses* (New York: Mesorah Publications, 1989), p.241.
16. Ibid., p.242. Italics in original.
17. Ibid.
18. Bab. Tal., *Avot* 5:20.
19. Bab. Tal., *Bava Metzi'a* 59b.
20. Joseph Soloveitchik, *Halakhic Man* (Jerusalem: Sefer ve Sefel Publishing, 2005), p.80.
21. Bab. Tal., *Avot* 1:18.
22. 'Israel': literally, 'one who strives with God'.
23. This was in response to my piece 'Standing Up Against Antisemitism' on the comment-is-free website, *Guardian*, 22 April 2009, in which I supported the delegate walkout in Geneva during the speech by Mahmoud Ahmadinejad, President of Iran, at the UN Conference Against Racism. Evidently, I crossed a line on 'the left'. On one listserv, a respected academic remarked that I had joined the ranks 'of those who use accusations of anti-Semitism to deflect criticism of Israel'.

CHAPTER EIGHT

On Saying that Israel has a Right to Exist

THE INDISPENSABLE CONDITION

'Nobody does Israel any service by proclaiming its "right to exist". It is disturbing to find so many people well-disposed to Israel giving currency to this contemptuous formulation.' These were the opening sentences of 'The Saudi Text', an article that appeared in the *New York Times* on 18 November 1981. Given present Israeli policy, it might come as a surprise to know that the author was Abba Eban, Foreign Minister in Israel's Labour government from 1966 to 1974.[1] Labour was in opposition when Eban's article was published, and perhaps even more surprising is the fact that his withering words were not aimed at Menachem Begin, leader of the right-wing Likud party (headed today by Prime Minister Benjamin Netanyahu), which had come to power four years earlier. Far from it: on this point, at least, the two adversaries were wholly in agreement. Presenting his newly-elected government to the Knesset in June 1977, Begin had made the following firm avowal: 'I wish to declare that the Government of Israel will not ask any nation, be it near or far, mighty or small, to recognize our right to exist.'[2]

Neither Begin nor Eban, of course, meant to imply that Israel does *not* have a right to exist. Their point was that this right should be regarded as a given, as something taken for granted. It was precisely for this reason that they rejected the idea that Israel needs other people to bestow it or confirm it. 'Israel's right to exist', Eban continued, 'like that of the United States, Saudi Arabia and 152 other states, is axiomatic and unreserved. Israel's legitimacy is not suspended in midair awaiting acknowledgement by the royal house in Riyadh.'[3] In the same vein, Begin went on to say in his speech to the Knesset: 'It would not enter the mind of any Briton or Frenchman, Belgian or Dutchman, Hungarian or Bulgarian, Russian or American, to request for his people recognition of its right to exist. Their existence per se is their right to exist. The same holds true for Israel.'[4]

But today, the formulation that Eban called 'contemptuous' has become ubiquitous. It is the price of admission, the ticket to ride, in two different (though overlapping) arenas. One is the world of international diplomacy where, since Hamas' victory in the January 2006 Palestinian elections, the Quartet (US, UN, European Union and Russia) have isolated the party until it passes three political tests, including 'recognition of Israel'.[5] Israel itself has set the same condition for any prospective 'partner for peace'. As is evident from the discourse in diplomatic circles, 'recognition of Israel' means more than implicitly acknowledging the fact that the state exists. For one thing, it refers to the *right* – not just the *fact* – of its existence, as George W. Bush (who was US President at the time) underlined: 'The Hamas party has made it clear that they do not support the right of Israel to exist. And I have made it clear so long as that's their policy, that we will not support a Palestinian government made up of Hamas.'[6] For another, in order to satisfy the condition, it is not enough for Hamas (or anyone else) to *imply* recognition: it has to be stated explicitly: it has to be *said*.

In the public square, many people 'well-disposed to Israel' (in Eban's phrase) make a similar stipulation. Their unwritten law, which applies both to groups in civil society and to private individuals, is roughly as follows: 'Criticize Israel as much as you like, provided you proclaim Israel's right to exist.' Thus, the rule of entry is the same in both arenas. If you are Hamas and you wish to receive aid from the Quartet; if you are an interested party and seek a place at the negotiating table; or if you are just a plain private person with a beef about Israel: then, like Ali Baba in the story, you must say the magic words if you want the door to open. If he were alive today, it would surprise Eban to know the extent to which his 'contemptuous formulation' has become the indispensable condition.

I come to this topic not as a politician but as someone with views about Israel and the Israeli–Palestinian conflict which, from time to time, sometimes as an individual and sometimes together with others, I express. It is in this connection that I have encountered the 'indispensable condition'. I shall, accordingly, focus on the debate in the public square rather than on the world of international diplomacy. Although the two arenas overlap, and some of the argument carries across from one to the other, I shall not try to do justice to the complexities of the diplomatic scene. Diplomacy is like a game in which the players play cat-and-mouse with each other, employing different strategies at different times in pursuit of political goals at home and abroad – goals that are often flexible and mutable: all of which calls for analysis on its own terms. I focus instead on the debate in the public square because it is the immediate context of my concern; I know it from first-hand experience, and it is my experience that has motivated this chapter.

As a preliminary to the main discussion, and so as to throw the topic into sharper relief, let us put the case of Israel temporarily to one side and consider the phrase 'a right to exist'. As a legal concept applied to sovereign states, what does it mean? In international law, sovereign states have various rights vis-à-vis each other, many of which can be traced back to the principles laid down in Article 2 of the UN Charter, the fourth of which is this: 'All members shall refrain in their international relations from the threat or use of force against the territorial integrity or political independence of any State, or in any other manner inconsistent with the Purposes of the United Nations.'[7] Article 51 of the UN Charter specifies the 'right of self-defence' against an armed attack.[8] Resolutions, declarations and treaties have, over the years, added other specific rights (and corresponding obligations) to the list, so that we can speak of a state having, say, a right to territorial integrity, a right to security, a right to live in peace within recognized boundaries, and so on. (I have expressed these rights roughly and loosely.) Now, in a given case, all these rights presuppose the existence of the state – a non-existent state could not possess any rights – but whether the state has its existence by right is another matter.

Unless, of course, 'a right to exist' is nothing more than shorthand for the inventory of specific rights that a state possesses. This would make its 'right to exist' reducible to its rights to its territory, security, self-defence and so on, in which case there is nothing esoteric about 'a right to exist'. But then it does not mean anything to single it out – for there is nothing to single out. If, however, there is more to a state's 'right to exist' than the set of its specific rights (or some basic subset thereof), what is it? Stripped of all specification, what is a bare 'right to exist'? What distinctive state of affairs does the word 'exist' pick out – such that it can be the subject of a discrete right? Kant famously argued that existence is not a 'real predicate' because when we predicate existence of a thing we do not add to our concept of that thing.[9] Although he made this argument in a rather different context, his analysis comes to mind now. Territorial integrity, living in peace, self-defence, and so on: each of these attributes adds to (or qualifies) our concept of some state; existence does not. Each is a *mode* of a state's existence, a way in which the state can be. Existence itself or per se is not (nothing is a mode of itself) – which, on the face of it, makes it an odd candidate for being a legal right in its own right.

But perhaps 'a right to exist', understood as a legal term applied to sovereign states, means neither one specific right among others nor a set (or subset) of specific rights, but the *legitimacy* of a state, where this means that the state conforms to the rules (such as they are) of international law either in the manner in which it was created or its reception into the international community or its compliance with its obligations under the terms of the UN Charter or a combination of these factors.[10] Understood this way, whether a given state – such as Israel – has 'a right to exist' appears to be a juridical – not a political – question.

But Hamas is neither a court of law nor a society of international jurists. Nor, for that matter, am I. Nor are the vast majority of people who participate in the arena of international diplomacy or in the general debate in the public square. Yet any of us is liable to find ourselves asked to give a ruling on whether Israel has 'a right to exist' – and to be judged by our verdict. Furthermore, none of us is likely to be faced with the equivalent question by, or on behalf of, any other state. In fact, I can think of no other example of a state insisting upon its 'right to exist' and demanding that others explicitly recognize this right. (It is partly for this reason that the phrase is opaque: its meaning has not been determined or clarified by use.) This is particularly striking when we bear in mind how many states have come into existence in the recent past. James Crawford reminds us: 'At the beginning of the twentieth century there were some fifty acknowledged states. Immediately before World War II there were about seventy-five. By 2005, there were almost 200 – to be precise, 192.'[11] Israel is thus only one of 117 newly-created states. The legal legitimacy of many of these states is a matter for debate, yet I can think of no other case where the question is posed in terms of 'the right to exist'; only Israel.

Taken together, these circumstances suggest that the 'right to exist' that is insisted upon by Israel (along with many of the people who see themselves as its supporters) is not a *legal* concept, or not primarily. If it is about legitimacy, the legitimacy is not a matter of conformance with rules of international law, or not au fond. Something else is at stake. Some other agenda or concern (or set of concerns) is driving this insistence forward. When we look into this further, we find that the 'indispensable condition' deforms the whole shape of the debate about Palestine and Israel. Partly, this is because it tends to use up all the oxygen, emphasizing the 'existential threat' to Israel and deflecting attention away from the predicaments of the Palestinians (let alone the security anxieties of neighbouring states). Partly, it is because the content is a tissue of confusion: 'Israel has a right to exist' is, in each part and as a whole, as vague as a cloud (or as slippery as an eel).

The clock is ticking; and the more time passes, the more urgent it becomes to clear the air and come to grips with the impasse in the

Middle East. It is with this urgency in mind that I have written this chapter. As a Jew living in Britain, I am also mindful of the impact of the debate about Israel on Jewish life in the wider world. The chapter, as I have already implied, is not an exercise in jurisprudence. Focusing on the public square, I shall discuss the rhetoric of the phrase 'Israel has a right to exist' and its widespread use as a political litmus test. Like Abba Eban and Menachem Begin, I regard the 'indispensable condition' as indefensible, though I daresay my reasons are different from theirs.

A TISSUE OF CONFUSION

Let me begin with a personal anecdote. In February 2007, a number of people living in Britain – all of us Jewish – launched an initiative called Independent Jewish Voices (IJV). Largely with an eye to the Israeli–Palestinian conflict, we drafted a statement, 'A Time to Speak Out', and invited fellow Jews in Britain to join us in signing it. The core of the statement is a set of five principles of (social) justice and human rights: principles that are either universal in themselves or in the spirit of universality.[12] We held that these principles, rather than the principle of group or ethnic loyalty, should come first. We tested the draft statement in advance on a few trusted friends and acquaintances. The advice we received from one quarter was emphatic: 'You need to begin with an explicit declaration of support for Israel's right to exist and flourish.' Otherwise, he warned us, we would not 'get a hearing' in the British Jewish mainstream. He was reminding us of the 'indispensable condition'.

His advice was given in a spirit of goodwill and, in a way, it was sound. (He is both prominent in the Jewish world in Britain and has his finger on the pulse of the Jewish mainstream.) But precisely to the extent that he was right, he was wrong; for if, in order to 'get a hearing', this is what we had to say, then our message would not have been heard. Our own words would have drowned it out. Taking his advice, we would have been in contradiction with ourselves. This is not because we were asserting that Israel does *not* have 'a right to exist'; we were not asserting the negative any more than the positive. We were proclaiming universal principles that transcend partisan support for one side against another and calling for the debate about the Israeli–Palestinian conflict to be based on the premise that these principles must be applied, in an even-handed way, to all parties. Singling out Israel, declaring our support for its right to exist, would have conveyed a completely different message – or a muddled one. We would have proven our credentials to one particular constituency – admittedly a large one in the Jewish world – but at the cost of our credibility. Of course we would have gained a hearing; but we would have lost the independence of our voices.

But suppose we would have complied with the advice and prefaced our statement by uttering the obligatory words: What would these words have said to the people who need us to say them before we get a hearing? To put it another way: What kind of a 'hearing' would they have given us? They hear us say 'a right to exist': Although it is unclear precisely what *kind* of right they take this to be, it must, as we have seen, be more than merely legal. Call it a *moral* right. But unless and until we know what they regard as the moral *basis* for this right, we do not really know what they are hearing us say (for they are hearing us affirm the source of moral authority that *grounds* this right). And before we can clarify *this* point, we need to know what they understand by the name 'Israel'. What *is* Israel? What is the nature or identity of the bearer of this moral 'right to exist'?

Israel, to be sure, is a state; that is, a sovereign political entity within a specified territory. And now there are two complications. The first is that this territory is *not* specified. For what are Israel's – legally binding – borders? The matter has never been settled.[13] What does it mean to say that a state has 'a right to exist' if we do not know the extent of the territory over which its right is exercised? And, since the question of borders is one of the burning issues in the Israeli–Palestinian conflict, this is not something that we can quietly gloss over. But perhaps all we are being asked to say (by the people who want us to say it) is this: 'Israel has a right to exist somewhere between the Mediterranean Sea and the River Jordan', leaving it vague as to what its boundaries might be. Perhaps this is what they mean; perhaps not. But let it pass, for there is a deeper problem when we turn to the second complication with the name 'Israel'. Israel is a state. But does the name 'Israel' denote the state *as such* or does it denote the state *as Jewish*? Does it (to take this one step further) denote the state *as the state of the Jews*? Saying 'Israel has a right to exist', what would be we saying? What would we be *heard* to be saying by the people for whose benefit we were saying it? We would be speaking about Israel: but *in which sense*?

In his landmark foreign policy speech at Bar Ilan University on 14 June 2009, Prime Minister Netanyahu left his audience – the world – in no doubt about what *he* means when he says 'Israel'. Over and again, he called the country 'the state of the Jewish People' or 'the national homeland of the Jewish People'. Muddying the waters while rubbing salt into the wound, he persisted in referring to the West Bank as 'Judea and Samaria', the biblical names for the region (which is also official Israeli terminology), even as he placed the onus on the Palestinians and enunciated the 'indispensable condition'. 'We need', he said, 'the Palestinian leadership to rise and say, simply, "We have had enough of the conflict. We recognize the right of the Jewish People to a state [of] its own in this land. We will live side by side in true peace."'[14]

For how many people in the Jewish mainstream does 'Israel' mean what it means for Netanyahu? It is hard to say. My impression is that a majority would accept the caveat that by 'Israel' they mean 'a Jewish state', but whether they are clear about what *this* means is another matter. For one thing, do they have an idea about who should count as 'Jewish'? (The State of Israel itself does not seem to be sure. Thus, among the immigrants from the former Soviet Union who were awarded citizenship as Jews, hundreds of thousands 'are considered non-Jewish' by Israel's rabbinic courts.[15] Yet these courts are 'an arm of the Israeli justice system'.[16]) For another, do they think (at one end of the spectrum of possibility) that 'a Jewish state' means a state whose public culture reflects the ethnic and religious identity of the majority of Israelis – who, as it happens, are Jewish? Or (at the other end) do they mean a state whose laws, institutions and official practices discriminate in favour of Jews? Furthermore, how many of them would distinguish the idea of 'a Jewish state' from Netanyahu's full-blown notion of Israel as 'the state of the Jewish People'? Or would they see this as a distinction without a difference? There would, I imagine, be a good deal of vagueness or uncertainty on this point; it might not be a point to which they have given any thought. But, if pressed, I suspect that a sizable number of Israel's Jewish 'supporters' would endorse the view that Israel is 'our state'. If *this* is what Israel is, then 'Israel' means 'the state of the Jewish people'; in which case, saying 'Israel has a right to exist' is not just saying that this state has a certain right; it is saying that a certain people has a right to this state. This is a rather different matter. And it brings us, I believe, closer to the heart of what is driving the demand that is under discussion in this chapter.

If this *is* what Israel is to the people who need us to say the obligatory words ('Israel has a right to exist'), then (to get back to an earlier point that I left dangling), they will hear us saying something else implicitly: they will hear us affirming the source of moral authority that *grounds* this right. Once again, it is not altogether clear what they take this to be; nor do they all necessarily give the same grounds. And yet, by and large, the various reasons given are variations on certain themes. Netanyahu, in his speech in June 2009, struck a familiar chord when he said: 'The right to establish our sovereign state here, in the Land of Israel, arises from one simple fact: Eretz Israel is the birthplace of the Jewish People.'[17] (This leaves the Palestinians where? According to Netanyahu, it places them 'in the heart of our Jewish Homeland'.) Treating Genesis as a historical document, he spoke of the 'connection of the Jewish People to the Land' going back 'more than 3,500 years' and referred to 'Judea and Samaria' as 'the places where our forefathers Abraham, Isaac and Jacob walked'.[18] This is hiding the divine light under a bushel: citing the Bible without invoking God. Begin was more direct: 'We were granted our right to exist by the God of our fathers, at the glimmer of the dawn of human civilization, nearly four thousand years ago.'[19]

Examples could be multiplied and there are other themes that could be exemplified. But, for the purposes of this chapter, it is beside the point to go further into the stock of arguments. The point is this: Suppose we would have complied with the advice we were given and had prefaced the IJV statement with the words 'Israel has a right to exist': given the way these words are likely to be heard by the audience for whom we would have been saying it, we would, in effect, have been signing on to a whole political ideology, the ideology of Jewish nationalism centred on Palestine. But we would not have known it in advance.

To put it another way: Declaring support for Israel's 'right to exist' is like signing a blank cheque, for it is a form of words, the content of which is intrinsically unclear. However, the likelihood is that the cheque will be cashed in favour of some version or other of a fully-fledged theory about the state: a theory that is not merely about its *existence* but its *essence*. It then becomes impossible to say, for example, 'I support Israel's right to exist but I propose that it redefine itself as "the state of the Israelis" rather than "the state of the Jews".' You cannot say this if 'belonging to the Jewish people' is written into the very concept of the state and if you have underwritten this concept – as you will have done, whether you meant to or not, in signing the blank cheque. Your proposal might be intended to secure the future of the state, but you will stand accused – by many 'supporters' of Israel – of seeking its 'destruction'. (Proposing, say, a bi-national state would put you further beyond the pale.) The precise meaning of 'Israel' determines what counts as 'exists', and therefore what satisfies its *'right* to exist'. Thus, if you fall in with the demand to proclaim Israel's 'right to exist', you may find yourself more restricted than you would like when you enter into a debate about the future. Furthermore, the continual focus on the *right* to its existence insinuates that Israel faces a continual *threat* to its existence – either from the Palestinians or from other states in the region. This tends to reinforce a whole outlook – 'us against the world' – and the militaristic approach that naturally accompanies it. It suggests that no other issue in the conflict matters as much as *this* does; that the conflict might come to an end if only the enemies of Israel would take their collective boot off Israel's throat; and that this constant 'existential threat' justifies every illegal act that Israel performs and every controversial policy that it adopts.

Take, for example, Operation Defensive Shield. In spring 2002, Israeli troops entered the West Bank in force. Television viewers and newspaper readers across the globe were assailed with scenes of devastation in Jenin, Ramallah and elsewhere. But, seen through the eyes of Ariel Sharon, it might have been the other way round: Palestinians laying waste to Tel Aviv or Ashdod – or the Warsaw ghetto. 'This is a battle for survival of the Jewish people', declared the man who was Israel's Prime Minister at the time, 'for survival of the state of Israel.'[20]

Survival. Existence. These words point, I believe, in the direction of what ultimately is driving the 'indispensable condition' – at least for many ordinary Jewish people who take part in the general debate in the public square. They are not cogs in the machine of the Israel lobby, told what to think by Zionist apparatchiks. They are drawing on something deeper than ideology: memory. And if there is one word tattooed into their memory it is this: 'existence'. A right to exist; a right to exist as Jewish; a right, as a Jew, to exist: this was denied for millions of people in Europe. It is an existential horror that occurred within the living memory of many Jews – and the collective memory of an untold multitude. This gives the theme of existence a 'specific gravity' that is transferred to Israel seen vaguely as 'the Jewish state'.

In this light, it is not surprising if the debate over Israel is peculiar in its focus on existence. And it is understandable if, asked to endorse its 'right to exist', people of goodwill instinctively say 'Yes' – even if this is misguided and they are giving the nod to a tissue of confusion.

FROM RHETORIC TO REALITY

Perhaps the deepest confusion of all in this entire debate is the failure to distinguish clearly between a state and an individual. I do not know whether, or in what sense, a sovereign state has 'a right to exist'. But, if it does, this right is neither inherent nor absolute. An individual, in contrast, does have an inherent, absolute right to exist; it is called 'a right to life' and, as I read the UN Declaration of Human Rights, it is grounded in 'the dignity and worth of the human person'.[21] The state *belongs* to 'human persons' but it is not itself a living, breathing human being. It is not endowed with dignity purely by virtue of being a state. And whatever worth it has is purely a function of how valuable it is to the people to whom it belongs. I long to hear the 'supporters' of Israel switch their emphasis from Israel's 'right to exist' to its 'duty of care': a duty it owes all its citizens equally – and to everyone under its sway.

Certainly, it would not be prudent for any state to ignore the aggressive language of another state, even if this turns out to be mere sabre-rattling. I am alluding to the hostile speeches of President Ahmadinejad of Iran. But prudence is not the same as paranoia; and reality is the realm of differences. If Israel cannot alter its posture of warrior, if the mentality of perpetual war where every border skirmish is a battle for the survival of the Jewish people persists, then the consequences will be as fatal for Israel as they are lethal for others. Israel's rhetoric of 'existence', which is part of its posture of warrior, puts its very existence at risk.

In order to secure its future, Israel does not need anyone – not Hamas, nor you nor I – to recognise its 'right to exist'. UN Security Council Resolution 242, passed shortly after the June war of 1967, speaks of 'a just and lasting peace' that is based, inter alia, on the principle that every state in the area has a 'right to live in peace within secure and recognized boundaries free from threats or acts of force'.[22] The same wording occurs again in 'Frameworks for Peace', signed jointly by Anwar Sadat and Menachem Begin at the Camp David Summit in 1978.[23] Similar language is used in the peace treaties between Israel and Jordan (1994).[24] In other words, *specific* rights are what states require in reality. The 'right to exist' either speaks for itself – or says nothing useful.

It is time to end this preoccupation – if not obsession – with Israel's 'right to exist'. Israel should be treated like any other country. It has the rights that (all other things being equal) every existing state possesses. But no state is exempt from challenges to its constitutional arrangements, whether those challenges are made by its citizens or by others. This extends to the question of whether the state should break up or, conversely, enter into a union with another state. These are perfectly legitimate and proper issues that people ought to be free to discuss, having an eye to what is best for every 'human person' affected by the question; for it is people that matter, not states, not in themselves. But it is impossible to conduct the kind of open discussion that is urgently needed for the sake of all inhabitants of the region if first – as a sine qua non – you have to say, 'Israel has a right to exist'.

I gave Abba Eban the first word in this essay. Let it be the last word too, subject to a friendly amendment. The people of Palestine and Israel, Jewish and non-Jewish alike, desperately need to work out a better future together: a state of affairs that enables them to co-exist and flourish. Nobody does them any service by proclaiming Israel's 'right to exist'.[25]

NOTES

1. Abba Eban, 'The Saudi Text', *New York Times*, 18 November 1981, http://www.nytimes.com/1981/11/18/opinion/the-saudi-text.html. Eban was responding to 'the Fahd Plan', put forward by Saudi Crown Prince Fahd ibn Abd al-Aziz, August 7 1981.
2. 'Statement to the Knesset by Prime Minster Begin upon the presentation of his government, 20 June 1977', available at the Israel Ministry of Foreign Affairs: http://www.mfa.gov.il/MFA/Foreign%20Relations/Israels%20Foreign%20Relations%20since%201947/1977-1979/1%20Statement%20to%20the%20%20Knesset%20by%20Prime%20Minister%20Begi.
3. Eban, 'Saudi Text'. There are now 192 states belonging to the United Nations.
4. Begin, 'Statement to the Knesset'.
5. This was the phrase used by UN Secretary General Kofi Annan when he read out the Quartet's statement ('Hamas rejects unfair aid demand', BBC News, 31 January 2006, http://news.bbc.co.uk/1/hi/world/middle_east/4664152.stm). The other two tests are: 'non-violence' and 'acceptance of previous agreements and obligations, including the roadmap'.
6. 'President Bush Remarks on Hamas Election Victory', 30 January 2006. Available at Jewish Virtual Library: http://www.jewishvirtuallibrary.org/jsource/US-Israel/bush20106.html.
7. 'Charter of the United Nations (1945)', in Malcolm D. Evans (ed.), *Blackstone's International Law Documents* (London: Blackstone Press, 2001), p.9.
8. Ibid., p.16.
9. Immanuel Kant, *Critique of Pure Reason* (Indianapolis: Hackett, 1996 [1787]), pp.582–3, A 598/B 626. Kant at this point is arguing for the impossibility of an ontological proof of the existence of God.
10. Article 2 (2): 'All members, in order to ensure to all of them the rights and benefits resulting from membership, shall fulfil in good faith the obligations assumed by them in accordance with the present Charter', 'Charter of the United Nations', in Evans (ed.), *Blackstone's International Law Documents*, p.9. I am grateful to Victor Kattan for his observations on this point.
11. James Crawford, *The Creation of States in International Law* (Oxford: Clarendon Press, 2006), p.4. Crawford's 870-page tome is the authoritative work on statehood.
12. The text of the IJV statement is available on the IJV website at http://jewishvoices.squarespace.com.
13. John V. Whitbeck, 'What "Israel's right to exist" means to Palestinians', *Christian Science Monitor*, 2 February 2007, http://www.csmonitor.com/2007/0202/p09s02-coop.html.
14. 'Full text of Netanyahu's foreign policy speech at Bar Ilan', *Haaretz*, 14 June 2009, http://www.haaretz.com/hasen/spages/1092810.html.
15. Anshel Pfeffer, 'This Conversion Row Could Hit Us All', *Jewish Chronicle*, 30 May 2008, p.27.
16. Gershom Gorenberg, 'How Do You Prove You're a Jew?', *New York Times* (Magazine), 2 March 2008, http://www.nytimes.com/2008/03/02/magazine/02jewishness-t.html.
17. 'Full text of Netanyahu's foreign policy speech'. 'Eretz Israel' means 'the Land of Israel'.
18. Ibid.
19. 'Statement to the Knesset'.
20. 'Sharon vows to fight on', BBC News, 10 April 2002, http://news.bbc.co.uk/1/hi/world/middle_east/1918861.stm.
21. 'Universal Declaration of Human Rights (1948), in P.R. Ghandhi, *Blackstone's International Human Rights Documents* (Oxford: Oxford University Press, 2002), p.22.
22. Walter Laqueur and Barry Rubin, *The Israel–Arab Reader: A Documentary History of the Middle East Conflict* (London: Penguin Books, 2001), p.116.
23. Ibid., p.223.
24. Ibid., p.478.
25. A version of this chapter appears (in German) in S. Deeg and H. Dierkes (eds), *Bedingungslos für Israel – nur bedingt für Menschen und Völkerrecht* (Cologne: Neuen ISP, 2010).

CHAPTER NINE

The State of Zionism

On 20 June 2006, at the thirty-fifth World Zionist Congress, Israel's Prime Minister Ehud Olmert welcomed the delegates – representatives of Jewish organizations from around the world – to 'Jerusalem, which is Zion, the beating heart, and the object of yearning and prayers of the Jewish people for generations'. Recalling the first congress, convened by Theodor Herzl in 1897, Olmert said: 'There is a straight line between Basel and Jerusalem, the line of political Zionism, whose aim was the return of the Jewish people to the stage of history as an independent and sovereign nation, which takes its fate into its own hands, in the Land of Israel, the heritage of our forefathers.'[1]

Herzl's seminal 1896 pamphlet *Der Judenstaat* ('The State of the Jews') was subtitled 'An Attempt at a Modern Solution of the Jewish Question'. The second indefinite article is misleading. Herzl wrote to Bismarck, 'I believe I have found the solution to the Jewish Question. Not *a* solution, but *the* solution, the only one.'[2] Decades later, Nazi Germany pursued its own 'only' solution to the Jewish Question: extermination. This gruesome project and its grisly success – the murder of roughly two-thirds of European Jews and the destruction of Jewish community life on much of the continent – propelled Herzl's proposal to the foreground of international affairs. Within three years of Hitler's defeat, the State of Israel was created. But has this settled the question?

Not according to Olmert. In his address to the World Zionist Congress, he declared that the question will not be resolved until 'every Jew in the world' comes to live in Israel and 'all the peoples of the region' accept Israel's 'right to exist as a Jewish state'. Since neither condition has yet been met, 'we must gather to discuss the "Jewish question" here at the thirty-fifth Zionist Congress as well'.[3]

Must we? Or must we, on the contrary, stop giving legitimacy to the question itself, which tends to insinuate that we Jews are a problem people, like a problem child? And even if the question was inescapable in Herzl's day, even if Europe forced it on Jews by alternately offering and withholding emancipation, and promoting or permitting antisemitism, is this the question that faces us – Jews and non-Jews – today? Or is it not Herzl's solution that is in question?

Every element in Olmert's address to the Zionist Congress is questionable, beginning with the slide from Zion, ancient religious and poetic heart of Jewish dispersion, to Zionism, modern political movement for the liberation of the Jewish people. Could it be that Zionism, whose aim was 'the return of the Jewish people to the stage of history', is caught in a time warp? Could Israel, in the grip of its founding ideology, be continually undermining itself, while millions of Jews have no choice but to be implicated in its policies? (Is this what is meant by a nation 'which takes its fate into its own hands'?) What, in short, if our 'liberation' has entrapped us?

Furthermore, contrary to Olmert, the line that leads from Basel to Jerusalem has been anything but straight. Since its birth more than a century ago, Zionism has veered from secular to religious and from left to right, with tangents that have not altogether disappeared. It has led to a fight against British imperial power, while it has resulted in the dispossession and dispersion of Palestine's indigenous Arab population. And the Jewish state created by the Zionist movement has become increasingly woven into the tangled web of western influence in the Middle East, with Israel now serving as a Mediterranean Fort Laramie in America's 'war on terror'.

Tragically, the same line has led from the walled ghettos of Europe to the West Bank barrier, separating Jews from the surrounding Arab population; and it has failed to secure Israel's integration into the region. Not that integration is entirely within Israel's control. No modern state could adapt sufficiently to satisfy the extreme demands of radical Shiite fundamentalism, and no prudent state could disregard the bellicose pronouncements of the Iranian President (and Holocaust denier) Mahmoud Ahmadinejad. Nonetheless, Israel's existence has been accepted, however grudgingly, by most of its neighbours. In March 2007 the Arab League reiterated its commitment to peace and normal relations if Israel withdraws from the land it has occupied since 1967 and agrees to both the creation of a Palestinian state and a 'just solution' for displaced Palestinians. Yet Israel has largely dismissed the Saudi peace initiative since its launch in 2002 and persists in behaviour that entrenches its isolation.

With the fortieth anniversary of the occupation this month (June 2007), Zionism, the official ideology of the Jewish state, is in crisis.[4] The crisis threatens the future of Israel as a 'normal' state, deepens the oppression of the Palestinians, fuels conflict in the region, feeds Muslim–Jewish tensions abroad and (as recent controversies in the US, UK and elsewhere demonstrate) rancorously divides Jew against Jew. For all these reasons, we need to understand the trajectory of this movement. Where did it begin? What has it become? Whither now?

MOVEMENT AND STATE

In the early days of Zionism, two different trends, cultural and political, jostled with each other, as Bernard Avishai reminds us in *The Tragedy of Zionism*, his magisterial retelling of the movement's development, now available in its second edition. In the first place, 'Zionist theories, institutions, and language ... were meant to advance a wide-spectrum revolution: against Rabbinic scholasticism, anti-Semitism, Yiddishkeit, softness.'[5] Like communism and other ideologies to which European Jews flocked, Zionism sought, for better or worse, to transform the whole character of Jewish life. In the second place, there was the aspiration for a homeland. But on the most basic constitutional question – to be or not to be a Jewish state – opinion was divided.

Thus, in the 1930s, the radical Labour Zionist party Ha'Shomer Ha'Tzair (The Young Guard) supported a bi-national state with Palestinian Arabs. Among other Zionists who shared this view was Judah Magnes, first chancellor of Hebrew University, and philosopher Martin Buber. Even David Ben-Gurion, the key figure in Labour Zionism, the man who was to become Israel's first Prime Minister, 'did not at first reject the idea'.[6]

With the creation of the State of Israel, proclaimed on 14 May 1948, the die was cast. But it was a crucially ambiguous moment: Was this the culmination of Zionism or its reinvention as a state? It turned out to be the latter. 'It would be wrong', says Avishai, 'to confuse Israel with the movement that produced it.'[7] Indeed, he describes Labour Zionism as 'a good revolution that long ago ran its course'; elsewhere he criticizes those who have 'missed how radically, and for the better, historic Zionism has changed Jewish culture'.[8] Be that as it may, this confusion between movement and state is precisely the 'tragedy' to which, as I read his book, his title refers.

The confusion goes both ways. On the one hand, the State of Israel is not just a state; it is the focal point of a movement. Any normal country should be a home for its citizens, enabling them to get on with their lives. But Israel is something more than this for many Jewish people around the world (and something less for millions of Palestinians who live within its extended borders): It is a transcendent ideal, 'the state of the Jews', an object of their unqualified love.

On the other hand, the movement turned into a state. Zionist concepts and principles were incorporated into national institutions, public policy and basic laws, notably the Law of Return, which allows any Jew in the world to 'make aliyah' and automatically become a citizen. This has driven a sharp wedge between Jewish and non-Jewish citizens, creating, according to Oren Yiftachel and others, an 'ethnocracy': a country that effectively belongs to one ethnic group.[9] Others describe Israel as an 'ethnic democracy'. For Palestinian citizens of the Jewish state, it comes to the same thing: They are second-class citizens, subject, as novelist David Grossman said at the Rabin memorial ceremony in Tel Aviv in November 2006, to a 'deeply ingrained institutionalized racism'.[10] Some steps have been taken in recent years to mitigate these inequalities. Nevertheless, Israel remains 'the state of the Jews'.

Because of this confusion (or fusion) between movement and state, Zionism was reinvigorated when, after the 1967 war, Israel suddenly found itself in control of new territories, the so-called Jewish heartland of biblical Judea and Samaria. The capture of these territories and the 'unification' of Jerusalem were understood as national restitution by many secular Zionists for whom the Bible is a national epic. And, as Avishai observes, many religious Jews, such as the leaders of Gush Emunim, 'young men with gleaming eyes', believed that 'the Promised Land was united and the Messiah was at hand'.[11] Within a short time, settlements were being established by religious Jews who viewed themselves as heirs of the original *chalutzim* – with a wink and a nod from Israel's Labour government. It was a turning point in the history of the movement and of the state.

I remember the period well. It was as if all of Jewry had linked arms and was dancing the hora together. (For a while I, too, was part of the joyful circle.) But this embrace between the religious and the secular was not merely a marriage of convenience. The bonds were more than skin-deep; they were inscribed in the flesh of the movement by the circumstances of its birth and by the language in which it told its own story.

DESPAIR AND HOPE

Zionism is a hope born of despair. Taking ethnic nationalism as its rubric, it is a child of its times. But fundamentally, it is the stepchild of antisemitism. As Jacqueline Rose observes in *The Question of Zion*, 'no discussion of Zionism can make sense' if it does not start here.[12] Only then can we begin to understand the hold that Zionism has over its adherents and its resistance to any whisper of self-doubt. As Rose writes: 'How do you begin to address ... the problem of a political identity whose strength in the world ... relies on its not being able, or willing, to question itself?[13] The title of her book (a homage to Edward Said's *The Question of Palestine*) can be heard as an elliptical expression of a wish: Would that Zionism could become a question! The question of Zion is a desideratum.

Rose's conundrum can be put this way: How do you address an identity when people fear they will fall apart without it? How do you ask them to be uncertain about something they affirm precisely because it relieves them of uncertainty: the predicaments and insecurities of existence as a Jew? 'We are a nation now, and there's an end to it!' says the collective voice. How do you get a hearing when this voice is so insistent and when you are unsettling an idea that was supposed to have settled the issue once and for all, an idea that is practically sacred: Israel, seen not merely as the 'solution' to 'the Jewish question' but (recall Olmert's opening words to the Zionist Congress) as the answer to a Jewish prayer?

I say 'prayer'. Call it, if you will, a hope; but when hope is conceived in the midst of despair, then it amounts to prayer, even if it is not addressed to heaven. It becomes, in Rose's phrase, 'a secular prayer'.[14] 'I am totally secular', said David Grossman in his Rabin memorial speech, 'and yet in my eyes the establishment and the very existence of the State of Israel is a miracle of sorts.'[15] A miracle (of sorts) in answer to a prayer (of sorts): The hold of Zionism, with Israel as its expression, is not intelligible unless it is seen in this light.

Zionism arose from disillusionment with European modernity, or, more precisely, with Europe as the site of the modern. (In a way, when Herzl spoke of a 'modern solution' what he meant was this: 'If we Jews cannot have Europe in Europe then we shall have it in another place.') The foundations for despair had been laid for centuries. But the sense of betrayal had become unbearably acute by the late nineteenth century, with the intensification of pogroms and the rise of anti-Jewish legislation in Eastern Europe, the formation of openly antisemitic political parties in western Europe, and the Dreyfus case in France. And none felt more betrayed than secular, assimilated Jews, such as Herzl.

On the face of it, the ambitions of early Zionism could hardly be more different from – even opposed to – the age-old messianic hope in Judaism for divine intervention. The 'wide-spectrum revolution' of which Avishai speaks was, by and large, aggressively secular. This implied not only rejection of religion in general but also a specific quarrel with Jewish particularism: the idea of the Jews as a people apart, quietly existing as *am hasefer*, patiently suffering until the coming of the Messiah in God's good time.

For this reason, as Yakov Rabkin explains in *A Threat From Within*, rabbis generally spurned the new movement.[16] (Some strands, especially among the Ultra-Orthodox, still do, as Rabkin meticulously documents: a useful reminder at a time when it almost seems as if Judaism has converted to Zionism.) It is true that, virtually from the outset, there was a small religious presence within the Zionist movement in the form of the Mizrachi Organization, and that Rabbi Abraham Kook, the spiritual ancestor of the post-1967 religious settlers, gave the movement his blessing. But the aim of the Zionist revolution was, in large part, to put an end to the old way of life; not just to create a new future for Jews but to craft a 'new Jew' for the future. The new Jews would not speak Yiddish, much less Arabic or Ladino, but Hebrew, a properly 'national' language, the language of the ancestors. Jews would be like other people; they would be normal. This sounds like a contradiction. But normalization was the hope that animated the mainstream of the Zionist movement.

However, as Rose perceptively points out, 'messianism colors Zionism, including secular Zionism, at every turn'.[17] This colouring affects its most basic vocabulary. 'Zion', in the Bible, initially the name of one of the hills of Jerusalem, refers poetically to the city itself and by extension to the whole of the Promised Land – indeed, it refers to the land *as promised* in the context of an eschatological narrative of return. Other ingredients in the messianic discourse – 'ingathering of the exiles', 'redemption of the land' – are part and parcel of the political lexicon of this movement-cum-state. The genius of Zionism is that it speaks the familiar language of tradition with a modern revolutionary accent. This makes its message ineluctably poetic: it constantly stirs the waters beneath the surface of its words, stirring up emotions that, in their ambiguity and volatility, unite left and right, religious and secular – even when, like *mishpochoh*, they are at each other's throats. In unison, all rise to sing the national anthem, the title of which, 'Hatikvah', means precisely 'the hope'.

In short, Zionism at heart is, as Rose writes, a 'collective passion', an authentic reaction (one among several) to antisemitism, one whose flexible language has enabled it to evolve after 1967 from secular left to religious right.[18] Its variety has not disappeared, nor are the differences between the various camps immaterial. But they are apt to merge with each other, or adapt to each other, as circumstances change and as passion dictates.

THE NATIONAL SCRIPT

Just as Zionist concepts and principles were translated into Israeli law and institutions, so its passion – its 'prayer' – persists in its national script, shaping national policy, systematically deforming Israel's dealings with the Palestinians and neighbouring Arab states. For who are the Palestinians – who are the Arabs? – in a worldview transplanted from an antisemitic Europe to a region that, for its own reasons, is hostile to the presence of a Jewish state? Certainly, as neighbours and enemies, the Arabs are real. But simultaneously they are demonic characters in a recurring nightmare: Cossacks on horseback attacking the shtetl, jackbooted Nazis enacting another *Kristallnacht*. It is difficult enough to make peace with flesh-and-blood enemies. But how do you negotiate with ghosts? How can a phantom be a partner for peace?

And what is Israel in this phantasmagorical landscape? Not merely a state at odds with its neighbours but the persecuted 'Jew among nations', as Alan Dershowitz and others argue.[19] The trouble with their argument is that the more it succeeds as a defence of Israel, the more it fails as a defence of Zionism; for if Israel is the old Jew writ large, an eternal victim of an eternal antisemitism, then the movement has failed its own test. Herzl's plan was not to export the so-called Jewish question from Europe to the Middle East but (as Olmert reminded the Zionist Congress) to 'solve' it.

There are, to be sure, critics of Israel who are motivated by hatred of Jews, just as there are Arab and Muslim opponents of the state who have embraced *The Protocols of the Elders of Zion* and Holocaust revisionism to underwrite their hostility. But, by and large, both the fate of the state and its reputation are more in its own hands than we are led to think by 'defenders' of Israel who, lovingly polishing its image as if this were its very being, cannot bear to hear that Israel is ever culpable. Not that they view the Jewish state as powerless in its own defence; on the contrary, the critical difference between the 'new' Jew and 'old' (as they see it) is that tough Israel does not go like a lamb to the slaughter. But nor (they insist) does it go like a slaughterer to the lamb; not even when the Israeli air force launches strikes against targets in densely populated civilian neighbourhoods in Gaza or invades Lebanon and lays waste to its infrastructure. In the dominant mindset that I am describing, Israel's hand is forced by hate-filled enemies and nothing it can do will assuage that hate.

Thus, paradoxically, the reliance that Israel places on power derives from its sense of powerlessness: the conviction that it is condemned to be hated, that every apparent thaw in its relations with its neighbours is a cunning Arab stratagem and that the Palestinians are simply waiting to throw the Jews into the sea. This, mutatis mutandis, is the same conviction about Europe that gave rise to Zionism in the first place. Sticking to its stock narrative of the Jewish past, this state-cum-movement is frozen in time on the shifting 'stage of history' (in Olmert's phrase)

In his recent account of the Arab–Israeli conflict, *Scars of War, Wounds of Peace*, former Israeli Foreign Minister Shlomo Ben-Ami observes: 'Israel could never really decide whether she was an intimidating regional superpower or just an isolated and frightened Jewish ghetto waiting for the next pogrom to happen.'[20] Deep down it is both: the 'old' Jew within the 'new', the implacable despair coiled like an incubus inside the Zionist hope.

Yet according to the national script, it is hope triumphant: The wandering Jews have come home, and the Citadel of David has fallen into their hands. In *Booking Passage*, a study of the 'poetics of exile and return' in the modern Jewish imagination, Sidra DeKoven Ezrahi locates Zionism on the mental map of a people who, for 2,000 years, have seen themselves as 'on the road', forever longing for Jerusalem.[21] What happens when spiritual longing is replaced by material fulfilment? What becomes of Zion, 'the beating heart' (Olmert) of the Jewish people, when it is possessed; when its status changes from poetic centre to capital city? Can its heart continue to beat? Or does it atrophy into a trophy that must not, at any cost, be surrendered? The Zion of the Psalms lies on the horizon, where heaven and earth appear to meet. 'When this poetic image denies its status as poetry', writes Ezrahi, 'it makes such claims on the political imagination that the "final status" of Jerusalem becomes non-negotiable.'[22]

If, in this triumphalist script, Arabs in general are the foil to the 'miracle' of Israel's birth, then the 1.4 million Israeli citizens who are Palestinian (about a fifth of the population) are the remnant within. They are 'insider outsiders', a phrase with historical resonance for Jews. (The four million Palestinians in the occupied territories and East Jerusalem, neither inside nor outside, are left in limbo.) Thus, the national script divides the Israeli people against itself. As do the symbols of state. Hundreds of thousands of Arab children in Israeli schools 'are expected to sing an anthem that ignores their very existence', as veteran peace activist Uri Avnery wrote after this year's Yom Ha'atzmaut.[23] There are many Israelis for whom 'Hatikvah' means despair.

Yet Palestinian citizens of Israel ('Israeli Arabs') are not just figments in another people's narrative. As Ezrahi points out, they are themselves 'narrating subjects' with a stake in the country they call home: Israel.[24] In an eloquent appeal for inclusiveness, she refers to 'the Arab voices that have begun to be heard'.[25] But when those voices call for Israel to become 'a state of all its citizens', they are liable to be heard as hostile to their own country.[26] Yuval Diskin, head of the Shin Bet security service, has reportedly gone so far as to describe Israeli Palestinians as a 'strategic threat' to the state.[27] And recent documents calling for recognition and equality, such as the 'Future Vision' report by the Committee of Arab Mayors in Israel, have largely fallen on ears deafened by fear.[28]

These documents are not the last word on how Israel should reconfigure itself. But the fear they inspire inhibits open debate. Au fond, it is Israel's fear of abandoning its script; fear of being a normal country, one that belongs to all its citizens; fear of equality, of an inclusive and open-ended society that evolves into something that is and is not Jewish. But if Israel cannot give up this fear, what hope is there for the future? A state that does not believe in its own possibility, except as a perpetual interloper at odds with its neighbours, has no future.

ENDING IN HEBRON

Nor does a people. The Jewish people (or Jewry or Jews in general or however we express the collective) does not have a future, or a future worth having, if it cannot believe in its own possibility except as the world's perpetual pariah. When such a state and such a people tie the knot so tightly that they become inseparable, then their predicaments are compounded. This, in a nutshell, is the crisis in Zionism today. In his welcoming speech to the thirty-fifth World Zionist Congress, Olmert affirmed 'the unification of the Jewish people with the State of Israel'.[29] This, the nub of Zionism, the core principle of the movement and its state, is also the heart of its crisis.

For forty years, Israel's occupation has dominated both the national agenda and the international perception of the state. In one way, this has been a distraction from the deeper question of self-definition and the national script. But ultimately it concentrates the mind for, as

Avishai argues, it is 'the persistence of Zionist principles – or at least over-simplified versions of them – which engendered the political climate in which the West Bank settlers took up their cause'.[30]

Zionism is not all of a piece. There are Zionists strongly opposed to the settlers and the occupation. And if the national script divides the Israeli people against itself, there is an antidote in an unexpected place: the Declaration of the Establishment of the State of Israel, where the principle of equality, like a shining light, burns a hole through the middle of the document. The text proclaims 'complete equality of social and political rights to all its inhabitants irrespective of religion, race or sex'.[31] If someone wants to say that this is what they mean by Zionism, they are welcome to the word; but it does not change the main trajectory of the idea. The fact is that the line that began in Basel has led to Hebron. The momentum of the movement has brought it to this pass; and, as I have seen for myself at first hand, that way lies madness.

Which way forward? I like to think that forty years from now, under the aegis of complete equality, Arab and Hebrew cultures (among others) will thrive and mingle together in the area currently called Israel and Palestine, whether there are two states or three states or one. It seems like a pipe dream. But a phrase of Herzl's comes to mind: *Wenn ihr vollt, Ist es kein Märchen.* 'If you will it, it is not a dream.'[32] His motto gives us hope that beyond the troubled state of Zionism, beyond 'the state of the Jews', there is a future.

NOTES

1. 'Israel Prime Minister Olmert Addresses 35th Zionist Congress', 20 June 2006. Available at Israel News Agency: http://www.israelnewsagency.com/zionistcongressisraelolmertaliya4848 0620.html.
2. From Herzl's *Diaries*, vol. 1, p.118, quoted in David Vital, *The Origins of Zionism* (Oxford: Oxford University Press, 1975), p.245.
3. 'Israel Prime Minister Olmert Addresses 35th Zionist Congress'.
4. This chapter is adapted from the review essay with the same title that appeared in *The Nation*, 18 June 2007. The theme of the issue was 'forty years of occupation'. The four books that were the subject of review are the ones by Avishai, Rose, Rabkin and Ezrahi discussed in the chapter.
5. Bernard Avishai, *The Tragedy of Zionism: How Its Revolutionary Past Haunts Israeli Democracy* (New York: Helios Press, 2002), pp.xv–xvi.
6. Ibid., p.118.
7. Ibid., p.xxvii.
8. Ibid., p.xxviii; Bernard Avishai, 'Saving Israel From Itself', *Harper's Magazine* 310, 1856 (January 2005), p.34.
9. Oren Yiftachel, *Ethnocracy: Land and Identity Politics in Israel/Palestine* (Philadelphia, PA: University of Pennsylvania Press, 2006), passim.
10. 'David Grossman's speech at the Rabin memorial', *Haaretz*, 6 November 2006, http://www.haaretz.com/hasen/spages/784034.html.

11. Avishai, *Tragedy of Zionism*, pp.287, 278.
12. Jacqueline Rose, *The Question of Zion* (Princeton, NJ: Princeton University Press, 2005, p.115.
13. Ibid., p.152.
14. Ibid., p.55.
15. 'David Grossman's speech at the Rabin memorial'.
16. Yakov Rabkin, *A Threat From Within: A Century of Jewish Opposition to Zionism* (London: Zed Books, 2006), p.20.
17. Rose, *Question of Zion*, p.28.
18. Ibid., p.17.
19. Alan Dershowitz, *The Case for Israel* (Hoboken, NJ: Wiley, 2003), p.222.
20. Shlomo Ben-Ami, *Scars of War, Wounds of Peace* (London: Weidenfeld & Nicolson, 2005), p.330.
21. Sidra DeKoven Ezrahi, *Booking Passage: Exile and Homecoming in the Modern Jewish Imagination* (Berkeley, CA: University of California Press, 2000), pp.8, 3.
22. Ibid., p.238.
23. Uri Avnery, 'A Hope not Lost', 28 April 2007, available at Gush Shalom: http://zope.gush-shalom.org/home/en/channels/avnery/1177848858.
24. Ezrahi, *Booking Passage*, p.23.
25. Ibid.
26. Azmi Bishara (leader of the Balad Party and a former member of the Knesset), claims that this is why he has been accused of 'aiding the enemy': see Azmi Bishara, 'Why Israel Is After Me', *Los Angeles Times*, 3 May 2007, http://www.latimes.com/news/opinion/commentary/la-oe-bishara3may03,0,5123721.story.
27. Yoav Stern, 'PMO to Balad: We will thwart anti-Israel activity even if legal', *Ha'aretz*, 17 March 2007, http://www.haaretz.com/hasen/spages/838660.html.
28. Isabel Kershner, 'Noted Arab Citizens Call on Israel to Shed Jewish Identity', *New York Times*, 8 February 2007. http://www.nytimes.com/2007/02/08/world/africa/08iht-web.0208 israel.4516756.html.
29. 'Israel Prime Minister Olmert Addresses 35th Zionist Congress'.
30. Avishai, *Tragedy of Zionism*, p.xix.
31. 'Declaration of the Establishment of the State of Israel (May 14, 1948)', in G.S. Mahler and A.R.W. Mahler (eds), *The Arab–Israeli Conflict: An Introduction and Documentary Reader* (Abingdon: Routledge, 2010), p.107.
32. Motto of Herzl's *Altneuland*. Quoted and translated in Ezrahi, *Booking Passage*, p.3.

CHAPTER TEN

A Time to Move On

THE CONVENTIONAL DOCTRINE

There is a view about the relationship between Jews in general and Israel, 'the Jewish state', that I shall call 'the conventional doctrine'. It is a blend of political and cultural Zionism and can be summed up this way: *Jews, whoever they are and wherever they live, constitute a single nation – the Jewish people – and Israel is the state that both belongs to this nation and is the centre of its collective life. Thus, those Jews who do not live in Israel inhabit the periphery of Jewish national life.* This is simultaneously a doctrine about identity and status: it asserts that Jewish identity and Israeli identity are each at the heart of the other and that the status of 'the diaspora' is lower than that of the State of Israel. (The term for Jewish immigration to Israel, aliyah, means 'ascent', as though the state were not only the centre but also the summit.)

A personal anecdote illustrates how deeply the conventional doctrine has penetrated into Judaism. In February 2005 I had occasion to visit the London Beth Din, the court of the Chief Rabbi. As I entered the building, my eye was caught by a framed poster on the wall that included a list of the six core 'values' of the United Synagogue, the largest organization of Orthodox synagogues in the UK. Five items on the list were values that would have been familiar (in some shape or form) to Jews anywhere and at any time in history: 'spiritual growth and practice', 'lifelong Jewish learning', and so on. But the sixth stood out as something new: 'the centrality of Israel in Jewish life' – as if this were on the same level as the other five values. Moreover, the United Synagogue evidently saw no tension between *this* item and the *first* on the list: 'the welcoming of every Jew' into the synagogal community – as if necessarily every Jew puts the State of Israel at the centre of Jewish life.

But there is no necessity about it. A report published in January 2008 by the Jewish People Policy Planning Institute notes that 'the notion of the Jewish people comprised of Jewish communities around the world with a core state in Israel is one which shows signs of weakening'. (This statement is featured on the cover of the report, reflecting the degree of seriousness that the authors attach to it.[1]) Research in the US suggests that, with each successive generation, fewer American Jews see Israel as pivotal to their lives.[2] 'Young Jewish Adults in the United States Today', a report produced by the American Jewish Committee in 2006, noted: 'There is a consensus among several studies that Israel is not central to young people's Jewish identity.' The authors remark that 'the distancing from Israel by young Jews ... is a serious concern'.[3] Certainly it is something to be taken seriously; but why exactly is it a concern? The answer, of course, is that this development flies in the face of 'the conventional doctrine', the view that, despite the evidence that I have just cited, continues to maintain a tenacious hold in much of the Jewish world.

It might be conventional to hold this view today but it has not had much traction until relatively recently in Jewish history. Two questions arise: Why is it so *hard* for us Jews to confront this doctrine? And do we really *need* to confront it? I shall look briefly at each question in turn.

It is hard to confront because it puts into question a set of arrangements that were intended to be a solution, 'a Modern Solution to the Jewish Question', to quote from the subtitle of Theodor Herzl's seminal 1896 pamphlet *Der Judenstaat* (published in English as *The Jewish State* but better translated as 'The State of the Jews'). The question to which Herzl believed he had found the solution was not academic; he was not Einstein formulating an equation in physics or Wittgenstein propounding a proposition. It was a question posed by the salience of European antisemitism; or so he understood it. As the twentieth century swept on, like a river in flood, there appeared to many Jews to be only two solutions to this question: either Herzl's or Hitler's, either life or death. And Jews, ever obedient to Moses, 'choose life' (Deut. 30:19).

To understand the hold of 'the conventional doctrine' we need to remember that it was in the midst of this existential drama that the State of Israel came into being. Following a catastrophe on an unprecedented scale in Jewish experience – the murder of roughly two-thirds of the Jews of Europe and the wholesale destruction of Jewish community life on much of the continent – the creation of Israel represented more than just a refuge or safe haven. It was, fundamentally, the creation of a new Jewish identity, one that was meant to revive Jewish life and secure the Jewish future. Small wonder that it is so hard for us to confront the relationship between Jews and Israel!

Yet, confront it we must, for this is 2008, not 1948, and yesterday's solutions were not designed for today's needs.[4] Nor can we brush away the problems to which those solutions, in turn, gave rise. It is time to move on. But when people are in the grip of an idea, they *cannot* move on: they stand in their own way. Where to begin? Rabbi Tarfon's words in the Mishna come to mind: 'The day is short, the task is great.' He observes, 'You are not obliged to complete the task, but neither are you free to give it up.'[5] In the spirit of this admonition, I shall try to make a small start on what I see as a massive collective task: disentangling concepts and identities whose confusions sustain 'the conventional doctrine'.

A PEOPLE OF TIME

A cryptic remark by the Israeli author David Grossman in a conversation with Amos Oz in 2003 seems a promising place to begin: 'We have been unable to decide: Are we a people of place or of time?'[6] While I cannot quite grasp what the question means, somehow it seems to go to the heart of the matter. This makes it a question in the finest tradition of mind-bending Jewish conundrums. For a Jewish philosopher, this is doubly irresistible. I shall try à la Socrates to follow dialectically in the footsteps of Grossman's remark to see where it leads.[7]

Like all such questions, Grossman's question begets another question: Who does he mean by 'We'? He appears to mean Jews in general and to assume that 'we' are a people. We (you and I) shall need to revisit this assumption later. But, for the sake of argument, let us go along with his question, the gist of which is this: In what *sense* are we, the Jews, a people: is it 'of place' or 'of time'? Here is his response to his own question: 'In the Diaspora we decided we were a people of time. An eternal people.' When he says 'we decided' he cannot mean that a plebiscite was held among the Jews scattered across the face of the earth. He must be referring to the traditional self-understanding of Judaism over nearly 2,000 years: that the Jewish people will remain in exile until the coming of the Messiah at the end of days. Until then, wherever we are, we are a people without a place; that is to say, the place where we truly belong lies always in the future.

That this *is* what he means is confirmed by what he goes on to say: 'Take note of the name: the Promised Land. That's a grammatical form that continues into infinity. It's not the land of promise or the land that was promised, it's the land that is eternally promised. It's a land that one never reaches.' But if it is a land that one never reaches, how come we got there – as he seems to say we did? For he also says: 'But even after we came to this place, we were still unable to crystallize for ourselves a feeling of identity as a people of place.' *Who* came to *which* place? *Jews* came to *Palestine*; that is to say, Jewish people did. They came to the territory on which the State of Israel was created. This might be the *site* of the Promised Land but, as Grossman implies, to say that Jewish people came to 'this place' is not the same as saying that *the* Jewish people reached the Promised Land; as a 'people of time' they could not and therefore did not.

The point is not that the Promised Land is metaphorical or imaginary, a Never Never Land or Shangri-La. The land in question (the Land of Israel or Palestine) exists. It is tangible. You can find it on a globe or in an atlas. It is part of the physical geography of planet Earth; and as such it *can* be reached and *has* been reached, by non-Jews and Jews alike, for countless years. The point, rather, is the peculiar place that place occupies for the Jewish people as a 'people of time'. For such a people, a people that sees itself in an enduring state of exile, the land can be reached only *as land*; as *holy* land perhaps, but not as the fulfilment of an eternal promise. From the point of view of this people (the Jewish people of old), exile is exile, wherever you live on the face of the earth, be it Timbuktu or Tel Aviv, Harrow-on-the-Hill or Jerusalem – until the end of days.

To repeat: Grossman says that 'even after we came to this place, we were still unable to crystallize for ourselves a feeling of identity as a people of place'. But, ex hypothesi, a feeling of identity as 'a people of place' is not an option for a 'people of time'. It was, however, a possibility for those of his compatriots who came as Jews to Palestine (later Israel) and who sought to claim the land as their place. *This* 'we' is an assortment of individuals with an array of ethnicities and a variety of attitudes towards Judaism. It includes religious Jews, secular Jews, atheist Jews, Jews who sought to leave their Jewish identities behind and so on. It is not the 'we' of the 'people of time'. Grossman slides from the one 'we' to the other. His undifferentiated 'we' straddles a difference that is not merely numerical but categorical: the *logical* difference between a bunch of Jews and the Jewish people.

But my point is not that Grossman equivocates. My point is that neither he nor we – his readers – *notice* this equivocation unless we stop and think and compel ourselves to analyze what he says. Why is this? Why is his elision so elusive? It is because it is so familiar. It is much the same blurring or fusing of identities that is expressed in 'the conventional doctrine' about the relationship between Jews in general and the State of Israel, a doctrine that solders all varieties of Jewish identity into one big – national – 'we'.

THE SENSES OF DIASPORA

This soldering is accomplished via the subtle alchemy of words. For, while Zionism talks the talk of a 'return to history', it speaks the language of 'the end of days'. Key words and phrases in its vocabulary bespeak the frame of eternal reference of the 'people of time', the Jewish people of old; except that the new frame is the now – the here and now of the State of Israel. This spices up the content of the ideology for many Jews (as well as Christians of a certain millenarian stripe). After so long in limbo, waiting and waiting for the Day of the Lord, who can resist the carrot of instant gratification that the rhetoric of Zionism dangles?

A key term in this rhetoric is 'diaspora'; it is also a prime example of the confusion that this rhetoric engenders and a mainstay of 'the conventional doctrine'.[8] In the modern sense, the word 'diaspora' means the dispersion of any people from their native country. The Irish, for example, have a diaspora, as do the Italians and the Palestinians. So does Israel: at least 350,000 Israelis living in the New York area, for example, are part of it.[9] But I (a British Jew or Jewish Brit), for example, am not.

But am I not part of the *Jewish* diaspora? Here is where the picture gets complicated. The term 'diaspora' goes back to the Septuagint (the Greek version of the Hebrew bible that was produced two or three hundred years before the Romans crushed the Judeans in the first century CE). Within Judaism, it acquires the meaning of exile; not just physical banishment but alienation, as it were, from God's favour. In *this* sense, the condition of diaspora is constitutive of the Jewish moral universe. Life in the here and now, on the traditional Jewish under-standing, is suspended between alienation and redemption, exile and return. So (still speaking in the first person singular), insofar as I identify as a Jew *this way*, then, yes, I understand my existence as diasporic. (Not that you have to be religious exactly to see yourself this way; it is available to anyone who, drawing from the well of Jewish culture, either adopts or adapts this orientation to life.) It's just that (with the greatest of respect) this is not a state of exile from which the government of Israel can rescue me.

Leaving me aside, there are Jews who live outside the State of

Israel who do not have a diasporic sensibility or outlook: they are neither part of the *Israeli* diaspora nor (in their own eyes at least) are they part of the *Jewish* diaspora. They might or might not see themselves as part of the Jewish people; and there are different ways in which a group can be thought of as a people, or think of themselves as a people; or see themselves as Jews. This diversity of possibilities goes to the heart of the quarrel that some of us, as Jews, have with 'the conventional doctrine': it is like a straitjacket that restricts the Jewish spirit, or a uniform that you are required to don if you are to count – fully – as a Jew.

Taken to an extreme (though an extreme that was a norm in classical Zionism), 'the conventional doctrine' leads to the view that you cannot count – fully – as a Jew unless you live in Israel. The Israeli novelist A.B. Yehoshua told an American Jewish audience in 2006 that *their* Jewish identity, unlike *his* as an Israeli, was incomplete. Speaking to the *Jerusalem Post*, he said: 'It seems to me obvious that our Jewish life in Israel is more total than anywhere outside Israel.'[10] What chutzpah! What chauvinism! But above all, what dogmatism! And how completely false to the actual picture in the wider world!

UNTYING THE GORDIAN KNOT

The insistence that the State of Israel must be the centre of Jewish life, or the idea that 'every Jew in the world' should 'make aliyah' (as Israeli Prime Minister Ehud Olmert reiterated at the Thirty-Fifth World Zionist Congress in June 2006), or that Jews are self-hating if they do not show 'solidarity' with Israel, or that Jewish identity in 'the diaspora' is incomplete, all of which is contained in 'the conventional doctrine', prevents a normal conception of life, as a Jew, outside Israel.[11] So does the fear-filled belief that Israel exists to protect Jews everywhere. We certainly do not need the kind of 'protection' given by Olmert when he gave a video address to an American audience during the 2006 conflict with Lebanon. 'This is a war', he said, 'which is fought by all the Israelis.' A slight pause for dramatic effect, then he continued: 'I believe that this is a war that is fought by all the Jews.'[12] Think about this claim: he said that he *believed* it. What would lead him to believe such a thing? Not, I suggest, empirical evidence. It is an article of faith, an a priori conviction, a corollary of the axiom that Israel represents Jewry as a whole. On this basis he, the Prime Minister of Israel, implicated Jews around the globe in a military campaign that (rightly) inflamed the opinion of millions of people. Tarring all Jews with the brush of Israel's controversial foreign policy does not promote our general well-being. (As our grandparents might have said, 'It's not good for the Jews.')

By the same token, Israel is hamstrung by its self-definition as *der Judenstaat*, the state of the Jews. It needs to become the state of the Israelis. Here in England it might savour of chauvinism to cry 'England for the English' or 'Britain for the British'. But 'Israel for the Israelis' would be a liberating slogan for a country unable to settle down to the task of making its home in the region that it inhabits. Israel needs to shed the burden of Jewish fears and hopes that led to its creation and become its own state pursuing its own good for its own people, all of them equally, non-Jew and Jew alike; just like a normal country. Only on this basis can it make peace, not only with its neighbours and with the Palestinians but with its (plural) self.

A normal conception of life. A normal country. Such poignant phrases! Zionism was a movement that sought to normalize life for Jews in a world (or Europe) where, time and again, their status or their treatment was, at best, peculiar and frequently worse. Now it stands in the way of achieving its own goal. Like any successful ideology, it tends to cling with unyielding tenacity to the minds and hearts that it conquers. But, like other ideologies that burst into existence in the strident and strife-torn twentieth century, it might yet turn out to be ephemeral. Judaism, like the vault of the heavens, is as vast as it is ancient, whereas Zionism is a Yonni-come-lately. Jews, one way and another, have been around for millennia – long before Jewish nationalism emerged as a Big Idea. You cannot be on this planet for such a length of time, nor wander on its surface so far and wide, without seeing every Big Idea – including your ideas of yourself – subverted. You could almost say that in Judaism, funnily enough, nothing is sacred – nothing on earth, nothing finite, no object or idea. Setting up something finite as infinite: what is this if not the essence of idolatry? And what is Judaism if not the overturning of idols, especially one's own, be they sticks or stones, statues or states? (Perhaps this is why self-mockery is a staple of Jewish humour.)

In short, Zionism – the nationalization of Jewish identity – has had its day. It is time to do the Jewish thing and move on. Not that it is a simple matter to dismantle a view as entrenched as 'the conventional doctrine'. If Jewry and the State of Israel are central to each other's identity, then the one keeps leading into the other. It seems seamless. How do you pry apart a Gordian knot, a knot that has no ends? Not easily. But a people, in time, might just do (or undo) it, if they are willing to acknowledge the places where the thread is fraying thin.

Sensible, hard-headed readers will react impatiently to this chapter. They will see an unworldly philosopher sunk in his armchair, splitting hairs about the meaning of words. In my defence I call upon Moses who, as we all know, was pre-eminent among prophets, but who also invented philosophy while he was on Mount Sinai, a fact that is less well known. Why do I call Moses a philosopher? Because for long periods – forty days and forty nights at a stretch – he had his head in the clouds. He was the original Wondering Jew. With a philosopher leading them, is it surprising that the Children of Israel got lost on their journey to the Promised Land? They – we – are still searching.

NOTES

1. The Jewish People Policy Planning Institute (JPPPI), 'Annual Assessment 2007', p.7. The JPPPI is a Jerusalem think tank established by the Jewish Agency for Israel. Its mission is 'to help assure a thriving future for the Jewish people and Judaism with Israel as their core state': see the 'Mission Statement' page on JPPPI's website: http://www.jpppi.org.il/.
2. Anthony Weiss, 'Attachment to Israel Declining Among Young American Jews', *Forward*, 5 September 2007, http://www.forward.com/articles/11550/.
3. Jacob B. Ukeles et al., *Young Jewish Adults in the United States Today* (New York: American Jewish Committee, 2006), pp.34, 92.
4. This chapter is adapted from the essay with the same title that appeared in Anne Karpf, Brian Klug, Jacqueline Rose and Barbara Rosenbaum (eds), *A Time to Speak Out: Independent Jewish Voices on Israel, Zionism and Jewish Identity* (London: Verso, 2008), pp.286–96.
5. Bab. Tal., *Avot* 2: 20–1.
6. 'Elective Affinities/Reality Bites' (conversation between David Grossman and Amos Oz), *Ha'aretz*, 10 January 2003, available at the Jewish Agency for Israel: http://www.jewisha gency.org/JewishAgency/English/Jewish + Education/Compelling + Content/Eye + on + Israel/Current + Issues/Society + and + Politics/Elections2003/Elective + Affinities.htm.
7. The earliest version of the argument in this section formed the basis of a talk to the Oberlin Zionists, Oberlin College, Ohio, in December 2003. I am grateful to Jacqueline Shields (now Turk), president of the society at the time, for the invitation.
8. For the discussion of some other terms in the language of Zionism, see Chapter 7, 'The Climate of Debate about Israel in the Jewish World', and Chapter 9, 'The State of Zionism'.
9. 'Growing Israeli Diaspora', *Jewish Chronicle*, 24 February 2006, p.15.
10. Nathan Guttman, 'A.B. Yehoshua Sparks Uproar in US', *Jerusalem Post*, 4 May 2006, http://www.jpost.com/servlet/Satellite?cid=1145961275054&pagename=JPArticle%2FSho wFull.
11. 'Israel Prime Minister Olmert Addresses 35th Zionist Congress', 20 June 2006. Available at Israel News Agency: http://www.israelnewsagency.com/zionistcongressisraelolmertaliya48480 620.html.
12. Video recording available at Ynetnews website: http://www.ynetnews.com/articles/0,7340,L-3287851,00.html. For transcript, see 'Video Speech to the United Jewish Communities By PM Olmert', 7 August 2006. Available at Prime Minister's Office: http://www.pmo.gov.il/ PMOEng/Archive/Speeches/2006/08/speechujc070806.htm.

CHAPTER ELEVEN

Next Year in Hackney

Revised version of a talk given at Hackney Limmud, September 2008.

THE SPEAKER'S REMARK

During the discussion at a recent seminar in London organized by the Institute for Jewish Policy Research (JPR), one of the speakers, an eminent scholar at a prominent centre for Jewish Studies in the US, dropped a thought that caught my ear and drilled itself into my consciousness. He said: 'The destiny of the Jewish people is that it has left Europe. It has left for two dispensations: sovereignty in Israel and pluralism in America.'[1] It is a striking remark: elegant, succinct, clear, assured, decisive and profoundly misconceived.

I shall give a brisk critique of the speaker's remark, a brief portrait of British Jewry today, and a rough sketch of a possible model for the future.[2] I emphasize 'brisk', 'brief', and 'rough'. It will be said that I paint in brushstrokes too broad, make generalizations that are too hasty, and leave gaps in the argument large enough for a full-grown camel to fall through with room to spare; all of which is true. I wish I could be as pithy as the speaker at the London seminar but I shall have to settle for being bitty. My aim is limited to one thing: to spark your imagination. For we need to be able to imagine a future that attracts us; and I, for one, am not captivated by the prospect contained in the speaker's remark.

My title alludes to the phrase 'Next year in Jerusalem', the wish or prayer contained in the Haggadah, recited towards the end of the Seder, after the repast, having just downed the final cup of wine, which ought to be drunk leaning to the left (though by this point in the proceedings, if you have been diligent in your observance of the law, you will have quaffed three previous cups and be leaning in every direction), and which sometimes is sung to a tune with an upbeat tempo. Such is the state of the celebrants at this juncture that they might be feeling upbeat regardless of whether they know what they are saying. But what are they saying? What do we mean by 'Next year in

Jerusalem?' Do we mean what we say? My title is not meant to imply that Jerusalem was builded here in Norf London's green and pleasant land. Hackney happens to be where I live. But if your home is elsewhere, feel free to substitute your address. 'Hackney', as I am using the name, stands for 'here', and 'here' is wherever you are – and plan on being next year. In short, I wish to point a direction for the Jewish future, pointing not to one or two places on the planet but everywhere (every here).

That said, if my father were alive he would find it odd to think of Hackney in the future tense. For him, Hackney was decidedly last year, not next. He was born in the East End and grew up in this area, as did my mother. Both my parents went to Newington Green School. My father's family belonged to the United Synagogue congregation in Poet's Road, while my mother's went to the (very *frum*) Addas shul in Burma Road. But, like many other Jewish families, they left Hackney behind them and migrated across London in a north-westerly direction. My sibs and I grew up in Finchley and Hendon. Hackney, to us, although not many miles distant, was practically a mythical place, a place that existed only in our parents' reminiscences, and Clissold Park, where they played when they were young, sounded like a children's *Gan Aden*. But after Reva and I moved here a few years ago, Hackney became real to me – like the earthly city of Jerusalem.

Let us examine the speaker's remark, looking at each element in turn. To begin with, Jews, as a matter of fact, have not abandoned Europe: around two million are alive and well and inhabiting over forty European states.[3] There is reason to think that, far from heading en masse for the exit doors marked 'America' and 'Israel', they are, by and large, at home in Europe and that Jewish life is flourishing again on the continent. Certainly it is in Britain. The title of a magazine founded in 2001, *Jewish Renaissance*, captures this quality of renewal. So does the headline of an article in the *Jerusalem Post* earlier this year: 'Jewish Life in Britain is Thriving'. Written by Henry Grunwald, President of the Board of Deputies of British Jews, the article describes how 'Jewish life in the UK is teeming with vibrant educational and cultural activity, robust political involvement and demonstrable pride in Jewish identity'.[4] Henry and I were at university together as undergraduates and, now as then, are often on opposite sides of the political fence. But on this point we are shoulder to shoulder.[5] And, while conditions vary from state to state, it appears that the UK is not untypical. 'The revival of European Jewry over the last 20 to 25 years', explained the Policy Briefing for the selfsame seminar at which the speaker made his remark, 'is one of a number of remarkable developments in Jewish history since the Holocaust.' In part, this revival is religious, but it is also much broader. 'It's more accurately a cultural revival encompassing informal Jewish education, day-schools, the revival and renewal of Jewish music, Jewish film festivals, Jewish book festivals and fairs, theatre, art, crafts, genealogy, publishing, heritage travel, and much more besides.'[6] 'The destiny of the Jewish people is that it has left Europe', proclaimed the speaker. As a European Jew, I am reminded of what Mark Twain supposedly said when he heard the news of his own demise: 'The reports of my death have been greatly exaggerated.'[7]

Moreover, migration is a two-way street. If in one direction Jews are leaving Europe, they are returning in the opposite. In a recent essay in the *Jewish Chronicle*, David Shneer, Director of the Program in Jewish Studies at the University of Colorado at Boulder, points out that 'as Europe becomes a vibrant social and economic home for global Jewry, some Israelis are even reclaiming old European identities and moving to places such as Berlin and London'.[8] In his book *New Jews*, co-authored with Caryn Aviv, we come across this little nugget of information: 'In 2003, the year of the most recent migration statistics, more Jews moved *to* Moscow *from* Israel than vice versa.'[9] The vagaries of mere facts can play cruel havoc with our grand theories of 'destiny'.

Furthermore, the idea of an entire people with a single destiny, something into which all Jews can be folded, a unity that moves out of one continent into another, savours of reification, as though the Jewish people were one big blob. Perhaps this is making too much of what is just a manner of speaking. But I am on safer ground when I say that the speaker was thinking of Jews as constituting, like, say, the Basques or Kurds, an ethno-national group. Whether either term ('ethnic' or 'national') applies to Jewry, however, is a moot point. For one thing, whatever my cousins in Stanmore have in common with the Falashas of Ethiopia, ethnicity is not it. For another, many Jews do not conceive of their Jewishness in national terms at all. For some, it is a purely cultural identity. For others, the phrase 'the Jewish people' is a collective noun with only a vague collective subject: a name that loosely denotes Jews in general, synonymous, perhaps, with 'Jewry'. Besides, nationhood can mean different things. For many Jews, Jewish nationhood or peoplehood is sui generis; it is neither an anthropological category nor a political one but, so to speak, Jewish, a product of Judaism itself, a take on 'the people of God' in the Torah: a people bound together by commitment to a covenant. By any account, we are a strange lot; but on this – common and even core – interpretation, Jews are not so much a peculiar people as a people in a peculiar sense.

For these reasons, the idea of the Jewish *people* exercising *sovereignty* is intrinsically problematic. In the specific case of Israel, it is doubly so in the light of the fact that there are secular Israelis 'who do not identify as Jews but see themselves as Israelis'.[10] A 2007 report by the Van Leer Jerusalem Institute cites a poll of Israeli opinion in which only 48 per cent of respondents said that they feel they 'belong to the Jewish people at large'.[11] (The context makes it clear that they were all ostensibly 'Israeli Jews'.) Bearing in mind that you don't have to be Jewish to be Israeli, and that at least 20 per cent of the citizens of Israel are *not* Jewish, the idea is still less tenable. You *could* say that in Israel Jews (or Jewish people but not *the* Jewish people) enjoy the dispensation of being in the *majority*. But sovereignty is another matter. If democracy is the will of the people, and if Israel is a democratic state, then it seems to follow that sovereignty is vested in the *Israeli* – not the *Jewish* – people.

As for pluralism, it is certainly a dispensation that Jews have encountered in America and one in which, on the whole, they have prospered. But first, pluralism is not singular: different societies are plural in different ways. (Israel itself is, in its own way, a superb example of a rainbow society – and would be even if its entire population were Jewish.) Second, the implied contrast with Europe is false. It suggests a stereotypical view of Europe as a continent of ethnic nationalisms and monocultural societies where Jews live on sufferance, their rights like straws in the wind. But in the new Europe, the one that began to emerge from the ashes of the Second World War and which, despite setbacks from time to time, continues to grow both in strength and extent, pluralism, though not on American lines, is of the essence. Moreover, Jews have been prominent in promoting a pluralist vision of the new Europe. Steven Beller observes, 'Many of the champions of liberal pluralism in post-war Europe were, not coincidentally, Jewish ... It is also the case that many of the more enthusiastic proponents of the EU have been Jews.' Why 'not coincidentally'? Because a pluralist Europe is 'definitely good for the Jews'.[12] Which brings us back to where we began, for it might help explain why, in point of fact, Jews are *not* leaving in droves and heading for the exit doors marked 'Israel' and 'America'.

Despite all this, many Jews today will be drawn to the speaker's remark. Resonating to its mythological form, they hear a recognizable tale in which the biblical people, like the patriarch Abraham, journeys from one site to another in the wilderness in search of the best encampment. Vaguely or otherwise they recollect the verse 'A wandering Aramean was my father' (Deut. 26:5). And have not the Jews moved on from place to place, from continent to continent, in the course of more than 2,000 years? Thus, the story told by the speaker rings a bell; it has the *sound* of authenticity to Jewish ears that are primed – by education and culture – to hear it.

In addition, to *American* ears, a story about Europe as the place of the past, the place left behind, has the ring of truth; it is an integral part of a founding myth about America and its role in the 'destiny' of the human race. Nor would it be surprising if the speaker's remark were to appeal to Israeli and American Jews, since it affirms their position as the two Jewish populations that are (currently) the largest on the planet. But perhaps the most receptive audience comprises all those Jews, wherever they live, who subscribe to a certain post-Holocaust doctrine: that the State of Israel is the home of the Jewish people and that Europe is its graveyard.

To sum up: the striking remark made by the speaker at the London seminar is false, incoherent, probably complacent and certainly mythological in form. And if it appeals to some Jewish people, for others – particularly those of us who are working out our destiny as Jews in the European so-called graveyard – the view of the future that it contains is precisely an *impediment* to the future. We need an alternative view of Jewry; otherwise we shall not be able to contemplate our future without burying it in advance. For, if it were true that the destiny of the Jewish people is that it has left Europe, where would that leave *us*?

A PORTRAIT OF THE PRESENT

A good place to start is by examining the facts on the ground to see whether a picture forms that suggests an alternative view. Take, for example, Britain. Apart from the fact that it is the country that probably all of us in the room know best, there is the fortuitous existence of a cornucopia of information in the form of a recent report published by JPR. The report gives a clear picture of the state of Jewish life in Britain, a picture that turns out to be suitably suggestive of a different prospect for the future.

The JPR report contains a 'snapshot' based on the 2001 Census that included, for the first time, the question 'What is your religion?' 'Jewish' was one of eight boxes that respondents could tick. This was in addition to the question 'What is your ethnic group?' Although the latter did not include a separate 'Jewish' category, it did give respondents the opportunity to write in their ethnicity and, if they so wished, describe themselves as Jewish. Taken together, the answers to these two questions provided researchers with two ways of determining whether a respondent identified as Jewish. The result, in the words of the authors of the report, is 'the widest ranging quantitative demographic study ever undertaken on Jews in Britain'. This wide range, like a wide lens, gives a startlingly different picture: 'Its scope and detail have revolutionized our analytical understanding of the [Jewish] population.'[13]

It is worth underscoring the point the authors make about the *scope* of the census data. Previous social surveys of British Jews 'were based on relatively small samples of Jewish households'. Such surveys endeavour, of course, to be representative. But they 'work within confined parameters and definitions, as a consequence of which they will miss many people who consider themselves to be Jewish'. The authors observe: 'They [sample surveys] are inherently biased towards reaching those Jews who have institutional connections ... or who live in the more densely Jewish parts of the country; they have been less effective at reaching Jews who do not formally affiliate to the community or who have minimal contacts with the "mainstream".'[14] Although it is difficult to quantify, it could be that as much as 40 per cent of the total British Jewish population is 'non-affiliated' (do not belong to a communal organization, such as a synagogue, club, school or charity).[15] Not all of these individuals will have been covered (or uncovered) by the census. But many of them – people who previously have not shown up on the radar screen of social scientific research into British Jewry – are now visible.

As a result, the face of the Jewish population that shows up in the JPR 'snapshot' looks substantially different from the one that we are accustomed to seeing. Many of the results, say the authors of the report, are 'truly fascinating and mould-breaking'. 'The analysis', they say, 'lays bare the complexity of the Jewish population, and puts to rest several popular myths.'[16] For example, the census data 'have done away with any remaining illusions of Jewish uniformity. This is a socially diverse group.'[17] It is also geographically spread out: although Jews continue to tend to concentrate in certain urban areas, they inhabit all but one of the 408 Local Authority Districts in the United Kingdom (the exception being the Isles of Scilly).[18] And their home life is diverse: a variety of domestic arrangements, including cohabitation and 'exogamous relationships' contribute to 'the complex nature of Jewish partnerships'.[19]

In effect, what we see is not *one* face but *many*; and this is perhaps the principal finding of the JPR report: diversity. 'Whether one looks at location, age, nationality or any other marker', say the authors, 'there is no single "Jewish community" but a complex array of overlapping tiers.'[20]

One reaction to this multifaceted portrait of Jewish life in Britain is panic: fear of loss of 'Jewish continuity', of communal cohesion, of collective solidarity. From this point of view, the census is like an alarm bell, warning that Jewish identity is fading away; or perhaps a death knell heralding the eventual demise of the British branch of the Jewish people. The trouble with this perception (I am happy to say) is that it happens to be false. The opposite is true: Jewish life is flourishing in Britain today in every way – far more so than when I was a child. This very event, Hackney Day Limmud, is a living illustration; there was nothing comparable when I was growing up in London. Nor was there anything like the peripatetic Wandering Jews ('a self organising collective'), or the outrageous Jewdas ('radical voices for the alternative diaspora'), or the enterprising Glasgow Jewish Educational Forum, to choose a few disparate examples.[21] Thus, from a different point of view, the census is full of the sound of a population that is confident enough to depart from its own customary norms. This is not the *waning* of Jewishness but its *waxing*.

I do not say (because I do not know) that Jewish life throughout Europe is flourishing. As it happens, I do not think that the British case is so exceptional, but the argument I am developing is not based on a generalization and therefore does not turn on this question. Using the British case as a springboard, I want to invite us to make a leap of imagination into a possible future. This will mean, taking a hint from the JPR report, rethinking what we mean by 'the Jewish community' – and even 'the Jewish people'. For, if the people is defined in such a way as to diminish or negate Europe as a site for Jewish life, how does it include *us*?

A MODEL FOR THE FUTURE

Entering into the spirit in which the speaker at the London seminar made his remark, let me say something that is too bold and too sweeping (though not as neat): The direction of the Jewish future is undetermined. It can be determined according to two models: 'centre and periphery' or 'diversity and parity'. Both these models operate at two levels, globally and nationally (which, though distinct, are closely linked), as I shall roughly and hastily outline.

Globally, as Sander Gilman observes, 'the overarching model for Jewish history has been that of the center or core and periphery'.[22] However, what interests me here is not the role this model plays in Jewish historiography but its function in structuring the way we think about the relationships between Jewish populations across the globe. Since at least the middle of the last century, the main organizing principles have been supplied by Zionism, and in almost any version of Zionist thought the dominant model is what Aviv and Shneer call 'the simple diaspora–Israel dichotomy', with Israel as the centre and the diaspora as the periphery.[23] (It is possible that the speaker's remark implies a *bicentric* view, with America alongside Israel as a global hub. But to the rest of us – those who live neither in Israel nor America – it makes little difference: whether one centre or two, we are consigned to the rim.) The concept of 'the diaspora', of course, predates Zionism. But the concept has been transformed by the shift from the *land* of Israel to the *state*. This has not just been a simple substitution (state for land) but a systematic change in the whole structure – cultural and political – of the Jewish universe.[24] 'The emphasis on "diaspora" and "Israel" ', say Aviv and Shneer, 'has prevented Jews from exploring the diversity of Jewish experience and the ways that Jews craft their identities at home in the places they live.'[25] Nonetheless, on the strength of their field research, they see extensive evidence that this emphasis is fading. They envisage 'a new map for the Jewish world, one that has multiple homelands, that does not break the Jewish world into a dichotomous relationship between "diaspora" and "Israel" '.[26] On the new map, diaspora morphs into diversity, and a level surface replaces disparity in status. 'Diversity and parity': this is the emergent model for the Jewish future. Not that there is anything inevitable about it – any more than there is an iron destiny that takes the Jewish people out of Europe.

A similar map is coming into being at the country level where, in analogous fashion, there are signs that the old model of 'centre and periphery' is being superseded by the new. In Britain, for example, the old model is reflected in the standard concept of the 'Jewish community' as a single entity or bloc that, whatever its internal complexity, presents a common face to the outside world via its dual ambassadors: the Board of Deputies of British Jews (whose byline is 'The voice of British Jewry since 1760') and the Chief Rabbinate (comprising the Chief Rabbi and his cabinet).[27] On the standard view, Jews who are 'unaffiliated' are seen as inhabiting the margin of British Jewish life. And there is a tendency in the so-called mainstream to think that such people have less right to speak *as* Jews – especially if they are breaking ranks on the subject of Israel or challenging a Zionist worldview. (Notice the link here between the two 'levels' – global and national – on which the 'centre and periphery' model operates.) It is as if living on the margins of the 'Jewish community' makes you a marginal Jew or marginally Jewish. But it does not. It makes you *differently* Jewish. Furthermore, in the light of the JPR 'snapshot', the very idea of a margin in relation to a mainstream is problematic. This is not to deny that some forms of Jewish life, or some expressions of Jewishness, are less conventional than others; it is only to assert that less conventional does not mean more 'peripheral' and less valid.

To an extent, the old model has never fitted the facts of Jewish life in Britain. Neither is the Board the sole secular voice, nor is the Chief Rabbi the sole religious voice, of the British Jewish population as a whole. Nor *could* they be, for there *is* no such whole. In particular, the Chief Rabbi is not, nor has he ever been, the Jewish Pope or Archbishop of Canterbury. He has never had the authority to speak for all religious Jews in Britain, not even for all *Orthodox* Jews. He is the religious head of the United Synagogue (a group of Ashkenazi Orthodox congregations), full stop.[28] But this has not prevented the general public from perceiving him as representing the religion of Judaism in this country – just as the Board has the ear of the Government and other public bodies on secular matters as though it were (which it is not) the Jewish equivalent of Parliament.[29] Such is the power of a dominant paradigm: its hold over the mind is so strong that it can defy the facts.

But on the ground, in Britain and elsewhere, the facts they are a-changin'. Jewish sons and daughters (to continue this nod in the direction of Dylan) are beyond the command of their elders and betters. The order is rapidly fadin'. What Aviv and Shneer discovered in the course of their travels is that Jews are developing 'new forms of Jewishness'.[30] At the end of their groundbreaking, heart-warming, thought-provoking book, they conclude that 'Jews are a group of diverse peoples with many cultures, many homes, and infinitely creative ways of expressing what it means to be at home, as Jews'.[31] This idea – that Jews comprise peoples in the plural rather a people in the singular – is moot and calls for close scrutiny. But we should keep an open mind: it might turn out to be necessary to insist on the plural in *one* sense (say, sociological), breaking up the fictive unity that was the subject of the London speaker's remark, in order to recover the singular in *another* (say, Jewish).[32] With all this in mind, I say loudly and firmly, 'Next year in Hackney'.

Where does the argument leave Jerusalem? This June, as it happens, Reva and I were there. Immersed in the warren of the Old City, we could almost think, if we closed our eyes and listened to the cacophony, that we were back in multicultural Stokey.[33] It was the morning of Shavuoth and, as we strolled along, one of the locals, draped in a flowing *tallis*, was urgently striding down the crowded narrow street, oblivious to everyone else, practically muttering, like the White Rabbit, 'Oh dear! Oh dear! I shall be too late!' Early the following day, hours before our flight back to London, we ascended *Har HaZeitim* under a luminous sky. Craning our necks like camels, we gazed down from the summit and took in the entire silent panorama. A black-robed group was burying its dead in the Jewish cemetery. Christian pilgrims, perhaps at Mary's tomb, were milling about. And, perched like a rising sun, the golden vault of the Dome of the Rock dominated our field of vision. At that moment, it was possible to believe that we were granted a glimpse of eternity. The prospect was breathtaking, heavenly even. And had the phrase entered my head I might have been heard uttering softly, 'Next year in Jerusalem'.

L'shonoh habo'oh!

NOTES

1. The seminar, 'Making More of Europe: Perils and Prospects of European Jewish Advocacy', was held on 22 February 2008. Subsequently, the speaker verified in private email correspondence that he had made this remark.
2. This chapter is adapted from a talk I gave at Hackney Day Limmud, September 2008. The talk in turn was based on an essay published (in German) in 'Zwei Szenarien zur Zukunft des Judentums', *Aufbau*, 13 April 2008, pp.13–17, in a special issue devoted to the question of 'the Jewish future'.
3. Antony Lerman, 'A Changing European Jewry', presentation at the World Conference of Jewish Communal Service, 14 November 2003 (typescript), confirmed in private email correspondence.
4. Henry Grunwald, 'Jewish Life in Britain is Thriving', *Jerusalem Post*, 24 February 2008, http://www.jpost.com/servlet/Satellite?cid=1203847455740&pagename=JPost%2FJPArticle%2FShowFull.
5. We are 'shoulder to shoulder' on the assertions I have quoted. He goes on in the same sentence to specify 'Salute to Israel Parades' and does not mention public displays of criticism of Israel by Jews. Yet the fact that Jews in Britain can openly and publicly disagree over Israel is much better support for his assertions than this one-sided evidence.
6. Antony Lerman, 'Making More of Europe: Perils and Prospects of European Jewish Advocacy: Policy Briefing', London: Institute for Jewish Policy Research, 22 February 2008, p.2.
7. This is one variation on the theme of the remark popularly attributed to him.
8. David Shneer, 'We Are All Global Jews Now', *Jewish Chronicle*, 15 August 2008, p.29.
9. Caryn Aviv and David Shneer, *New Jews: The End of the Jewish Diaspora* (New York: New York University Press, 2005), p.xv; see also p.49.
10. Aviv and Shneer, *New Jews*, p.174.
11. Cnaan Liphshiz, 'Report: Israel–Diaspora relations sink to a new low', *Ha'aretz*, 14 December 2007, http://www.haaretz.com/hasen/spages/929743.html. The poll was conducted in 2001.

12. Steven Beller, 'Is Europe Good for the Jews? Jews and the Pluralist Tradition in Historical Perspective', London: Institute for Jewish Policy Research, April 2008, p.9.
13. David Graham, Marlena Schmool and Stanley Waterman, 'Jews in Britain: A Snapshot from the 2001 Census', London: Institute for Jewish Policy Research, May 2007, p.99.
14. Ibid., pp.9, 11–12.
15. Private email communication from Antony Lerman, Director of JPR, 30 August 2007.
16. Graham, Schmool and Waterman, 'Jews in Britain', p.99.
17. Ibid., p.78.
18. Ibid., p.24.
19. Ibid., p.99.
20. Ibid., p.100.
21. Wandering Jews: http://www.wanderingjews.co.uk/; Jewdas: http://www.jewdas.org/; Glasgow Jewish Educational Forum: http://gjef.wordpress.com/. Association of Jewish Humanists, Jewish Book Week, Jewish Community Centre for London, Jewish Council for Racial Equality, Jewish Gay and Lesbian Group, Jewish Socialists' Group, Independent Jewish Voices, Limmud (national), Tzedek, UK Jewish Film Festival: these are a few more examples of how Jewish life is flourishing in new ways in Britain.
22. Sander Gilman, 'Introduction: The Frontier as a Model for Jewish History', in Sander L. Gilman and Milton Shain (eds), *Jewries at the Frontier: Accommodation, Identity, Conflict* (Urbana, IL: University of Illinois Press, 1999), p.1.
23. Aviv and Shneer, *New Jews*, p.172.
24. See Chapter 10, 'A Time to Move On', for an extended discussion of the topic of diaspora.
25. Aviv and Shneer, *New Jews*, p.xvi.
26. Ibid., p.xv.
27. For the Board's 'byline', see their website: http://www.bod.org.uk/. The Chief Rabbi's full title is 'Chief Rabbi of the United Hebrew Congregations of the Commonwealth'.
28. On the office of Chief Rabbi, see Geoffrey Alderman, 'The British Chief Rabbinate: a Most Peculiar Practice', *European Judaism*, 13, 2 (1990), reprinted in his *Controversy and Crisis: Studies in the History of the Jews in Modern Britain* (Boston, MA: Academic Studies Press, 2008).
29. 'Although the Board of Deputies of British Jews is recognized by the British government as the Jewish community's representative body, over the last twenty to thirty years the number of other organizations pursuing their own concerns with government or local authorities, or simply expressing an independent voice, has grown enormously.' Antony Lerman, 'Touching a Raw Nerve', in Anne Karpf, Brian Klug, Jacqueline Rose and Barbara Rosenbaum (eds), *A Time to Speak Out: Independent Jewish Voices on Israel, Zionism and Jewish Identity* (London: Verso, 2008), p.154.
30. Aviv and Shneer, *New Jews*, p.xiv.
31. Ibid., p.176.
32. There is a discussion of the concept of the people in the Prologue, 'The People of God – The Very Idea', and in Chapter 10, 'A Time to Move On'.
33. Stoke Newington, a district in the borough of Hackney.

Part 2
Angles on Identity

Introduction

In the general introduction I explained that I am using the word 'justice' in roughly the same way that Socrates uses it in Plato's Republic: 'doing what, in the broadest sense, is right'. Rather than pin the word down too far in advance, my preference has been to let its meaning find its own level in different contexts. Several chapters in Part 1 have shown that the question of what is right often points over its shoulder to a prior question in the background: identity: who or what we are. (So, for example, in Chapter 1, where I explored the rights and wrongs of joining the Israel Solidarity Rally, I did so in the context of what it means to be Jewish.) This logical connection – between questions of identity and questions of justice – recurs again and again in the following chapters.

If the first part of the book dwells on Jewishness, especially vis-à-vis Zionism and the State of Israel, the second roams across a range of identities, approaching them from various angles. Perhaps 'other angles on other identities' would be a more accurate title for Part 2, except that Jewishness continues to be very much in the frame. In one way, the wider scope represents a departure, since the book moves on from its initial preoccupation in 'Approaches to Zion'. In another way, it fills out the picture, showing the place that this preoccupation occupies. For Judaism, as I care to receive it, is never a retreat into itself so as to escape from its surroundings. If, in some sense, it holds itself apart, this is not to keep its distance but, on the contrary, to re-establish its involvement. For there are two opposite ways of being lost to the world: either staying aloof and aloft, losing sight of the ground, or being too close to the action and losing your bearings. A people apart? But only in order to collect itself so as to be (or become) thoroughly an inhabitant of – a presence in – this world.

Not only the scope, but the texture of the second part of the book is different from the first. Whereas the previous chapters are relatively close knit, there is a looser weave from this point on; the spaces (so to speak) between chapters are wider. Yet there is a discernible development.

Part 2 continues from the point where Part 1 ends, with two new angles on Jewish identity. First, examining the 'ethnic question' on the 1991 UK Census form (Chapter 12), I deliberate over a personal dilemma: Do I, as a Jew, tick the box marked 'White'? At stake in this decision is a general question about what it means to divide up common humanity into the groups listed on the form, as well as a specific question about the space filled by being Jewish. I then discuss the case of Arthur Balfour, 'protector of the Jews', who spoke of Jews collectively as a 'race'. What (asks Chapter 13) did he mean and how did this impinge upon his politics? In the next two chapters the scene shifts to the US. How (to take another angle) does the difference between 'Black' and 'White' play out in multi-ethnic America (Chapter 14), and what bearing does it have on the complex relations between Jews and Blacks (Chapter 15)?

I said in the general introduction that these chapters are 'chapters from my life' and that the topics they discuss 'forced themselves on my attention'. Some did, perhaps, more than others. The shock of hearing naked antisemitism on the airwaves of a black radio station late one night as I was driving home on Lake Shore Drive in Chicago propelled me into the thick of things (Chapter 15). Likewise, the next two chapters owe their existence to a blow to my equanimity. This time it took the form of a campaign in Britain in the 1980s against Muslim and Jewish methods of killing animals for food. I felt put on the spot and pulled in contrary directions by this campaign. For, on the one hand, it was waged in the name of animal welfare, a cause for which I have advocated, while, on the other hand, it targeted two minority groups, including mine (even if meat per se is not exactly kosher for vegetarians like me). So, I felt compelled to look into the issue. First, I investigated the rhetoric against 'ritual slaughter' (Chapter 16). Then I researched the reality of 'humane slaughter'; and I do mean reality, as I descended into the bowels of Britain's abattoirs and witnessed for myself the shambles within (Chapter 17).

The next two chapters continue to pursue the change of direction from, as it were, race to species. Via two stories (one by Francis Bacon and another by H.G. Wells) about imaginary islands run by scientists, I move from the slaughterhouse to the lab. Neither chapter debates the rights and wrongs of particular uses of animals. Rather, by interrogating the culture of science (Chapter 18) and the view of animals as mere 'organisms' (Chapter 19), they attempt to clear the ground for approaching such issues.

Then what *is* an animal? And are *we* not animals? Are animals like us – only not quite as developed? Are they like children? How *should* we approach the question of whether we treat animals well or badly? There is such a thing as racism; so, is there something akin called 'speciesism'? Do animals have rights too? Do children? But what is a child? These questions seem to come tumbling out of the previous three chapters; and although they overlap they are roughly allotted one chapter per kind of identity: animal, human and child. First, I examine the concept of speciesism, rejecting the analogy with racism (and antisemitism and sexism), which distorts our sense of animals as 'fellow creatures', simultaneously familiar and alien – like the self-confident kangaroo who assailed me one morning on the coast of Australia (Chapter 20). This leads to reflection on what it means to see ourselves as human and to a critique of Peter Singer's 'new vision of who we are': his view that 'we are animals too': *human* animals. Not that we're not. It's just that (to speak in the idiom of Genesis) we are made in the image of God. In dismissing the Genesis account, he misses a vital point. A small menagerie of pigs, piggons and piggles – a mixture of real and not-yet-real fellow creatures – helps me make this point (Chapter 21).

Finally, drawing on Peter Pan (both the story and the play) by J.M. Barrie, I explore the concept of the child (Chapter 22). Now, there is more going on in this concluding chapter than meets the eye. For, in the process, I am revisiting two of the themes that resound through this book: being human and being Jewish. Not that there is anything to indicate this within the text itself. Nor can I elucidate the point adequately here. But I would ask the reader to recall the Prologue, where I present the Jewish people in a certain light. 'Seen in this light', I argued, 'the Jewish people are to the rest of humanity what an instance is to a universal: an example'. But the Jewish people identify with the children of Israel. And the Israelites are children not just by virtue of being descendants of Jacob (Israel) but also as the people of God: God, whose omnipresent countenance is decidedly parental, alternately severe and benign. From these premises it follows inexorably that, in the scriptural view of things, all of us grown-ups are still *kinder* (children): we are all in a state of arrested development. Or, to place the accent in a different place, we adult humans are not fully ourselves unless, from time to time, we come out and play.

The chapter itself ends on a whimsical note. At the risk of causing offence (and in the certain knowledge that the parallel I draw is absurd), I juxtapose Peter's island, the one to which Wendy and the boys are spirited away, with Jerusalem – not the earthly place in the here and now but the city that exists just beyond it. This is the Jerusalem that appears for a moment at the close of Part 1 in 'Next Year in Hackney', whose title precisely recalls the perennial prayer in the Haggadah, 'Next year in Jerusalem'. 'Next year in Neverland' ends by looking back to that pivotal moment of looking forward. It is the right time to call it quits – for emphatically this is a book of life.

CHAPTER TWELVE

The Language of Race

Originally a keynote address given at an international conference to mark the thirtieth anniversary of the founding of the journal Patterns of Prejudice, *London, December 1997.*

THE EXAMPLE OF SOCRATES

I wish my grandmother could see me today.[1] I say this for a particular reason. My brother Harold tells the story of how she used to read the *Jewish Chronicle* from cover to cover every week, and then complain, 'There's nothing else to read.' So he introduced her to *Patterns of Prejudice*. You have to understand that my grandmother came over from Poland when she was still in her teens and that she had no formal schooling. But she was so pleased with her copy of the journal that she asked him to take out a subscription in her name. This was in the late 1960s, when *Patterns of Prejudice* was in its infancy; and so a list of subscribers at the time would have included university libraries, academic institutes, distinguished professors – and grandma. Education or no education, she could tell the difference between a mere *shmata* and the real McCoy. And *Patterns of Prejudice* she knew was no rag. 'Darling', she would say to Harold when he visited her on weekends and they discussed the latest issue of the journal together, '*this* is *knowledge*.'

I imagine her now, sitting in the front row, interrupting me even as I speak, asking rhetorically, 'Was I right or was I right?' Well, grandma, you weren't wrong. For thirty years, *Patterns of Prejudice* has countered ignorance with knowledge, bigotry with reason, racism with responsibility. When I say 'responsibility' I mean both academic – meeting the highest scholarly standards – and social, covering issues that span the world. And today, friends of the journal have come from near and far to celebrate this thirtieth anniversary in the appropriate manner: conferring together, across nations and across disciplines, about the forms that prejudice takes, the patterns that keep recurring and entrapping us the world over.

Mentioning disciplines gives me pause, for if it is clear what history or sociology or political science or anthropology can contribute to our understanding of prejudice and discrimination, what about my own discipline, philosophy? What can philosophy contribute to what my grandmother called 'knowledge'? Well, naturally, it all depends on what you mean by philosophy. And, of course, this is something about which philosophers are always arguing. At one extreme, philosophy is seen as the queen of the sciences, the one that occupies the throne of knowledge. On this view, the philosopher is the wise don at the top of the ivory tower who, looking down from on high, studies the whole shebang (to paraphrase Aristotle), gathering findings from the particular sciences and putting them all together to form Knowledge with a capital K. At the opposite pole is the dishevelled Socrates, wandering about in the streets, like a lunatic at large, stopping people in their tracks and leaving them thoroughly confused. Not that he does this wantonly or maliciously, for, as he says to Meno, when Meno complains that Socrates has addled his brain, 'I do not have the solution when I make others perplexed, but I am totally perplexed myself, and as a result I produce perplexity in others.'[2] In other words, Socrates thinks he has nothing to offer people other than to show them that they are as thoroughly confused as he is. On this view, philosophy is not so much queen as charlady who, with mop rather than sceptre in hand, goes around peeking under rugs, looking for the messes that have been swept there. Whether this sort of intellectual housekeeping is a contribution to knowledge, I could not say.

But I take my cue from Socrates: when I use the language of race, I know I am confused. I suspect, moreover, that some of the confusion is not merely in my head but out in the world, swept under its rug, so to speak. And today I should like to raise some dust. I shall speak, not from above the fray, but in the midst of it, where all of us are situated when we step out of our academic gowns and emerge on the street. My contribution will be less academic than anecdotal. I shall be speaking about experiences, my own and other people's, drawing attention to two different but connected sorts of confusion. The first is about words and what they mean – words like 'racial', 'ethnic', 'white', 'black', and so on. The second is about practice: about what to do and what not to do; what is and what is not a responsible reaction to racism. In the process I shall stray into the territory of the social sciences. However, I do not mean to trespass on someone else's academic turf. In speaking about the language of race I shall try to imitate the example of Socrates and, disclaiming any expertise, stick to what I do not know.

THE ETHNIC QUESTION

Every ten years the United Kingdom conducts a census. The last census was held in 1991. For households in Great Britain, the census form included, for the first time, an ethnic question (as it has been called), question 11, which asked about the 'ethnic group' to which each resident belonged. You were given nine choices, and an instruction in the margin asked you to 'please tick the appropriate box'. These were the choices, in the order in which they appeared on the form: White, Black-Caribbean, Black-African, Black-Other, Indian, Pakistani, Bangladeshi, Chinese, Any Other Ethnic Group. If you ticked 'Black-Other', you were asked to 'please describe' your black otherness, if I may so put it, and given two lines beneath the box in which to do this. The same provision was made if you ticked 'Any Other Ethnic Group'. There was one other instruction in the margin, as follows: 'If the person is descended from more than one ethnic or racial group, please tick the group to which the person considers he/she belongs, or tick the "Any Other Ethnic Group" box and describe your ancestry in the space provided.'[3]

Although I have not stated all this from memory – I needed to get hold of a copy of the 'ethnic question' in order to be able to describe it accurately – I do recall clearly the moment when I read it for the first time as I dutifully filled out the form for myself. I was stunned. I think there were two components to this reaction. First, it was a shock to see the British population chopped up into nine 'ethnic or racial' boxes, each with a neat label summing somebody – everybody – up. It seemed like an assault; that was how it struck me in the moment. Second, where was I in this scheme of things? Where did I fit in? There was something faintly familiar and vaguely sinister about this latter sensation.

I realize that my reaction could seem odd if not extreme. It needs explaining. Ironically, the explanation has to do with the very thing about which question 11 was supposedly asking: my heritage or background. More specifically, it has to do with upbringing. My sister Francesca expressed this eloquently in a recent round-table discussion on Black–Jewish–Muslim relations in Britain, the transcript of which has appeared in *Jewish Quarterly*. I cannot do better than quote her. She said, 'I was brought up to understand myself and my family as part of a minority community along with several other obviously identifiable minority communities, all of whom have suffered from one common factor, and that is racism. I was brought up to understand

what racism was, over and above everything else, including maths and
algebra.'⁴ She went on to say, 'So everything I say is in that context
because I don't know how to approach it any other way.' And in the
same vein: 'What I learned as a child, and what I hope to try to build
on, is the only thing I understand. Everything else I change my mind
about.' Her words speak for me too. And, bearing in mind that filling
out the census form is required by law, when I saw question 11,
dividing people along 'ethnic or racial' lines, classifying them according
to their 'ancestry', some ancestral part of me shivered in its shoes.

I shall try to explain what pondering this question was like. To begin
with, it was weird how the form moved so smoothly from questions
about name, marital status, type of accommodation, and the like, to
this one – as if your being white or black or whatever were just
another personal datum. One minute you were answering a question
about central heating in your house, the next you were stating your
race. First 'Are you warm?', then 'Are you white?' They were separate
questions, but it was as if they could have been combined – 'Are you
warm and are you white?' or 'Are you white and are you warm?' –
without it making any real difference, since the form uttered them, so
to speak, in the same matter-of-fact tone of voice. *There* were the questions, *there* were the little boxes, and in every case a flick of the pen
would record the simple fact with a tick.

However, this appearance of logical parity was an illusion. Consider
the instruction, 'Please tick the appropriate box'. Where the question
was about facilities, there was one fact, and one fact only, that counted.
If, for example, you had installed central heating in your house, then
the appropriate box was the one that corresponded to that fact, full
stop. But when it came to your 'ethnic group', which box was the right
one? Was it 'appropriate' to tick the box into which others – people in
general perhaps – would put you? Should you ask yourself, 'How do
others see me?' Or was it how you see yourself that counted? The instruction 'Please tick the appropriate box' slid over this issue, as though
it did not or could not exist. However, the subordinate instruction in
question 11, the one that applied to people 'descended from more than
one ethnic or racial group', said 'tick the group to which the person
considers he/she belongs'. Note the word 'considers'. In other questions the form did not ask 'What do you *consider* your name to be?' or
'Do you *think* you are married or single?' or '*In your view* do you live
in a house that has central heating?' It asked simply 'What is the case?'
or 'Is it so?', and in each case something either was so or was not so.
If the ethnic question were on the same logical plane as these other

questions, then the instruction would have read, simply, 'tick the group
to which the person belongs' and not 'tick the group to which the person *considers* he/she belongs'. I take this wording to mean that what
counts is how the person sees themselves, not how others see them. If
the main instruction in question 11 is taken the same way (and it is
reasonable to do so), then 'Please tick the appropriate box' means tick
the box that corresponds to that group in which you place yourself.
That, at any rate, is how I interpreted the instruction. That this needed
to be clarified is a measure of how question 11 was different – logically
– from other questions on the form. That it was *not* clarified, or
clarified only indirectly, by inference from the subordinate instruction,
suppressed that difference. In suppressing that difference, in making
the ethnic question look as straightforward and as 'factual' as any other
question on the form, it suppressed the questionableness of the
question.

What exactly was question 11 asking in asking you to place yourself in one of the nine boxes on offer? Take the box marked White.
What does it mean to say you are white? A Chinese colleague and
friend, born in Taiwan and living, as I am now, in Chicago, recently
surprised me with a query. 'Are Jewish people white?' she asked. (She
was thinking, of course, of Jews in America, whose extraction is
predominantly European.) After a pause, she answered the question
for herself. 'I think they're not', she said, 'in the real white white sense.'
Her remark prompted the thought that we have conflicting ideas about
what whiteness in a person consists in. On the one hand, there is physical appearance, primarily complexion. In this respect, broadly speaking,
Jews in America are like any other group that derives from Europe; so
Jews are 'white'. On the other hand, there is historical experience, the
Jewish experience of being foreigners in Europe for nearly 2,000 years;
so Jews are *not* white. Physical appearance suggests one answer,
historical experience suggests another. Hence the paradox: Jews are
not 'white white'. Now, I can understand a third party, especially someone who does not know I am Jewish, looking at me and saying
unhesitatingly, 'You're white.' That's as may be; but when I look in the
mirror I do not necessarily see a white face, for 'white' is not just about
physical features; it is partly a matter of history, and history does not
necessarily show up in the glass.

What would it have meant, then, to tick the box marked White in
question 11 on the census form? On the face of it, it would have been
merely a matter of choosing one box from among nine separate boxes,
where all the boxes were the same shape and the same size – separate

but equal, so to speak. As it happens, the box marked White was first
on the list. To be more precise, the boxes were arranged as a column,
White at the top. But so what? After all, *one* of the boxes had to come
first, and it could have been any of them. True, but it *was* the one
marked White. I have no idea whether this is the norm with forms in
Britain, but it is my impression that, over and again, White is the first
option in ethnic questions on official forms in the US. The one exception was when I applied for a social security card: the box marked
White came, not first, but last. I have never seen White on an official
form in the middle of a list, with other descriptions on either side.
Now, in itself, this is neither here nor there; the order in which the
boxes appear means nothing intrinsically. But in context, the larger
context of society, it resounds with historical connotation. Regardless
of what was in the minds of the people who formulated question 11
on the 1991 UK census form, there is a rhetoric associated with the
word 'white' and with the fact that White came first and came top. I
heard that rhetoric, silent as white noise, when I read the question. I
do not say that I put what I heard into words at the time. I am not sure
that I could have done. I shall try to do so now.

I would be less able to do this were it not for an article in *Patterns
of Prejudice* by Roger Ballard.[5] Ballard's article, which analyses the
ethnic question on the 1991 census form, had been excluded from a
volume of commentary published by the Office for National Statistics.[6]
Consequently, we owe a debt to our editors for giving it a home, for it
is a fascinating piece, a jewel in the crown of the journal. Ballard points
out that there was, in effect, a colour scheme running through question
11. He says: 'the layout of the boxes seemed implicitly to invite
respondents to sort themselves into one or another of three broad
categories: "White", "Black" and (even though the explicit colour
identifier was omitted) "Brown".'[7]Actually, if he was going to add
Brown, then by the same token he should have added Yellow, since the
boxes he groups under Brown include Chinese.

Ballard glosses over the fact that only White and Black were
explicitly mentioned, but it is worth taking a moment to reflect on
this. I was discussing the subject of this talk with a friend who is
European-American, Jewish, and married to a Chinese-American. She
pointed out to me that people do not call themselves 'yellow'. I
suppose it is obvious but it had never occurred to me before. Nor, to
the best of my knowledge, do people call themselves 'brown'. Other
people call other people 'brown' and 'yellow'; whereas people do call
themselves 'black' and 'white'. Moreover, it is a feature of the words

'black' and 'white', in contrast to 'brown' and 'yellow', that they can be used as nouns, singular or plural, to designate an individual or a group. Consider, for example, the language in this sentence from a report published by the Policy Studies Institute in 1984: 'In areas of relatively dense black residence the proportion of *whites* saying *blacks* are treated better rises to a quarter' (emphasis added).[8] The report could not have contained a similar sentence about the proportion of *browns* saying *yellows* are treated better, since the words 'browns' and 'yellows' are not names for groups of people. To which you might say: 'So what? The report could have used the phrases "brown people" and "yellow people" to get round this grammatical point.' But the point, unless I am much mistaken, is that anyone who used these particular phrases would not be writing for the Policy Studies Institute; that to speak about 'brown people' or 'yellow people' savours of prejudice, whereas speaking of 'black people' and 'white people' does not.[9] Not that the expressions 'black' and 'white' are on the same logical footing. Think, for example, of the different connotations of the slogans 'Black Power' and 'White Power', or the phrases 'black leadership' and 'white leadership'.[10] All of this shows that the colour terms used in the language of race are not logically equivalent. But this is an aside.[11]

To return to Ballard's point regarding the ethnic question on the 1991 census form: having observed that the boxes on the form seem to fall under three headings, White, Black and Brown, he goes on to say, 'Beyond this the "White" category offered no further subdivisions, while respondents identifying with the other two were invited to identify themselves further in ethno-national terms, permitting as well additional write-in answers.'[12] If I understand him correctly, Ballard thinks that when the majority of the population ticked the White box, they were, in effect, making the negative point that they did not belong in any of the other boxes, meaning they were not 'different'. The 'not' implies that 'white' is normal, and not just normal but neutral, a sort of zero state, so that ethnicity is something that other people have.[13] Indeed, next to the box, on the other side from the label White, was an actual zero. While no number was assigned to the two open categories Black-Other and Any Other Ethnic Group, the rest of the boxes were numbered from 1 to 6. I sent Roger an email about this, asking him to clarify what was going on, and why this particular numbering system was used. He explained that the numbers relate to the coding frame that enable the census takers to turn the ticks into statistics. He added: 'as far as I can see 0 is being understood as normal, and in that sense "not ethnic" by the Census classificatory system'.[14] Be that as it may, the point remains that the language of question 11 combined with its format, the privileging of the White box and the peculiarity of the coding, seem to insinuate that people divide into White and Not White, insiders and outsiders. Accordingly, this, in effect, is what I heard question 11 asking me: Did I see myself, ethnically speaking, as part of the 'in-crowd'?

Obviously not. If the question was about 'ethnic group', and that is how it was billed, and if this has anything at all to do with family and roots, with exodus and exile, with life in the Pale of Settlement and death beyond the pale, death for not being Aryan, not being 'white white', then, even in the safe haven of London, how could I possibly tick the box marked 'in crowd'? So I didn't. I ticked the 'Any Other Ethnic Group' box and wrote, in the space provided, 'Jewish'. Alas, if Roger Ballard is right, I need not have bothered. In answer to a question I put to him he replied: 'if you wrote in anything such as Jewish, English, pink, or what-have-you, you would have been recoded as a nought'.[15] Then all my agonizing literally came to nought. And thus our scruples are ground into dust, and our frank responses become grist for the statistician's mill.

OBJECTION AND REPLIES

By now, I imagine, there is some restlessness in the room, and I seem to hear an objection, one that has been building for some time. So let me try to give it voice. It goes something like this:

> It is all very well for you [meaning me] to have scruples, and I am sure we are all fascinated by your agonizing over whether or not to accept the offer of the box marked White. No doubt we applaud the purity of your decision. But there are those for whom this offer is not open; those whose agonies are felt not in filling out a form but in living out a life, or trying to, in a real world where prejudice is ubiquitous and discrimination slams doors in faces because they look different. They are the ones for whom the ethnic question was designed, not you; and not for the purpose of answering metaphysical questions about personal identity. The point of the question is precisely to get grist for that mill that you mention, which is not as Satanic as you seem to think. Statistics are an instrument, a tool. Without them, how are we going to combat racism? We need to know the facts – about poverty, housing, education and jobs – so we can protect minorities and promote social justice. You keep

asking what the ethnic question was asking. It is obvious what it was asking: are you or are you not a member of one of the minority groups in Britain that, because they look different, are liable to be treated differently? You talk about being frank. Frankly, it really does not matter, in the great scheme of things, if your response to the ethnic question got lost in the works. If you think the question can be improved, say so. If not, sit down.

Such, as I seem to hear it, is the objection.

To which I reply: point taken. It is no harder for me to take the point than to make it, since the point is mine. It is the voice of the activist within; and the protest is so loud in my ears that it almost persuades me that I should end my talk here – that that would be the decent thing to do. However, if you will allow me a little more time, I wish to enter some reservations concerning the objection. All I shall do is indicate a number of lines of thought that need developing. But I think this is the least I should do, for things are not as simple as the objection makes out. In the first place, assuming for the sake of argument that the ethnic question on the census form was introduced with the best of intentions, there is nonetheless the danger that it perpetuates the very thing it is intended to combat. In the second place, there are deep confusions lying under the surface of the objection, and they need to be brought out into the open. I have five observations to make.

1. The objection assumes that because the motive behind the ethnic question is good – to protect minorities and promote social justice – the information it yields will be put to a benign use. But this does not necessarily follow. Patricia Williams, in her 1997 Reith Lectures for the BBC, furnishes an example. In the US, the Fair Housing Act is designed to prevent banks from practising 'red-lining', a form of discrimination in which some people, because of their 'race', are refused a mortgage to purchase a home in certain neighbourhoods. The Act monitors the lending record of banks by requiring all mortgage applicants to fill out a Fair Housing form which includes a box for 'race'. Williams observes, 'The Fair Housing Act thus tracks the race of all banking customers to prevent such discrimination. Unfortunately, some banks also use the racial information disclosed on the Fair Housing forms to engage in precisely the discrimination the law seeks to prevent.'[16]

   She is speaking from first-hand experience. She relates what happened when she tried to buy a house in another state, conducting the negotiations with the bank by phone. Because of her excellent credit record, her professional status as a lawyer and a professor of law at Columbia University, and because her voice sounds, in her own words, 'like a white person', she secured the loan without any difficulty.[17] When the forms arrived in the post, she discovered that the loan officer at the bank had jumped to conclusions and ticked the box marked White on the Fair Housing form. She corrected the mistake, ticked the Black box instead, and returned the amended form, assuming it was, as she puts it a 'done deal'. Here is what happened. 'Suddenly said deal came to a screeching halt. The bank wanted more money as a down payment, they wanted me to pay more "points", as certain extra charges are called, they wanted to raise the rate of interest. Suddenly I found myself facing greater interest and much more debt.'[18]

The bank blamed falling property values in the neighbourhood. And what caused this sudden catastrophe? Williams explains: '*I* was the reason the prices were in peril.'[19] She continues, 'The bank was proceeding according to demographic data that show any time black people move into a neighbourhood in the States, whites are overwhelmingly likely to move out.' Thus racial discrimination crept in through the back door of economics – thanks to the ethnic question on the Fair Housing form.

2. I have explained why, physical appearance notwithstanding, I did not tick the box marked White on the UK census form. But you don't have to be Jewish to feel the same way. What I said about the word 'white' barely scratched the surface, barely scraped the crud, you might say, with which the word is encrusted. And even if you were descended from Vikings, you might shrink from ticking that box – so as not to legitimize the category White. What, in any case, is the category White doing in a question called 'ethnic', alongside such categories as Black-Caribbean, Indian and Bangladeshi? It all seems a bit of a hodgepodge, a mishmash of different concepts, a case of what Gilbert Ryle called 'a category mistake', where ideas belonging to one category are represented as belonging to another.[20] Not only is this confused, it is also invidious, for it seems to give credence to an idea that lies at the heart of what has been called the 'new racism': the idea that Whites are united by a common cultural heritage that is as powerful a bond as anything in their genes.[21] Williams captures what could be called the 'new whiteness' well. She says, 'Whiteness is a kind of sociological clubhouse, a weird compression of tribal and ethnic animosities, some dating back to

the time of the Roman invasions, all realigned to make new enemies, all compromised to make new friends.'[22] It is at least arguable that by including White as a category, the ethnic question on the census form tends to reinforce the idea in people's heads that they belong to this clubhouse, keeping its doors slammed shut in the faces of others (to adapt a phrase taken from the objection).

3. The objection asks if the ethnic question can be improved. You might think that the thing to do is to clean up its act and turn it into a genuinely *ethnic* question. That is what Ballard thinks should be done. He points out that the 'pre-set categories on the Census form were an ad hoc mixture of ethno-national and skin-colour identifiers'.[23] He proposes rectifying this by removing what he calls 'the racial options' and replacing them with 'a considerably wider range of ethnic identifiers'.[24] In particular, he thinks 'the catch-all category "White" could be unpacked'. By this he means breaking it down into English, Welsh, Scottish and Irish, and either creating one box for all these groups or, preferably, a separate box for each. The virtue of the latter proposal, if I understand him correctly, is that it would allow the form to show that all ethnic groups are, as he puts it, 'hyphenated Brits'.[25] Thus you would get English-British, Welsh-British, Scottish-British, Irish-British and, to continue the series, Indian-British, African-British, Chinese-British and so on.[26]

It is a neat solution, but, I fear, too simplistic. Take someone like Ian Wright, the striker who plays for Arsenal and for England.[27] He plays for England: does that not make him English-British? So is this the box that he should tick? Or, being black, should he tick African-British or Caribbean-British? Alan Shearer also plays for England, but in his case there would be no comparable quandary. Perhaps I am not doing Ballard's proposal justice, but it seems to me that the hyphen makes it look as if English-British and (say) African-British are logically on a par, when they are not. And what would the 'African' in African-British signify exactly? Ethnicity? Or, in so many words, race? If F.W. de Klerk were to pack his bags and emigrate to Sussex – and somehow that is where I imagine he would go – would he be African-British? And so the questions multiply.

4. Ballard's proposal, as I have indicated, is based on the premise that it is possible to separate out the racial from the ethnic. If this were so, it would make life, both at the level of theory and practice, much easier. But I fear that what we have is a conceptual mess, and it is best to sweep it out from under the rug. On the street, so to speak, people tend to use the words 'ethnic' and 'racial' interchangeably,

as if they were synonymous. At the same time, they also use 'ethnic' as a *euphemism* for race – which they could not do if the two words were indeed identical in meaning. No doubt this is all confused, but the confusion is not merely something in the minds of 'ordinary people' as opposed to academic experts; it is in the words themselves. There are, I dare say, several strands to this confusion. I shall try briefly to identify two.

First, the word 'race' has many different meanings, as the dictionary will testify. If there is, so to speak, a core meaning, a concept that informs all the different meanings of the word, it is this: a race comprises living things of the same kind. The profusion of meanings arises from the fact that living things, especially people, can be sorted under different heads. So, for example, 'the human race' is humankind as distinguished from animals. But there are different kinds of human beings, as Charles Lamb points out in his Elia essay 'The Two Races of Men', positing 'two distinct races, *the men who borrow* and *the men who lend*'. People also comprise *peoples*, as in 'the English race' or 'the German race'. This last example brings us to the edge of that use of the word 'race' at which we all flinch: classifying people according to supposedly distinct physical types which are supposedly accounted for by genetic inheritance. The reason why we all flinch at this latter idea is not so much because it is bad biology (although it is), but because historically speaking 'race' in this sense was not merely a term of biology but also ideology: the 'types' into which people were divided were not merely physical but also mental, intellectual and cultural. This is the use of the word 'race' that is in itself racist. It is how the word 'race' was used in the ideologies of Nazism and apartheid.

However, not everything we call 'racist' is rooted in this particular use of the word 'race'. In the background is a wider sense of the word, the sense in which it is possible to apply it to people on the basis of nationality or ethnicity or certain other distinguishing features. This complication affects the scope of 'racial discrimination' covered by the UK Race Relations Act 1976 and the definition of a racial group. The Act states that a 'racial group' is 'one defined by reference to one or more of the following: colour, race, nationality (including citizenship) or ethnic or national origins'.[28] When I read this I thought at first that it was both circular and contradictory. It seemed circular because the phrase 'racial group' is defined (in part) in terms of 'race'. It seemed contradictory because it is also defined in terms of factors – like nationality and ethnic origins – which, being listed *alongside* race, presumably are *not* racial. I now think that what is going on in this definition is something like this: 'racial', in the *definiendum*, is being used in a wider sense of the word, and 'race', in the *definiens*, in a narrower sense. Which narrower sense exactly, I am not sure. But as a result, the definition is unclear, not to say confusing. (A similar complication occurs in the definition of 'racial discrimination' in the International Convention on the Elimination of All Forms of Racial Discrimination, adopted by the UN in 1965.[29])

Second, the confusion is compounded by the semantics of the word 'ethnic'. It is not only on the street that the two words 'race' and 'ethnic' are closely linked, but also in the dictionary. For example, according to my *Cassell's New English Dictionary*, 'ethnic' means 'pertaining to or characteristic of a race or people'.[30] Admittedly, this dictionary, which I was given as a bar mitzvah present, is not so 'new' any more, but more up-to-date dictionaries make the same sort of connection between the words 'ethnic' and 'race'. The two words keep turning into each other, so to speak, and this is not something that can be rectified by fiat: by decreeing that henceforth and for ever more they shall stand for two distinct concepts.

5. Finally, the objection – the one made by the 'activist within' – makes it seem as if my quarrel with the instruction in question 11 of the 1991 UK Census form was a quibble. The instruction was to 'tick the appropriate box', and I said that the word 'appropriate' left it crucially unclear as to whether you should tick the box into which others put you or the box into which you put yourself. The objection makes it seem as if this were not crucial at all – except for the likes of me. But the problem is a more general one, as this extract from an article in the *New Yorker* demonstrates:

> A National Center for Health Statistics study found that 5.8 per cent of the people who called themselves Black were seen as White by a census interviewer. Nearly a third of the people identifying themselves as Asian were classified as White or Black by independent observers. That was also true of seventy per cent of people who identified themselves as American Indians. Robert A. Hahn, an epidemiologist at the Centers for Disease Control and Prevention, analyzed deaths of infants born from 1983 through 1985. In an astounding number of cases, the infant had a different race on its death certificate from the one on its birth certificate,

and this finding led to staggering increases in the infant-mortality rate for minority populations ... over what had been previously recorded.[31]

The article concludes with a comment by Representative Thomas Sawyer, Democrat of Ohio, who chaired congressional hearings in 1993 on the ethnic and racial categories used in the US census. He sums things up as follows: 'We act as if we knew what we're talking about when we talk about race, and we don't.'[32]

THE RACE QUESTION

We don't and we do, because even as we stumble over the language of race and cringe at its ugliness, we know perfectly well what we are talking about au fond: racism, however you define it. What we seek is a way of speaking about the subject responsibly. But as I have tried to indicate, it is difficult to find a way of doing this that is neither confused nor implicated in the very prejudices we oppose. Because of this we can feel torn – as my brother Tony was in my final anecdote. Some years ago a questionnaire was circulated to all staff at Tony's place of work, Amnesty International, here in London. The form included a question on the racial or ethnic origin of each person. This was being done in the spirit of good equal opportunities policy, which, of course, Tony fully supported. But try as he might he could not bring himself to answer the question. (It runs in the family.) It brought to mind for him the occasion in 1970 when, on behalf of the UK National Union of Students, he was flying from apartheid South Africa to Ian Smith's Rhodesia, an illegal racist regime. As the plane was due to land, he was confronted with 'the race question' on the visa form. He was conscious of the fact that his fellow passengers were of various 'races'. Tony describes his predicament: 'I paced up and down the aircraft, thinking and – more to the point – trying to see how others had filled this question in.' In the end, he says, he filled in the word 'human' – and was refused entry.[33]

For thirty years *Patterns of Prejudice* has sought to speak about 'the race question' and keep the language human. It is work in progress. I trust that progress will continue to be made, and that thirty years hence, when friends of the journal gather to celebrate its sixtieth anniversary, the voice of a certain ancestor of mine will be heard in the room, saying truthfully, 'Darlings, *this* is *knowledge*.'

NOTES

1. This chapter, slightly amended, appeared with the same title in *Patterns of Prejudice*, 33, 3 (1999), pp.5–18. The original essay was a lightly-revised version of the paper written as a keynote address for the conference 'Racism and Responsibility', London, 1997.
2. Plato, *Meno* 80c.
3. Fax from Office for National Statistics, Census Population and Health Group, Census Division: extract from *1991 Census – Definitions Great Britain* (London: HMSO, 1992), p.88. In March 1999 the government published a White Paper, 'The 2001 Census of Population', which sets out proposed changes to the ethnic question. The proposed changes mainly affect the question as it will be asked in England and Wales. The government also proposes to introduce an ethnic question for Northern Ireland, which will be along similar lines to the one used in Scotland. While these developments are not insignificant, the discussion in this paper applies, mutatis mutandis, to the revised versions of the ethnic question in the White Paper.
4. '"Braithwaite, Silverstein and Shah": A Roundtable Discussion on Black–Jewish–Muslim Relations in Britain', *Jewish Quarterly*, 166 (1997), pp.24–5.
5. Roger Ballard, 'Negotiating Race and Ethnicity: Exploring the Implications of the 1991 Census', *Patterns of Prejudice*, 30, 3 (1996).
6. Ibid., p.3, n.1.
7. Ibid., p.15.
8. Colin Brown, *Black and White Britain: The Third PSI Survey* (Aldershot: PSI, 1984), p.87.
9. There are contexts in which the savour of prejudice is absent, yet it seems to me that there is always something either stilted or vapid in such cases. As an example of what I mean by vapid, here is a sentence from a current NAACP appeals letter: '"Colored" people come in all colors; black, white, yellow and brown' (undated, received via US Mail 3 September 1998).
10. Kathleen Alaimo has drawn my attention to an article describing the emergence of 'whiteness studies' in the US (Margaret Talbot, 'Being White', *New York Times Magazine*, 30 November 1997, pp.116–19). Whatever 'whiteness studies' is, or proves to be, is it comparable to Black Studies? Could it be?
11. The statements I have made in this aside are rather terse; they are little more than a starting point for a discussion of the vocabulary of colour in the language of race.
12. Ballard, 'Negotiating Race and Ethnicity', p.15.
13. Ibid., especially pp.9, 23–4, 27.
14. Private email correspondence, 1–2 December 1997.
15. Ibid.
16. Patricia J. Williams, *Seeing a Colour-Blind Future: The Paradox of Race* (London: Virago, 1997), p.37.
17. Ibid., p.33.
18. Ibid., pp.37–8.
19. Ibid., p.38.
20. Gilbert Ryle, *The Concept of Mind* (Harmondsworth: Penguin, 1963), p.17.
21. See, for example, Paul Gordon and Francesca Klug, *New Right, New Racism* (London: Searchlight, 1987).
22. Williams, *Seeing a Colour-Blind Future*, p.50.
23. Ballard, 'Negotiating Race and Ethnicity', p.21.
24. Ibid., p.31.
25. Ibid., p.25.
26. Ibid., p.13.
27. Alas, Wrighty plays for Arsenal no more, having been transferred to West Ham.
28. Home Office, *Racial Discrimination: A Guide to the Race Relations Act 1976* (London, 1977), p.4.
29. Michael Banton, 'The Relationship between Racism and Antisemitism', *Patterns of Prejudice*, 26, 1–2 (1992), p.18.

30. *Cassell's New English Dictionary*, 19th edition (London: Cassell, 1960).
31. Lawrence Wright, 'One Drop of Blood', *New Yorker*, 25 July 1994, p.53.
32. Ibid., p.55.
33. Private email correspondence, 1 and 3 December 1997.

CHAPTER THIRTEEN

The Other Arthur Balfour

'PROTECTOR OF THE JEWS'

There appears to be a conundrum about Arthur Balfour.[1] On the one hand, his name is inseparable from the Declaration he signed as Foreign Secretary on 2 November 1917, which read in part: 'His Majesty's Government view with favour the establishment in Palestine of a national home for the Jewish people, and will use their best endeavours to facilitate the achievement of this object'.[2] On the other hand, as Prime Minister he brought in immigration controls aimed specifically against Jews from Eastern Europe. So, which was he: friend of the Jews or foe? Some say that there is no riddle: keeping Jews out of Britain and packing them off to Palestine were just two sides of the same antisemitic coin. But this would be too hasty and too cynical. It would not do justice to the man. The truth is both more complex and more intriguing.

Let us begin with the question of motivation vis-à-vis Zionism. Why did Balfour lend his name to the November 1917 declaration? Two kinds of motives appear to have been at work. First, there were *raisons d'état*. At the decisive meeting of the War Cabinet on 31 October 1917, Balfour opened the discussion of item 12, 'the Zionist Movement', by stating that 'from a purely diplomatic and political point of view, some declaration favourable to the aspirations of the Jewish nationalists should be made'.[3] It was natural that Balfour, as Foreign Secretary, should see things from this point of view, especially at a critical juncture of the war when, as Jon Kimche remarks wryly, 'it was the British Empire that needed help more urgently than did the Jews'.[4] But why did Balfour think that the cause of empire would be advanced by winning the support of the Zionists? The answer to this question will begin to take us into the mind of the man on the subject of the Jews.

Broadly speaking, there were two wartime considerations that exercised Balfour. One was a passage to India, which currently was blocked by Ottoman holdings in the region and which a Jewish homeland in Palestine under British sponsorship might secure. The second consideration was foreign support: he wanted to keep Russia in the war and draw the US into it. In this latter connection, following his opening remarks at the War Cabinet meeting, Balfour continued as follows: 'The vast majority of Jews in Russia and America as indeed, all over the world, now appeared to be favourable of [*sic*] Zionism. If we could make a declaration favourable to such an ideal, we should be able to carry on extremely useful propaganda both in Russia and America.'[5]

There are two remarkable claims contained in Balfour's argument to the War Cabinet, one explicit, the other implicit. The first is about the extent of global Jewish support for Zionism. Historians find it hard to determine Jewish attitudes to the Zionist movement at the time. David Fromkin tells us: 'As of 1913, the last date for which there were figures, only about one percent of the world's Jews had signified their adherence to Zionism.'[6] In America, Jewish support for the movement only began to grow later. 'In 1919', says Fromkin, 'membership of the Zionist Federation grew to more than 175,000, though Zionist supporters remained a minority group within American Jewry'.[7] He goes on to say that the movement 'still encountered fierce opposition from the richer and more established Jews – opposition that was not really overcome until the 1940s'. So, the facts are not altogether clear, but it appears that in 1917, Jewish nationalism was not a popular cause among Jews. Yet Balfour believed that the 'vast majority' of Jews 'all over the world' were Zionists. Nor was he alone in thinking this. 'British Intelligence reports indicated a surge of Zionist feeling during the war in the Pale of Russia, but there were no figures either to substantiate or to quantify it.'[8] The idea that Jews in general were strongly in support of Zionism seems to have been widely held in British Government circles. But why?

Perhaps light can be shed on this when we turn to the second remarkable claim made in Balfour's argument to the War Cabinet: the *implicit* claim that Jewish influence was worth winning; that it was a major factor in the affairs of the world. This view was commonplace in the British corridors of power. It was not based on a sober analysis but merely, or mainly, on the connotations of the word 'Jewish'. British officials widely believed that Jews (or 'the Jews') were behind Bolshevism in Russia, imperialism in Germany, and the Turkish Government too. A case in point was Colonel Sir Mark Sykes, who was chief adviser to the Foreign Office on all Middle Eastern questions and who played a major role in converting the War Cabinet secretariat to the Zionist cause.[9] But did Balfour *himself* see Jewry this way? We shall come to this question in due course. For the time being, suffice to say that 'the Foreign Secretary', in the words of one of his biographers, Sydney Zebel, 'greatly exaggerated Russian Jewry's influence, just as he over-estimated the influence of America's Jews'.[10] This reinforced his conviction that, for reasons of state, the British Empire should embrace the Zionist cause.

However, Balfour's interest in Zionism exceeded the bounds of duty and the demands (as he saw them) of practical politics. It was, says his biographer Max Egremont, one of his 'greatest and most far-reaching enthusiasms'.[11] Chaim Weizmann relates that when he talked with Balfour on 12 December 1914 and explained 'the Jewish tragedy' in Europe, the British statesman was 'most deeply moved – to the point of tears'.[12] Balfour's niece, Blanche Dugdale, wrote: 'Near the end of his days he said to me that on the whole he felt that what he had been able to do for the Jews had been the thing he looked back upon as the most worth his doing.'[13] Towards the end of his life, Egremont tells us, Balfour 'came to relish his role as protector of the Jews, even writing to golf clubs in the Home Counties in an attempt to remove their ban on Jewish membership'.[14] This affectionate regard was reciprocated at his death. 'Telegrams from Jewish communities and expressions of regret were sent from all over the world.'[15]

It comes, therefore, as a surprise to discover that this 'protector of the Jews' presided over the passage of the 1905 Aliens Act, the main object of which was to limit the entry into Britain of Jews from Eastern Europe. Not that the Act referred to Jews explicitly; it dealt with aliens – foreigners – in general. 'Nevertheless', writes Tony Kushner, 'it is clear that the major purpose of the Act was to stop the flow of East European Jews into Britain.'[16] This emphasis is reflected in the popular agitation that called for legislation, in the Report of the Royal Commission on Alien Immigration (1903), and in the debate in Parliament.

Bernard Gainer, in his classic study of the 1905 Aliens Act, points out that in the twenty years or so leading up to the passage of the Act (from about 1880 onwards), 'immigrant' and 'Jew' 'became synonymous terms'.[17] The title of Gainer's book, *The Alien Invasion*, reflects a phrase that was current in the anti-immigration rhetoric of the period. So, for example, a book by W.H. Wilkins, secretary of the newly-founded Association for Preventing the Immigration of Destitute Aliens, had the same title.[18] In the same year in which Wilkins's book appeared (1892), Balfour, speaking for the British Government, used the same word, 'invasion', in connection with immigration. Responding to rumours that an overwhelming number of Russian Jews were about to flee Russia for England, he said: 'we quite appreciate the gravity of the matter and we are watching it most carefully, for we feel that such an invasion as has been suggested ... would be an intolerable abuse of the system of emigration'.[19] Gainer tells us that from mid-May to July 1891, 'the Evening News had screamed incessantly "Shut the Gates" against "The Jewish Invasion" '.[20] He adds, 'On 23 May 1891, it stressed that "nineteen-twentieths" of the immigrants were Jewish.'[21] Notice the slide from 'the alien invasion' to 'the Jewish invasion'.

Let us look briefly at this 'invasion' and its causes. Jews had been migrating to Britain, without let or hindrance, ever since Oliver Cromwell readmitted them in 1656. Throughout the nineteenth century, the Jewish population in Britain grew steadily, partly due to the number of Jews – notably from Poland – who immigrated year by year.[22] Then beginning in 1881, events in Russia precipitated a mass exodus of Jews from Eastern Europe. On 13 March, Czar Alexander II was assassinated by a group of revolutionaries; a Jew was among those implicated; and the entire Jewish population of the Russian empire paid the price. 'The following month, a wave of terror began which engulfed the Jewish inhabitants of the Pale of Settlement to which Russian law restricted them.'[23] A series of Orders, the 'May Laws', were issued in 1882, 'attacking the basis of Jewish economic life in Russia'.[24] (We are accustomed to making a sharp distinction between 'economic migrants' and 'asylum seekers'. But in the case of the émigré Jews who left Eastern Europe a hundred years ago, this is a distinction without much difference. The historian David Feldman observes, 'In view of the legal disabilities under which all Russian Jews lived, any definition of who was or was not a refugee contained an arbitrary element.'[25]) The situation did not improve, either in Russia or elsewhere in Eastern Europe, over the next few decades. Expulsions, pogroms and legal disabilities made life intolerable for Jews, who emigrated en masse. Between 1880 and 1914 over 2,000,000 Eastern European Jews left their homes and migrated to other parts of the world, mainly the US.[26] The level of desperation can be gauged by one remarkable event in 1900: 3,000 Jews left Romania and trekked across Europe on foot 'until they arrived on British soil'.[27] Thousands of other Romanian Jews who took part in the same 'march of despair' went elsewhere.[28] Between 1881 and 1905, about 100,000 Jews from Eastern Europe, seeking escape from persecution and poverty, settled in England.[29] Then in 1905, the same year in which the notoriously antisemitic 'Black Hundreds' was founded in Russia, Parliament, under the guiding hand of the Prime Minister, Arthur Balfour, decided to curtail Jewish immigration into Britain.[30]

The Aliens Act of 1905 broke with a long-standing tradition in which Britain granted asylum to all-comers. It initiated 'modern immigration law' and has 'formed the basis for all subsequent restrictions'.[31] Under the Act, new arrivals were denied admission to the country if they were deemed 'undesirable'. For example, someone who could not 'show' that they possessed, or were able to obtain, 'the means of decently supporting himself and his dependents' would be an 'undesirable'.[32] Similarly, someone who, due to illness or infirmity, appeared 'likely to become a charge upon the rates or otherwise a detriment to the public' was an 'undesirable'.[33] By these criteria, a large number of Jewish arrivals from Eastern Europe were potentially 'undesirables'. Much of the debate in Parliament centred on the principle of asylum, which critics of the Aliens Bill referred to as a 'right'. The bill, in its final form, did include certain exemptions.[34] But they were carefully qualified and opponents felt that they were too narrow.[35] In any event, the bill passed its third reading on 19 July with a majority of 90. It received the Royal Assent on 11 August and came into effect on New Years Day, 1906.[36]

Balfour played a prominent part in steering the Act through the House of Commons. His speeches show that he was well aware of the conditions of life for Jews in Eastern Europe. When the Aliens Bill came up for its second reading on 2 May, he denounced 'the bigotry, the oppression, the hatred the Jewish race has too often met with in foreign countries'.[37] Later that week, the *Jewish Chronicle* gave a stinging rejoinder. Leonard Stein writes that the paper 'invited Balfour to explain how his sympathy with persecuted Jews could be reconciled with a policy which led him "to refuse asylum to Jewish religious refugees" '.[38] Balfour had, in effect, given his answer just before the question was put to the House: 'In my view we have a right to keep out everybody who does not add to the strength of the community – the industrial, social, and intellectual strength of the community.'[39] The clear implication – strongly contested by opponents of the bill – was that some Jewish immigrants did not 'add to the strength of the community'; that their misery and distress were a burden to society as a whole; and that their numbers were significant enough to warrant legislation.

Setting aside the question of whether there was any validity to this case, how can we make sense of the fact that Balfour, the 'protector of the Jews', was one of the people making it? For his argument would seem to exclude precisely those Jews who came to these shores in most need of his protection. Furthermore, although the legislation was ostensibly about 'aliens' (non-citizens) in general, it induced a 'widespread uneasiness among English Jews'.[40] The *Jewish Chronicle* had summed up this feeling the previous year. Attacking the 1904 version, 'the paper stressed that the bill would end up creating animosity against the Jews, as Jews'.[41]

It almost seems as if there were two Arthur Balfours at two different times: a later Balfour who saw himself as protecting Jews against their enemies, an earlier one who sought to protect Britain against Jews – or against those 'undesirable' Jews who did not 'add to the strength of the community'. And yet the government that introduced the Aliens Act also offered Theodor Herzl – in 1903 – the prospect of a Jewish homeland in British East Africa: the so-called Uganda proposal, which has been called 'the first Balfour Declaration'.[42] In the debate in Parliament over the Aliens Bill two years later, Balfour tried to make capital out of this offer. He used it to refute the charge of 'inhumanity' and to prove that he was not 'indifferent to the interests' of 'the Jewish race'. Specifically, he said this: his government had 'offered to the Jewish race a great tract of fertile land in one of our possessions in order that they might ... find an asylum from their persecutors at home'.[43] Given the context, the word 'asylum' seems carefully chosen.

'A PEOPLE APART'

To recap: There were two kinds of motives that appear to have led Balfour to lend his name to the November 1917 declaration. On the one hand, as Egremont puts it, he was a 'ruthless practitioner of power in the defence of what he saw as his country's interests'.[44] On the other hand, there was his sympathy – even enthusiasm – for the Zionist idea. The latter was rooted in his view of Jews – or 'the Jews' – and of Jewish history. To this I now turn.

In the same sitting on the Aliens Bill in which he invoked the Uganda proposal in defence of his humanity, Balfour, referring to 'an alien immigration which was largely Jewish', gave a revealing glimpse of his view of Jews. He said:

> a state of things could easily be imagined in which it would not be to the advantage of the civilization of the country that there should be an immense body of persons who, however patriotic, able, and industrious, however much they threw themselves into the national life, still, by their own action, remained a people apart, and not merely held a religion differing from the vast majority of their fellow-countrymen, but only inter-married among themselves.[45]

Previously, he had argued that the bill 'only excludes, broadly speaking, those who are likely to become a public charge'.[46] But in this imaginary scenario, the people he deemed undesirable were neither shirkers nor spongers. He was no longer referring to Jews as immigrants but as a 'body of persons' who lead a distinctive way of life; not as 'aliens' in the technical sense of non-citizens but aliens in the mythic sense of strangers, outsiders, 'a people apart'. The question had changed: it was not about who adds to 'the strength of the community' but who belongs.

Who *does* belong? Balfour had a particular view of what it means to be part of the British nation – or of what it means for the nation to remain itself – which suggests that race, in some shape or form, played a part in his idea of nationhood. Consider this curious argument that he made during the debate on the second reading of the Aliens Bill:

> If there were a substitution of Poles for Britons, for example, though the Briton of the future might have the same laws, the same institutions and constitution, and the same historical traditions learned in the elementary schools, though all these things might be in the possession of the new nationality, that new nationality would not be the same, and would not be the nationality we should desire to be our heirs through the ages yet to come.[47]

Since many of the 'Russians' who were migrating to Britain were Poles, and most of these Poles were Jews, his illustration could hardly have been more appropriate. That aside, what, we might ask, would be the crucial difference between the 'old' and the 'new' nationalities in his 'example'? He did not say. At one point, he made a contrast between immigrants and 'Englishmen, Britons' whom he referred to as 'our own flesh and blood'.[48] He frequently used the expression 'the Jewish race'; but the language of race was commonplace and did not necessarily imply (any more than it does today) a fully-fledged theory of difference based on biology. Balfour admired the way America took 'men of many distinct nationalities and many races' and turned them 'by a process of natural alchemy' into 'citizens of the United States'.[49] He called this 'a marvellous power'; but added that 'it has its limits'.[50] What determines those limits is left unclear. However, he believed that there was 'an unbridgeable abyss' between black and white: 'the white and black races ... are born with different capacities which education cannot and will not change'.[51]

Although the precise role played by race is unclear, Balfour's idea (or ideology) of nationhood was a fundamental part of his political credo. It lies in the background of his view of Jews as 'a people apart'. If he admired the Zionists, it is partly because he held 'strong views about the inspiring power of true nationalism'; and he regarded theirs as authentic.[52] 'What was at the back of the Zionist movement', he told a meeting of the War Cabinet on 4 October 1917, 'was the intense national consciousness held by certain members of the Jewish race.'[53] The Jews, he told the House of Lords in his maiden speech on 21 June 1922, have maintained 'a continuity of religious and racial tradition of which we have no parallel elsewhere'.[54] Furthermore, he thought that the Jews 'are the most gifted race that mankind has seen since the Greeks of the fifth century'.[55] 'The Jews are too great a race not to count', he wrote to his sister in July 1918, 'and they ought to have a place where those who had strong racial idealism could develop on their lines as a nation and govern themselves.'[56] Thus Jewish nationalism, for Balfour, was not only authentic, it was exemplary.

It was also, he thought, vital – not only for Jews but also for the sake of Europe – that the Zionist movement should achieve its goal. For, as he saw it, the very virtue of Jews – their 'intense national consciousness' – was also the root of the 'problem' that they posed for the nations among whom they dwelt: the problem of refusing to blend into the general populace, of remaining 'a people apart'. In an Introduction written specially for Nahum Sokolow's *History of Zionism* (1919), Balfour explained the double value of Zionism:

> If it succeeds, it will do a great spiritual and material work for the Jews, but not for them alone. For as I read its meaning it is, among other things, a serious endeavour to mitigate the age-long miseries created for Western civilization by the presence in its midst of a Body which it too long regarded as alien and even hostile, but which it was equally unable to expel or to absorb.[57]

As this passage shows, Balfour had some sympathy for the predicament in which, as he saw it, 'Western civilization' was placed by the Jewish 'Body' in its midst. In January 1917 he met with Lucien Wolf, of the Conjoint Foreign Committee, 'the recognised spokesman of the British Jews in matters affecting Jewish communities abroad', to discuss discrimination against Jews in Russia.[58] He acknowledged that 'the treatment of the Jews was abominable beyond all measure'. But he went on to point out that 'the persecutors had a case of their own'.[59] Here is how he saw that case:

> Wherever one went in Eastern Europe one found that by some

way or other the Jew got on, and when to this was added the fact that he belonged to a distinct race and that he professed a religion which to the people about him was an object of inherited hatred, and that, moreover, he was ... numbered by millions, one could perhaps understand the desire to keep him down and deny him the rights to which he was entitled.[60]

Wolf notes that he 'did not say that this justified the persecution'. But Balfour does seem adept at putting the case of the persecutor. Furthermore, when he met with Weizmann three years earlier, he mentioned a conversation with Cosima Wagner, the composer's widow, and said he 'shared many of her anti-semitic postulates'.[61] (The conversation with Cosima Wagner was during a visit to Bayreuth in the late 1890s.[62]) He was, according to Colonel Edward House, President Woodrow Wilson's chief aide, 'inclined to believe that nearly all Bolshevism and disorder of that sort is directly traceable to Jews'.[63] And in a letter to Lloyd George, he wrote that 'the Jews undoubtedly constitute a most formidable power whose manifestations are not by any means always attractive'; though he went on to say that 'the balance of wrong doing seems to me on the whole to be greatly on the Christian side'.[64] Indeed, during the debate over the Aliens Bill, he declared with passion: 'The treatment of the [Jewish] race has been a disgrace to Christendom, a disgrace which tarnishes the fair fame of Christianity even at this moment'.[65] And his niece remembers 'imbibing from him the idea that Christian religion and civilization owes to Judaism an immeasurable debt, shamefully ill repaid'.[66]

Balfour's attitude to Jews has been called ambivalent.[67] But he was not ambivalent about seeing them as larger than life: a people with unique qualities (good and bad) and possessing special significance for the world. For they were, in the first place, the people of the Bible. His ideas about Jews were rooted in the Old Testament brand of Christianity on which he was raised by his Evangelical mother.[68] It seems likely that, as the 'strongest single influence' on the young Arthur, she transmitted to her son the idea of the Jews as a special people and the ideal of restoring them to their ancient land.[69] Opinion is divided over whether there was a 'mystical' element in Balfour's commitment to the Zionist cause.[70] Be that as it may, no other 'nationality' could have the same cachet for him as the Jewish. No other nationalism could be more 'true'.

Given his concept of nationhood, there were only two possible solutions to the problem that, as Balfour saw it, afflicted both the Jews and the countries where they lived. He put it succinctly to Weizmann when they met in London in December 1914. The 'problem', he said, 'would not be solved until either the Jews became completely assimilated here or a normal Jewish society came into existence in Palestine'.[71] (Significantly, Balfour 'was thinking more of the West European Jews than of those of Eastern Europe'.[72]) The third alternative – remaining in Europe as 'a people apart' – was not a possible solution; for, in his eyes as well as Weizmann's, this was precisely the 'Jewish problem' that needed solving.

A true-life vignette captures Balfour's perception of the 'Jewish problem'. Once, some years prior to the Parliamentary debate over the Aliens Bill, he paid a social visit to the Sassoons. Describing the experience in a letter to a friend he said that the house was 'peopled with endless Sassoon girls'.[73] He continued: 'I believe the Hebrews were in an actual majority – and though I have no prejudice against the race (quite the contrary) I began to understand the point of view of those who object to alien immigration.'[74] The English house, brimming with 'endless Sassoon girls', the house where 'the Hebrews' were 'in an actual majority', was a microcosm of the imaginary Britain in his speech in the Commons: a nation that housed 'an immense body of persons who ... remained a people apart'. For Balfour, the basic problem was the presence of a Jewish 'Body' that the British nation was 'equally unable to expel or to absorb'.

In conclusion, the alien on Balfour's mind was not simply the immigrant; it was the Jew. And far from being contradictory, the 1917 Balfour Declaration and the 1905 Aliens Act were two sides of the same coin. However, to call the coin 'antisemitic' would be simplistic. Call it 'nationalist', perhaps. At any rate, the conundrum is solved. There was no 'other Arthur Balfour'.

NOTES

1. This chapter was adapted from a talk given to the Jewish Historical Society, Manchester, 12 February 2006. The talk was expanded from an essay with the same name that appeared in Stephen W. Massil (ed.), *The Jewish Year Book 2005* (London: Vallentine Mitchell in association with the *Jewish Chronicle*, 2005), pp.xi–xviii.
2. The letter is reproduced as a frontispiece in Leonard Stein, *The Balfour Declaration* (New York: Simon & Schuster, 1961).
3. Jon Kimche, *The Unromantics: The Great Powers and the Balfour Declaration* (London: Weidenfeld & Nicolson, 1968), p.41.
4. Ibid., p.43.
5. Ibid., p.41.
6. David Fromkin, *A Peace to End All Peace: The Fall of the Ottoman Empire and the Creation of the Modern Middle East* (New York: Avon Books, 1989), p.294.
7. Ibid., p.300.

8. Ibid., p.294.
9. Ibid., p.293.
10. Sydney H. Zebel, *Balfour: A Political Biography* (Cambridge: Cambridge University Press, 1973), p.248.
11. Max Egremont, *Balfour: A Life of Arthur James Balfour* (London: Phoenix, 1980), p.204.
12. Leonard Stein, *The Balfour Declaration* (New York: Simon & Schuster, 1961), pp.154–5; Ronald Sanders, *The High Walls of Jerusalem: A History of the Balfour Declaration and the Birth of the British Mandate for Palestine* (New York: Holt, Rinehart & Winston, 1983), p.120. Previous meetings between the two men were in January 1905 and January 1906 (Stein, *Balfour Declaration*, pp.147, 151.)
13. Egremont, *Balfour*, p.296.
14. Ibid., p.313.
15. Ibid., p.339.
16. Tony Kushner, *The Persistence of Prejudice: Antisemitism in British Society During the Second World War* (Manchester: Manchester University Press, 1989), p.11.
17. Bernard Gainer, *The Alien Invasion: The Origins of the Aliens Act of 1905* (New York: Crane, Russak & Co., 1972), p.1.
18. Ibid., p.85.
19. Ibid., p.171.
20. Ibid., p.169.
21. Ibid., p.276.
22. David Englander, *A Documentary History of Jewish Immigrants in Britain, 1840–1920* (Leicester: Leicester University Press, 1994), p.7.
23. Gainer, *Alien Invasion*, p.1.
24. Ibid.
25. David Feldman, *Englishmen and Jews: Social Relations and Political Culture 1840–1914* (New Haven, CT: Yale University Press, 1994), p.301.
26. Ibid., p.141.
27. Robert Winder, *Bloody Foreigners: The Story of Immigration to Britain* (London: Little, Brown, 2004), p.176.
28. Ismar Elbogen, *A Century of Jewish Life* (Philadelphia, PA: Jewish Publication Society of America, 1966), pp.361–2.
29. Stein, *Balfour Declaration*, p.78.
30. Strictly speaking, the organization founded in 1905 was the Union of the Russian People, while the 'Black Hundreds' were the armed bands recruited by this organization and by similar societies. See Norman Cohn, *Warrant for Genocide: The Myth of the Jewish World Conspiracy and the Protocols of the Elders of Zion* (London: Serif, 1996), p.120, n.2.
31. Christopher Vincenzi, 'The Aliens Act 1905', *New Community*, 12, 2 (Summer 1985), p.275.
32. Aliens Act 1905, clause (3) (a), reproduced in Englander, *Documentary History*, p.279.
33. Aliens Act 1905, clause (3) (b), reproduced in Englander, *Documentary History*, p.279.
34. For the relevant clauses, see Englander, *Documentary History*, p.279.
35. See Gainer, *Alien Invasion*, p.196, and Feldman, *Englishmen and Jews*, p.290.
36. Gainer, *Alien Invasion*, p.196.
37. *Parliamentary Debates*, 4th Series, vol. 145, col. 795.
38. Stein, *Balfour Declaration*, p.150, quoting from the 5 May 1905 issue of the *Jewish Chronicle*.
39. *Parliamentary Debates*, 4th Series, vol. 145, col. 804.
40. Stein, *Balfour Declaration*, pp.79–80.
41. David Cesarani, *The Jewish Chronicle and Anglo-Jewry, 1841–1991* (Cambridge: Cambridge University Press, 1994), p.98.
42. Fromkin, *Peace to End All Peace*, pp.273–4.
43. *Parliamentary Debates*, 4th Series, vol. 149, col. 178.
44. Egremont, *Balfour*, p.339.
45. *Parliamentary Debates*, 4th Series, vol. 149, col. 155.
46. Ibid., vol. 145, col. 801.
47. Ibid., vol. 145, col. 796.
48. Ibid., vol. 145, col. 805.
49. Ibid., vol. 145, col. 796.
50. Ibid.
51. Egremont, *Balfour*, p.215.

52. Mrs Edgar Dugdale, *The Balfour Declaration: Origins and Background* (London: Jewish Agency for Palestine, 1940), p.29.
53. Doreen Ingrams, *Palestine Papers 1917–1922: Seeds of Conflict* (London: John Murray, 1972), p.11.
54. *Parliamentary Debates*, 5th Series, vol. 50, House of Lords, col. 1017.
55. In conversation with Sir Harold Nicolson in 1917, as recalled by the latter, quoted in Stein, *Balfour Declaration*, p.157.
56. Egremont, *Balfour*, p.295.
57. Arthur Balfour, 'Introduction', in Nahum Sokolow, *History of Zionism 1600–1918*, vol. 1 (New York: Ktav, 1969), p.liv.
58. Stein, *Balfour Declaration*, p.172. The Conjoint Foreign Committee was formed in 1878 by the Anglo-Jewish Association and the Board of Deputies of British Jews.
59. Ibid., p.164.
60. Ibid.
61. Ibid, p.154.
62. Egremont, *Balfour*, p.204.
63. Colonel Edward M. House, quoted in Tom Segev, *One Palestine Complete: Jews and Arabs Under the British Mandate* (New York: Henry Holt & Co., 2001), p.119.
64. 19 February 1919, in Ingrams, *Palestine Papers 1917–1922*, pp.61–2.
65. *Parliamentary Debates*, 4th Series, vol. 145, col. 795.
66. Blanche Dugdale, *Arthur James Balfour*, vol. 1 (London: Hutchinson & Co., 1939), p.325.
67. Kenneth Young, *Arthur James Balfour* (London: Bell & Sons, 1963), p.258; Stein, *Balfour Declaration*, p.165; Gainer, *Alien Invasion*, pp.117, 119.
68. Young, *Arthur James Balfour*, pp.257, 387; Egremont, *Balfour*, pp.296, 340.
69. Egremont, *Balfour*, p.18.
70. Stein says no (Stein, *Balfour Declaration*, p.158), Egremont says yes (Egremont, *Balfour*, p.313).
71. As related by Weizmann to Ahad Ha'am two days later, quoted (and translated from the Russian) in Stein, *Balfour Declaration*, p.154.
72. Ibid.
73. Sanders, *The High Walls of Jerusalem*, p.119. The friend was Lady Elcho.
74. Ibid.

CHAPTER FOURTEEN

Old Ghosts in the New World

Revised version of a talk given at Saint Xavier University, Chicago, April 1995.

SCHLESINGER THE HISTORIAN

In speaking as a Brit among Yanks, I am conscious of my foreign accent.[1] And as a relative newcomer to the US, I would think myself presumptuous to be speaking about America to Americans were it not for the fact that this country has seen itself as a nation of newcomers; or, in the phrase that John Kennedy used for the title of an essay that he wrote in the 1950s (and which he was revising at the time of his assassination in 1963), 'a nation of immigrants'.[2]

How is such a thing – a nation of immigrants – possible, given the variety of nations from which these immigrants have come? For Arthur Schlesinger, a special adviser to President Kennedy, the answer boils down to one thing: the melting pot. His essay *The Disuniting of America* is a spirited defence of the 'idea of a melting pot' against the 'cult of ethnicity'.[3] The essay does not suffer from excessive nuance. It is essentially a polemic: articulate, forceful, provocative. If it hits hard it frequently hits home. It is also one-sided and simplistic – but that is part of being a polemic.

Schlesinger is a historian, someone who writes stories about the past. But the story he tells at the beginning of the first chapter, a story that is carried forward throughout the rest of the book, is not so much history as myth. It is a creation myth for the American nation, an idealized account of how the nation came into existence. The opening sentence recalls the opening words of Genesis: 'At the beginning America was seen as a severing of roots, a liberation from the stifling past, an entry into a new life, an interweaving of separate ethnic strands into a new national design.'[4] In this familiar myth of origin, America was not created out of nothing: it emerged out of elements that existed in 'the stifling past', transforming them into a new – and enlightened – order

of things. 'And the future was America – not so much a nation', Herman
Melville said, 'as a world.'[5]

The unofficial 'motto' of this New World was 'Never look back.'[6]
But looking back is precisely what the 'cult of ethnicity', in
Schlesinger's account, insists on doing. And in so doing, it 'threatens
to become a counter-revolution against the original theory of America
as "one people", a common culture, a single nation'.[7] In other words,
in opposing the 'ethnic revolt against the melting pot', Schlesinger is
writing in defence of the American revolution and the integrity of the
nation against a divisive and mortal enemy within.[8] It is *that* kind of
book.

Schlesinger's front-line rhetoric and his grand optimistic vision of
America lend vigour to his writing. But the effect is more rousing than
inspiring. This has something to do with the shallowness of the overall argument, such as it is. I say 'such as it is' because, although the
author often succeeds in scoring points, what informs the essay is not
so much a coherent argument as an animus against certain tendencies
in modern America. As a result, his enemy is never quite in focus.
Consider, for example, the following sentence: 'The cult of ethnicity has
reversed the movement of American history, producing a nation
of minorities – or at least of minority spokesmen – less interested in
joining with the majority in common endeavor than in declaring their
alienation from an oppressive, white, patriarchal, racist, sexist, classist
society.'[9] The causal connection is, to say the least, obscure: why should
a cult of *ethnicity* produce people who regard American society as
patriarchal or *sexist* or *classist*? The thought carries no weight; what
carries the sentence forward is the grumpiness. And what Schlesinger
is really reacting against here is not a 'cult of ethnicity' but a certain
sort of contemporary politics on the left, sometimes called 'radical' or
'correct'. It is a rule of rhetorical combat that he practices again and
again: When two or more opponents raise their heads, collapse them
into one.

For that matter, the word 'white' in the sentence just quoted is logically odd too. In his Foreword Schlesinger explicitly states that the
'cult of ethnicity' he is attacking 'has arisen both among non-Anglo
whites and among nonwhite minorities'.[10] But a 'non-Anglo white',
such as an ethnic Italian or Pole, inclined towards ethnic chauvinism,
is hardly going to feel alienated from society because society is *white*.
Again: the thought as it stands makes little or no sense.

It does, however, make better sense if we read into it the meaning
that predominates in the essay as a whole. For Schlesinger is primarily

concerned with two developments: 'the rising flow of non-European immigrants' and, above all, Afrocentricity among American Blacks.[11] Much of the book is directed against the 'uncritical glorification' of African history and 'the Afrocentric campaign' to change the public school curriculum.[12] He laces his text with choice quotations from a number of 'Afrocentric ideologues', focusing especially on two sources: the 'African-American Baseline Essays' conceived by the black psychologist Asa Hilliard, and a report submitted in 1989 to the New York State Commissioner of Education by the Task Force on Minorities: Equity and Excellence.[13] Here is where Schlesinger scores most of his points.

However, he makes Afrocentricity seem more eccentric than it is. Misleadingly, he speaks of 'the five ethnic communities into which the New York state task force wishes to divide the country'.[14] The five groupings are as follows: African-American, Asian-American, Puerto Rican/Latino, Native American and White. What he fails to mention is that these categories, for better or for worse, are not desiderata on a wish list drawn up by the Task Force or by 'Afrocentric ideologues': they correspond, almost exactly, to the five classifications laid down by the federal Office of Management and Budget in 1977 under Statistical Directive 15: four racial (Black, Asian-American and Pacific Islander, Native American, White) and one ethnic (Hispanic). In other words, the federal government has already divided the country (if you wish to put it that way) into five 'communities'; the New York Task Force was only following Washington's lead. As I discovered recently when I paid a visit to the Social Security Administration Office downtown, you are asked to tick one of these five boxes on Form SS-5 when you apply for a social security card. (Don't ask me which box I ticked.[15]) These same five classifications are used by the federal Census Bureau, by the Center for Disease Control, and by agencies that monitor compliance with civil rights laws.[16]

Furthermore, Schlesinger picks out the zaniest or most extreme ideas and treats them as though they were typical. (This is another of his rhetorical devices: to use a few rotten apples to spoil the barrel.) Scoring points against easy targets is worth doing if it leads to insight. But, on the contrary, he does not put the sort of thinking he attacks into context; or rather, the context he provides is wrong. On the one hand, he writes in full awareness of the 'curse of racism' in American history and in particular the 'bitter experience' of Blacks.[17] On the other hand, he describes the 'black American predicament' as 'another variation on the familiar theme of nationalism'.[18] But it is not. It is

even misleading to bracket together, under the term 'racism', the treatment of Blacks in the US and bigotry towards such immigrant groups
as the Chinese or Mexicans. It is certainly not the case that black
separatism is just another example of the 'cult of ethnicity'. And this
points to the blindness at the heart of Schlesinger's essay.

At the heart of the essay, as I have earlier mentioned, is the idea of
'the melting pot'. Schlesinger is vague about what this implies for the
make-up of American society. While upholding 'the old American ideal
of assimilation', leaning heavily on metaphors of melting and dissolving, he also speaks in terms of integration; he celebrates the 'splendid
diversity of the nation'; and he explicitly embraces 'cultural pluralism'.[19]
Then again, when discussing Horace Kallen's 1915 essay, 'Democracy
Versus the Melting-Pot', he presents the doctrine of cultural pluralism
as the express rejection of the ideal of the melting pot.[20] If all this is
somewhat confusing, he is reasonably clear on one point: the glue that
holds the melting pot together is 'a shared commitment to common
ideals'.[21] These ideals are the unofficial articles of what, borrowing a
phrase from Gunnar Myrdal, he calls 'the American Creed'.[22] They are
the ideals of the American Revolution, *liberal* ideals to which
Schlesinger himself subscribes: 'the ideals of the essential dignity and
equality of all human beings, of inalienable rights to freedom, justice,
and opportunity'.[23]

But what, in America, constitutes a human being? To be human, on
Schlesinger's account, is to be an individual: a free-standing being making choices between things. Thus he says, the 'American Creed envisages
a nation composed of individuals making their own choices and
accountable to themselves, not a nation based on inviolable ethnic
communities'.[24] It turns out that what this means is that being an
individual means *not* being, in any serious sense, a member of an 'ethnic
community'. He speaks of ethnicity as something a person can 'shed',
as though it were an accessory; or as though that is what it ought to
be in America, the New World, the best of worlds.[25] And clearly he
welcomes the fact (if it is a fact) that most Americans 'see themselves
primarily as individuals and only secondarily and *trivially* as adherents
of a group' (emphasis added).[26]

The blindness of which I speak consists in this: for Schlesinger,
ethnicity is nothing more than either an atavistic (and un-American)
attachment to the past or a kind of accessory. Seen this way, ethnicity is
ethnicity, whatever its specific flavour. And all forms of social injustice
involving racial or ethnic discrimination amount to the same thing: the
failure to ignore a mere accessory and to treat the individual as an

individual. Hence on Schlesinger's account the position of Blacks in the US is fundamentally the same as that of any other ethnic group, even if, as he acknowledges, the black experience has been incomparably harsher. In this reckoning, the racism suffered by Blacks is essentially an aberration: a temporary lapse from the liberal ideals of the 'American Creed'.

I say 'temporary' because in Schlesinger's eyes it is in the very nature of the US to improve and progress: 'The steady movement of American life has been from exclusion to inclusion.'[27] This is, in effect, a corollary of the myth with which the essay opens: an America where you forget the ghosts of the past and step out into an enlightened future. But what if those ghosts are American? What if America is itself the past that you need to forget? And what if the present contains continual reminders of that past – as if it were not the past merely but a portent of the future? And if someone were to appeal to you using the very same words – citing the selfsame ideals – that stood for the nation to which your ancestors were forcibly brought and in which you have been systematically degraded precisely because of your ancestry, would you be reconciled? Or might you retort in the same vein as this particular black woman did, recalling the 1984 centennial of the Statue of Liberty: 'What I got angry about, when you had your hundred years of that Statue of Liberty and I got damned mad because it was sickening to me. That was not made for me. We didn't come through Ellis Island. Do you understand what I'm saying?'[28]

What she is saying, I take it, is that black Americans with African ancestry were not in the same boat – not metaphorically and not literally – as the tired, poor and huddled masses that emigrated to the New World yearning to be free. (The first ship bringing Negro slaves to America reached Jamestown in 1619, one year before the Mayflower docked at Plymouth Rock.) The founding myth of *her* America runs counter to the one that Schlesinger recites at the opening of his essay (though there are haunting echoes). It goes, I suppose, something like this: 'At the beginning America was seen as a severing of roots, a suppression of a once-thriving past, an entry into a new life of captivity, a dissolving of separate ethnic strands into a new generic blackness.' And the future was America – not so much a nation as a hell.

In other words, for Blacks in the US oppression and disadvantage are not temporary aberrations. The 1964 Civil Rights Act was an aberration. Affirmative action is an aberration. Social justice is an aberration. These are aberrations, not merely because they depart from the normal course of events but because they deviate from the very nature of

America – the other America which also came into existence 'at the beginning' and which has not ceased to be.

This is not to derogate from the liberal ideals that Schlesinger cherishes. Nor is it to deny their power to inspire across the racial divide. Indeed, Schlesinger underestimates the extent to which these same ideals give impetus to some of the very tendencies in contemporary America, including black America, that he deplores. Apparently he is blind to the fact that these ideals can, in their way, divide as well as unite. (Or you could say that their best promise is to unify the nation by being the issues over which people argue.) He writes as if there were basically two camps: the camp of the 'American Creed' versus the camp of the 'cult of ethnicity'. This language – of creed versus cult – imparts an oddly religious hue to the whole affair; as does the apocalyptic vision in the Foreword of an entire planet threatened by ethnic conflict. In short, the battle lines are clearly drawn in this polemic. Schlesinger is a believer, a defender of 'the American democratic faith', fighting the good fight against the 'multicultural zealots'.[29]

While this makes for good melodrama, the trouble with reducing all the questions to a single, simple either-or is that it flattens and distorts the issues. In support of his position, Schlesinger quotes a number of black intellectual and political figures who criticize Afrocentrism. But the debate in black circles over black culture and black politics does not divide neatly into two sets of opposing views: the melting pot versus black cultural nationalism. There are tensions and complexities at every turn. And you cannot even begin to analyse them if you start from the false premise that Schlesinger adopts: the notion that Blacks are basically just another group of individuals moving from the margins of American society to the centre, from exclusion to inclusion. In a sense, no group or population has been more intimate to the place. All along, Blacks have been incorporated into American society: as the negative, so to speak, of the positive. If you could take a snapshot of the contemporary US a double image would show up. It would show that black separatism is, in its way, as American as apple pie – and not just another nasty outbreak of Old World ethnocentricity.

Speaking of which, Schlesinger rather meets himself coming in the opposite direction towards the end of his essay. The champion of America becomes the champion of Europe. Europe, he states, is 'the source – the *unique* source – of those liberating ideas', the ones that unify America. In case the reader has not grasped the point he adds: 'These are *European* ideas, not Asian, nor African, nor Middle Eastern ideas, except by adoption.'[30] There follows a series of contrasts all of

which reflect well on 'the West', badly on everywhere else. In this connection, he observes: 'There is surely no reason for Western civilization
to have guilt trips laid on it by champions of cultures based on
despotism, superstition, tribalism, and fanaticism. In this regard', he
thinks, 'the Afrocentrists are especially absurd.'[31] He expands on the
latter remark. 'What the West would call corruption is regarded
through much of Africa as no more than the prerogative of power.'
The 'rule of law', we are admonished, is 'alien to African traditions'.
It was 'the West', he says, that led the charge against slavery. He adds,
with magnificent condescension: 'Those many brave and humane
Africans who are struggling these days for decent societies are animated
by Western, not by African, ideals.'[32] It is nice to see someone rooting
for his side. But coming from the man who has just spent 120 pages
warning that ethnic chauvinism threatens to disunite America – this is
a bit rich.

It is also a bit cheeky, given Schlesinger's frequent homilies against
the abuse of history. History – particulate, accurate, textured recounting of the human story – is conspicuous by its absence in his essay. The
past comes into the picture only in a form that fits the narrow scheme
of things that he brings, ready-made, to the world. Or to put it differently, Schlesinger substitutes a simple and immutable myth of America
(and to some extent of Africa) for the complex reality that changes
over time. On this showing, the author of *The Disuniting of America*
is no historian.

SLEEPER THE NEW YORKER

One of Schlesinger's observations about the role of history is this:
'history is to the nation rather as memory is to the individual'.[33] It is a
potentially interesting remark – *potentially* because he does nothing
actually interesting with it. It raises, to my mind, a question about
where the historian is situated when writing history. And I venture that
if you thought the remark through it would sit uneasily with another
Schlesinger aphorism: 'The use of history as therapy means the
corruption of history as history.'[34]

This is my cue to turn to *The Closest of Strangers* by Jim Sleeper.
The book focuses on New York but covers much the same territory as
The Disuniting of America. By trade, Sleeper is a journalist. But this is
not the capacity in which he writes. He writes, he says, as a New
Yorker, as 'a citizen of a city' with which he has 'fallen in and out of
love several times'.[35] He describes his book as a record of a 'journey'

in which he set out to put some of his 'assumptions about racism and the politics of race through a tortuous reexamination'.[36] He tells his story via a retelling of stories about the city with which he is so involved. The book has the passion, the disillusionment, the candour and ultimately the faithfulness of a first-rate novel.

It is this quality – of concernful involvement – that separates Sleeper's work from Schlesinger's. He is no less 'American' in his vision of a liberal democratic society that transcends racial identity; no less critical of the follies and fallacies of black separatism. Often both authors seem to be making the same points (for example in evaluating the 1989 New York State Task Force report.[37]) Yet there is a world of difference. The difference is that in Sleeper's case *there is a world* – and he is in it. The world, as he presents it, is rough and unrounded; it is full of 'the complexity of the human truth' (to borrow a phrase from the book).[38] Where Schlesinger is above the fray, complacent and cantankerous, dispensing his solutions from on high, Sleeper takes you down into the neighbourhoods and on to the streets, arguing at every turn – as much with himself as with any opponent. He writes from the inside, working things out.

For example, the second chapter opens with a vivid vignette in which Sleeper – who describes himself as white, Jewish and middle class – runs up against a 'well-dressed black woman' one cold winter morning at a newsstand on a crowded street corner.[39] Each seems to think that the other has cut in front and neither gives way. The woman jabs Sleeper with her elbow – twice. They look daggers at each other. Sleeper writes:

> From my lips, unpremeditated, leaps a sentence I hadn't known was in me. 'I didn't do it to ya, lady.' I find myself breathing in a low, portentous register, shaking my head slowly from side to side. With a start, I realize that I'm referring not to the jostling but to the three hundred years of oppression and pent-up rage I've decided went into her elbow.[40]

Sleeper reports the woman's reply. ' "Well", she hisses back, without missing a beat, "it was your kind." ' And then he reflects on her words and on the incident as a whole:

> Never mind that barely seventy years before our encounter at the newsstand, 'my kind' were shivering in peasant hovels in a czarist Baltic province. Never mind that, given my mood that morning, the same rude jostling could have occurred with a Jewish woman

> or anyone else this side of Hulk Hogan crossing my path. The
> fact remains: I understood intuitively what the black woman was
> thinking; she knew that I knew; and as we acknowledged it, the
> earth seemed to open at our feet to reveal the depths of the
> wound.[41]

This perfectly illustrates Sleeper's gift for taking an isolated moment and removing the wraps so as to disclose the depths of the past – and the pain – packed inside. Moreover, the mere act of recollection in this case – recognizing the ghosts on the sidewalk – seems to clear the air a little, to effect some repair to the present tattered state of things.

Some of the moments Sleeper recalls are taken from his own biography and some from the city's; often the same moment belongs to both. Take, for example, his account of the Howard Beach incident in 1986: a black man was run over and killed after white youths had assaulted him and two black companions, following which the white motorist whose car was involved was put on trial. Sleeper analyses the racial politics that surrounded the trial, condemning what he sees as the dishonest strategy of the two black attorneys representing the victims. At the same time, he describes the subtle but profound change that took place in his relationship with Dan, a black friend and former mentor, whom he called on the phone to discuss the case.[42] If there is much to learn, there is also a lot to query, in his treatment of such moments and events. But the enterprise – uncovering the past for the sake of recovery in the present – deserves to be called history. Moreover, while this is not 'the use of history as therapy', history of this stripe could conceivably be called therapeutic. And as you read Sleeper's brand of history you realize that fiction, fantasy and honest confusion are part of 'the complexity of the human truth'; that ideological solutions like Schlesinger's solve nothing; and that there is no substitute for the salve of arguing.

In a sense, the whole of Sleeper's book is argument – not as product but as activity. He launches the argument in the Introduction with two questions: 'Do frontal assaults on racism ... really have any remaining purchase against blacks' suffering? If not, what are the alternatives?'[43] The rest of the book, directly and indirectly, pursues these questions. His views are intricate and cannot easily be summarized. But, broadly speaking, he answers the first question with a frontal assault on frontal assaults on racism. As he puts it in the chapter 'Folly on the Left': 'sometimes the only way to address racism, to break its spell, is to stop casting events as purely or primarily racist in character. Not because racism isn't real and destructive, but because we can't get at it by oversimplifying it this way.'[44]

The folly – the 'oversimplifying' – is threefold. First, expanding the definition of 'racism' to the point where there are 'intimations of racism in every leaf that falls'.[45] Second, dismissing a priori the fears and reactions of 'white ethnics' as racist, even though they might, in part or in whole, be legitimate.[46] Third, placing the primary emphasis on racial identity. The third oversimplification 'represents a fateful, typically American dodging of the reality of social class divisions, which are arguably more fundamental than racial divisions in perpetuating social injustice'.[47]

Sleeper is continually arguing – not least with former allies and fellow activists, as well as those white radicals and black militants whom he believes have betrayed the very constituencies for whom they claim to speak. As his anecdotes reveal, he speaks from the heart and from first-hand experience; but not with hostility and not without understanding. He is no less hard-hitting than Schlesinger. But his harshness is more a lamentation than a sneer, a prophetic reproach to a backsliding people, than an outburst of uncomprehending bitterness. Perhaps ultimately *that* is what separates the two books. Call it tone.

Calling it tone should not imply that the difference is cosmetic, a mere matter of coloration. On the contrary, the difference goes to the heart of the question with which both these books are concerned: How can the US, with a population whose ethnic traditions and histories are so diverse, sustain a society that is both civilized and just? The question is not merely academic; nor is the writing in either of these works. More than just political texts, both works are political acts: they are interventions, through writing, in the public debate (such as it is) about contemporary America. Hence the difference in tone makes *all* the difference: it thoroughly affects what each work is *doing*.

Schlesinger's tone of voice in his essay – peevish, sarcastic, smug – is divisive: it can only contribute to the further disuniting of America. If you were to squeeze the pages of his book dry, the juice you would extract would be essentially sour. The fact that he scores a number of intellectual points is not a saving grace; it only makes matters worse. That is to say, the tone of his criticisms, whether they are valid or not, is such that they sour the debate. Whereas with Sleeper, criticisms do not merely make a point, they seek a response. As he puts it in the Introduction, 'This is a conversation with fellow New Yorkers to which anyone is welcome to listen'.[48] Whether his analysis is faulty and whether his politics are sound, the author of *The Closest of Strangers* is thoroughly what he says he is: a citizen, a New Yorker to the core, with the New Yorker's odd mix of hard-nosed realism and romantic hope. And his book, for all the astringency, is an act of reconciliation; it is a neighbourly act, an act of goodwill. This is part of what I mean by 'the salve of arguing': it is a paradox of human relations that arguing brings strangers closer together.

THE MAP OF AMERICA

Nearly thirty years ago, Martin Luther King observed, 'We are confronted with the fierce urgency of *now*.' He punctuated the point with an ominous image: 'Over the bleached bones and jumbled residues of numerous civilizations are written the pathetic words: "Too late".'[49] Towards the end of his book *Race Matters*, Cornel West, consciously or otherwise, recalls King's admonition. He remarks, 'I believe it is late – but maybe not too late – to confront and overcome the poverty and paranoia, the despair and distrust that haunt us.'[50] In other words, the *now* to which King spoke has not passed; it is the same *now* with the same fierce urgency. For the same ghosts from America's past – the ghosts of slavery, segregation, discrimination – continue to haunt, or rather possess, the body politic. These are home-grown ghosts, made in America. They were not imported from the Old World: they are indigenous to the New. And neither brilliant refutations nor magic incantations, such as 'Never look back', will expel them. Then what, now, will avail?

Perhaps more of the sort of history that Sleeper gives us – the kind in which he takes a moment of confrontation in the present and shows the internal structure given it by the past – would not go amiss. To put it another way: ghosts, whether personal or political, cannot be exorcized unless they are seen for what they are. Schlesinger's criticisms of Afrocentrism rankle because he does not see the ghosts of America's past in their true light. In his passion for assimilation, he practices what he preaches: he assimilates the black experience to that of any other disadvantaged 'ethnic group' entering these shores. This travesty of their *then* cannot help us in our collective *now*.

Which brings me back to *A Nation of Immigrants*, the little book by Schlesinger's hero, Kennedy, that I mentioned at the start. It was, at the time, quite a heroic effort, written to support reform of the explicitly racist 1952 Immigration and Nationality Act. In the second chapter of his book, Kennedy reviews the variety of reasons that led to different national and ethnic groups coming to America. He does not lump them all together. In particular, he singles out the case of Blacks who were brought as slaves from Africa; who came because they 'were bought and sold and had no choice'.[51] In the Chronology of Immigration appended to the text, the first arrival of Blacks, as slaves, is duly recorded. But when you turn to a map indicating 'the general distribution of immigrant groups in the US', African-Americans do not show up.[52] In Florida we find Spanish, Greeks and Cubans; in South Carolina, French; in Alabama and Mississippi, English; and so on. But Africans are nowhere to be seen. What has happened? Is this just an oversight on the part of either the author or the editor? Or is it perhaps because the word 'immigrant' is not a good fit for the historical experience of Blacks who came from Africa because they were 'bought and sold'? But, in that case, the map is right, and the title and the text of the book are wrong: America is not 'a nation of immigrants'.

For that matter, Poles but not Apaches, Czechoslovaks but not Cherokees, show up on the map – which therefore is not a map of the nation. If America is a nation, it is a nation of immigrants, of former slaves, and of conquered peoples. This is the complex reality that confronted the 1989 New York Task Force. It is surely not an ignoble aim to seek to develop a curriculum for public education that does justice to the complexity, preparing children for the problems of living in a society that cannot be united by a single national creation myth. Naturally, proposals for such a curriculum will contain excess and idiocy – *naturally* because the capacity for being idiotic and excessive is universal: it is one of those universals that transcend all differences of culture and ethnicity. It unites us all, not only Americans, making humanity one.

Not all of us, however, are on the same legal footing, and I am conscious that, as a 'green card' holder, my status in the US is that of a resident alien. So, in closing, let me say: Greetings from my world to yours! And thank you for bearing with my accent.

NOTES

1. This chapter is adapted from a talk I gave as a Lilly Workshop for the Center for Educational Practice, Saint Xavier University, Chicago, 19 April 1995. The talk was based on a review essay, 'Old Ghosts in the New World: Racism and Ethnicity in the Contemporary United States', *Patterns of Prejudice*, 29, 2–3 (1995), 113–22. The two books that were the subject of the review are the ones by Schlesinger and Sleeper discussed in the chapter.

2. John F. Kennedy, *A Nation of Immigrants* (New York: Harper & Row, 1986).
3. Arthur M. Schlesinger, Jr, *The Disuniting of America: Reflections on a Multicultural Society* (New York: W.W. Norton, 1992), p.15.
4. Ibid., p.23.
5. Ibid., p.24.
6. Ibid., p.23.
7. Ibid., p.43.
8. Ibid., p.133.
9. Ibid., p.112.
10. Ibid., p.15.
11. Ibid., p.120.
12. Ibid., p.80. See Chapters 2 and 3, passim.
13. Ibid., p.75.
14. Ibid., p.74.
15. See Chapter 12, 'The Language of Race', for how I dealt with a similar choice when filling out a UK Census form.
16. Lawrence Wright, 'One Drop of Blood', *New Yorker*, 25 July 1994, pp.46–55; National Public Radio, Morning Edition, 'Census Bureau Wants More Racial Categories Added', 1 August 1994, transcript no. 1401, segment no. 10.
17. Schlesinger, *Disuniting of America*, pp.14, 132.
18. Ibid., p.71.
19. Ibid., pp.130, 138, 74.
20. Ibid., pp.36–7.
21. Ibid., p.117.
22. Ibid., p.27.
23. Ibid.
24. Ibid., p.134.
25. Ibid., p.131.
26. Ibid., p.112.
27. Ibid., p.134.
28. Maggie Holmes, quoted in Studs Terkel, *Race: How Blacks and Whites Think and Feel about the American Obsession* (New York: Doubleday, 1992), p.145.
29. Schlesinger, *Disuniting of America*, pp.136, 117.
30. Ibid., p.127.
31. Ibid., p.128.
32. Ibid., p.129.
33. Ibid., p.45.
34. Ibid., p.93.
35. Jim Sleeper, *The Closest of Strangers: Liberalism and the Politics of Race in New York* (New York: W.W. Norton, 1990), p.21.
36. Ibid., p.21.
37. Ibid., pp.227–32.
38. Ibid., p.187.
39. Ibid., p.21 for Sleeper's self-description.
40. Ibid., p.68.
41. Ibid., p.69.
42. Ibid., pp.183–8; also pp.192, 202–4. 'Dan' is a pseudonym.
43. Ibid., p.28.
44. Ibid., p.254.
45. Ibid., p.313; see also pp.28, 36, 174.
46. Ibid., pp.122, 129–32, 169–70, 249–50. Chapters 4 and 5 discuss the subtleties and complexities of this point, partly in connection with crime and partly in connection with housing.
47. Ibid., p.160.
48. Ibid., p.21.

49. Martin Luther King, Jr, *Where Do We Go From Here: Chaos or Community?* (Boston, MA: Beacon Press, 1968), p.191.
50. Cornel West, *Race Matters* (New York: Vintage Books, 1994), p.158.
51. Kennedy, *Nation of Immigrants*, p.7.
52. Ibid., p.84. The map is on pp.86–7.

CHAPTER FIFTEEN

Spring Fever in Chicago

APPROACHING MIDNIGHT ON LAKE SHORE DRIVE

20 May 1988. It is a little after 11 pm. I am on my own, speeding south on Lake Shore Drive, punching the buttons on the car radio, searching for something to keep me awake at the wheel.[1] A genial voice comes floating over the airwaves. 'Okay, thanks for calling. This is WVON. 591 5990 is our number. We want to hear from *you*, Chicago. Well, what do you think about that hit list? Is there such a thing and what does it mean?' The phrase 'hit list' catches my ear. The genial voice is alluding to the lead story, 'Alderman Streeter on Jewish "Hit List" ', on the front page of the May issue of Streeter's ward newspaper, *The Alderman Speaks*. The story has lit a fuse in the city. Streeter claims that there is a Jewish 'hit list' that names several prominent black leaders, including himself, with a view to their being 'silenced' or removed from public office.[2] The mellifluent voice on the radio suddenly sounds less congenial: 'Well, they're using the term "hit list" but of course we're not talking – hopefully – about bloodshed. What they're talking about is targeting certain people that, well, don't have their interests at heart – or at least that's what they think ... 591 5990 is my number. Give us a call, Chicago.' I am cured of my drowsiness and for the next two hours, first in the car and then at home, my ears are burning.

The phone-in talk show I have stumbled upon is 'On Target'. The genial host is Norm Ungar. Anyone in the Chicago area can listen in, but I feel like an eavesdropper since WVON is a black radio station. There again, the topic under discussion, in a manner of speaking, is me; or more precisely, my kind, the Jews. So I listen. And I record.[3]

One caller points out that the so-called Jews are not really Jews at all. But, whoever they are, these 'Jews' had a lot of influence in the civil rights movement. Another says cheerily, 'Now they have the hit list here. Yeah, I believe there's a hit list. But if [there is] one thing that Afro-Americans have never learned: the dollar, that mighty dollar. A lot of people have read the *Protocols of the Elders of Zion*. That is a blueprint of the Jewish people to control things by controlling that dollar.' Perhaps wary that the likes of me might be monitoring the broadcast, he adds, 'There are some things that I don't want to say on "On Target".' Anyone wanting to hear more is invited to a forthcoming meeting of the United American Progress Association. (Who?) A woman caller airs her grievance: 'We know that the Jews are not going to let go of running black people's affairs, even though we are sick and tired of them running us into the ground and using us as a stalking horse. The Jews have all the money and all the power and they are determined to keep black people in subjugation around the world.' In a burst of misplaced pride, painful to listen to, she asserts:

> nothing is going to stop the march of black people. We are not going to continue to answer to the Jews. They were not put here as our guardians. We are human beings in our own right. We are just as smart and intelligent as they are. And the reason that we black people don't have anything – any money – that we don't have anything to call our own – is because of the Jews.

She concludes by going on the counteroffensive: 'My last thought is this: that while the Jews are compiling hit lists, I think we had better be compiling some hit lists against them.' 'Well there's an interesting proposal', our genial host responds. 'Fight fire with fire.'

Over the two hour period, only one person ever questions the assumptions that seem to underlie the programme. 'This Jewish–Black thing is getting out of hand', says the caller derisively. 'I've been black as long as Alderman Streeter ... I don't have a problem with the Jews.' I suppose it is a relief to hear this, though I have a problem with the syntax: imagine a Jewish person saying 'I don't have a problem with the Blacks.' Still, better to not be a problem than to be one.

Around midnight, Steve Cokely, local activist and one-man cause célèbre, comes on the air. Among other things, he calls in order to set this sceptical caller straight. He is treated as a superstar by Ungar, who keeps him on the line for another hour while taking other calls intermittently. Cokeley explains that the question of Jewish–Black relations can be settled by 'research'. He talks darkly about 'the beginning of time, the origin of life on earth and the beginning of the races'. And he supplies an image for how 'they' behave in going after the black leadership: 'Just imagine a beast hidden in the cave and part of his strength was his hidden nature and that no one could ever see the attack coming because the beast was hidden or submerged.'

Two hours into this incendiary broadcast my ears are still burning, but I am chilled to the bone.

THE NOT SO MERRY MONTH OF MAY

Last May was not a merry month in Chicago, and the controversy surrounding the said Steve Cokely is among the reasons why. The broadcast on WVON, although it threw me at the time, did not come out of the blue. Several highly-charged events led up to it and contributed to the sense that Black–Jewish relations are in a state of crisis. But, if so, what exactly does this crisis consist in? And what is to be done?

Eugene Kennedy, Professor of Psychology at Loyola University, Chicago, takes the view that the crisis is essentially moral. In a recent article in the *New York Times*, he writes 'Virulent antisemitism has gripped Chicago's black community. Nobody morally powerful enough to try to combat it, including the Reverend Jesse Jackson, who lives here, has attempted to do so.'[4] As I heard for myself on the night drive home in May, the antisemitism of which he speaks is not imaginary. But his way of describing it is both misleading and overdrawn. The events in question did not take place in a vacuum. They occurred against a local background of interracial conflict and a national background of tension between Blacks and Jews. Jackson is himself part of this background. And when we take a closer look at what happened in Chicago in May, we discover a complicated pattern of events in which prejudice is interwoven with politics. Kennedy's view – that the crisis is essentially moral and that the solution calls for the exercise of moral authority – turns out to be simplistic at best; at worst, his view is inflammatory.

In recounting the events of last May, I am bound to be selective. The story I shall tell will purposely single out the thread of antisemitism that runs through the events. I shall then fill out the picture by adding some of the missing detail and by attempting to situate the story against its (local and national) background. In this light, I shall offer an analysis of the animosity towards Jews expressed by some Blacks in the city.[5]

The events of last May clustered around two consecutive incidents. The first of these concerned the political fate of Steve Cokely, a 35-year-old mayoral aide who served as community liaison officer. On 1 May the *Chicago Tribune* ran a front page story reprinting hardcore antisemitic remarks made by Cokely in four lectures he gave between August 1985 and November 1987. The lectures were delivered to audiences at the Final Call Building in Chicago, headquarters of the Black Muslim splinter group, Nation of Islam, led by Louis Farrakhan.

Tape recordings of the lectures were on sale at a south side bookstore run by the group. Cokely's remarks sound as though they might almost have been lifted from the *Protocols*, the book recommended by the 'On Target' caller. He was reported as affirming the existence of a powerful international conspiracy that sets out to oppress Blacks and to achieve world domination on behalf of Jews. To quote a remark from one of his tapes: 'The Jew hopes to one day reign forever.' Another of his allegations, that Jewish doctors have spread AIDS by injecting Blacks with the virus, recalls medieval charges that Jews caused the Black Death by poisoning wells.

Some of Cokely's invective was aimed at Whites in general and not Jews in particular. He struck out at a number of prominent Blacks as well, but he attacked them on account of their Jewish connections. He criticized Jesse Jackson for having Jewish advisers; likewise Harold Washington, who had been mayor of Chicago from 1983. Cokely also took Washington to task for having recently (November 1987) toured Jewish businesses and synagogues on the north side where windows had been smashed by a neo-Nazi group on the anniversary of *Kristallnacht*. Cokely, referring to Washington derisively as 'this nigger', dismissed the vandalism as having been done 'by some Jew'.

Apart from reproducing some of Cokely's inflammatory statements, the *Tribune* report mentioned that in early April the Anti-Defamation League (ADL) had brought his speeches to the attention of the mayor, Eugene Sawyer. (Sawyer, who is black too, was appointed interim mayor after Washington died in office last November.) Furthermore, according to the report, top mayoral advisors had been alerted to Cokely's doings and sayings by City Hall officials several months earlier, soon after the new mayor had taken office. Thus the report did more than expose the bigotry of a minor city official. It caused eyebrows to be raised about the judgment of the mayor and his advisers. This was the bone of contention throughout the controversy: not Cokely but the reaction, or absence thereof, to Cokely once his antisemitism had been exposed.

Over the next few days the silence from City Hall was deafening. On Thursday 5 May a front page story in the *Tribune* appeared under the headline 'Mayor's silence heating Cokely crisis to a boil'. The effect of the mayor's silence was reinforced by the voices raised in some quarters of the black community. Revd Al Sampson sermonized, 'I trust Sawyer will remember his roots and maintain Cokely within the administration and not sacrifice him for thirty pieces of silver.'[6] More fuel was added to the fire by suggestions that the substance of what Cokely said might be true. Lu Palmer, an influential writer and commentator in radical black circles in Chicago, said on television, 'I think it is certainly possible that Jews, not just Jews but whites, are in a conspiracy to rule the world.'[7] And a widely respected figure, Revd B. Herbert Martin, who was Harold Washington's pastor at the Progressive Community Church, was reported as saying that there was a 'ring of truth' to Cokely's allegation of a worldwide Jewish conspiracy. Cokely began to look like the tip of an ominous iceberg.

Finally, on Friday 6 May, Chicagoans read in their newspapers that the mayor had taken the plunge and fired his troublesome aide. Sawyer delivered his verdict the previous day at a news conference, surrounded by black and Jewish civic leaders, and issued a call for 'healing'. But by this point the crisis had boiled over. Among Jews, attention had shifted from Cokely to the fact that the administration had dragged its heels and that leading figures in the black community appeared to be giving credence to his antisemitic views. The spotlight fell in particular on Revd Martin, the mayor's nominee for Executive Director of the Commission on Human Relations. At the same time, according to the *Tribune*, after he was fired Cokely 'was enthusiastically received at an emotional West Side rally where residents supported what they said was his "right to freedom of speech" '.[8]

There were, however, exceptions to the rule among Chicago's black leaders. These included three aldermen who had publicly called upon the mayor to dismiss Cokely. These aldermen found themselves caught in the crossfire. On the one hand, they were criticized in Jewish circles for having waited until the eleventh hour before speaking out. On the other hand, they were seen by some Blacks as breaking ranks. Farrakhan, who came to Cokely's defence and offered him a job, condemned them as 'traitors'.[9]

Into this climate of agitation and recrimination there came, from out of the blue, the second incident. A student at the prestigious School of the Art Institute, 23-year-old David Nelson, had painted a portrait – whose apparent intention was satirical – of the late Harold Washington attired in lingerie. On the morning of Wednesday 11 May he hung the picture in a corridor at the school as one of his entries in the annual fellowship contest for final year students. The exhibition was not open to the public, but word of the painting's existence reached the ears of the City Council, in session a few blocks away. Several black aldermen ('the group of eight') left the chamber and went directly to the school to remove the painting. Precisely what occurred there is not entirely clear. But somehow in the scuffle the canvas incurred a gash. It was eventually removed from the premises by policemen acting at the behest of the aldermen. The matter was promptly taken up by the Chicago office of the American Civil Liberties Union (ACLU), who said that they would file suit on Nelson's behalf, citing his First Amendment rights of freedom of expression.

In the heated public debate that ensued, no one had a good word for the offending canvas. But opinion was divided over whether the school was culpable and whether the action taken by the aldermen was justified. Coming in the wake of the Cokely affair, opinion tended to divide along racial lines. On Friday 13 May a 'unity' meeting of 'One Hundred Pastors for Peace and Tranquility in Our City' took place at the headquarters of Operation PUSH, the organization that Jesse Jackson formed in 1971. All the participants were black. Mayor Sawyer attended and joined with the pastors in demanding an apology from the student and from the school. Sawyer also assured the meeting that he would stand behind Revd Martin's nomination for Executive Director of the Commission on Human Relations. Revd Willie Barrow, Executive Director of PUSH, made the link between these two subjects explicit, calling Nelson's painting 'the latest in a series of escalating attacks and insults against the black community'. Summing up their position, she said: 'A united black community should not continue to have to defend itself against questionable charges of anti-semitism and racism. Those who seek to hold us down paint with too broad a brush.'[10]

In the circumstances, the metaphor was artfully chosen. But who exactly are the people who 'paint with too broad a brush' and why should David Nelson have lent his talents to their cause? Alderman Allan Streeter (one of 'the group of eight') had a ready explanation: 'The fellow who drew that picture is Jewish', he averred, the day after the incident. He saw a connection between the painting and the outcry against Cokely. 'The Jewish community tried to keep our people silent, [yet] we cannot speak out against an injustice. That's what worries me.' He continued, 'It's all related. I don't feel it's a coincidence. I feel the fellow is a Jewish person who is defaming the mayor that I love.'[11] On this occasion the alderman's feelings led him astray. I have a friend who teaches at the School of the Art Institute. A couple of phone calls established that Nelson is no more Jewish than Streeter himself, a finding that was quickly verified.[12]

Streeter was not alone in seeing a double standard. In a televised panel discussion with Harvey Grossman, Legal Director of the ACLU, Alderman Robert Shaw turned to Grossman and said, 'When there's a question of Whites and Blacks, you fellows at the ACLU take the side of Whites all the time.'[13] (This claim is about as credible as saying that the Confederation of British Industry always sides with workers against employers.) In another televised appearance, Shaw asked Jay Miller, Executive Director of the ACLU, 'How many instances can you cite where the ACLU ... cut against the grain of the Jewish community? How many times have you offended prominent Jewish people?' Miller replied, citing cases. Shaw got more specific: 'How many times have you defended a Black, taking their side against a Jewish person?' The programme ended before Miller could do justice to the question.[14]

This anti-Jewish rhetoric was given an added boost a week after the School of the Art Institute incident with the publication of the May issue of Streeter's ward newspaper with the front-page article about a so-called Jewish 'hit list'. The list, supposedly drawn up by the ADL, was said to include, besides Streeter himself, Farrakhan, Cokely and others. Streeter was quoted as saying, 'Now it looks like Reverend Herbert Martin is on the list.' 'We can't allow other groups to choose our leaders', he said. What other groups did he mean? The article mentions that at a meeting with CBS, the broadcasting company, he referred to 'intense attempts of certain Jewish groups to remove him from office by providing extensive financial backing to his opponents'. Streeter also touched on 'the issue of continued Jewish dominance of the news media and the ongoing portrayal of anyone who speaks out as "Antisemitic" '.[15]

But it was the so-called hit list that attracted most attention in the city's media. The rumour was that the ADL had given the mayor a copy. The ADL denied possession of a 'hit list' and Sawyer said he had not seen one. The rumour, however, persisted and was the subject of the 'On Target' phone-in talk show that I tuned into by chance late at night on 20 May as I headed south on Lake Shore Drive, scouring the airwaves for something lively, something to keep me alert.

THREE LEVELS OF ANALYSIS

What are we to make of Chicago's 'spring fever'? Does it mean that, in Kennedy's words, 'virulent antisemitism has gripped Chicago's black community'? It has certainly gripped Cokely, for whom it is a comprehensive ideology. Moreover, antisemitism is undoubtedly a force within certain sections of the black community in Chicago, not least among a number of vocal activists. This fact is both chilling and disturbing. But it is hardly news. Chicago has been the headquarters of the Nation of

Islam since Farrakhan formed the group in 1978.[16] It is true that anyone who listened, as I did, to the programme on WVON would have gained the impression that antisemitism is rampant in the black community. But an impression based on selective sources and partial information, howsoever persuasive when taken on its own, can be misleading: a self-selected audience contributing to a radio phone-in constitutes a highly specialized sample of the population. A *Tribune* poll in June found that only 8 per cent of Blacks in Chicago thought that Cokely should have been allowed to keep his job.[17] This hardly settles anything. But it is enough to insinuate a question mark into the mind of the observer and to suggest that it is necessary to look at this story again.

A case in point is that of Revd Martin. Kennedy, in his article published in July, refers to 'the continuing defence of Mr Cokely by black political activists and other spokesmen of the black community such as the Reverend B. Herbert Martin'. But Martin has not continued to come to Cokely's defence; nor, it turns out, did he ever do so. After the initial press report of his comments, in which he was attributed with the remark that Cokely's views have 'the ring of truth', he publicly dissociated himself from Cokely's antisemitism and said categorically that it 'cannot be tolerated'. In the same interview he explained what it is that concerns him, and what he had intended to convey originally, namely, that for a growing number of Blacks, especially young Blacks, Cokely's statements have the ring of truth. In other words, he was talking about the *perceptions* of young people in his community. The point he had been seeking to make, rightly or wrongly, was that this is more worrying than the views of a Steve Cokely.[18] In fact, as President of the Chicago South Side branch of the National Association for the Advancement of Colored People (the largest in the country), Martin had sent a telegram to Mayor Sawyer calling for Cokely to resign.[19] It would appear that Martin's words were plucked out of his hands and set ablaze by the political fire sweeping the city. Roughly, he meant the opposite of what he was taken to mean.[20]

Martin's assessment of the trend in black attitudes towards Jews is not idiosyncratic. Sober studies lend support to his view that there is cause for concern.[21] At the same time, everyone I have interviewed on the subject, including Martin, rejects out of hand the notion that antisemitism is rife among Blacks in Chicago. Lawrence Bloom, a Jewish alderman who represents a ward that is 75 per cent black, said he found that Cokely's antisemitism was as 'absolutely reprehensible to blacks as to whites'.[22] Robert Lucas, a black civil rights activist, considered that the number of black people supporting Cokely 'might represent 1 or 2 per cent. That's all.'[23] This might be an underestimate. But it is a useful check on any tendency to overstate the extent of black antisemitism at the present juncture.

Lucas also called for Cokely's dismissal early on. However, the fact that he was in a small minority among prominent Blacks needs explaining. The explanation has less to do with black antisemitism than it has to do with the specificities of Chicago's tumultuous politics and the rivalries among black aldermen following Washington's sudden death.

When Washington was elected mayor in 1983 it was a landmark event. He was not the first candidate to defy and defeat the old Democratic machine. But he was the city's first black mayor. It was, however, a pyrrhic victory, since he did not have a working majority on the floor of the council. For nearly three years the aldermen were locked in 'council wars'. The mayor stood his ground; black political factions held together; and alliances were nurtured among Hispanics and white liberals, notably Jews. In 1986, aldermanic elections gave Washington's bloc a slim majority, but it was not until Spring of 1987, when Washington was re-elected and further gains were made in the wards, that effective political power was finally attained. After years of political struggle, it was a moment for Chicago's black population to savour, a moment of arrival, a moment filled with the promise of genuine control over the city's resources for the first time in the city's history. That promise, however, was snatched away almost at once when Washington dropped dead of a heart attack in November.

The problem was that there was no obvious successor. This posed a potential threat to the black movement in three ways. First, it created a window of opportunity for the Old Guard, the rump of the white Democratic machine, to resume their efforts at political sabotage. Second, it jeopardized the alliances that Washington had formed and which were held together partly by the sheer force of his personality and the astuteness of his political touch. The same qualities were in evidence in holding together the diverse elements that comprise the black movement. So, the third threat to the movement was itself: its own internal divisions and the danger that it would fall apart at the seams without a Harold Washington to keep it intact.

In short, the movement faced a crisis as a result of losing its leader. And, predictably, the first reaction to this crisis was a schism, precisely over the question of succession. Eugene Sawyer, the old campaigner, emerged the victor over the young progressive, Tim Evans, and was appointed interim mayor – but only by virtue of the support he received from those white aldermen who had opposed Washington. Thus Sawyer did not inherit Washington's legacy whole. The meaning of his mayoralty was, and is, ambiguous; and his position precarious.

Despite the means by which he won, Sawyer had a useful entrée into radical black circles via one of his aides, Steve Cokely, whose nationalist credentials were above reproach and who nonetheless staunchly defended the mayor. This fact alone would be enough to motivate his reluctance to dismiss Cokely: without Cokely he would lose touch with a small but influential constituency.

But there was more to it than constituency-building. Partly because of the nature of the support that secured his victory over his rivals, Sawyer needed to demonstrate, to friend and foe alike, his capacity to stand up to pressure from 'outsiders'. Moreover, in view of its fragile internal state, the black movement was supersensitive to any hint of external interference. It is true that the liberal Jewish vote was a crucial element in Washington's mayoral victories, both in 1983 and in 1987.[24] But at the heart of the movement that elected Washington was the cause of black political empowerment – and Jews are not Blacks. When Cokely came under fire for having made statements offensive to Whites in general and to Jews in particular, it triggered, in the climate of political crisis that reigned at the time, a reflex action within the divided black leadership: ranks closed in the blink of an eye. It was blind politics – rather than blind prejudice – that took over.

At this (first) level of analysis, the reaction to the Cokely crisis on the part of the mainstream black leadership had nothing to do with Jews per se. Blacks did not close ranks in defence of Cokely's anti-semitism but rather as a gesture of defiance, a way of achieving unity, by resisting what was perceived to be the pressure that the traditional external enemy – white power – was seeking to exert over them. Viewed in this light, Jews are just another shade of white.

But there is another layer to these events, one that puts Jews as Jews very much at the centre of the picture. Local black aspirations in Chicago do not exist in splendid isolation from black aspirations nationwide. And black aspirations nationwide have for some years been focused on the person of Jesse Jackson and the coveted prize of the Democratic nomination for President. Twice Jackson has gone after the prize, once in 1984 and again in 1988; twice the prize has eluded him. On both occasions he has come up against entrenched opposition from Jews: not only from the extremist group 'Jews Against Jackson' but also from mainstream Jewish organizations and from a broad spectrum of Jewish voters. I do not intend to open up the Pandora's box of Jackson–Jewish relations in this essay, but merely point out the fact that, by and large, Jews as Jews have opposed Jackson's bid for power. In so doing, they have in practice placed themselves as an obstacle in the path of the movement Jackson leads. This might not be the intention; it is nonetheless the effect. And, as a result, Jews, who fought with Blacks in the 1950s and 1960s for civil rights, now appear to Blacks to be opponents of the principal goal on their current agenda: political empowerment.

All this was very much in the foreground at the time of the Cokely affair. Following a string of sensational successes, Jackson's nomination campaign had just come to grief (in April) in New York: the black movement nationwide had suffered a major setback. Moreover, the disappointment came in the wake of calculated efforts by Mayor Koch, the powerful Jewish mayor of the city with the largest Jewish population in the country, to undermine Jackson's support, saying that Jews and friends of Israel would be 'crazy' to cast their votes for Jackson. Given what Jackson represents and the role that he plays, the effect of Koch's statement was to pit Jew, as Jew, against Black – in a bizarre caricature of the dire prophecies of people like Farrakhan and Cokely.

There is, however, a crucial difference. If Koch takes issue with Jackson it is not because of the eternal war between heaven and hell but because Jackson once embraced Yassir Arafat. In this respect, Koch illustrates what has happened in Black–Jewish relations during the last twenty years or so. Since the late 1960s, Jews and Blacks have found themselves on opposite sides of the fence over a range of issues, from the question of quotas and affirmative action to relations between Israel and South Africa; issues that both communities deem vital to their own interests. Naturally, this has given rise to a degree of mutual hostility. This hostility, to the extent that it is the product of a conflict of collective interests, whether real or merely perceived, is neither racist (on the part of Jews) nor antisemitic (on the part of Blacks).

Thus, at the second level of analysis, the reaction of mainstream black leaders to the Cokely crisis reflected a wider quarrel with Jews: Jews as an ethnic community (so to speak) whose agenda cuts across theirs – if not locally then nationally.

It is only at the third level, at the depths plumbed by Farrakhan and Cokely, that we find antisemitism proper – in which Jews are cast in the role of demons and the limited agenda of a small minority is blown up into a blueprint for world domination.

All of this is on the plane of theory. The real world, however, does not divide neatly and conveniently along lines of analysis, and in the rough and tumble distinctions become blurred. This was all the more true in Chicago this Spring when events came fast and furious. Reviewing those events, it is hard to make out the precise patterns traced by the intersection of politics and prejudice. Consequently, it is difficult to know what's to be done. But it cannot avail to single out the failings of one group – anti-Jewish bigotry on the part of black people – and to overstate the scale of this failing. Such a move is liable to exacerbate tensions, rubbing salt into wounds. Kennedy calls for someone 'morally powerful enough' to step in and 'combat' black antisemitism. Certainly antisemitism, like anti-Black racism, ought to be combated wherever it occurs. But, unless this is seen as just one factor in a multi-factored approach to the question of Black–Jewish relations, Kennedy's prescription is merely moralistic. And if it were applied to attitudes that are not, at bottom, antisemitic at all – hostility that arises on one or other of the first two levels of analysis – then it is dangerously misconceived.

To the extent that Jews are 'just a different shade of white', the question of Black–Jewish relations merges into the wider question of the future of 'race relations' in a deeply segregated city and in a larger society where Blacks continue to be systematically disadvantaged.

Insofar as Jews and Blacks have different agendas that conflict (or appear to do so), what is needed is an initiative aimed at reconciling these different agendas, to the extent that this is possible, and at restoring the political alliance that flourished under Harold Washington. Steps have already been taken to this end. A Black–Jewish Dialogue has been formed that brings together several prominent and active members, both clerical and lay, from the two communities.[25] And Chicago's Commission on Human Relations is developing a programme to foster mutual understanding between Jews and Blacks in the city.

This leaves the third level: black antisemitism. Here Kennedy's plea is apropos; but even here it can only go so far. Farrakhan is heeded because he articulates grievances that are real. This is what prepares the mind of his audience for his message of hate against Jews. It is an old story. But these are old grievances, and as long as they persist I doubt that even a whole army of 'morally powerful' individuals could deprive Farrakhan of his audience. However, he and his ilk *can* be deprived of legitimacy – simply by being spurned. Ultimately, this is a matter for the black movement itself. A strong movement can afford to do without antisemites; a worthy movement cannot afford to include them in its ranks.

A LETTER TO REVEREND MARTIN

In the middle of the not very merry month of May, as tempers rose to fever pitch, the much-maligned Revd Martin reminded everyone of a different past as a template for a better future: 'Blacks and Jews marched together and died together for civil rights in this country. In the early seventies we stopped talking to one another. History has brought us to the point [where] we don't know one another. We stopped talking because we thought everything was okay. Everything is not okay. We can never take that for granted.'[26] He subsequently took over the reins of the Commission on Human Relations. Mindful of his reminder, I sent him, several months later, a copy of the front cover of the April 1988 issue of *Jewish Currents*, which featured Martin Luther King, Jr, on the front cover. In the accompanying letter, dated 20 September 1988, I wrote as follows:

> I have given further thought to our conversation over lunch, with particular reference to next week's meeting at Temple Beth-El and the task you face of establishing contact with a Jewish audience.[27] You say that you are willing to offer an apology for any offence you might unintentionally have caused. But you are anxious that this might fall on deaf ears. I agree that this is a real possibility.
>
> The question seems to me to be this: What does such an audience want and need to hear *first*, if you are to gain their ear? The deep problem here is that suspicion has taken the place of trust. Jewish people in Chicago have gained the impression that black leaders, yourself included, tolerate hatred directed at Jews. They feel bewildered by what appears to have been a surge of anti-semitic feeling (the sort of thing I heard at length on WVON) coming out of the blue and without provocation. And they feel exposed by what they perceive to be the animosity of most leaders of black opinion in a city with a black administration.
>
> It might help to put this in a wider perspective. The sort of thing that has happened in Chicago is archetypal in Jewish history. To Blacks, Jews might appear to be just another shade of white. But to Jews, black power is gentile power under another name. Despite antisemitic myths of Jewish power, the predominant Jewish experience, for two thousand years, has been that of a small and vulnerable people exposed to the unpredictable hostilities of an overwhelmingly non-Jewish world. The Nazi

Holocaust is only the most recent, if most devastating, demonstration of this. It spawned the slogan, 'Never again'. And it gave
rise to a deep mistrust of any temporal power, whether white or
black or any shade in between.

In this connection, I recall the first of our telephone conversa-
tions last May, and I remember the relief I felt when you said to
me, 'There is no way under heaven that I subscribe to Steve
Cokely's remarks' (regarding Jews). At that precise moment, I
knew I was not talking to someone who was my enemy. My gut
feeling is that this, rather than an apology, is the crucial factor: the
need to hear words that restore confidence and dispel fear: to actually hear them spoken by *you* to *them*, just as you said them to
me. Otherwise any attempt at reconciliation is likely to fall on
stony ground. And such a reaction would be natural: how can
one become reconciled with someone whom one fears – fears as
an enemy? I think the first thing to do is to put the minds of your
audience to rest by convincingly denouncing the notions and sentiments that threaten them. Then their hearts might soften.

If that is the first thing that needs doing, I am by no means sure
that asking for forgiveness is the second. Perhaps you would get a
better response if before *they* have to give *you* something (forgiveness), *you* give *them* something – something positive they can
willingly accept. Perhaps something tangible, such as a commitment in connection with the work of the Commission on Human
Relations. Or an assurance that in future civic leaders will take
swift action against racial bigotry of any variety in their midst.
Furthermore, I think you have something better than an apology
to offer: inspiration: a call for people of goodwill to rally round.
My guess is that most people, Jewish, Black or otherwise, would
gladly exchange hope for despair, and amicableness for hostility,
if given reason and opportunity to do so. And since both hope and
communal harmony are the goals you are pursuing, deep down
your audience is on your side! That should give *you* hope!

I suppose what I am saying is that forgiveness cannot be sought
and given in a vacuum. The ground must first be prepared so that
an apology can be accepted in the spirit in which it is given. An
apology might well *seal* the process of healing, but I am inclined
to think that in the current climate of fear and distrust it is
unlikely to *begin* it.

Finally, by way of providing one perspective on conflict
between Blacks and Jews, I remember being in a second-hand

bookstore in Hyde Park when the 'Cokely affair' was at its height, and I could not help overhearing a rather loud conversation between two people who were discussing the controversy. One of them, a woman, mentioned that she was Jewish and said how much she deplored what Cokely had said. The full force of her remarks hit me when I stepped into the aisle she was in and I saw that she was black. We forget that there are such people. What anguish it must be, for a black Jewish person, to see Jews and Blacks at daggers drawn. That woman personifies for me the tragedy of Black–Jewish conflict. Thinking of her should humble any antisemitic Black or anti-Black Jew. If only we could all, Jews and blacks alike, identify with her – then we would no longer be divided.

If only she, rather than Cokely, had been the superstar on the WVON programme on the night of 20 May, when I was haring home on Lake Shore Drive, desperately seeking a stimulant! I would still have sat bolt upright on the drive home – but later I might have slept more peacefully in my bed.

NOTES

1. This chapter is adapted from the essay, 'Springtime in Chicago: A Pattern of Politics and Prejudice', that appeared in *Patterns of Prejudice*, 22, 3 (1988), pp.36–46. This opening section, which was not part of the original essay, is based on portions of two separate pieces: 'Farrakhan of Worms', *Jewish Socialist*, 14 (Autumn 1988), pp.7–8, and 'The Philosophy of Cleaning Clothes', *Searchlight* (November 1988), pp.19–20.
2. This is the opening sentence: 'Alderman Allan Streeter recently revealed that he and several other prominent African American leaders are among those listed on a Jewish "Hit List" of people to be removed from public office or silenced, according to recent news media reports.'
3. The quotes in this section are transcribed from the cassette recording that I made direct from the radio after returning home to my apartment in Hyde Park. There was an interval of a few minutes – between parking the car and reaching my apartment – in which I did not catch the broadcast.
4. Eugene Kennedy, 'Antisemitism in Chicago: A Stunning Silence', *New York Times*, 26 July 1988.
5. This analysis bears some comparison with the analysis in Chapter 2, 'The Collective Jew', of Arab and Muslim hostility to Israel.
6. Salim Muwakkil, 'Harold Washington's Fractured Legacy', *In These Times*, 25 May 1988.
7. 'Chicago Tonight', WTTW Channel 11, quoted in *Chicago Tribune*, 5 May 1988.
8. Ann Marie Lipinski and Dean Baquet, 'Sawyer Fires Cokely as Aide', *Chicago Tribune*, 6 May 1988.
9. James Strong and Jerry Thornton, 'Cokely Sorry Mayor Had to Bow to Pressure', *Chicago Tribune*, 10 May 1988.
10. Ray Hanania and Tracey Robinson, 'Sawyer Refuses to Back Off on Picking Martin', *Chicago Sun-Times*, 14 May 1988; Robert Davis and Maria Hunt, 'Clergy Urge Review Plan at Art Institute', *Chicago Tribune*, 15 May 1988.
11. John Camper and Ann Marie Lipinski, 'Cokely Furor Ends the Honeymoon between Chicago's Blacks and Jews', *Chicago Tribune*, 15 May 1988.

12. Interview with Harvey Grossman, ACLU, 25 May 1988; Toni Schlesinger, 'The Mayoral Painter's Fifteen Minutes of Fame', *Chicago Tribune*, 22 May 1988.
13. 'Newsmakers', WBBM-Channel 2, 15 May 1988.
14. 'Face to Face', WLS-Channel 7, 22 May 1988. During this period the ACLU received numerous enquiries as to whether it was a Jewish defence organization, along the lines of the American Jewish Congress or the ADL (source: Derryl Woods, Director of Public Information, ACLU, 26 September 1988).
15. 'Alderman Streeter on Jewish "Hit List" ', *The Alderman Speaks*, 2, 7 (May 1988), p.1.
16. 'Louis Farrakhan', *ADL Facts*, 29, 1 (Spring 1984), p.22. The original Nation of Islam was founded by Elijah Muhammad in the 1930s.
17. Widely cited, as in Dirk Johnson, 'Black–Jewish Hostility Rouses Leaders in Chicago to Action', *New York Times*, 29 July 1988; and in 'Chicago Takes Another Bum Rap', *Chicago Tribune*, 30 July 1988. Kennedy refers to this poll in his article but does nothing with it. He merely observes that it is to the 'credit' of 'the overwhelming majority of the black community'. He does not consider the possibility that the finding belies the gist of his article.
18. Leslie Baldacci, 'Martin Explains His Response to Cokely's Remarks', *Chicago Sun-Times*, 14 May 1988.
19. Interview with Revd Herbert B. Martin, 27 September 1988; Revd Herbert B. Martin, panel discussion on Black–Jewish relations, Temple Beth-El, Chicago, 28 September 1988.
20. A simple moral to be drawn is that first impressions can be misleading. Compare, in this respect, the discussion in Chapter 3, 'A Plea for Distinctions', of the Coffrini image.
21. Garry A. Tobin, *Jewish Perceptions of Antisemitism* (New York: Plenum Press, 1988), pp.43–4; Camper and Lipinski, 'Cokely Furor Ends the Honeymoon'.
22. Ann Marie Lipinski and James Strong, 'Mayor's Silence Heating Cokely Crisis to a Boil', *Chicago Tribune*, 5 May 1988; see also Johnson, 'Black–Jewish Hostility Rouses Leaders in Chicago to Action'.
23. Lipinski and Baquet, 'Sawyer Fires Cokely as Aide'.
24. Interview with Al Raby, former Executive Director of the Chicago Commission on Human Relations, 26 September 1988; Robert G. Weisbord and Richard Kazarian, Jr, *Israel in the Black American Perspective* (Westport, CT: Greenwood Press, 1985), pp.183–4; Johnson, 'Black–Jewish Hostility Rouses Leaders in Chicago to Action'; 'Around the World', *Jewish Currents*, 42, 9 (September 1988), p.45.
25. Johnson, 'Black–Jewish Hostility Rouses Leaders in Chicago to Action'.
26. Baldacci, 'Martin Explains His Response to Cokely's Remarks'.
27. Founded in 1871, Temple Beth-El is one of the oldest Reform congregations in the Chicago area. The panel discussion on Black–Jewish relations was held on 28 September 1988.

CHAPTER SIXTEEN

Ritual Murmur in Britain

FLYING THE FLAG FOR ANIMALS

A tender concern for the weak and the vulnerable might not be a conspicuously fascist trait. Nonetheless, the National Front (NF), along with other groups on the extreme right wing of British politics, fly the flag for animals, and have been doing so throughout the 1980s.[1]

Although these organizations attack a variety of practices, including hunting and vivisection, there is one item on the animal rights agenda which, more than any other, commends itself to the cause of nationalism: the campaign against so-called 'ritual slaughter' of animals. The special appeal of this campaign resides in the fact that Jews and Muslims are on the receiving end of it. The NF have produced a slick leaflet on the subject, 'Stop This Evil!', which has been widely circulated over the last four or five years.[2] In September 1984 they held a march in Brighton to protest against 'ritual slaughter'. Martin Wingfield, regional organizer at the time, said the protest 'is part of our overall policy against cruelty to animals'. He repudiated the charge of anti-semitism, adducing as evidence a familiar defence: some of his friends are Jews.[3]

'Ritual slaughter', otherwise known as 'religious slaughter', is a colloquialism used to refer to the Muslim and Jewish methods of killing animals for food. All animals slaughtered for food in Britain today are killed by an incision made with a knife. Under existing law, the general rule is that animals must be stunned (rendered unconscious) before the incision is made. Stunning is done by various means. The animal is either electrocuted, gassed or shot in the head with a steel bolt fired by a pistol. All these means infringe the religious laws governing *shechita* (the Jewish method), and most Islamic jurists in Britain take the same view with respect to *dhabh* (the Muslim equivalent).[4] This is reflected in the law of the land: the relevant statutes do not require animals slaughtered for kosher and halal meat to be unconscious when the incision is made.[5]

In January 1988, the NF backed a candidate in a local council by-election in Havering, Essex. The candidate, M. Griffin, stood under the rubric of 'Havering Animal Welfare'. One of his leaflets attacked 'the barbaric practice of ritual slaughter of animals'. The leaflet reproduced the name, address and logo of a well-known national animal rights organization, Compassion in World Farming (CIWF), which has been in the forefront of protest against 'ritual slaughter' throughout the 1980s.[6] CIWF reacted vigorously. They said that they were 'horrified' at having their name coupled with that of the NF; that they had never heard of Griffin; and that they 'condemn his attempt to use animal welfare to try to gain support for the obscene racist policies of the National Front'.[7] There were no ifs and buts about their reaction. They said bluntly, 'We want nothing to do with the National Front.'[8]

Consistent with this position, CIWF have been at pains to say that the issue of religious slaughter is entirely about the treatment of animals and that race does not enter into it. In this connection, they have a favourite argument that they use to establish the credentials of their campaign: 'Ritual slaughter is prohibited in Iceland, Norway, Sweden, Switzerland and parts of Austria. All these countries have a reputation for liberal human rights, which makes further nonsense of the idea that this is a racist issue.'[9]

Reduced to its essentials, the argument comprises two premises and a conclusion; and as syllogisms go, it is beguilingly simple:

1. Norway, Sweden, etc. have banned religious slaughter.
2. Norway, Sweden, etc. are not racist states.
3. Therefore, religious slaughter is not a racist issue.

You could call this 'innocence by association'. I wonder, however, about the spotlessness of the precedents. Austria has not exactly distinguished itself over the years by its benign attitude towards Jews. In Switzerland, Norway and Sweden the ban was imposed in 1893, 1929 and 1937 respectively: we would need to know about the circumstances at the time.[10] As for Iceland, it is difficult to believe that legislation was passed with the Jewish and Muslim communities in mind since, to the best of my knowledge, no such communities have ever existed there.[11]

But even if the two premises were rectified, the conclusion is a non sequitur. This can easily be seen by juxtaposing an argument that runs parallel, but in the opposite direction:

1. Nazi Germany banned religious slaughter.
2. Nazi Germany was a racist state.
3. Therefore, religious slaughter is a racist issue.

Formally, the two arguments are identical, yet their conclusions are contradictory. It follows that the reasoning in neither case is valid. Both these arguments are really skirting the issue. But there is no short cut here; it is necessary to examine the facts: to look at the actual character of the protest against religious slaughter in the Britain today. Only then is it possible to evaluate the claim made by CIWF that it is 'nonsense' to suggest that religious slaughter is a 'racist issue'.[12]

THE CONTROVERSY IN BRADFORD

Looked at one way, the issue of 'ritual slaughter' concerns an aspect of Muslim and Jewish culture. Looked at another way, it is about the treatment of animals. The strategy used by neo-fascist groups is to try to merge these two points of view.

A case in point is the controversy in the Yorkshire city of Bradford, where in 1983 the town council became the first local authority to introduce halal meat into school meals for Muslim children.[13] The Bradford Animal Rights Group (BARG), which was formed a year earlier to confront animal abuse, took the council to task. Their quarrel was solely with the fact that the meat was obtained from animals that had not been stunned before being killed. This quickly turned into a heated local controversy and put Bradford under the national spotlight.[14] The NF entered the fray in their own right, distributing their 'Stop This Evil!' leaflet. Eventually, in March 1984, the matter came before the full council. The debate was held under the watchful eyes of two packed public galleries, the opposing lobbies sitting on either side.[15] The council's decision, by fifty-nine votes to fifteen to continue the halal meals service, was received with applause on one side. On the other, in the version given in *National Front News*, the vote was greeted with 'cries of shame from animal welfare and National Front supporters in the public gallery'.[16] Notice the crucial equivocation in the phrase 'animal welfare and National Front supporters'. Does this refer to two completely separate groups of people whose 'cries of shame' happen to intermingle? Or does it mean that there was a body of people who exclaimed with one voice, the voice of a single cause: the unified cause of animal welfare and the National Front?

No doubt the syntax is self-serving. Nonetheless, the ambiguity was not wholly a figment of the NF's grammar, as a closer look at the opposition to halal meals in Bradford reveals.

Speaking candidly about the controversy, nearly three years after the events in which she herself had played a leading part, the treasurer of BARG put her own perspective on the issue this way: 'Animal rights to me is an extension of human rights.' All the organizers of the group, she said, felt the same way. But their campaign attracted people whom she referred to as racists. These people swelled the ranks of BARG and left the group once the halal meat issue was lost. Or they supported the group's campaign from the outside, signing petitions and writing letters to the local press. She distinguished between two sorts of racists. There are the ideologues, such as the NF, who subscribe to a theory of race. And then there are the run-of-the-mill xenophobics. The fairweather supporters of BARG, if I understood her correctly, were of the latter variety: people who, while not devoid of feeling for animals, were also actuated by bigotry and prejudice. On this account, there is no reason to think that BARG had been either 'infiltrated' or 'hijacked' by the NF. But the sort of people whom she described might well have lent an ear to the Front's policies on race and immigration. And it is not farfetched to suppose that some of those 'cries of shame' in Bradford Town Hall on the night of 6 March 1984 did double duty.[17]

Take the case of A.P. of Great Horton. He was there that night. In his letter to the Bradford *Telegraph and Argus* (*T & A*), he referred to the Muslim method of slaughter as 'this inhumane way' of killing animals. He saw the council's decision as a 'blatant and cynical example of the sacrificing of compassion' for 'Muslim votes'. He wrote: 'As a vegetarian and spectator in the public gallery of the Council Chamber, I witnessed and admired the fifteen councillors ... who refused to trade integrity for expediency.' The letter concluded unabashedly, 'I am tempted to vote BNP' (British National Party, a neo-Nazi group).[18]

A.P. had neither the first word nor the last on the subject. As the newspaper mentioned a few days prior to the council meeting on 6 March, the controversy over halal meat 'has been raging in the letters columns of the *T & A* for months, with hundreds of impassioned letters pouring in'.[19] And they have not stopped. A peek at some of the letters in the Bradford local press over the years affords a glimpse of the kinds of passions poured into those letters; at the same time it gives an idea of what the cause of animal welfare meant to many of the people opposed to 'ritual slaughter'.

To begin with the minimalist version: on the day of the March council meeting, a letter from a member of BARG stated emphatically on behalf of the group, 'We are *not against* halal meat – we simply want the animals pre-stunned before this religious rite is carried out in order to alleviate some of the suffering these animals are subjected to.'[20] This goal – the alleviation of some suffering – is a somewhat modest basis for what the *T & A* subsequently called 'a remarkable and seemingly never-ending campaign against Islamic methods of slaughtering animals'.[21] And it is fair to say that the campaign would not have enjoyed so much popular support if the issue had been seen in these minimalist terms.[22] On the contrary, correspondents reach for the sky to find superlatives sufficient for the task of expressing the cruelty of 'ritual slaughter'. It is 'ruthless killing', 'merciless', 'a hellish way of dying', 'needless and terrifying cruelty', 'the systematic torture of animals', and so on.[23] These epithets go together with a lurid and tendentious version of what the method of slaughter consists in: bleeding animals slowly to death while they are fully conscious.[24] Almost invariably, this is represented as being in stark contrast to the standard methods of slaughter used in Britain today, which, in the words of one correspondent, are 'as humane as slaughter could be', or at least incomparably kinder.[25]

Typically, this contrast – between cruelty and kindness – is embedded in another, wider, contrast: the civilized versus the primitive, or the advanced versus the backward, or the new versus the old. Often as not, no distinction is made between these different oppositions, as though whatever is ancient is also (or thereby) barbaric and inferior. As one correspondent asked: 'Where there is a modern way to slaughter in a civilized country, why adhere to the only method known 1,400 years ago in far flung villages?'[26] I wonder: far flung relative to where? To Bombay or to Bradford?

In any event, 'a civilized country' refers to contemporary Britain. And it is a popular perception of many of the opponents of 'ritual slaughter' that Britain is synonymous with the cause of animal welfare. In the words of L.H.H. of Beechcliffe, 'We, as a nation of animal-lovers, abhor needless and terrifying cruelty to animals.'[27] Or, as A.B. of Bradford proudly stated, 'British people down through the years have fought and struggled to stop all forms of cruelty to our animals, and the fight still goes on.'[28]

Against whom? It requires only a slight turn of the screw for this entire rhetorical ensemble to become an issue of 'Us' (we who are humane, civilized, progressive and modern) versus 'Them' (outsiders whose standards and practices are retrograde by comparison). Notice, in this connection, how A.B. referred to *our* animals; M.M.G., also of Bradford, called them 'our helpless animals'.[29] For E.M.F., of Bradford again, they are 'British animals'.[30] It is as if the animals themselves participate in the quality of being British, whereas citizens of Asian extraction do not. Referring to the council's position on halal meat,

A.B. (cited above) cautioned, 'Maybe it will make the Muslims in our city happy to be here, but I'm sure it will make the majority of Bradfordians less happy to have them here.' L.H.H. (also cited above) warned, 'There will always be ill-feeling and animosity to the minority who make animals suffer in the name of religion.'

Speaking of religion, LHH pointed out in his letter that 'England is mainly a Christian society, and as such the laws of the country are made, and not even non-Christians should be above the law.' Where Christianity is invoked, and it frequently is, it tends to slip easily into the rhetorical structure of Us versus Them. The Reverend J.T., a Dewsbury clergyman of the Anglican persuasion, was 'disgusted to read that halal meat is now to be served in schools'. He wrote, 'I see no reason why animals should not be painlessly stunned before these primitive rituals occur within our modern slaughterhouses.' And he asked, 'As Christians, are we going to sit back, and in due course sanction such barbaric innovations?' He saw a biblical analogy: 'All that is necessary for heathenism to return and barbarity to prevail is that we sit back and wash our hands, like Pilate tried to do with Jesus.' Presumably, the Reverend thought he was practising Christian charity when he said this about catering for the special dietary needs of Muslim schoolchildren: 'If this is the price for racial tolerance, then I shall remain intolerant.'[31]

All of this is but a whisker away from the sort of letter R.G.H. of Keighley wrote. Opening with the popular aphorism, 'When in Rome, do as the Romans do', he ran the usual rhetorical gamut and finished up with a twist on his opening line: 'If you don't like the way the Romans behave, don't go to Rome!'[32] Again, 'Don't come here' is a fraction of an inch short of saying 'Go home'; which is the policy of the NF.

THE POPULAR POLEMIC NATIONWIDE

Throughout the 1980s, local disputes over religious slaughter have proliferated across the country. Apart from the issue of halal school meals, local communities and local authorities have debated such questions as whether to introduce halal meat into hospital meals and meals-on-wheels, and whether to grant licences to slaughterers and slaughterhouses for performing *shechita* or *dhabh*.[33] There have also been isolated incidents, such as the notorious occasion in Roehampton in September 1984 when an Iranian diplomat slaughtered a sheep in the street.[34] And in 1985 the debate went national when the Farm Animal Welfare Council (FAWC) published its review of religious methods of slaughter.[35] Whatever the occasion, or the specific point at issue, time and again the selfsame patterns of rhetoric that appeared in Bradford re-appear elsewhere, with the same momentum carrying the polemic from 'reduce animal suffering' to 'wogs go home'. As utterly diverse as these two sentiments appear to be at first sight, there are mediated by clichés about Britain and progress and Christian civilization and what-have-you. Thus the one shades into the other, imperceptibly but ineluctably. And what starts out as a purely technical question about different methods of slaughter turns into a stark confrontation between Us and Them.

The crux of the technical question is this: what difference, if any, does it make to the suffering experienced by an animal if it is killed by the Jewish or Muslim method rather than by the normal alternatives? In practice, a lot turns on the state of the equipment and on the proficiency of the slaughterer. Mishaps can and do occur with any method. But as to the superiority of 'secular' over 'religious' methods in principle, experts argue the toss and impartial authorities disagree.[36] Although at times one side or the other might appear to have the edge, the argument over the years has been something of a stalemate. Neither side would care to admit this in public. But a 1979 RSPCA internal document written by J.K. Dow, the member of their veterinary department with special expertise in this area, puts the debate into historical perspective. Referring to the fact that the 1904 Admiralty Committee Report came down against *shechita*, he points out, 'The decision was reached after considering evidence from two distinguished physiologists, Sir Michael Foster and Professor Starling, but their views were in direct conflict with those of the equally eminent Professor Lovatt Evans and Sir Leonard Hill.'[37] He observes that the evidence at the time was obviously 'at best incomplete and at worst controversial'. And he adds, 'Sadly, three quarters of a century later, we are little further forward. We have only a few established facts to help us.' In the Summary he frankly concludes, 'There is no evidence that either method, correctly applied, is more or less painful to the animal.'[38]

The stand-off at the turn of the century, with impartial authorities ranged on either side, continued to be the position in subsequent years, up to and including the 1980s.[39] Nor is this a well-guarded secret: the conflicting evidence has been brought before the public repeatedly.[40] Nonetheless, a note of absolute conviction has always been a hallmark of the popular polemic against 'ritual slaughter'. As R.R. stated baldly in her letter to Belfast City Council in 1981, 'There is irrefutable scientific proof that this method of slaughter causes intense suffering.'[41]

The 'proof', however, is not so much scientific as semantic. Phrases, not facts, are what motivate the continual murmuring against the Jewish and Muslim methods of killing animals. For they are not merely methods, they are icons, symbols of a moral or metaphysical opposition: the 'ritual' versus the 'humane'. The connotations of these two words reverberate throughout the popular rhetoric on the subject. In general discourse, the word 'ritual' has come to be used routinely as a pejorative term to imply 'pointless' and 'heartless' – as in one newspaper editorial that appeared under the headline 'Ritual Slaughter of Animals'. This turned out to have nothing to do with *shechita* or *dhabh*. It was about a man who 'beat his dog to death in front of his own son'.[42] Because this was a cruel and mindless thing to do, it was called 'ritual'. And because 'ritual' and 'humane' define what is vaguely felt to be a fundamental antithesis, exaggerated claims are made about the beneficence of 'humane' slaughter, the horrors of 'ritual' slaughter, and 'irrefutable scientific proof' on the subject. By the same token, the issue is blown up out of all proportion to the plight of animals in the modern industrial world of factory farming and factory slaughtering.

The semantics of the controversy do not end there. The antithesis between 'humane' and 'ritual' is continued in a variety of synonyms. 'Humane slaughter' is also known as the 'Western', 'Christian', 'British', or 'English' method. 'Ritual slaughter' is called 'Jewish', 'Muslim' and 'Semitic'.[43] Thus the very labels lend themselves to a polemic that opposes Us to Them, Our methods to Theirs.

The combined effect of these purely semantic aspects of the controversy is that Our methods *by definition* are superior to Theirs. The correspondents who quote the adage 'When in Rome do as the Romans do' rarely leave it at that. Almost invariably, in the same breath, they condemn 'ritual slaughter' as barbaric (or backward or cruel) – as though this were one and the same argument. What they mean is better put by Jack of Oldham who says, 'In England do as the English do.'[44] For, after all, as A.S. of Bradshaw exclaims, 'This is England!'[45] 'Rome' was just an ancient city but 'England' is a moral category. And when the *Oldham Evening Chronicle* remarks, 'Ritual slaughter can have absolutely nothing to commend it in English eyes', this is tantamount to a truism, given the linguistics of the debate: the virtual equivalence in meaning between 'English' and 'humane' on the one hand, and the opposition between 'humane' and 'ritual' on the other.[46]

In view of the terms in which the issue is conceived, terms that are as complimentary to Us as they are derogatory to Them, it is not surprising that the protest against 'ritual slaughter' enjoys such broad and vociferous support. When 'an Islamic abattoir' was opened in Kids-grove in Staffordshire in 1985, one local councillor was reported as saying that 'he had never known such a public outcry in the town as over this issue'.[47] A few months later, when the Lancashire town of Bolton was faced with the question of whether to provide Muslim children with halal meat, the *Bolton Evening News* commented: 'Our postbag is bulging with letters from Boltonians absolutely appalled by the idea.' The newspaper called it 'one of the most controversial local issues for a long time'.[48] And a grateful Hon. Sec. of the Bolton branch of the RSPCA declared, 'In the past I have accused the townspeople of apathy but the overwhelming support we have received on this issue has moved me to believe that they do care.'[49]

It is striking how people who care – and they care passionately – reflect the entire spectrum of attitudes towards the treatment of animals. At one extreme there is the moral outrage of hunting enthusiasts; such as M.W.B. of Little Horwood, Bucks, who wrote, 'Fox hunting by comparison with ritual slaughter is a gentle, compassionate and pleasant death for an animal.'[50] At the other extreme are vegetarians, among whom Dr Alan Long, Hon. Research Adviser to the Vegetarian Society of the United Kingdom, is a prominent opponent of religious slaughter. Dr Long, who has been described by the environment correspondent of the *Independent* as 'one of the best informed enemies of the meat production business', aligned himself with certain slaughtermen in a letter to *Farmers Weekly* attacking *shechita*.[51] Inveighing against 'slavish interpretation of Mosaic law', he quoted the men as saying that religious slaughter is 'sheer bloody murder'.[52] In another letter, he alluded to 'Jewish sophists' and spoke of 'the Jews and Muslims still demanding their grisly sacrifices'.[53] Elsewhere, in a lengthy article in the *Vegetarian* that provoked a heated correspondence, he referred to *shechita* as 'debauchery', and called upon Muslims and Jews in Britain to abandon 'such alien practices'. Citing restrictions that 'Muslims' impose on 'their visitors', he wrote, 'We may sincerely ask them to desist here from practices offensive to the traditions of the British population.'[54] Dr Long, as a proselytizing vegetarian in a society where eating meat, especially at certain seasons of the year, is an entrenched practice, makes an unlikely champion of British traditions. Be that as it may, as this sample of his invective illustrates, he does not fare well, measured by the standard set by CIWF: 'It is, of course, essential that this campaign is conducted solely on animal welfare grounds.'[55]

Nor, as it turns out, do CIWF. Shortly after the FAWC report was published in July 1985, they wrote as follows in their magazine,

Agscene: 'A letter to *The Times* on 19 August sums up much of the argument. It includes this statement: "One must respect other people's religious law, but it is not proper that a minority's custom should be allowed to offend the moral sense of the majority." '[56] As for showing respect for other people's religion, CIWF accuse Muslims of using religious freedom 'as a cloak for big business'; they say that *dhabh* 'should certainly not be called religious slaughter' because it is 'just diehard tradition, nothing more'; that the Jewish and Muslim methods 'mock the name of religion'; that 'ritual slaughter is a cruel and savage custom'; that Muslims who insist upon it are 'a minority of fanatics' who 'defile their religion and aggravate racism'; and so on.[57] Apropos this last point, they criticize Bradford Council 'and its imitators' for providing a halal meals service, on the grounds that this will lead the Muslim community to make other demands, such as 'separate swimming for girls and boys and single sex classes'. This, they say, 'is encouraging racial segregation'.[58] If nothing else, this line of argument does not carry the campaign forward 'solely on animal welfare grounds'.[59]

The appeal of the campaign also crosses political lines, finding favour on the left as well as on the right. One letter containing the usual smattering of phrases ('We, the indigenous population', 'our own Christian children', 'a civilized country', 'this barbaric form of killing', 'offensive, sickening', 'the only civilized method') came from the pen of the Chairman of the Derbyshire County Labour Party.[60]

In short, when it comes to the slaughter of animals by Jews and Muslims, all manner of people care. This is not to say that there are no dissenting voices. But for those in the 'indigenous population' who are so disposed, the issue of 'ritual slaughter' is a rallying point. All internal differences are transcended as hands join in a united protest against the generally felt affront committed by the outsider. It is reminiscent of what footballers do when they take the field in order to consolidate eleven individuals into a team: it is called bonding. And when you scan the press and find the same formulaic phrases occurring over and over again, like a constant drumbeat, you begin to acquire an uncanny sense that people across the country are participating, through their common murmuring, in, dare I say it, a primitive communal ritual.

THE VERDICT

When I wrote to CIWF to express concern about aspects of their propaganda over 'ritual slaughter', they replied, 'sometimes it needs a little emotive language to get people steamed up to campaign on the subject'.[61] This, in a way, gets to the heart of the matter: the nature of the emotion aroused in people by the language of protest against Muslim and Jewish methods of slaughter.

In this connection, the treasurer of BARG made a number of telling comments about the abortive campaign in Bradford against halal school meals. 'We didn't see it', she said. 'We didn't realize that all this racism was there.' She recalled the crowd that had come to the Council meeting on the night of 6 March 1984 to lobby for BARG's position: 'There were people – all their nastiness had come out, it was boiled up into this one thing.' Her final verdict was this: the exercise 'hurt the Muslim community and didn't help the animals'.[62] Her testimony belies the claim made by CIWF that it is 'nonsense' to suggest that 'ritual slaughter' is 'a racist issue'. It is, on the contrary, hard to see how a public campaign along these lines could be otherwise.

The movement for animal rights sees itself as appealing to the best in people. But the evidence shows that the campaign against 'ritual slaughter' tends to bring out the worst. And it seems disingenuous for CIWF to say, 'We want nothing to do with the National Front' while at the same time pursuing a campaign that effectively invites them to climb on board.[63]

POSTSCRIPT

Campaigns against 'ritual slaughter' take different forms at different times. In June 2010 the European Parliament approved new regulations that would, in effect, require meat from animals killed by orthodox Jewish and Muslim methods to be labelled 'meat from slaughter without stunning'. (At the time of writing, this measure has yet to come before the Council of the European Union.) Providing consumers with information about the products they buy is, in principle, a good thing. However, the proposed measure singles out one fact among many that affect the question of animal suffering at the point of slaughter. For this reason alone it is misleading. Furthermore, the consumer is liable to assume that meat that does not bear this label comes from animals that died painlessly or without suffering, 'humanely' put to sleep. Even in ideal conditions, this assumption is false; and conditions are rarely ideal in the real world of a killing factory dedicated to maximising 'output' – as I discovered for myself when I ventured behind the scenes and embarked on an odyssey of visits to slaughterhouses (see Chapter 17).

NOTES

1. See, for example, *National Front News*, March 1984 and April 1985; *Nationalism Today*, October 1984 and June 1985; 'Animal Welfare', a leaflet produced by *Combat* ('White Nationalist paper for youth'), August 1983.
2. See also *National Front News*, May 1984, September 1984, March 1985 and October 1985. The tradition on the far right of attacking *shechita* goes back at least as far as the Britons in the 1920s. See note 52.
3. *Evening Argus*, Hastings, 18 and 22 September 1984.
4. For stunning methods, see G. Eikelenboom (ed.), *Stunning of Animals for Slaughter* (Boston: Martinus Nijhoff, 1983). For the orthodox Muslim and Jewish positions in Britain respectively, see 'The Muslim Response', Islamic Cultural Centre, 1985, and 'Comments by the Jewish Community', Office of the Chief Rabbi, November 1985. Both pamphlets affirm the principle of minimizing suffering to the animal.
5. The Slaughterhouses Act, 1974, clause 36; the Slaughter of Poultry Act, 1967, clause 1. *Shechita* and *dhabh* are, however, subject to other conditions, including the stipulation that they be performed 'without the infliction of unnecessary suffering'.
6. *Jewish Herald*, 21 January 1988; *Brentwood Review*, Essex, 29 January 1988; *Searchlight*, 152 (1988), p.5. In 1985 the NF candidate for Sevenoaks East, Carol Addison, was described as 'an active anti-vivisectionist and Animal Rights campaigner' (*Sevenoaks Chronicle*, 12 April 1985).
7. *Jewish Chronicle*, 15 January 1988.
8. Quoted in 'The Truth about Havering Animal Welfare', a leaflet produced by the Romford Labour Party (January 1988). CIWF sent a solicitor's letter to Griffin's agent, G. Williamson, deputy chairman of the NF, complaining of defamation and demanding that no further leaflets be distributed. Griffin's leaflet also implicated the British Union for the Abolition of Vivisection (BUAV), who obtained a High Court interim injunction restraining Griffin and Williamson from distributing the leaflet. BUAV were equally forthright in disassociating themselves from the NF (BUAV Press Release, 14 January 1988; *Daily Telegraph*, 21 January 1988; *City Limits*, 21 January 1988; *Jewish Chronicle*, 22 January 1988). I am not aware of any family connection between Griffin and Nick Griffin, who contested the seat of Croydon North West for the National Front in 1981 and 1983 and later became leader of the British National Party.
9. CIWF leaflet, 'The Slaughter Ritual'. The argument is used frequently. See, for example, the letter from Carol Long of CIWF in the *Guardian*, 28 August 1985.
10. Michael Metcalf explores this question in 'Regulating Slaughter: Animal Protection and Antisemitism in Scandinavia, 1880–1941', *Patterns of Prejudice*, 23, 3 (1989), pp.32–48. See also I. Lewin, M.L. Munk and J.J. Berman, *Religious Freedom: The Right to Practice Shehitah* (New York: Research Institute for Post-War Problems of Religious Jewry, 1946).
11. The Chief Veterinary Officer of Iceland has informed me that there is no Jewish or Muslim community there (letter from Pall A. Palsson, 27 October 1988).
12. This chapter is a lightly edited version of 'Ritual Murmur: The Undercurrent of Protest Against Religious slaughter of Animals in Britain in the 1980s', *Patterns of Prejudice*, 23, 2 (1989). For a review of this controversy over the long term, see T. Kushner, 'Stunning Intolerance: Opposition to Religious Slaughter in Twentieth Century Britain', *Jewish Quarterly*, 133 (Spring 1989), pp.16–20. See also R. Charlton and R. Kaye, 'The Politics of Religious Slaughter: An Ethno-Religious Case Study', *New Community*, 12, 3 (Winter 1985–86), pp.490–503.
13. D. Harrison, 'Whose Rights in Bradford?', *Guardian*, 5 March 1984.
14. The controversy was given extensive coverage in the British media locally and nationally. See, for example, Diane Spencer, 'How Bradford Held On to Its Lead in Race ...', *Times Educational Supplement*, 7 October 1983; Wendy Berliner, 'Bigotry Boils Up over Asian Meat', *Guardian*, 26 March 1984.
15. 'Halal – The Dispute that has Split Bradford', *Meat Trades Journal*, 22 March 1984.
16. *National Front News*, May 1984. Compare the *Observer*'s description of the same scene: 'The result was greeted with cries of "shame" from animal rights campaigners and extreme right-wingers' (11 March 1984).
17. Interview with Alison McKay, 15 November 1986. The committee of BARG, in a letter repudiating people who 'made racialist comments' in support of their campaign, wrote as follows: 'If you truly care for animals but not for humans, we fail to understand you, but at least do the animals the service of staying out of the pre-stunning issue' (*Telegraph & Argus*, Bradford, 13 March 1984).

18. *Telegraph & Argus*, 15 March, 1984.
19. Ibid., 2 March 1984.
20. Ibid., 6 March 1984.
21. Quoted in D.G. Wright, 'Ritual Slaughter', *Times Educational Supplement*, 21 October 1983.
22. BARG had 7,400 signatures on a petition against the slaughter of animals without prior stunning (*Telegraph & Argus*, 26 January 1983). A subsequent petition against the council's halal school meals policy 'on moral grounds' had over 9,000 signatures (*Telegraph & Argus*, 2 March 1984).
23. *Telegraph & Argus*, 2 April 1982, 5 October 1983 and 8 August 1983; *Keighley News*, 29 November 1985 and 21 February 1986.
24. *Telegraph & Argus*, 19 October 1983.
25. *Keighley News*, 16 September 1983.
26. *Telegraph & Argus*, 31 August 1983.
27. *Keighley News*, 29 November 1985.
28. *Telegraph & Argus*, 28 February 1984.
29. Ibid., 26 July 1983.
30. Ibid., 16 September 1983.
31. Ibid., 1 August 1983.
32. *Keighley News*, 16 September 1983.
33. This chapter is based in part on my review of newspaper coverage of local disputes over religious slaughter in various places apart from Bradford, including the following: Basingstoke (1988), Birmingham (1985, 1989), Bolton (1985), Boston (1985), Brent (1983), Clwyd (1986), Hexham (1982), Islington (1987), Leicester (1987), Northampton (1988), Oldham (1984), Peterborough (1987), Rochdale (1984, 1987), Rotherham (1985), Stoke-on-Trent (1985), Waltham Forest (1985), Walton-on-the-Hill (1986), Wolverhampton (1988).
34. *Morning Star*, 24 September 1984; *Guardian*, 25 September 1984.
35. The Farm Animal Welfare Council (FAWC) is an advisory body set up by the government in 1979. FAWC have produced three reports on the treatment of animals at slaughter, all of them highly critical of existing practices. Only the third, *Report on the Welfare of Livestock When Slaughtered by Religious Methods* (London, 1985) deals with *dhabh* and *shechita*. FAWC recommended repeal of the statutory provision enabling Jews and Muslims to slaughter without stunning, on the grounds that 'humane slaughter can best be achieved by effective stunning' (par. 76). The government has taken the view that this would impose an unjustifiable burden on Muslims and Jews (Ministry of Agriculture Press Release, 29 October 1987; *Hansard*, 29 October 1987, 410). This decision is based in part on the fact that there are differences in scientific opinion (letter from Donald Thompson, Junior Agriculture Minister, to Ivan Lawrence, MP, 17 December 1987).
36. FAWC's report on religious slaughter has been faulted for omissions in its review of the scientific literature. See, for example, 'Comments by the Jewish Community'.) Recently, Temple Grandin has found that a skilled shochet could cause over 95 per cent of calves 'to collapse immediately like animals shot with a captive bolt'. This rate is 'similar in performance to stunning' (T. Grandin, 'Humane Slaughter System', *Vealer* [May 1987], pp.6–9). The British Veterinary Association support FAWC's position (*Guardian*, 27 June 1986). However, I have found opinion to be divided among the veterinarians and slaughterhouse personnel I have consulted on this question. See Chapter 17, 'The Kiss of Death', for an account of my visits to various kinds of slaughterhouses.
37. *Report of the Committee Appointed by the Admiralty to Consider the Humane Slaughtering of Animals* (London: HMSO, 1904).
38. J.K. Dow, 'Ritual Slaughter' (January 1979). Nonetheless, the RSPCA has campaigned energetically, from time to time, against 'ritual slaughter'. Their opposition dates back at least as far as 1855 (RSPCA, *Annual Report*, 1856) and continues to the present day (see note 62).
39. The literature is too large to summarize here. For some leads in one direction, see M.L. Munk and E. Munk (eds), *Shechita: Religious, Historical and Scientific Aspects* (New York: Gur Aryeh, 1976), p.109. For the opposite orientation, see L. Macnaghten, *Pistol Versus Poleaxe: A Handbook on Humane Slaughter* (London: Chapman & Hall, 1931), Chapters 10 and 11. See also the proceedings of two symposia organized by the Universities Federation for Animal Welfare: *Humane Killing and Slaughterhouse Techniques* (1971) and *Humane Slaughter of Animals for Food* (1986).
40. Conflicting evidence surfaces in the course of the debate conducted through letters and articles in the press. The Board of Deputies of British Jews has produced, over the years, a

number of leaflets and pamphlets citing research results and expert testimony in defence of *shechita*, such as 'The Jewish Way' (1987).

41. Quoted in M. Gaisford, 'Religious Slaughter', *Farmers Weekly*, 5 June 1981.

42. *South Wales Argus*, 19 July 1988.

43. *Dhabh* and *shechita* are also referred to as 'ritual slaying', 'ritual killing', 'ritual animal killing', 'animal slaughter ritual', 'Arab religious slaughter', 'halal ritual' and 'the kosher ritual'. Muslims and Jews who carry out the practice are called 'ritual killers' and 'ritual slaughterers'. In this chapter I have not explored the overlapping connotations of these expressions. (But see note 52.)

44. *Manchester Evening News*, 31 July 1985.

45. *Oldham Evening Chronicle*, 2 August 1984.

46. Ibid., 24 August 1984.

47. *Wolverhampton Express & Star*, 8 March 1985.

48. *Bolton Evening News*, 30 July 1985.

49. Ibid., 7 August 1985.

50. *Bedfordshire Times*, 13 November 1986. See also J.F.O.'s letter in *Loughborough Echo*, 30 January 1987.

51. *Independent*, 2 December 1986. The description is by Richard North, the newspaper's environment correspondent.

52. *Farmers Weekly*, 12 June 1981. Compare S.M.H. of Dudley: 'The whole business of murdering animals to conform to antiquated and alien dogmas is repugnant (*Wolverhampton Express & Star*, 6 January 1987). The Britons produced a pamphlet, 'Jews' Ritual Slaughter' (London, n.d.), divided into two parts. Part 1 was entitled 'The Religious Murder and Torture of Animals for Food'. Part 2 was called 'Ritual Murder' and propagated the medieval charge that Jews kill Christians and use their blood in religious rites. The murderer, in these stories, is often a shochet and the victim is frequently killed by a gash in the throat. See 'Blood Accusation' in *The Jewish Encyclopedia* (New York: Funk and Wagnalls, 1906). See also C. Holmes, 'The Ritual Murder Accusation in Britain', *Ethnic and Racial Studies*, 4, 3 (July 1981), pp.265–88. Holmes speaks of 'that most resilient element of antisemitism, the dark myth of Jewish sadism and ritual murder'. Phrases like 'ritual killing' and 'ritual killers' mediate the two notions of 'ritual slaughter' and 'ritual murder', since they apply to both. Furthermore, there are pronounced similarities in the popular rhetoric of both these obloquies against Judaism. With this in mind, Francesca Klug (in conversation) has referred to the outcry against 'ritual slaughter' as 'the blood libel of the twentieth century'.

53. *Farmers Weekly*, 4 October 1985.

54. A. Long, 'For God' Sake Stop this Slaughter!', *Vegetarian* (November/December 1981). He argued along the same lines in a feature article, 'Taking the Horror out of the Ritual Slaughter of Animals', *Independent*, 28 August 1987.

55. *Agscene*, 82 (March 1986), p.6.

56. Ibid., 80, (October 1985), p.10.

57. CIWF leaflet, 'Ritual Slaughter'; *Agscene*, 73 (November/December 1983), p.12; 81 (November 1985), p.3; 85 (September 1986), p.3; 69 (November/December 1982), p.9.

58. *Agscene*, 73 (November/December 1983), p.12.

59. I examine CIWF's language and mode of arguing at greater length in 'Overkill: The Polemic against "Ritual Slaughter" ', *Jewish Quarterly*, 134 (Summer 1989), pp.38–42.

60. *Star*, Sheffield, 13 December 1983.

61. Letter from Joyce D'Silva, 24 October 1988. She attributes this explanation to Peter Roberts, founder of CIWF and editor of *Agscene*.

62. Interview with Alison McKay, 15 November 1986. Compare the Bradford *Telegraph & Argus* on a report by the Bradford Community Relations Council: 'The debate about halal meat stirred up unprecedented animosity towards the Muslim community in Bradford, says a report just published' (12 May 1984). Despite the well-publicized example of Bradford, later that year the RSPCA annual general meeting voted unanimously to 'actively campaign' against 'ritual slaughter' (RSPCA, *161st Annual Report*, 1984, p.8; *Telegraph & Argus*, 28 June 1984).

63. Some prominent individuals and organizations in the animal rights movement have pointedly refrained from campaigning on this issue. Victor Schonfeld would not include it in his hard-hitting *The Animals Film* (1981 London Film Festival). John Bryant, chair of the council of Animal Aid had said, 'We are in no position to turn round to the Muslims and Jews and criticize them for being inhumane' (*Weekend Voice*, 30 April 1987).

CHAPTER SEVENTEEN

The Kiss of Death

MY FIRST SLAUGHTERHOUSE

My first slaughterhouse was a small affair on the outskirts of London. Not being an aficionado and having no connections in the trade, I turned to London's *Yellow Pages* and looked under 'Abattoirs'. The first entry was Llewellyn & Fisher Ltd. I looked no further and, hoping that I was not about to put my head on the block, dialled the number.

I was not in the market for meat at wholesale prices. Nor was I a farmer ready to cash in his livestock. I was an outsider to the hidden world of butchery, looking for a glimpse behind the veil. How do you introduce yourself to a slaughterhouse when you have no practical business to transact with it? How do you get the proprietors to invite you into their lair when you have no reason for being there – no reason that they are likely to recognize as any concern of theirs? The prospect seemed especially bleak at a time (the mid 1980s) when slaughterhouse premises were being fire-bombed, lorries sabotaged and staff held at knife-point by masked animal-rights guerrillas. 'Meat is murder', sang the Smiths, a slogan that was spray-painted on the walls of slaughterhouses across the country. In view of all this, it behoved me to think of an angle of approach and prepare my opening gambit carefully in advance. But what could I say that might do the trick? I simply took the plunge; and when, after a long hold, a gruff voice at the other end of the phone line suddenly uttered the slurred syllable 'Slawerous', it gave me quite a jolt.

The shock galvanized me into coming straight to the point and the brief conversation went something like this. I asked if I might come down to the abattoir and see how they do things. Did I mean that I want to watch the animals being killed? Yes, that was the general idea. Which species? I was interested in all of them, I explained. There followed a succinct schedule: Monday pigs, Tuesday beef, Wednesday lambs. I should be sure and come early. Click: the line was dead. It was over. I was in.

Or was I? It was with some uncertainty that I set out for my first slaughterhouse, first thing on the following Monday. Llewellyn &

Fisher was, as I say, on the outskirts of London, beyond the green strip of countryside that girdles the city like a giant belt round an enormous belly; and the drive out in the early July morning, on a clear road with a cloudless sky above, was invigorating. It was hard to keep my mind off the morning and on my destination, a shadowy far-off place about which I knew next to nothing. I knew only what it was called: a slaughter-house. Or should that be abattoir? Does the name make a difference? I did not know and could not care less. At that time of day the air is electric and the whole irrational creation seems to be instinct with life while discerning civilization is still sputtering in its bed. But there are some civilized activities that are exceptions to the rule; among these is slaughtering. Slaughterers are up with the birds. By the time I arrived on the scene, they were reaping their grim harvest.

Neither Mr Llewellyn nor Mr Fisher was there. So, after parking the car, I walked in and introduced myself to the slaughtermen as best I could. They did not seem to mind me. I was glad of it: a slaughterhouse is not the kind of place where you want to find yourself unwelcome. I do not say that they were positively pleased to see me. But the odd person hovers about the premises from time to time – a meat inspector, a state veterinary officer, and so on; and I suppose to the men I was just another odd person.

Once across the threshold I realized that I was not quite dressed for the occasion. In particular, looking down at my feet, I wondered if my lounge shoes would cope with the ooze on the floor of the slaughterhall. Gingerly I stepped across to where several pigs were crowded into a small pen. I counted fifteen but it was hard to be sure of the number because they were continually on the move, swerving to avoid the manoeuvres of the man who stood among them, implement in hand.

I placed myself just outside the pen, where I was out of harm's way, and watched. I was not altogether unprepared for what I was about to witness since I had seen the general procedure described on paper. But I needed, for the particular purpose that had brought me there, to see it in the flesh. The implement in question was a pair of scissor-like tongs. You could not tell at a glance what these tongs were for or what they were capable of doing. To an innocent eye they appeared quite innocuous. But they were connected to a transformer on the wall by a long wire flex through which an electric current of about eighty volts was constantly flowing. An electrode was fitted on the end of each arm of the tongs. The operator held the live implement at the other (insulated) end. His job was to try to catch each pig by the head with the tongs and hold it there for several seconds, thereby sending an electric charge through the animal's body. The object of the exercise was not to kill outright but to shock the pig into senselessness: to knock it out. This exercise is called an 'electrical stunning operation'. It is part of the practice widely known as 'humane slaughter'.

One thing was immediately apparent about this operation: the pigs did not consider they needed it. They were in the pink of health and conducted themselves accordingly. At first, when the pen was full, there was not much scope for them to avoid the tongs, which hovered over their heads like the angel of death, descending at random onto the nearest hapless skull. Gradually, however, the pen began to empty as one electrocuted animal after another was shackled by the leg to the elevator and hoisted on to the rail where, suspended upside down, it was despatched by the sticker (the man with the knife). As the pen began to clear, the remaining pigs had more scope for taking evasive action. I call them survivors for their adeptness at avoiding the operator (the man with the tongs). Their contrariness seemed to peeve him and he chastised them as though they were disobedient dogs refusing to do their master's bidding. The operator expected their full cooperation. And when they did not oblige he swore at them in a lusty vernacular without so much as a 'Pardon my French'. 'Get yourself out, you cunt', he told one animal whose hindquarters were wedged between the hoist and the wall of the pen. He encouraged the pig to free itself by repeatedly kicking it. 'Fuck you': this to an animal whose struggles made it difficult to position the tongs correctly. One survivor stood stock still in the middle of the pen squealing for all it was worth. 'I haven't touched you', said the operator reproachfully, as though the beast were being unreasonable. Then he applied the tongs to its head. 'Silly bastard.'

We call his sort of English 'bad language,' meaning that the words he used, taken in themselves, are crude, and because they are crude reprehensible. But it was not the obscenity as such that jarred. It was something like the lack of fit: the fact that his banter bore no relation to what the pigs were being made to undergo at his hands: their death. I could imagine him speaking in a similar idiom to his children at home. It is bath time, say; it is later than usual; supper is nearly ready; the kids are messing around and complaining, refusing to get undressed. One of them hits his head against the bathroom door as he tries to escape his dad. 'Silly bastard.' This might be said in anger or with affection. In any event, it has a natural setting. The fact that this vocabulary might be too coarse for some people's taste or education is neither here nor there. In a certain sort of household, such language is part of the domestic rough and tumble. It has a context. That context is provided by family ties and it includes a future. But between those creatures and that operator there were no ties; and the future is precisely what he was depriving them of. It was these incongruities that made his language grotesque.

There are many ways in which language can go bad. And I would not say that the worst language I encountered on my project was on the floor of the slaughterhall. Odd as this might sound, it was language, or a particular turn of speech, that had brought me to Llewellyn & Fisher. In the popular idiom, the usual way of slaughtering animals for food is called 'humane' on the grounds that the animal is rendered unconscious – 'stunned' – prior to being killed. This practice entails the use of techniques that, according to (all) Orthodox Jewish and (most) Muslim jurists, contravene the religious law of Judaism and Islam respectively and therefore may not be used for the production of kosher or halal meat. For this reason, their methods of 'ritual slaughter' are widely condemned as cruel by the advocates of 'humane slaughter', who seek to ban them. But what does it mean to call slaughter 'humane'? How does the phrase 'humane slaughter' fare when weighed by this standard Hamlet sets the players: 'suit the action to the word, the word to the action' (*Hamlet*, 3.2)? This is not something we normally stop to consider, for the phrase has become as conventional as the practice it names. Whenever language becomes set in its ways it is liable to languish, to lose its tone and therefore its cutting edge. Stock phrases like 'humane slaughter' can render our speech complacent. The thoughts we utter are not quite thoughts – or not quite ours. All this can happen – and still we retain the sensation of meaning what we say and the impression of thinking for ourselves, But language is chock full of stock phrases, and so the potential for being deluded is ever-present. We need to judge the fit of word to action: we need to *mind* our language – not for the sake of propriety but in order to appropriate our thoughts. But this need, though always with us, is rarely felt. In this case, the public campaign against 'ritual slaughter', in which two minority groups were fingered while the rest of the meat-eating public was off the hook, made the need palpable. Though I came to the slaughterhouse to watch, my purpose was not to see, merely. My watching was a species of listening. My aim was to make the phrase 'humane slaughter' ring in my ears; and I did not consider that I could judge this language – to pronounce it fair or foul – until I had the feel of the slaughterhouse in my bones.

On the Tuesday, which was beef day, I paid the price for arriving late – it was 8.30 when I got to the premises – by missing most of that morning's action. Still, it gave me the chance to introduce myself to Mr

Llewellyn and Mr Fisher. I explained, though a little more briskly perhaps than I have just set out, what it was that had brought me to their door. They were blunt-speaking men themselves with a taste for facts, not fancy talk. Their attitude toward me was one of mild curiosity with an admixture of sheer indifference. I seemed harmless; and good as a diversion in the lull between kills. But they were friendly enough and their advice to me was to enlarge my vision by seeing slaughter carried out on a larger scale. What about the protests over 'ritual slaughter' as against the standard way of doing it? They were in the trade: did they have an opinion? They had two between them. Mr Fisher took the view that the one way is as good as the other. 'Both are quick', he said. His partner Mr Llewellyn disagreed. He thought that the Jewish and Muslim methods were – his word – cruel. As for their own establishment, he took pride in the humanity of the place. He told me that all the slaughtermen that he and Mr Fisher employed were – his word again – animal-lovers.

He was right about Bill. The main thing I saw Bill do was give animals the knife at the killing or bleeding stage of the proceedings. He was the chief sticker. Although it was hard to pin down, there was something sympathetic about his demeanour. This is quite a compliment, bearing in mind that these were not surroundings in which it was easy for anyone to shine. I sought him out, when circumstances permitted, and we got chatting. He spoke unhurriedly about his own animals at home – he breeds dogs – and then he adverted to his job. He told me that sometimes, when he comes to work of a morning, he sees all the animals standing waiting and there is nothing he wants to do so much as let them all go. I asked him, 'How do you put the thought out of your mind?' 'You just get on with it', he said. And then an afterthought: 'You've got to live.' I was struck by Bill's unguarded answer. It contained no defence.

I asked Bill what he thought about the controversy over Jewish and Muslim methods. He deliberated for a moment and then said that the usual way of slaughtering, whereby the animals are first stunned, is 'the best way'. One of his fellow workers, the man who operated the electrical stunning equipment, put in his oar. Echoing what Mr Llewellyn had said, he called 'ritual slaughter' cruel. 'What we do', he assured me, 'is kind'. He also called it 'humane'. I am sure I was glad to hear it, especially from a man with his degree of experience in the art of killing with kindness. I nearly betrayed my ignorance by saying that, to my untutored eye, the pigs had not appeared too happy with the treatment they had received at his hands the previous day. I almost confessed that, to a layman like me, it did not seem kind to kick an animal about to die and already half-scared to death, as he had done before my eyes. But I was not there to argue the toss. I was there to learn. I made a mental note of what he said and kept it in mind when, on the Wednesday, I saw them do sheep.

I do not know when this species earned its reputation for acquiescence, and perhaps it was just the scent of a summer morning filtering through the putrescent smells of the slaughterhall – or perhaps it was the putrescence itself – but these sheep did not go like proverbial lambs to the slaughter. One animal was so reluctant to enter the pen, where the operator was waiting to greet them with electrified tongs in hand, that it had to be dragged in by the ears. Another managed to wriggle free from under the tongs and lived to be shocked a second time.

These animals were old enough to have acquired the shaggy coat that gives them that sheepish look. But they were not dying on their feet. They were young enough to want to scarper. There were about twenty in the batch that I saw done that day, and when they were all securely in the pen they began to crowd against the gate (now firmly closed), literally climbing on top of one another, facing the way they had come. This made it simpler for the operator, who peeled them off, one by one. Less prone than the pigs to dodging about, they were easier prey. Sheep are more vulnerable. Possibly this is why they have got a name for being more amenable to being killed; this, combined with the fact that, unlike the raucous pigs who make their outrage known, they do not scream. They do not, after all, have the voice. No matter how you bleat it, *meh* and *baa* will never be full of the sound of fury signifying something horrific. Quietly they succumbed to the last unnatural shock that flesh of their kind is heir to. The consummating knife followed soon after and, in the wake of the knife, the dismembering saws. They were sheep no longer.

These were my first glimpses of humanity in the slaughterhouse.

I agreed with Messrs Fisher and Llewellyn that I should set my sights on something bigger than their modest plant. They cautioned me, however, not to expect to walk carte blanche into another establishment. In other words, I had struck it lucky with my first slaughterhouse and now I was back at square one. Where should I go from here? I was stumped. I needed a fairy godmother, someone who, with a wave of her wand, could open abattoir doors throughout the land. And I found one. Her name was Mr Jolley.

MY FAIRY GODMOTHER

I discovered Mr Jolley by writing to the Association of British Abattoir Owners. Their reply referred me to the Deputy Chairman, who was also

General Manager of British Beef: Mr Jolley. He and I first got acquainted over the phone. We had a nice chat, in the course of which I asked him what he thought about 'ritual slaughter'. 'We don't believe the suffering of the animal is any greater', he said, adding that he did not want to see legislation against the Jewish and Muslim methods. 'I think I can speak for the trade', he said authoritatively. I told him about my limited exposure to conventional slaughtering and explained that I would like to observe it on a larger scale. 'Slaughterhouses are not meant to be children's tea parties', he observed solemnly. I intimated that I was willing to believe this on the strength of what I had seen, but I wondered nevertheless if he could arrange for me to visit another site. 'The whole thing is pretty gruesome', he continued gravely. 'It's not the sort of place you would take your maiden aunt to.' No doubt. Could he help? Mr Jolley thought he could. But subsequently, when I called to set things up, he invited me to his office instead. Nice as our chat had been, I could not see much scope for continuing the conversation. I could only think that in the interim Mr Jolley had come to think of me as something of a pig in a poke. With a slight shiver it dawned on me: the General Manager of British Beef wants to inspect me in the flesh. I am to be vetted by the Master Butcher.

I am not being fanciful when I refer to Mr Jolley as a master butcher. A certificate to this effect was framed on the wall of his office in West Smithfield, EC1. To be precise, on the sixth day of December in nineteen hundred and eighty four, the said Mr Jolley was 'Admitted to the freedom and livery of The Worshipful Company of the Art or Mistery of Butchers of the City of London'. I had a sense of the Mistery as I sat waiting for Mr Jolley to materialize. It was this delay that allowed me to survey the room and to breathe, as it were, the atmosphere of the man.

There was no photograph of him on the very solid desk, so I did not know what Mr Jolley looked like. But there was that about the vacant chair in front of it that conjured up the mental image of a formidable figure, a man who bulked large. The stamp of the man was on every object. A poster prominent on the wall, the *Farmers Weekly* Picture Guide to European Livestock, depicted 104 different breeds of cattle, sheep and pigs. You could almost smell them. What you smelt, in reality, were leather artefacts manufactured from the detritus of the slaughterhouse. There was nothing in that room that was not sturdy, either in mass or in design. There appeared to be an exception in the three cocktail mats on top of the desk. They looked like dainty flowers. But on closer inspection, hair was attached to the petals: the mats were made of hide and their texture was wholly animal. *La salle c'est l'homme même* (with apologies to Buffon). The room was the man himself. Nothing was out of place in it – except for me. By the time its rightful occupant crossed the threshold, that fact had sunk in.

I sprang to my feet – but even at full stretch I felt rather puny alongside my host. Mr Jolley was indeed a big man but not at all corpulent. His was the kind of size that implies physical strength in reserve. He was well dressed and clean-shaven. He spoke softly, as if someone or something needed placating. I had a mathematics teacher at school who used to talk like that. He did it to soothe his own temper.

Mr Jolley sat down behind his desk and I resumed my chair on the opposite side. The inspection began at once. I felt upon me the eyes of a man who, as he mentioned on the phone the first time we spoke, was forty-eight years in the meat business. I did not doubt that he had sized up a body or two in his time. What was he going to make of me? Not mincemeat; of that I was resolved. I do not recall exactly how our preliminary skirmish went. I know he tried one on: he said (shades of Mr Llewellyn) that people who work in abattoirs are all 'passionately fond of animals'. Did he imagine that he could pull the wool over my eyes? Or was he goading me? I tried stepping aside. But I felt myself being guided inexorably into a corner by an expert herdsman. I knew I was being put on the spot and sooner or later would have to turn and face. When the moment came, the question mark hanging over my head was as tangible as the electric tongs I had seen suspended over the pigs and the sheep. The question, which was never quite put into words, was this: Just what was I up to? Or to put it another way: Who exactly was I anyway and why should the Association go out of its way to help me? Up until now his tone was not hostile; but nor was it exactly friendly. Mr Jolley was ruminating on my place in his scheme of things.

I passed a piece of paper across the breadth of the desk. It was my sole credential: a letter of introduction from Robert Brown, President of the Food Animal Concerns Trust, Chicago. Mr Jolley picked up the letter deliberately and stared at it in silence, chewing it over and wondering what to make of this crud. It was obvious that the Trust, a small organization based several thousand miles away, meant nothing to him. And I could see that he was trying to look past the facade of the name to the underlying purposes of the Trust. I hoped that we need not go into that and tried to concentrate his mind instead on what the letter said explicitly. It testified to my being a member of the Advisory Board and it vouched for the fact that I was making bona fide enquiries on behalf of the Trust. On impulse, I drew his attention to the column on the left hand border of the letter, which listed the functionaries of the organization. I think I had a vague notion that if he saw my name in print, however small, it would elevate me in his eyes. It was a near-fatal faux pas. His eye was caught by the name of someone else, someone he knew and detested: a veterinary surgeon who was a vocal critic of British abattoirs.

The brows began to bulge: Mr Jolley was ruminating no longer. I was fair game now and he was going to get his quarry in his sights. He wanted to know everything about me. He noticed that there were letters after my name. Presumably I had gone to university? I had. Subject? Philosophy. I think he took this as a personal slight. If so, he was a glutton for punishment, as the next question proved. 'Are you a vegetarian?', he asked baldly. I stroked my beard and gingerly started to explain that the Food Animal Concerns Trust, which organization I represented, was concerned with various aspects of farming in the modern world, including the many difficult problems faced by small-scale producers, the quality of food from the consumer's point of view, and also certain aspects of animal husbandry with reference to the welfare of the animals as such. No pause. Was I a vegetarian? Yes, I was.

And how I regretted it. Never in my life have I felt so conspicuously uncarnivorous as at that moment, sitting in the office of the General Manager of British Beef, asking him the favour of fixing a visit to a slaughterhouse so that I could see how people like him kill animals for their flesh. Mr Jolley fell silent again. You could almost see the words *philosophy* and *vegetarian* fermenting inside him. The man was visibly suffering, like a cow that grazes on too much green forage and develops the bloat. I too kept quiet. I did not think it kind to utter another syllable. His head had rolled back on his shoulders as though he could not bear even to look at me, so repugnant was I to his way of thinking. Thus contorted, he spoke at last. It was not so much a sentence as a short series of snorts, like pockets of gas escaping under pressure. 'I'm ... trying ... to ... suppress ... my ... feelings ... of ... antipathy.' It was the moment of crisis in the interview and also the turning point, for I decided to take the bull by the horns. I was anathema to the man: I accepted this as the premise from which to restart the conversation. There was to be no more pussy-footing around. I would no longer conduct myself as though I were trying to sneak in through the cracks. I would state my business again and I would do so plainly and be barred or admitted on that basis alone. I spoke up. 'Perhaps it would help if I told you exactly why I have come and just what it is I am asking you to do', I said, or words to that effect. At the new sound in my voice Mr Jolley's head returned to its normal position. He looked directly at me and murmured something by way of concurrence. In fact there was nothing of any substance to add to what I had been telling him all along. I simply repeated myself, but in a manner more forthright. In the process, the nature of the encounter subtly changed. There were no more sinister secrets for him to ferret out. I was a known quantity. We were in open country and both of us, I believe, began to breathe more easily.

The rest of the interview was like a long process of exhalation. Mr Jolley, having exposed me for what I am, began to speak candidly about himself and his outlook on the universe. He was one of those people who, whether or not they have read a word of Darwin, take his metaphor to heart and really believe in those graphic phrases from Chapter 3 of *The Origin of Species*: the war of nature, the struggle for existence, the battle for survival. The very language was a kind of battle cry for Mr Jolley and, properly understood, an indictment of all things vegetarian. He did not so much *interpret* the text as sound like it. He had no need to fall back on books. He had been in the war, so he knew what nature was like. There are no rights in this life, he told me from first-hand experience; and therefore no *animal* rights. Only the fittest survive – and a vegetarian diet was not conducive to fitness. I might be in good shape at the moment but eventually my health was bound to deteriorate. This for one simple reason: I was not getting the *haemo* that the body needs to manufacture *haemo*globin. How long, by the way, had I been vegetarian? About eighteen years, actually. And I felt as red-blooded as the next Englishman.

Thus did we two sweetly strive together. And in the process, as is its wont, the awful truth came out: there was one in the family. It was his daughter who, like me, was in her thirties. She was about to embark on a university degree course. Subject? Philosophy, inevitably. Her conversion to vegetarianism was new. And she was taking it to such lengths that, as he ruefully observed, she 'won't have meat on the table'. No meat on the table – not even when her dad comes for dinner. *Quel scandale*: his own flesh and blood straying from the path prescribed by nature and falling into the mire of philosophy and vegetarianism. Such folly. Such evil to befall the House of Jolley! And here he was, entertaining in his private precincts a guest who must have seemed the very incarnation of the evil inflicting him and his family. Small wonder he had swelled with antipathy. Just being in his presence was tantamount to waving a red rag – or *the* red flag – directly under his nose. And on *his* turf too.

Such was the intimate nature of the crisis that had occurred in the interview. However, as I indicated earlier, by the time these facts had come to light the moment of crisis was passed. I was no longer the devil in Mr Jolley's personal hell; I had become more of a sparring partner. The fact that I reminded him so much of his daughter had assumed a new significance: I was practically part of the family now, a member of the fold. And in that spirit I put it to him that father and daughter might not be poles apart after all; that the apple might not have fallen far from the tree. In his disquisition on the nature of life, had he not displayed a taste for philosophy? May Socrates forgive me, but the remark seemed to go down well. The interview came to an end with Mr Jolley reaching for the phone and dialling a number. The manager of the slaughterhouse on the other end of the line, Mr Partridge, was someone he knew well – well enough to tell him to expect 'his friend' to pay a call and to show 'his friend' the works. His friend rose to leave and shook his hand – the beefy hand that waved the magic wand that causes doors to open. Benefactors and patrons come in all guises. But never was mortal creature blessed with so improbable a fairy godmother as I was with my Mr Jolley.

DRESSED TO KILL

The factory, which is how Mr Jolley referred to it, was situated on an industrial estate, somewhere in eastern England. Mr Jolley enjoined me not to identify the site, and so I may not be more precise. I still have the map he drew for me (in ink) with one landmark clearly indicated: a pub called The Angel. Once past The Angel I was to follow the road round, keeping left, until I reached a dead end. This was the factory.

There was ample parking space on the factory grounds. When I got out of the car I found myself facing a forbidding edifice with a flight of stone steps leading up to the main entrance. As I mounted them I felt as though I were going up in the world of butchery, graduating from a mere roadside shrine (my first slaughterhouse) to a full size temple of the Mistery. At last I was about to penetrate the veil.

I crossed the threshold and approached reception, which was attached to the main office. The place was a whirr of activity, in the midst of which Mr Partridge, the man in charge, was all of a flutter. The receptionist pointed him out to me. He was hovering over a desk behind her, snapping into the phone. 'We're trying to kill as many as we possibly can.' These were the first words I heard Mr Partridge utter and, as events were to prove, they might have served as the motto of the factory. He spoke them more in anger than in sorrow. I gathered he was speaking to head office – the factory was one of several owned by the same company – and it was apparent that someone there had ruffled his feathers by accusing the plant of under-production. Mr Partridge considered the charge most unfair. It was hard to find men to do the job: *that* was the problem and it was not his fault. In the circumstances, they were doing as well as could be expected. And so on.

Beyond a certain point, I did not find the conversation engrossing and my attention began to drift. My eye was caught by a colourful montage mounted on the drawer of a filing cabinet on the far side of the office. It comprised cut-out cartoon figures of farm animals. I noticed a mean-looking bull and a happy-looking moo-cow. Someone with a bent for humour had stuck them there, I reflected. There was also a pin-up: a photo of a scantily-clad muscle-bound Daley Thompson putting the shot. I was still waiting for Mr Partridge to come off the phone when several men in white coats trotted up the outside steps to the main entrance with bundles of papers in their hands. The bundles turned out to be copies of the daily tabloid *The Sun*, presumably for distribution to the workers; an attempt, perhaps, to bring some light into their darkness, or to treat their minds.

At last Mr Partridge prised himself free of the phone and came over and greeted me, briskly but civilly. There were no questions asked. I was under the aegis of Mr Jolley and this was good enough for Mr Partridge. What did I want to do? Look around? By all means. Alas, he was a busy man. He had no time to stand and stare himself. But he would see to it that I was taken care of. First, I had to be kitted out. His practised eye took in my (medium) build at a glance. What size wellies? He would send someone to fetch the gear. While we were waiting, I should come into his office. He darted inside, quick as a hawk, and I followed suit.

'It's a hellish business', confided Mr Partridge, picking up from the point where his conversation with head office left off. It is all a question of throughput, he explained. This means, quite literally, the rate at which animals are put through the mill. In a world where abattoirs are closing down all the time because they cannot break even, throughput is crucial. Throughput is the keynote: killing as many animals as you possibly can in order to stay in business. This was the thrust of his homily, and, for a while, I sat quietly and heeded. Eventually, however, I could not resist saying that it sounded to me like a cut-throat business: would he agree? I nearly shot my bolt with that particular quip. He cast me a quizzical look – as though I might need puzzling out – and I quietly chewed my tongue. Then he resumed his theme; and as I listened it struck me that this commercial battlefield was the world that Mr Jolley had called real. For Messrs Jolley and Partridge, reality is a scene of carnage in which slaughterhouses that cannot compete do not survive.

While we were talking, my uniform arrived and I began to change. There were three items of apparel: a white coat, freshly laundered and down to the knees, a pair of rubber boots and a hard hat. I was in the process of putting them on when several figures, all of them similarly attired, appeared in the doorway. They glided into the room like angels of mercy or like priests in attendance at a temple service. It was the management team. Mr Partridge begged my pardon: they would have to discuss the production schedule right away. Would I mind? I did not mind and he did not ask me to wait outside. Nor did he bother to introduce me to the others. He was a man who liked to get on with things; and he made no secret of his trade. He was the personification of a motto or adage that I found in *Meat Technology: A Practical Textbook for Student and Butcher*: 'Be open in everything – have no secrets of trade – Truth is not ashamed of the light' (quoted from *The Experienced Butcher*, 1816). The meeting began at once and without any formalities. There we all were, five or six of us, dressed to kill, helmets in hand and the Union Jack stitched onto our left breast pockets, manfully planning the slaughter of hundreds, if not thousands, of beasts. Having changed, I was, to all intents and purposes, one of them. As a novice, I stayed as silent as my coat was spotless, but still was wholly present in the inner sanctum of the factory, in worshipful company, privy to the mystery.

Mr Partridge was not a man to beat about the bush. He got right down to business; and in so doing gave a practical demonstration of the truths he had been impressing upon me. He wanted to know what quantity of lambs and pigs we were going to 'put in' that day. 'Put in' was not a euphemism: it was not an indirect reference to slaughter nor was it meant to sound sweeter or vaguer. It was simply manager's talk, direct and to the point: it was the action of the factory under the aspect of productivity. The men put in animals the way they put in hours; both time and beast were grist for the mill. 'Put in' was not the only expression that Mr Partridge used in place of 'kill'. Another was 'die'. 'How many cattle will die today?' he asked, as though death were spontaneous on the part of the cattle. But Mr Partridge was not choosing his words so as to evade the painful truth; he was not that sort of man. His mind was trained on the facts. He knew perfectly well that under his supervision hundreds of farm animals are deliberately done to death every day. He knew it for a fact. The cold fact that he knew it to be was part of the real world – the business world – in which he and his management team function. That world is governed by a formula along these lines: income depends on output and output on input. Anything, to count as a fact in the real world of profit and loss, must figure in this scheme of things; otherwise it remains an intangible, outside the cognizance of the management team. It was precisely the office of this team to translate intangibles, like animals, into palpable facts. This, the transubstantiation of flesh into fact, was the purpose of the meeting; it was the meaning of the mystery. Every morning, at the onset of the working day, in sessions identical to this, the same essential work was performed. It was not an idle ceremony. The office was a factory within a factory, producing the facts. And that was all that Mr Partridge was trying to do with his question. 'Put in', 'kill', 'die': they were just so many verbs to fill the same gap in a sentence. It made no odds to him which to use. 'Die' and 'kill' lacked the coloration that vivified them at other times and on others' lips. The cold facts were black and white. And Mr Partridge wanted to get at them.

'How many lambs next week?' Mr Partridge asked us, proving that verbs could be dispensed with altogether. 'About eleven hundred or so', was the reply. He was appalled. 'One thousand bloody lambs', he said with feeling. 'Bloody' was an expletive, not an adjective. His point was that 1,000 lambs were nowhere near enough. Having overheard his anguished conversation with head office a few minutes earlier, I understood what he must be going through. Eleven hundred lambs per week, as it turns out, was 400 under par for this abattoir. That translates into a sizeable chunk out of the overall throughput – unless the numbers could be made up with cattle or pigs. Pigs, cattle, sheep: they were just so many kinds of input to fill the same gap in the schedule. It made no odds which species to kill. It came down to the same thing in the end: throughput; and the factory needed as much of it as it could get.

Once the order of the day was decided upon, the management team dispersed to the four corners of the factory to spread the word and set the wheels in motion; all except Chris, the young production manager, into whose hands Mr Partridge entrusted me. As we strolled across the yard (to the extent that you can stroll in heavy rubber boots), Chris explained the set-up to me. Sheep and cattle shared the same slaughterhall while pigs were killed in an area of their own. Cattle were first on the agenda. I asked if I could see where they were kept in the period leading up to their slaughter, so he led us into the building the back way. There they all were, bunched inside their pens, standing around on the concrete floor. They were steers, between twelve and eighteen months old. I do not know anything else about them. I have no idea where they came from. Likely as not they hailed from different parts, converging on the same destination. Some might have come direct from the field. Others would have passed though market. Probably most of them were conveyed here in large cattle transporters, possibly double-deckered like municipal buses, into which and out of which they would have had to be goaded; for farm animals are averse to being uprooted and they are inexperienced passengers. But all of this is on reflection and by way of general knowledge. It formed no part of the impression the animals themselves made on me at the time. The fact is that in and of themselves they did not make much of an impression. I noticed not so much as the colour of their skin. No distinctive markings left their imprint on my memory lending poignancy to their fatal predicament. No one animal stood out from the crowd so as to individualize the fate of them all. They were stock and that was that. They were there and that was all. I saw them neither travel nor arrive. For all I knew, here was where they had come into the world and this was their place in the sun.

We had got there just in time. Already the men were preparing to get the cattle rolling. Chris ushered me down the length of the lairage, down the route the steers themselves were about to take, towards the blind end of the building. This was the site of the metal stunning box, which was the connecting link between lairage and slaughterhall. The animals would enter the stunning box one by one, as though it were a kind of Noah's Ark, via an alley called a 'race'. Chris hurried me along as he was anxious to go back the way we came: he was needed on the other side of the wall, in the slaughterhall. He left to play his part and I, in order to play mine, took up position on the ledge overlooking the narrow entrance to the steel box, like a lookout at death's door.

From this vantage point I was able to view the entire proceedings from beginning to end. I counted heads – there were forty-four that went past me – but lost track of the time. It seemed like an eternity as one animal after another, having travelled the length of the race, crossed the threshold of the stunning box and entered oblivion. But, of course, their progress was being clocked by the factory: they were put through at the rate of thirty to thirty-five beasts per hour. I make that 1.9 minutes in the box for each steer, although some were quicker than this and others took their time about it. The men did their level best to speed up the process, as though it were a race against time, urging every animal to go through its paces without procrastinating. The gates of each pen were opened in turn, and as the steers came spilling out they were shooed, shoved and shocked – by means of electric goads – down the central passageway that funnelled them into the final turn before the finish. They jostled one another, as if vying for position. At either end of the race the animals faced a solid steel door. The doors were of a guillotine design so that, like a portcullis on a medieval castle, they opened and closed vertically. Because of the pressure of bodies from behind, every time the doors were raised the steers would surge forward into the narrow gap, sometimes squeezing one another up against the sides of the passage, thus causing an obstruction. Countermanding their own orders, the men would try to reverse the flow and force them back. But the cattle could not, or would not, always comply. It often happened that some unlucky steer bore the brunt of this congestion, the guillotine gate slamming down on its back. A number of spirited animals, attempting the impossible, tried to turn round and go back the way they came. But the race was less than a metre wide, with high solid walls on either side. No amount of squirming helped: their bodies were too beefed up for such a manoeuvre. It was a one-way race; and inevitably, whether they snorted resistance or not, every nose ended up pointing forwards and every steer got to the finishing line under its own steam.

The box was a kind of walk-in open-top coffin. It was oblong, built to be big enough to accommodate a full-size bovine animal still standing. The fit was not perfectly snug: the box's dimensions permitted a small amount of movement, although turning around was still out of the question. The solid walls of the box rose sheer from the floor to a height that none of the occupants could ever reach or look over. This was not a good prospect for a steer. But, being without a top or lid, the interior afforded a clear view of the factory ceiling directly above, framing the face of the operator bearing down (should any animal incline to look). Ingress, as I have said, was by way of a guillotine door at one end. At first sight, there did not appear to be an alternative exit. But one of the side walls turned out to be a panel that opened at the crucial moment, dumping the contents of the box behind the scenes, like a prop in a vanishing act. If you were a steer awaiting your turn at the end of the race, this is what you would see: The animal in front of you enters a cubicle. As the door drops down behind it, it is sealed inside. There is a short interval, during which you hear a good deal of banging. Then the door to the box opens and lo: it is empty! You are struck dumb. It seems like a magic trick. Somehow, after you enter this mysterious chamber, you are spirited away from the face of the earth.

For the animal, the trick is to get shot in the head. Getting shot is not quite as easy as it sounds and some of the steers had difficulty doing it. At the last, after all the collective certainty of the pen and the passageway, each animal is left in the dark and on its own. While several of them seemed to take this in their stride, many balked, bucking wildly in their confinement as if human beings were on their backs.

Some literally climbed the walls, making the open spaces of the factory ring with the sound of hoof pounding on metal. One brute, the most animated of them all, roared and bellowed like a bull in clover, full of itself. It would not die down and enter into the spirit of the occasion. Perhaps its memory was green. This was not a bear being baited: those barbaric days are long gone. But as I stared down at the heaving form, it was as though I were peering into a pit.

The concrete floor of the pit was slanted, with an edge or curb running its length. This had its advantages. Once the subject was shot and the side wall had opened, the senseless body would roll out into the slaughterhall for the coup de grâce. On the other hand, the tilted, uneven surface made it difficult for the still-conscious steer to keep its footing. It is an occupational hazard of being shot in the box; and one clumsy animal made a complete hash of it. Hooves slid, limbs flailed and the massive body tumbled to the ground. There was a small gap between the floor of the box and the bottom of one of the sides – the panel capable of being opened and closed – through which the creature's legs contrived to stick out. It lay there panting, looking absurd, its position hopeless. It was completely stuck, incapable of freeing itself and beyond the reach of helping hands reaching down from above. Several men dropped what they were doing and hastened to its aid. They raised the panel and assisted the confused beast to its feet. Once righted, it steadied itself. Then it was shot and fell to the floor.

It collapsed like a punctured balloon, as if its breath had been taken away: it was, in a word, stunned. It was no longer of this world but not quite gone to meet its maker – although if souls leave bodies I suspect that the spirit of that steer started at the sound of the pistol. The pistol in question is no ordinary firearm but one designed expressly for its stunning effect on large domestic animals. It produces this effect by firing a steel bolt at their stationary heads at high velocity and zero range. It is a bolt from the blue that deals a crushing blow, penetrating the skull and entering the brain to a depth of three or four inches. Having made its mark, the projectile automatically retracts into the cylinder of the gun, to which it remains attached throughout. For this reason, the instrument is called a 'captive bolt pistol'. Being captive, the bolt can be used to bore a hole into head after head, like a worm that works its way through a barrel of apples. This instrument is also known as a 'humane stunner'.

The man who wielded the humane stunner stood adjacent to the box on a platform or pedestal that raised him above the animals. He looked the very picture of humanity as he lorded it over them, systematically putting them down. He could not quite do it at will: he would have to wait each time until the steer obliged by standing motionless, its head held high – though never so high that the man did not have to stoop low to shoot. When the moment was right, he would bend over, finger on the trigger, place the warm mouth of the pistol against the middle of the animal's forehead, and press. It was the kiss of death if the aim was true. If not technically dead, the animal was instantly transformed into a living vegetable, one step up from meat.

Sometimes something went wrong. From where I was standing, it appeared, on each such occasion, that the gun failed to fire. Whenever this happened, the operator had to wait his moment again; for the steer was no statue and its head was still working, turning this way and that. There was one case that I remember vividly. Neither the first squeeze of the trigger nor the second produced anything more than a harmless click. It was like watching a version of Russian roulette in which the player is oblivious of the game. For it was evident that the steer did not have the foggiest idea that each time the pistol was put to its head it brushed with death. It flicked away the muzzle of the gun as if it were a fly that twice alighted on its forehead. The steer was still busy with its life, acquainting itself with its new quarters, which it eyed inquisitively, as though the box were a new stall and it was about to take up residence. This continued, as I say, through two failed attempts at shooting it. The third, luckily, shattered the illusion.[1]

NOTE

1. This is an edited version of an unpublished typewritten manuscript written in the mid-1980s, shortly after I completed the fieldwork for my project. The abrupt ending is due to the fact that the manuscript was unfinished. I am content to leave it as is. I visited several other slaughterhouses and saw a variety of methods, both 'humane' and 'ritual', used with different species. None was more disturbing than the system used at a 'poultry plant', where the chickens were 'humanely slaughtered' on a conveyor belt from which each bird was suspended upside down by one leg. With every method there are degrees of expertise and forms of mitigation, But none of the practices I witnessed impressed me as anything other than a pitiful way to treat fellow creatures. I reached two main conclusions. Singling out Muslim and Jewish methods for banning is invidious. Dignifying conventional methods with the word 'humane' adds insult to the ultimate injury.

CHAPTER EIGHTEEN

Salomon's House on the Island of Bensalem

PROLOGUE: OF CHIMPS AND MEN

In the film *Escape from the Planet of the Apes*, three intelligent chimpanzees are stranded on planet earth somewhere in California in 1973. They are taken to the infirmary at the zoo in Los Angeles where they are placed in the charge of Dr Lewis Dickson, an animal psychologist. Dr Dickson is astonished to discover that the chimps can speak English. One of them introduces herself as Zira – Dr Zira, a research scientist. She explains that in her era and her country human beings are used as experimental subjects; she herself has made anatomical investigations with human subjects, both living and dead. Subsequently, the chairman of a Presidential Commission of Enquiry makes a public statement about the alien apes. He observes that (Dr) Zira's experiments with human beings would be called atrocities in twentieth-century America, even though, as he puts it, 'what apes would do to humans is the same as what humans do to beasts'.[1]

A TRUMPETER OF THE NEW SCIENCE

Humans do many different kinds of things to many varieties of beasts in the pursuit and application of science. Animals are used by the millions for diverse reasons, including basic research, applied research, product development and testing, education and training. Various types of institutions use animals for scientific purposes, including commercial labs, government labs, and labs in hospitals, universities and schools. Animals are used as research models and experimental subjects; as experimental controls; as examples and specimens; and as sources of new materials and resources – including breeding more of themselves. Much of this use involves techniques that are lethal or harmful or painful or otherwise distressful to the animals in question.

Although subject to regulation, the practice of using animals in the lab is something we tend to take for granted. This is not so much an evasion, nor a deliberate omission; it is more a kind of oversight. Our eyes are not accustomed to seeing anything questionable – despite the fact that our lives are full of the evidence of lab animal use. More than this: we are positively predisposed to overlook the evidence. In part, this has to do with certain longstanding attitudes towards animals that are ingrained in our culture. It also has to do with a modern mentality concerning science and technology.

To be sure, these two factors are not independent of each other; and they combine crucially in the seminal writings of Sir Francis Bacon, a seventeenth-century 'trumpeter of the new science'. Bacon's writings are peculiarly redolent of modern science and cast light on the routine use of animals in the lab. This practice is staunchly defended today; and not always with carefully reasoned argument. It can be hazardous to tender criticism, however tentative and mild, of lab animal use. Frequently you encounter entrenched resistance, exaggerated claims and righteous hostility from the practitioners of (and the apologists for) lab animal science. Up to a point, this might have something to do with promoting vested interest. However, I believe it goes deeper than that. The underlying idea – that in science we may use animals without any external constraints – is written into the constitution of modern science. And Bacon is, so to speak, one of the authors of this constitution.

Of all Bacon's works, there is one in particular that vividly articulates his vision of the 'new science'. I refer to the strangely prophetic *New Atlantis*, published in 1627. The work, for whatever reason, is conspicuously unfinished. However, there is a sense in which each of Bacon's many works is completed by all the others. The entire corpus of his writings is animated with the same spirit and promotes the same purpose: the advancement of the new science. Consequently, while focusing on *New Atlantis*, I will be casting sidelong glances to other works in which Bacon elaborates his mission and his message.

The words mission and message are not out of place. Bacon was no mere theorist. In the first place, we can call him a visionary. He envisaged a world in which applied science would enable humanity to gain mastery over nature. (We will shortly see what that means.) In the second place, Bacon was no recluse. During his lifetime he played a prominent part in the affairs of England, rising to the rank of Lord Chancellor, the highest legal office under the crown. He actively promoted his ideas, seeking royal approval and patronage for his scientific program. Bacon died in 1626. But eventually, inspired by his writings, British scientists combined forces to form the Royal Society of

London for the Promotion of Natural Knowledge (1662). William Leiss observes that Bacon 'was universally praised as the herald of a new order and was christened "the secretary of nature" '.[2]

Bacon's name is closely associated with the doctrine that knowledge, to be scientific, must be acquired by a process of inductive reasoning. But the 'new order' that he advocated amounts to much more than a new logic. Bacon's vision embraced what we might call the *culture* of science. This includes its myths (what science likes to think about itself and its origins), its methods (how science proceeds), its purposes (what science is for), its character (what the institutions of science are like) and its status (the place that science occupies in the life and affairs of society). I will try to trace the shape of this vision, since the total culture of science provides the setting within which we do what we do to animals in the lab.

AN OUTLINE OF *NEW ATLANTIS*

In *New Atlantis*, Bacon outlines an idealized scientific society. The book takes the form of a narrative in which the narrator is one of the characters in the story. Briefly, this is the plot: a group of Europeans set sail from Peru westwards towards China and Japan. Due to the caprice of the winds they find themselves 'in the midst of the greatest wilderness of waters in the world' (III, 129), without food and in despair.[3] They pray to God for deliverance; and the following day they espy an island in the distance. They discover that the island is inhabited. At first, the natives do not wish them to disembark; but they relent when the voyagers explain their distress. Eventually, the ship's crew and passengers are transferred to the House of Strangers, where they are well provided for. Their hosts supply them with pills for their sick 'who thought themselves cast into some divine pool of healing, they mended so kindly and so fast' (III, 135). The Governor of the House of Strangers pays them a visit. He explains that they have alighted on the island of Bensalem, whose existence is unknown to the rest of the world owing to its 'solitary situation' and its 'laws of secrecy' (III, 136). He recounts the history of the island and the manner in which the people were converted to Christianity. He singles out by name 'a King, whose memory of all others we most adore; not superstitiously, but as a divine instrument, tho' a mortal man; his name was Solamona: and we esteem him as the lawgiver of our nation' (III, 144). Solamona is remembered above all for having founded 'an Order, or Society, which we call *Salomon's House*' (III,

145): a research institute dedicated to 'the finding out of the true nature of all things' (III, 146).

The ship's company ventures into the city and environs. They admire the humanity and largesse of the people. Two of them attend a state function called the Feast of the Family, held in honour of a local patriarch (a man who has thirty living descendants above the age of 3). The narrator converses with a local enlightened Jewish merchant named Joabin. The highlight of their sojourn is a public parade in which the citizens pay their respect to 'one of the Fathers of Salomon's House' (III, 154). Subsequently, this dignitary formally receives the European strangers and, after giving the narrator his blessing, bestows upon him 'the greatest jewel I have. For I will impart unto thee, for the love of God and man, a relation of the true state of Salomon's House' (III, 156). There ensues a long monologue in which the Father describes the purpose of the institution; the laboratories and the equipment; the different kinds of work done by the various members or fellows of the House; and finally 'the ordinances and rites which we observe' (III, 156). The narrative ends abruptly at the conclusion of this speech – but not before the Father blesses the narrator again and gives him leave to publish his story 'for the good of other nations' (III, 166).

THE ISLAND OF BENSALEM

The Island of Bensalem, or New Atlantis, is a Utopia in both senses of the word: it is nowhere to be found and it is the best of places. Even the short outline I have given suffices to bring out three of the most salient features of this ideal state. First, it is Christian. Second, its chief institution is a scientific research establishment. Third, the people are both happy and good. Furthermore, I take it that these three features are interrelated, not to say interdependent.

Bacon is at pains to emphasize the well-being and the worthiness of the people of Bensalem. The island is 'happy and holy ground' (III, 136); the people are pious, generous, chaste, humane and peaceful. (The very name of the island, Bensalem, is adapted from the Hebrew and means 'son of peace'.) Although a Christian country, uniformity of religion is not required: there is a small Jewish population, which is free to practise the precepts of Judaism. However, so marvellous a place is Bensalem that even the Jews are of a superior sort: 'they are of a far differing disposition from the Jews in other parts'. For whereas Jews elsewhere 'hate the name of Christ, and have a secret inbred rancour against the population amongst whom they live: these (contrariwise) give unto our Saviour many high attributes, and love the nation of Bensalem extremely' (III, 151). In short, it is a land of plenty, of harmony, of virtue and goodwill; a country that brings out the best in its people and enjoys their loyalty. All things considered, it is no wonder that the European wayfarers considered 'that there was no worldly thing on earth more worthy to be known that the state of that happy land' (III, 136).

It is made abundantly clear that the state of that happy land is secured by its institutions. In this connection it is important to notice that the representatives of science and Christianity in *New Atlantis* give reciprocal endorsements. So, on the one hand, Salomon's House, the seat of Science, is said to be the 'noblest foundation (as we think) that ever there was upon the earth; and the lanthorn [lantern] of this kingdom' (III, 145). These words are spoken by the Governor of the House of Strangers – who is a Christian priest. On the other hand, the conversion of the islanders to Christianity was mediated by a member of Salomon's House. This is how it happened. One night at sea a pillar of light was seen, bearing upon it a large cross also formed of light. The islanders, awed by this spectacle, launched several boats to meet it and intercept it. Miraculously, none of the boats was able to approach beyond a certain point; save one. On board this singular vessel was 'one of the wise men of the society of Salomon's House' (III, 137). His boat, and his alone, was able to draw near to the divine apparition – which promptly dispersed, disclosing a small ark containing the Holy Bible. Thus it was that a scientist brought the word of Jesus Christ to the people of Bensalem.

Moreover, religion and science seem to meet in the person of the Father of Salomon's House. As we have seen, he twice blesses the narrator – although we have no reason to suppose that he is a priest. He is called 'Father' and he addresses the narrator as 'my son'. When he appears in public he holds up his hand 'as blessing the people, but in silence' (III, 155). He enters the city with all the appurtenances of a prelate. He sits alone, dressed in fineries, borne on a magnificent chariot and escorted by footmen. Behind his chariot, city officials and dignitaries march in procession. The people stand and watch with perfect decorum. It is the first time in twelve years that a Father of Salomon's House has made a visitation to their city.

Overall, we gain the impression of majesty that borders on holiness. However, we must not forget that this is a Christian state. In the kingdom of Bensalem, science is not the state religion. Science does not supplant Christianity; nor is it a purely secular affair. As I hope to elucidate,

Bacon's perspective on science is that ultimately it subserves and furthers the Christian religion.

Due allowance must be made for the fact that there were external constraints on seventeenth-century authors. It would have been difficult for Bacon to have published a book that did not make the proper Christian noises. Having said that, Bacon does not seem to me to be a closet atheist. The theme of Christianity resounds through his writings; it is no mere coda. Be that as it may, the fact of the matter is that Bacon marshals the resources of Christian doctrine and powerfully redirects them towards the promotion of the new science.

For one thing, though this is a minor point, Bacon suggests that the advancement of science fulfils a biblical prophecy (Daniel 12: 4).[4] It also fulfils a holy purpose by playing the part of 'the accepted and loyal handmaid of religion, for religion reveals the will of God, Natural Philosophy His power'.[5] (For *Natural Philosophy* read *natural science*.) If the Bible is 'the book of God's word' then a complete natural history would be 'the book of God's works' (III, 268). Consequently, it should be compiled 'with a most religious awe' since it is 'a kind of second Scripture' (IV, 261).

But Bacon is no monk. He is a man of action and he conceives of science accordingly. The primary way in which science serves a religious purpose is not as a form of contemplation but as a means of increasing the scope of human action and thus the extent of human power. This is a *religious* purpose because, as he puts it in one place, 'both heaven and earth do conspire and contribute to the use and benefit of man' (III, 294). However, this benefit does not accrue to us without our active intervention. It is up to us human beings to claim what Heaven intends as our due. Towards the end of the first book of the *New Organon*, Bacon declares magisterially, 'Only let the human race recover that right over nature which belongs to it by divine bequest, and let power be given it; the exercise thereof will be governed by sound reason and true religion' (IV, 115). That last qualifying clause is added to appease those who might object to the advancement of science on the grounds that it could be debased 'to purposes of wickedness, luxury and the like'. If I understand him correctly, Bacon is conscious of the duties we owe to ourselves and each other. In particular, he hints here at the Christian (and Jewish) obligation to love one's neighbour (Lev. 19:18), since applied science would be a means of promoting the welfare of our fellow human beings. However, this caveat in no way limits our rights relative to nature – and therewith relative to animals.

THE CHRISTIAN BACKGROUND

At this juncture, we need to take some stock of the scriptural passages and the Christian tradition upon which Bacon is drawing and to which he is appealing. This should shed some light on the status of animals in Bacon's scheme of things.

Above all, Bacon surely has in mind those verses in Genesis that seem to proclaim human supremacy in some sense or other over the rest of creation. Genesis 1:28 lays down that God, having created Adam and Eve in the divine image, blessed them, saying, 'Be fruitful and multiply, and replenish the earth, and subdue it: and have dominion over the fish of the sea, and over the fowl of the air, and over every living thing that moveth upon the earth' (King James version). God makes a similar-sounding proclamation to Noah, after the Flood, in Genesis 9:1–2.

These verses, especially when taken together with certain other biblical passages, are susceptible of diverse interpretations. However, there is a clearly discernible mainstream in the Christian tradition that renders these verses to mean that animals do not matter in their own right: that they exist, not for their own sakes, but for ours. John Passmore suggests that Christian doctrine took this direction early on under the impact of Greek influences.[6] Augustine in effect canonized Aristotelian teaching when he said that 'man ... is a rational being and therefore more excellent and outstanding than any other creature on earth'.[7] Aristotle had outlined a natural hierarchy in which animals, being non-rational, exist for the sake of human – rational – beings.[8] The same idea can be discerned in Augustine's view that it is our rationality which gives us a prerogative over animals and plants (none of which is rational). He says, 'by a most just ordinance of the Creator, both their life and their death are subject to our use'.[9] Thomas Aquinas cites these words of Augustine when he reformulates the traditional teaching as follows: 'According to the Divine ordinance the life of animals and plants is preserved not for themselves but for man.'[10] Once again, this seems to owe as much to Aristotle as it does to Genesis inasmuch as Aquinas presupposes the idea that human beings, and not animals, have intellect or reason. 'Accordingly', says Aquinas, 'intellectual creatures are ruled by God as though He cared for them for their own sake, while other creatures are ruled as being directed to rational creatures.'[11]

Bacon, of course, was no more an Aristotelian than he was a Catholic. But, first, the notion that human beings, and only human beings, are rational animals had long become entrenched in the minds of Europeans. Second, the status of animals was not exactly the rock upon which the

Church split. Bacon probably imbibed his ideas of the bible partly from his mother, who was a devout Calvinist. If so, he might have been familiar with Calvin's commentaries on Genesis, Chapter 1. Calvin refers to 'man' as 'lord of the world'. He explains that dominion over animals 'was not given to Adam only, but to all his posterity as well as to him'. He continues thus: 'And hence we infer what was the end for which all things were created, namely, that none of the conveniences and necessaries of life might be wanting to men.'[12] (Apart from recalling Aquinas, this is strikingly similar to something Bacon says in the course of his commentary on the Greek myth of Prometheus. Bacon sees the myth as a parable whose main point is this: 'that Man, if we look to final causes, may be regarded as the centre of the world'. Accordingly, 'Plants and animals of all kinds are made to furnish him either with dwelling and shelter or clothing or food or medicine, or to lighten his labour, or to give him pleasure and comfort; insomuch that all things seem to be going about man's business and not their own' [VI, 747].)

Luther, as it happens, does not reiterate the commonplace view that Adam had dominion over animals so as to satisfy his wants. He insists that Adam 'would not have used the creatures as we do today'. Adam and his descendants, says Luther, would have exercised their power over animals principally 'for the admiration of God and a holy joy which is unknown to us in this corrupt state of nature'.[13] But there's the rub: we live in the aftermath of the Fall. Noah and his descendants no longer conduct the choir of creation; they exploit its resources. Since the Flood, says Luther, 'the animals are subjected to man as to a tyrant who has absolute power over life and death'. Luther does not mean by this that we have usurped the rights of animals. He calls our tyranny an 'extraordinary gift' from God to us, an explicit concession that shows that God 'is favourably inclined and friendly toward man'.[14]

This 'extraordinary gift' is part of the divine bequest of nature that Bacon exhorts us to grasp. To grasp it, he says, we need equipment. To make equipment we need knowledge. Knowledge is the business of science. Science is the way in which we human beings employ our God-given intellect so as to pursue our sacred claim against non-rational nature: minerals, vegetables, animals. Such is the solemn purpose of Salomon's House on the ideal island of Bensalem.

KNOWLEDGE AND POWER

The very name of Salomon's House is saturated with all the connotations Bacon wants for science. We are told by the Governor of the

House of Strangers that the scientific order is named after the 'king of the Hebrews', the man who is celebrated in scripture as the wisest person on earth. Among other things, the biblical Solomon knew all there was to know about nature and creatures (1 Kings, 4:33); his understanding of animals, in particular, is legendary. Solomon's father, David, praised God for having granted humanity dominion over all of nature – all things and all animals (Psalm 8). The reign of Solomon over Israel is one of peace and abundance, distinguished by extensive public works. Nor does it escape us that Solomon built a house: a temple dedicated to the service of God.

On the island of Bensalem, Salomon's House honours God by researching into his works. Indeed, the order is also known as the College of the Six Days Works (III, 146). However, as we have seen, God intends his creation to be mastered, not merely known, by the human race. Hence the fundamental purpose of Salomon's House, as stated by the Father: 'The End of our Foundation is the knowledge of Causes, and secret motions of things; and the enlarging of the bounds of Human Empire, to the effecting of all things possible' (III, 156). Thus the 'great instauration' or reconstruction of science that Bacon proclaimed is simultaneously the 'great instauration of the dominion of man over the universe'.[15] The new science makes possible a restoration of the rights of humanity over nature that fell into temporary abeyance with the Fall (IV, 247–8).

In short, without knowledge there is no power. This is the crux of one of Bacon's most famous aphorisms: 'Human knowledge and human power meet in one' (IV, 47). Moreover, by and large, human power does not consist in the exercise of a subtle influence over things. We do not charm nature with our pipes. Human power involves the *subjugation* of nature – forcing nature into submission. Nature must be forced, so to speak, against her will. Bacon speaks of nature as a 'rebel'. This 'rebelliousness' is a consequence of the Fall. Nonetheless, nature is not 'altogether and for ever a rebel'; she can in some measure be 'subdued to the supplying of man with bread; that is, to the uses of human life' (IV, 248).[16] To accomplish this we have to overcome the anarchy inherent in matter. For nature is deeply recalcitrant; not merely passive, but perverse. This is how Bacon interprets the Greek myth of the wrestling contest between Pan and Cupid. Pan, according to Bacon, symbolizes nature; Cupid represents order or concord. Bacon explains: 'Matter is not devoid of an appetite and inclination to dissolve the world and fall back into the old Chaos, but that its force and malice is restrained and kept in order by the prevailing concord of things.' Thanks to 'the infinite goodness of God', Pan or nature 'has the worst of that contest and goes away defeated' (IV, 325–6).

That's dandy for Cupid. But in the meantime the human race has its own distinctive quarrel to settle with nature: the quarrel over dominion and rights. Bacon speaks as if humanity has a legal case against nature; and he proposes that we put her to the question. 'In other words, I mean (according to the practice in civil causes) in this great Plea or Suit granted by the divine favour and providence (whereby the human race seeks to recover its rights over nature), to examine nature herself and the arts upon interrogatories' (IV, 263). This examination of nature does not take the form of a polite enquiry. Bacon calls for an 'inquisition of nature' (e.g. IV, 7) that will disclose to use 'the secrets still locked in Nature's bosom'.[17] After all, nature, our wayward adversary, can hardly be expected to tell us her secrets willingly. There are of course some things that we can find out by simple observation. But 'nature betrays her secrets more fully when in the grip and under the pressure of art than when in enjoyment of her natural liberty'.[18] (For *art* read *design*: mechanical artifices and contrivances.) Accordingly, scientific knowledge of natural things – of minerals and vegetables and animals – is best elicited with 'nature under constraint and vexed; that is to say, when by art and the hand of man she is forced out of her natural state, and squeezed and molded' (III, 29). Bacon's meaning is that scientists should avail themselves of the new technology in order to pursue their research. These recent 'mechanical interventions', says Bacon, 'do not, like the old, merely exert a gentle guidance over nature's course; they have the power to conquer and subdue her, to shake her to her foundations. For the rule is that what discoveries lie on the surface exert but little force. The roots of things, where strength resides, are buried deep.'[19] Bacon compares the 'vexations' of scientific instruments with 'the bonds and handcuffs of Proteus, which betray the ultimate struggles and efforts of matter' (IV, 257). Nature, to be known, must be manipulated. Thus Bacon's aphorism concerning knowledge and power works in both directions: not only is there no power without knowledge but equally there is little or no knowledge without power.

Bacon sometimes employs a more deferential idiom. At one point he says merely that we should 'consult' nature (IV, 252). He speaks of humanity as 'the servant and interpreter of Nature' (IV, 47) and he advises sagely that 'Nature to be commanded must be obeyed' (IV, 47; also IV, 114). However, in view of the repeated severity and violence of his language it is difficult to view these locutions as being much more than charming, wry and ironic. Certainly, all talk of *obeying* nature rings rather hollow when we recall that Bacon's 'main object is to make nature serve the business and conveniences of man' (IV, 170). The wise old man in 'The Masculine Birth of Time' puts it in these terms: 'I come in very truth leading you to nature with all her children to bind her to your service and make her your slave.'[20] Bacon's intention is well captured by Kant in the Preface to the second edition of the *Critique of Pure Reason* (1787) – which work is preceded with a motto taken from Bacon. Reason, says Kant, 'must approach nature in order to be taught by it. It must not, however, do so in the character of a pupil who listens to everything that the teacher chooses to say, but of an appointed judge who compels the witnesses to answer questions which he has himself formulated.'[21]

This interrogation of nature must be remorseless and relentless. Bacon warns against anyone who imagines 'that the inquisition of nature is in any part interdicted or forbidden' (IV, 20). Anything goes. There are no holds barred when it comes to science. Solomon himself, the wise king of Israel and God's own anointed, is brought by Bacon to the witness stand to testify to the fact that no 'parcel of the world is denied to man's inquiry and invention ... when he saith, "The spirit of man is as the lamp of God, wherewith he searcheth the inwardness of all secrets." ' (III, 265)

REASON AND NATURE

If this is what it means for 'the spirit of man' to be like 'the lamp of God', then Bacon is saying that there is something God-like about the scientific inquisition of nature. No wonder the Father of Salomon's House is so revered: not only is his research approved by God, and even enjoined by God, but it is work that resembles the activity of God.

In *The Refutation of Philosophies* the invited speaker begins his address with these sentences: 'We are agreed, my sons, that you are men. That means, as I think, that you are not animals on their hind legs, but mortal gods.'[22] The terms of this contrast are significant: not merely that human beings are 'mortal gods' but also that we are precisely not 'animals on their hind legs'. However, there is something undeniably animal about us or within us. Bacon's account of this is reminiscent of Aristotle's doctrine of the hierarchy of things in nature. Bacon says, 'man has somewhat of the brute, the brute somewhat of the plant, the plant somewhat of the body inanimate; so that all things are indeed biform, being compounded of a superior and inferior species' (IV, 322–3). That last phrase makes it clear that what is animal in us is inferior to what is distinctively human.

Of equal vintage is the idea that the 'brute' part of us is associated with unruly appetites and lusts. Plato, in Book IX of the *Republic*, paints a grisly picture of 'the wild Beast in us' that inhabits our dreams at night and, casting off all shame and prudence, seeks to gratify its instincts (571b–572b; see also *Timaeus*, 70e). Bacon uses a strikingly similar image when he talks about passion or desire and the way it 'breaks forth into acts' (IV, 333). He writes:

> For it is never content with what it has got, but with infinite and insatiable appetite tries for something more, and ever craves for new triumphs. Tigers likewise are kept in the stables of the passions, and at times yoked to their chariot; for when passion ceases to go on foot and comes to ride in its chariot, as in celebration of its victory and triumph over reason, then is it cruel, savage, and pitiless towards all that withstand or oppose it. (IV, 334)

Notice the phrase 'victory and triumph over reason'. Elsewhere he refers to 'the continual mutinies and seditions of the affections' (III, 410) – treasons that are perpetrated against reason.

If this reminds us of how he characterizes nature – rebellious, malicious, tending to chaos – it is hardly surprising, since manifestly he is speaking of the nature within us. In his essay 'Nature in men', Bacon has advice for 'he that seeketh victory over his nature'. He cautions that nature within us 'is often hidden; sometimes overcome; seldom extinguished'. And he warns that no one should 'trust his victory over his nature too far: for nature will lay buried a great time, and yet revive upon the occasion or temptation' (VI, 469–70).

In short, the animal within us, like the animal outside us, is part of nature: something that human reason should suppress or master. I do not want to embark on anything like an evaluation of these ideas – although I wonder whether and in what sense anyone can recognize themselves in this fraught duality between intellect and instinct, reason and nature, the human and the animal. The point is that yet again Bacon is using the animal as a foil or contrast with which to set off the human. Let's recap. First, the animal is a creature that consists of the inferior parts and portions of a human being. Second, the animal is something outside of us over which we have a God-given right of subjugation – even a religious duty of inquisition. Third, the animal is something within us that cannot be trusted and which we ought to overcome or extinguish.

There is something else too, something that has to do with the interface between the various roles assigned to the animal. Seen in the round, scientific experimentation on animals has a double-sided merit. In one fell swoop, not only do we assert our God-given rights over the inferior beings outside us but in the exercise of our God-like intellect we rise above or own animal nature. Thus to take hold of an animal and in the cause of science to put it to the question – to 'squeeze', 'mold', 'constrain' and 'vex' it – is, in this view of things, ennobling. It is a kind of catharsis in which we go some way towards purifying ourselves of the taint of the beast within. This is the deeper meaning of that rule of detachment enforced in the laboratory. Any self-respecting researcher must be able to cause pain and harm to an animal subject; and to do so without flinching. This is most important. To flinch is to be deflected from the exercise of the pure intellect. The absence of flinching indicates an intellect purged of all interference from the urges and feelings that surge up from below. In other words, at a deeper level, this detachment is a measure of how good we are at severing – detaching – our higher human self from our lower animal nature. In a word: the inquisition of animals in the laboratory is *sublime*.

SALOMON'S HOUSE

Salomon's House on the island of Bensalem is well equipped to conduct the inquisition of nature on every conceivable front. This includes extensive facilities for controlled experimentation on animals. The Father of Salomon's House describes their research programmes – whose variety anticipates the proliferation of animal research today.

> We have also parks, and inclosures of all sorts of beasts and birds, which we use not only for view or rareness, but likewise for dissections and trials; that thereby we may take light what may be wrought upon the body of man. Wherein we find many strange effects; as continuing life in them, though divers parts, which you account vital, be perished and taken forth; resuscitating of some that seem dead in appearance; and the like. (III, 59)

What 'divers parts' of animals' bodies are removed in the interests of seeing whether the animal can survive without them? Bacon leaves this to the reader's scientific imagination. The Father goes on to say, 'We try also all poisons and other medicines upon them, as well of chirurgery as physic.' Also, the natural functions and properties of animals are engineered: their colour, shape, size, behaviour and reproductive capacities are all modified and new species are created.

At no point does the Father suggest that any research would be curtailed out of consideration for the welfare of the animals used. There is, it should be noted, one occasion in the *New Organon* (Book II, aphorism 41) where Bacon seems to rule out a procedure (cutting out the fetus from the womb of a living animal) on the grounds that it would be 'too inhuman' (IV, 202). However, this sentiment seems anomalous in the context of just about everything else he says that bears upon the question. In this connection, it is significant that he characterizes goodness of character as the desire to promote 'the weal of men', i.e. *human* welfare; he explicitly equates goodness with the Greek virtue of *Philanthropia*, literally the love of human beings (VI, 403). And although it could be argued that the text is ambiguous at this point, it seems to me that Bacon cites compassion for animals as an example of what he calls an 'error' in goodness. (If so, then once again his words echo the voice of Aquinas who maintained that 'charity does not extend to irrational creatures' since 'they have no fellowship with man in the rational life'.[23])

At any rate, time and again Bacon emphasizes that the whole purpose of scientific research and development is to promote the power and the welfare of humanity over and against animals and the rest of nature; that this purpose is a divine right and even a religious duty; that not only are animals inferior to us and subject to our use but that the animal side of our nature is something we must try to master and even expunge; that in order to gain scientific knowledge it is necessary to exercise power over animals (and nature), to manipulate them and coerce them into betraying their secrets; that God wants us to do this and that it is wrong to impose any limits on the enterprise of science and the conquest of nature. The cumulative effect of these ideas completely overwhelms any isolated reservations that Bacon might have had about specific scientific procedures that are detrimental to the welfare of the animals used. There is an unmistakeable thrust in his writings: to deliver animals, body and soul, into human hands for human ends.

On second thoughts, these are not mere human hands. They are the hands that belong to the distinguished 'Sons of Science'[24] and to that 'blessed race of Heroes and Supermen'[25] whose scientific inventions relieve and improve the human estate. Who among us would want to tie the hands of these, our betters and benefactors? On the contrary, says Bacon: if we are to imitate the good example set by the Bensalemites then not only will we honour and erect statues to our scientists (III, 166) but we will give them a free hand. Moreover, this free hand includes the right to withhold information from the public and even from the state. Salomon's House, although it is 'the very eye of the kingdom' (III, 137), is a closed order. The Father explains that the Society reserves the right not to publish its discoveries and inventions. The members 'take all an oath of secrecy, for the concealing of those which we think fit to keep secret: though some of those we do reveal sometimes to the state, and some not' (III, 165). There is something poignant about this secrecy, bearing in mind that the secrets were originally nature's own. The open secrets of nature become the closely-guarded secrets of science. And the people of Bensalem are more than content to render unto science the things that now belong to science – including animals for use in experiments.

THE CULTURE OF SCIENCE

Such, at least, is the dream that Francis Bacon dreamed. It lies outside the scope of this chapter to describe the extent to which this dream is a dream come true. However, I hazard a guess that Bacon, were he alive today, would not be too disappointed with the way things have turned out for the 'new science' he advocated. I have in mind not only the inventions that he anticipated in *New Atlantis* – including submarines, flying machines, laser beams, the telephone, hearing aids and artificial flavouring for food. I am thinking more of the setting, the culture within which modern appliances and technology have their sense. Bacon would be sure to notice the vast institutions of twentieth century science, their power and their standing in public policy, and the influence they exert on our lives and on our language.

At the same time, he might pause to reflect on what has happened to the Christian rationale he provided for the new science: his idea that the conquest of nature restores to humanity our God-given rights over animals and nature. As Passmore sees it, 'the idea of "restoration" can be quietly dropped so as to leave behind it an ambition the most secular-minded of scientists could happily share'.[26] One wonders how anything so weighty could be dropped so quietly. I am more inclined to say, on the contrary, that the idea of restoration (of our rights over nature and animals) was quietly *taken up* into secular science. I do not mean that it was taken up *as* an idea – in the form of a proposition or thesis about the recovery of our rights. But, almost by a process of osmosis, the vitality in the idea was communicated to secular science. Secular science was conceived in a Christian crucible. It was thus able to tap – some would say sap – the energies of the Christian tradition, to absorb them into its marrow. So, when science turned secular it did not so much *reject* religion as *discard* it – as a snake will shed its skin.

As we read Bacon, we can practically see this metamorphosis starting to take place before our eyes. In *New Atlantis* we find the transition personified in the ambivalent figure of the Father of Salomon's House. Who or what is this man? Is he a scientific priest or a priestly scientist? It is impossible to say, for he is not a possible man: he is a character in a myth that Bacon invents in order to bring old traditions to a new beginning. The figure of the Father harks back to the authority of the Church; but also looks forward to the beneficence of the laboratory. He is at once the priest who knows about nature and the scientist who works miracles. The ambiguity here is what counts. It gives Bacon a cutting edge for teasing the past and the future apart – teasing the past with intimations of the future. The crucial point about this is that Bacon does not merely force a separation. He exercises his craft in such a way that the new science is nourished and enriched by the old religion from which it emerges. Or to put it another way: Bacon's work disturbs the very distinction between the secular and the religious. This distinction has become a blur and a problem. Sometimes we are unsure, concerning the institutions and practices and attitudes of modern science, whether to say that we are dealing with the secular or with the religious.

Modern science learned in its infancy that it has a mission to perform; that this mission has to do with benefiting humanity by conquering nature; that nature is raw material for us to use as we wish – and also an adversary that we must fight and defeat; that we need knowledge of nature in order to conquer her; that nature keeps this knowledge from us in the form of secrets that we must wrest from her by force; that doing this ennobles us and makes us more truly human; that the people who do this (the 'Sons of Science') should be publicly supported, honoured and revered; that the affairs of state should be guided by science; and that scientific institutions should be autonomous. All this science learned while it was still a babe in Christian arms. And this is what remains implicit in science now that it is fully-fledged and grown up.

It remains *implicit* because what science learned was not a lesson but a culture (a way of learning lessons). The use of animals in the lab is embedded in the total culture of science: its myths, methods, purpose, institutions and the place science occupies in the life and affairs of society. Moreover, the lab animal symbolizes the virility of this culture: it embodies the mastery to which we aspire. Ideally, we design it, we produce it, we utilize it for our purposes and then we dispense with it: total control. We *like* the fact that we can do this. It feels good.

With all this in mind, it should come as no surprise when research scientists close their ranks – and slam their doors – against any interference from 'outsiders'. They know in their bones that they ought to have a free hand to use animals as they see fit. As one professor of biology and director of a laboratory at Yale University was recently quoted as saying, 'These animals have no rights at all, and those people who think they do are ... grossly deficient.'[27] His animals, he says, are 'the raw materials of the lab'. These are not the words of a *callous* man, but of a *cultured* man – a man who speaks from and within the culture of science. And because this is our culture too, we, who are no more callous than he is, are disposed to hear him. Our ears are attuned to what the doctors of science have to say. None of them advocates using animals frivolously or gratuitously. They tell us that it is 'necessary' to paralyze monkeys or rear them in isolation chambers; to immerse rats in boiling water or stun them with electric shock; to expose dogs to radiation and to burn the eyes of rabbits with sodium hydroxide. We are good listeners. When they use this word 'necessary' we understand tacitly that they are alluding to the well-being of the human race. We might still have queries and reservations. But this word 'necessary' stills our tongue and strikes a chord deep within us. We soon shake our heads and say, 'Well, if it's necessary, it's necessary.' We are good at repeating our lessons. And this is a lesson we learn repeatedly, whether from textbooks or from popular books, magazines or commercials. Wherever we look, this 'necessary' is written between the lines; it is written into our culture and we learned it – like science itself learned it – in our formative years. We are educated readers. Therefore we are easy to persuade.

The conviction that we *must* use lab animals – that it is *necessary* to use them – is overlaid with connotations that pervade our education at its core. At the core of our education is a way of orienting ourselves towards the natural world around us. It is this orientation that primes us to see lab animals as pieces of equipment, as tools of the scientist's trade. Animals are not simply the raw materials of the lab; they are part of the 'deep structure' of the dream of science – *our* dream of conquest, of remaking nature in our image and extending our reach so as to encompass all things within our grasp. There is romance and hope and challenge in this dream. Furthermore, it is no mere fantasy: every day our grasp grows wider, our grip becomes stronger. This is why it is hard for us to broach and to think about and to discuss the questions that underlie laboratory animal use. How do you take issue with a dream – especially when you are caught up with it yourself?

There again, what kind of people are we if our dream requires, every year, tens of millions of animals to be put to the question? We do not pause to reflect. The inquisition of nature and of animals proceeds apace; and we have ways of making them talk.

EPILOGUE: ET TU, BRUTE

In the film *Conquest of the Planet of the Apes*, the year is 1991 and apes are trained by people to be slaves. There is one ape, a chimpanzee named Caesar, who has the ability to speak English. Caesar conceals this from the (human) authorities, who would kill him if they found out. Eventually, Caesar comes under suspicion and he is detained. However, he pretends to be just another dumb animal and the authorities need to be certain that he is indeed the talking chimp. So, they decide to put him to the question. He is taken to a laboratory and subjected to intense electric shock. 'Talk!' demand his inquisitors. He talks.

NOTES

1. This chapter is an edited version of 'Lab Animals, Francis Bacon and the Culture of Science', *Listening*, 18, 1 (Winter 1983), pp.54–72. There were no subtitles in the original version.
2. William Leiss, *The Domination of Nature* (Boston, MA: Beacon Press, 1974) p.45. In addition to Leiss's book I found the following work a helpful stimulus in writing this chapter: Carolyn Merchant, *The Death of Nature* (New York: Harper and Row, 1980).
3. Those references to Bacon's works which are given in parentheses in the text pertain to the standard edition of his collected works: J. Spedding, R.L. Ellis, and D.D. Heath (eds), *The Works of Francis Bacon* (London: Longman, 1857–74). Spedding's collection is in seven volumes. There are many editions of this collection with identical volume and page numbering. I consulted the facsimile reprint published by Friedrich Fromann Verlag Gunther Holzboog (Stuttgart-Bad Constatt, 1963). I have not in each case given the title of the piece to which I refer. I provide only volume and page references; e.g. 'III, 129' refers to volume III, page 129. I have not indicated whether the piece in question was originally written in Latin or in English. Where the former, I reproduce Spedding's translation. However, Spedding does not provide a translation for all of Bacon's Latin texts. See note 4.
4. 'The Refutation of Philosophies', in Benjamin Farrington, *The Philosophy of Francis Bacon* (Chicago, IL: University of Chicago Press, 1966), pp.131–2. Farrington's book includes his translations of three of Bacon's Latin texts not translated in Spedding's collection (see note 3). I will cite Farrington's book and use his translation whenever I refer to these three texts.
5. 'Thoughts and Conclusions on the Interpretation of Nature', in Farrington, *Philosophy of Francis Bacon*, p.79.
6. John Passmore, *Man's Responsibility for Nature* (London: Gerald Duckworth & Co., 1974), Chapter 1.
7. Augustine, *The City of God against the Pagans*, ed. R W Dyson (Cambridge: Cambridge University Press, 1998), Book XXII, chapter 24, p.1161.
8. Aristotle, *The Politics* (Harmondsworth: Penguin, 1962), Book I, chapter 8, p.40.
9. Augustine, *City of God*, I, 20.
10. Thomas Aquinas, *Summa Theologica*, part II, question 64, article 1. See Tom Regan and

Peter Singer (eds), *Animal Rights and Human Obligations* (Englewood Cliffs, NJ: Prentice-Hall, 1976), p.119.

11. Thomas Aquinas, *Summa Contra Gentiles*, third book, part II, chapter 112. See Regan and Singer (eds), *Animal Rights and Human Obligations*, p.56.
12. John Calvin, *On the Christian Faith* (New York: Bobbs-Merrill, 1957), pp.131–2.
13. Janoslav Pelikan (ed.), *Luther's Works* (St Louis, MO: Concordia Publishing House, 1958), vol. I, p.71.
14. Ibid., vol. II, pp.132–3.
15. Bacon's subtitle for 'The Masculine Birth of Time'.
16. These are the closing words of *New Organon*, book II.
17. 'Thoughts and Conclusions on the Interpretation of Nature', in Farrington, *Philosophy of Francis Bacon*, p.96.
18. Ibid., p.99. See also Spedding, Ellis and Heath (eds), *Works of Francis Bacon*, III, 333.
19. 'Thoughts and Conclusions on the Interpretation of Nature', in Farrington, *Philosophy of Francis Bacon*, p.93.
20. 'The Masculine Birth of Time', in Farrington, *Philosophy of Francis Bacon*, p.62.
21. Immanuel Kant, *Critique of Pure Reason*, trans. Norman Kemp Smith (London: Macmillan, 1968), p.20.
22. 'The Refutation of Philosophies', in Farrington, *Philosophy of Francis Bacon*, p.106.
23. Thomas Aquinas, *Summa Theologica*, part II, question 25, article 3. See Regan and Singer (eds), *Animal Rights and Human Obligations*, p.120.
24. 'Thoughts and Conclusions on the Interpretation of Nature', in Farrington, *Philosophy of Francis Bacon*, p.88.
25. 'Masculine Birth of Time', in Farrington, *Philosophy of Francis Bacon*, p.72.
26. Passmore, *Man's Responsibility for Nature*, p.19.
27. Dr Clement Merkert, quoted in Calvin Sims, 'Yale Sacrifices for Science', *Yale Daily News*, 25 February 1982.

CHAPTER NINETEEN

In the Shadow of Dr Moreau

A MORAL QUESTION ABOUT ANIMALS

Consider the following question: May we ever perform experiments on animals that cause them harm or suffering, or kill them, or otherwise prevent them from living their lives?[1] By 'we' I mean human beings in general and research scientists in particular. By 'animals' I mean animals.

But what is an animal? And do we know one when we see one? The answer to this last question depends, I think, on the frame of mind in which we look; it depends on what Thoreau calls (in an entirely different context) the 'intention of the eye'.[2] I am interested in the bearing that 'the intention of the eye' has on the question about scientific research. I am concerned, in particular, with a certain kind of tunnel vision in science that subverts the question altogether, preventing it from being seen for what it is: a moral question about animals.

My purpose is to save the question, not to answer it. (So, I shall not discuss the pros and cons, the rights and wrongs, of using animals in scientific research.) I shall pursue this aim by examining the logic of the frame of mind that is blind to the question. To this end, I shall utilize excerpts from two works written in the second half of the nineteenth century that give expression to this frame of mind, one by a popular writer of science fiction, the other by a celebrated advocate of medical research. I shall begin with the fictional Dr Moreau, a figure that continues to cast a long shadow.

WHEN IS AN ANIMAL AN ANIMAL?

In *The Island of Doctor Moreau*, a novel by H.G. Wells published in 1896, Edward Prendick is marooned on a remote island somewhere in the Pacific. The island is uninhabited except for two Englishmen and a small population of malformed individuals who seem, to Prendick's eye, not entirely human. One of the two Englishmen is the 'prominent and masterful physiologist' Dr Moreau.[3] Moreau, a 'notorious vivisector', who was 'howled out of the country' on account of his experiments on live animals, continues to pursue his research in a laboratory he has built on the island.[4] One day Prendick, hearing cries of excruciating pain coming from the laboratory, barges in, only to recoil from the sight of 'something bound painfully upon a framework, scarred, red, and bandaged'.[5] It is an animal – a puma – upon which Moreau has been operating. Several bizarre chapters later, Moreau divulges the secret of his research to Prendick. He explains that the humanoid creatures on the island are (or originally were) animals that he has surgically altered. He exclaims, 'To that – to the study of the plasticity of living forms – my life has been devoted.'[6] Warming to his subject, and calling himself 'an investigator', he gives eloquent expression to the 'intellectual passion' that motivates his work:

> You cannot imagine the strange colourless delight of these intellectual desires. The thing before you is no longer an animal, a fellow-creature, but a problem. Sympathetic pain – all I know of it I remember as a thing I used to suffer from years ago. I wanted – it was the only thing I wanted – to find out the extreme limit of plasticity in a living shape.[7]

When Prendick protests, describing his work as 'an abomination', Moreau responds by saying, 'To this day I have never troubled about the ethics of the matter. The study of Nature makes a man at last as remorseless as Nature.'[8] What Moreau means by this is unclear. Is he saying that, given the scientific nature of his work, ethics is not his business? Or is he saying that he operates on a plane that is higher than mere morality: that he is, so to speak, beyond good and evil? The latter seems to be implied by the way he describes himself. He calls himself 'remorseless'. Now, remorselessness is not exactly a morally neutral state. (The fact that it is not morally neutral is one reason why the simile 'as remorseless as Nature' is fatuous.) Calling someone 'remorseless' suggests that the person is at fault for lacking compassion or for failing to regret the harm they cause others. However, this cannot be what Moreau means when he calls *himself* remorseless, since he derides compassion ('sympathetic pain'), referring to it as something he used to *suffer* from – as though it were a weakness or an affliction. So, rather than judging himself, he appears to be judging remorse: he appears to be saying, in effect, that such feelings would be a failing in an 'investigator' (in other words, a research scientist). It is not clear, then, whether he is saying that he is indifferent to 'the ethics of the matter' or that he is above them. But, either way, this much is clear: he is saying that the moral question of whether he should or should not pursue his research (or pursue it in the way that he does) does not concern him; and that it does not concern him because he is an 'investigator'.

Although the plot of the novel is pure invention, Dr Moreau is not necessarily – or perhaps simply – a figment of Wells's imagination. Wells, like his fictional character Edward Prendick, had studied under T.H. Huxley when he was a biology student in London.[9] He was certainly aware of the controversy surrounding the use of live animals in scientific research.[10] And Moreau's speech to Prendick is strikingly reminiscent of a passage from *Introduction to the Study of Experimental Medicine* written by Claude Bernard and published thirty years earlier, in 1865: 'The physiologist is not a layman, he is a scientist; he is a man gripped and absorbed by the scientific idea that he pursues: he no longer hears the cries of animals, he no longer sees the blood that flows, he sees only his idea, and perceives only organisms that conceal from him the problems he wants to solve.'[11]

The frame of mind or point of view is essentially the same as that expressed by Moreau – even some of the words are the same (allowing for the difference between Bernard's French and Moreau's English). Where there might seem to be a divergence is in connection with what Moreau calls 'the ethics of the matter'. Bernard poses the question explicitly and answers it forthrightly: 'Does one have the right to perform experiments on animals and to vivisect them? For my part, I think that one does, wholly and absolutely.'[12] It appears, then, that Bernard, unlike Moreau, has considered the moral question with which I began and that he has troubled about the rights and wrongs of experimenting on live animals. It *appears* that way, but in reality, as closer examination reveals, he has not. Later I shall discuss the argument he makes to support his position regarding 'the ethics of the matter'. But it is not necessary to examine his reasoning as such. It is enough to know the frame of mind or point of view. I shall argue that to look at animals from this point of view is to cease to see them *as* animals; and if animals are not seen as animals then the moral question with which I began disappears from view.

Before I embark on this argument I should explain why it is worth paying attention to Bernard and Moreau. After all, both figures are larger than life. Moreau is an anti-hero in the fictional tradition of Frankenstein: a human being more monstrous than the monsters he creates. Bernard, who is widely acclaimed as a founder of modern experimental physiology, was an innovator and pioneer. Neither man is typical of today's research scientists, most of whom are humble men and women performing routine experiments, and many of whom would regard Bernard and Moreau as callous. At the very least, most people in science today would find their language overblown. But it is precisely this latter quality that is useful. Bernard and Moreau might be guilty of hyperbole but their words have the merit of presenting, writ large, the perspective of the pure research scientist per se. Furthermore, in privileging this perspective, they express an attitude that people, both inside and outside science, often have without necessarily knowing it or admitting it. Bernard's case is, I believe, especially relevant because what applies to him applies also to many others who tend to take his position on 'the ethics of the matter'; that is to say, they *answer* the moral question with which I began without ever truly *asking* it. They do not take the question to heart. And they do not take it to heart because they approach it in the wrong mind – in the sort of mind expressed by Bernard in the passage quoted above.

I turn now to an examination of this passage. Notice, to begin with, to whom Bernard refers. 'The physiologist', he says, 'is not a layman'.[13] It is natural to suppose that he is speaking about himself. No doubt he is; but he writes in the third person and the subject of the statement is 'the physiologist', not Claude Bernard per se. (I shall use the word 'physiologist' as an umbrella term for scientists whose research could be in any one of a broad range of biological disciplines. I realize that this is an archaic use of the word but it is convenient to use it in the same way that Bernard and Wells use it.) The statement Bernard makes is general and not specifically about himself. Notice, however, that he speaks of *the physiologist* and not of *physiologists*; and when I say that his statement is general, I do not mean that he is making a *generalization*. That is to say, he is not making an empirical claim about how actual physiologists do in fact, or for the most part, think or feel. What he gives us is a *type*: he is describing what the physiologist is like *in principle*. He is saying, in other words, that this is what it means to be a physiologist; as if someone who did not feel or think along the lines that he describes would not be the real thing. He is giving us, in effect, a definition.

Bernard defines the physiologist as 'a scientist', a man who is 'gripped and absorbed by the scientific idea that he pursues'. Note how he characterizes a scientist: someone whose mind is on a certain kind of object and in a certain state. The object is an idea; specifically a *scientific* idea. The state is that of being 'gripped and absorbed' by this idea. Now, 'gripped and absorbed' might seem to be strong words to describe the state of mind of a scientist, which we tend to think of as detached and dispassionate. But Bernard's scientist *is* detached, as the rest of his description vividly asserts: 'he no longer hears the cries of animals, he no longer sees the blood that flows'. The point is that detachment is relative; that is to say, relative to the object of interest. Bernard's scientist is detached from the suffering of animals precisely because he or she is 'gripped and absorbed' by a 'scientific idea': these are two sides of one coin. There is, and there can be, no such thing as a mind that is *absolutely* detached – unless it is a mind that takes an interest in absolutely nothing. And the word that describes someone who takes an interest in nothing is 'apathetic', not 'scientific'.

However, there is a question about the *degree* of interest one takes in something; and it might be thought that Bernard's scientist takes an inordinate interest in research. The words 'gripped and absorbed' might well conjure up the stock figure of the mad scientist for whom science is an all-consuming obsession. But that would be to miss the point of Bernard's description. You could say that Bernard gives us a highly romanticized version of the pure research scientist. Alternatively, you could say, as I shall say, that what he gives us is a highly rhetorical account of what it means to take a purely scientific interest in a piece of research. On this reading, the words 'gripped and absorbed' serve to emphasize that the point of view that Bernard describes is pure (purely scientific). What he is saying in this passage amounts to this: that the physiologist, looking at animals in the laboratory from a purely scientific point of view, is interested only in data – data that bear upon 'the problem he wants to solve'.

Moreau, hell-bent on performing his diabolical experiments on animals in his secret island hideaway, comes closer to the stock figure of the mad scientist. I dare say he *is* crazy and that Wells meant to depict him this way. However, I am interested only in the logic of what Moreau says when he explains himself to Prendick, not in his character as such. And the logic of what he says is the same as that of Bernard. Like Bernard's physiologist, he is detached, in the sense that he experiences no feelings of sympathy for the animals on which he experiments. But he is certainly not without feeling of *some* kind, for he speaks of his 'intellectual passion' and of 'the strange colourless delight' of his 'intellectual desires'. As with Bernard, we are looking at two sides of one coin. That is to say, Moreau's feeling for his subject ('the study of the plasticity of living forms') is one side of the coin of which his lack of feeling for the animals on which he experiments is the other. It might not be clear how delight can be 'colourless', or passion and desire 'intellectual'; but the point is that it is *delight, passion* and *desire* of which he speaks. The adjectives ('colourless', 'intellectual') are cerebral and point to the scientific nature of the object of his interest: the 'problem' concerning 'the extreme limit of plasticity in a living shape'. The substantives ('delight', 'passion', 'desire') express the fact that the interest he takes in this problem is total; and, being total, he is only interested in whatever sheds light on his problem. By Bernard's definition, he is a physiologist to the core. In short, both men, Moreau and Bernard, give us a graphic picture of someone who single-mindedly looks at animals from the angle of one particular interest: physiology.

Approaching from this angle, what is that the physiologist sees? In Bernard's words, 'only organisms that conceal from him the problems he wants to solve'. Lurking in this metaphor of concealment is a Baconian view of science in which the researcher seeks to extract 'the secrets still locked in Nature's bosom'.[14] This puts the whole of what Bernard says about the physiologist in a certain light; and in order to understand him fully it is necessary to place his words within the larger context of the rhetoric associated with the rise of modern (experimental) science from the sixteenth century on.[15] However, this is not necessary for the present purpose. Rather, what I wish to draw attention to is the word 'organism', the word Bernard uses to refer to that which 'conceals' the scientific problem from the physiologist.

Is the organism an animal? Of course it is. Then why does Bernard not refer to it as such – as an animal? The answer is that the physiologist, according to Bernard, 'sees only his idea', and consequently is aware of the animal only in terms of that idea; and at the heart of physiology is the idea of the organism. And *is* not the animal an organism? Certainly it is. But it is also an animal. The physiologist, you might say, is not interested in the animal as such. That is what it means to say that the physiologist 'no longer hears the cries of animals' nor 'sees the blood that flows'. Bernard does not mean that people who study physiology suffer from impaired hearing or need their eyes tested. It is not that they do not hear the cries of pain; it is that they do not hear them *as* cries of pain. It is a matter of what they tune out (or what they are attuned to). By the same token, it is not that they are unaware of the blood but that they are aware of it only as, say, a bodily fluid composed of certain chemical constituents and performing certain organic functions – and not as an injury or loss suffered by the animal as such. Moreau puts it this way: 'The thing before you', he says, 'is no longer an animal, a fellow-creature, but a problem.' When he says 'before you' he means before *him*, Dr Moreau, the physiologist. And when he says that the animal 'is no longer an animal' he does not mean that by some alchemy or miracle it ceases to be what it is. He is saying that *to the physiologist* the animal is not an animal. It is not, that is to say, 'a fellow-creature'.

It is not a *fellow*-creature because there is no such creature – no such animal – as a physiologist. None was created on the sixth day. This is not to say that there are no physiologists in the world. It is only to say that all of them are human beings.

CALLING A QUESTION MORAL

This brings me to the crux of the matter. I began with this question: May we ever perform experiments on animals that cause them harm or suffering, or kill them, or otherwise prevent them from living their lives? I said that by 'we' I mean human beings in general and research scientists in particular. Now, the words *general* and *particular* are important here: they imply that research scientists are included in the same 'we' as everyone else. Singling them out does not make them a breed apart; does not exclude them from the category of human being. The sole reason for singling them out is that they are the ones among us who perform experiments on live animals. In performing these experiments, they are concerned with questions that are scientific in nature, questions that arise for them as scientists. But the question of whether it is right or wrong to perform these experiments at all is a *moral* question and it arises for them in the same way that it arises for everyone else: as human beings, not as scientists. This is not to say that technical and scientific considerations never complicate the moral question about using live animals in laboratory research; of course they do. It is only to say that the questions to which such considerations give rise are not themselves exclusively technical and scientific. There is always logical space for a moral question. That is because experts are never *merely* experts: they are, in the first place, human beings. Calling a question moral is to call attention to this fact: to the fact that we are human beings first, whatever the particular angle of our professional interest.

You could say that this is something about themselves that both Moreau and Bernard forget. (That is to say, they forget *themselves*.) But Moreau, in a way, understands the logic of his position better than Bernard does. He recognizes that, speaking purely as a physiologist, he is not concerned with 'the ethics of the matter'. Or to put it

another way, the question of whether or not Prendick is right in calling his work 'an abomination' is not a question within physiology: it
is not a physiological question. Moreau understands this. What is
disturbing about him is the fact that the question does not concern him
at all: does not concern him, that is, as a human being. So that when
he says, 'The thing before you is no longer an animal', it is as if *he*
were no longer a *man*. (This is what makes him, as I put it earlier, more
monstrous than the monsters he creates.) Bernard, however, as we
noted earlier, does concern himself with 'the ethics of the matter'; or
at least he purports to. He certainly takes a moral position, claiming
that he has the right, 'wholly and absolutely', to perform experiments
on animals. But, as we shall see by examining his argument, the position he takes is really nothing more than the refusal (or inability) to
relinquish the point of view of the physiologist: to see animals as anything other than organisms. His point of view is the same as Moreau's,
except that unlike Moreau he confuses physiology and ethics.

Bernard's argument depends on the contrast he draws between the
physiologist and the layman.[16] 'The physiologist', he says, 'is not a
layman, he is a scientist.' This means, on his account, that the physiologist is someone whose thoughts and perceptions are governed by a
special idea; that is to say, a *scientific* idea. Then what is a layman?
Bernard writes as if a similar sort of account can be given of what it
means to be a layman, except that the special idea that governs the
thoughts and perceptions of the layman is not scientific: it is lay:

> I understand perfectly ... that laymen, who are moved by ideas
> totally different from those that animate the physiologist, judge
> vivisection completely differently. It could not be otherwise. We
> have said in some part of this introduction that in science it is the
> idea that gives facts their value and their significance. It is the same
> in morals, it is the same everywhere.[17]

So, there are laymen and there are physiologists. The layman is
moved by one set of ideas, the physiologist by another. Both judge the
rights and wrongs of vivisection accordingly and come to incompatible
conclusions. And that's that: there is nothing more to be said; nothing
more that *can* be said, according to Bernard, since the moral disagreement between physiologist and layman is simply a function of the
different ideas that go with the two different points of view. Hence he
declares, 'I shall not try ... to justify physiologists against the reproach
of cruelty made by people who are strangers to science; the difference
in ideas explains everything.'[18] This might sound plausible at first but

the reasoning is doubly fallacious. In the first place, the concepts of physiologist and layman are not symmetrical. Being a layman is not, logically speaking, on a par with being a physiologist. A physiologist is someone who specializes in a particular field or discipline, namely, physiology. But there is no field or discipline that corresponds to being lay; no point of view either. The concept is purely negative; or, rather, it is purely relative to some profession or other. The layman of whom Bernard speaks is simply someone – anyone – who is *not* a physiologist. Non-physiologists do not compose a group; they do not belong to the same clubs, go to the same places, share the same tastes and come to the same conclusions. They do not all agree about the rights and wrongs of vivisection. Nor, for that matter, do all physiologists. This brings me to the second fallacy in his reasoning. For even if all physiologists were unanimous on this score, their opinion would not flow from the principles of physiology; only *moral* principles can lead to moral conclusions.

What about the moral conclusion for which Bernard argues, namely, that he has a right, 'wholly and absolutely', to perform experiments on animals? Where does this come from? Well, on his account, given the contrast that he draws between physiologist and layman, and since he is the one and not the other, it follows that this moral conclusion is supposed to spring from the premises of his discipline. This is asking for the logically impossible; it is what I meant when I said that Bernard confuses physiology and ethics. It is also what I was alluding to when I said that he never truly considers the ethics of the matter. Here is how he concludes the portion of the *Introduction* with which I have been dealing:

> After what has preceded, we consider all discussion of vivisection futile or absurd. It is impossible for men who judge the facts with such different ideas ever to agree; and as it is impossible to satisfy everybody, the scientist should be concerned only with the opinion of scientists who understand him, and should extract rules of conduct only from his own conscience.[19]

Given 'what has preceded' (that is to say, given his argument so far), when Bernard refers to 'the opinion of scientists' he can only mean their opinion *as* scientists. This makes the use of the word 'conscience' positively weird, since conscience is a moral category, not a scientific one. What he is doing, in reality, is substituting the dictates of his discipline for the dictates of conscience. And when he asserts his absolute right to perform experiments on animals, his argument boils down to this: there is nothing in physiology against it. This is not exactly a knockdown moral argument. In short, what Bernard does is to take an imperative of his research (or what he sees as an imperative) and turn it into an absolute right – without giving any *moral* argument whatsoever.

RETURNING TO OUR SENSES

Once we have got the dust of Bernard's confusion out of our eyes, we can see clearly that his real position regarding the moral question with which I began is bound to be essentially the same as Moreau's, since it is inherent in the frame of mind or point of view that they share. That is to say, the question does not concern them. It does not concern them as physiologists who are looking at animals and thinking about them purely in terms derived from their science. But as human beings it *does* concern them; which is to say, it *should* concern them; it should concern *us*. This means restoring the very frame of mind or point of view that the physiologist, qua physiologist, suspends. It means turning Moreau and Bernard on their heads. If, in Moreau's words, 'The thing before you is no longer an animal, a fellow-creature', then it must once again become one in our eyes. If, in Bernard's words, the physiologist 'no longer hears the cries of animals' and 'no longer sees the blood that flows', then we must hear those cries once more: hearing them as cries of pain, of anguish and distress; we must see that blood again, seeing it as a loss sustained, an injury inflicted. And, hearing and seeing such things, we must wince. Normal human sensibility must be resumed; otherwise a person is not in a position to think about right and wrong.

This leaves open the moral question with which I began – which was precisely the aim of this chapter: to open a question that tends to be closed down in advance by the mental disposition that I have been describing. True, the question has been copiously discussed by innumerable people on countless committees of enquiry. It is possible, however, to discuss a question at length without ever getting it; and in this case you do not get it unless it gets to you. To grasp the question that I put at the outset we must feel it grasp us – which we cannot do for as long as we allow ourselves to be jaded by copious discussion. To ask this question we must take it to heart: stepping out of the shadow of Dr Moreau, and (as Thoreau did in an entirely different context), literally returning to our senses.[20]

NOTES

1. This chapter is adapted from the essay 'Can We See a Moral Question about Animals?', in Andrew Linzey and Dorothy Yamamoto (eds), *Animals on the Agenda: Questions about Animals for Theology and Ethics* (London: SCM Press, 1998), pp.206–15.
2. H.D. Thoreau, 'Autumnal Tints', in W. Harding (ed.), *The Selected Works of Thoreau* (Boston: Houghton Mifflin, 1975), p.709.
3. H.G. Wells, *The Island of Doctor Moreau* (London: Everyman, 1993), p.32.
4. Ibid., pp.33, 32.
5. Ibid., p.48.
6. Ibid., p.69.
7. Ibid., p.73.
8. Ibid., p.73.
9. Ibid., p.27, re. Prendick.
10. Wells's article, 'The Way the World is Going', justifying animal experimentation, was published in the *Sunday Express*, 24 July 1927. George Bernard Shaw's reply, 'These Scoundrels', was published in the same newspaper, 27 August 1927. See E. Westacott, *A Century of Vivisection and Anti-Vivisection* (Ashingdon: C.W. Daniel, 1949), p.589.
11. Claude Bernard, *Introduction à l'étude de la médecine expérimentale* (Paris: Cres et Cie, 1926), vol. 2, p.41. Translations from the French are mine, although I consulted the translation by Henry Copley Greene (New York: Macmillan, 1927). I owe knowledge of this passage to J. Vyvyan, *In Pity and In Anger: A Study of the Use of Animals in Science* (London: Michael Joseph, 1969), p.44.
12. Bernard, *Introduction*, p.38.
13. 'Le physiologiste n'est pas un homme du monde.' Greene translates '*un homme du monde*' as 'a man of fashion'. Vyvyan translates the phrase as 'an ordinary man'. I have chosen 'layman' as closest to what I think Bernard is saying in the larger context of his discussion in this portion of the book. The male gender – 'layman' rather than 'layperson' – reflects the French '*homme*'. I am grateful to Kathleen Alaimo for her advice on this point of translation. See also note 16.
14. Francis Bacon, 'Thoughts and Conclusions on the Interpretation of Nature', in B. Farrington (ed.), *The Philosophy of Francis Bacon* (Chicago, IL: University of Chicago Press, 1966), p.96. The original essay, in Latin, was written in 1607.
15. See William Eamon, *Science and the Secrets of Nature* (Princeton, NJ: Princeton University Press, 1994). I discuss Bacon's rhetoric, and its relevance to animal experimentation, in Chapter 18, 'Salomon's House on the Island of Bensalem'.
16. See note 13. If '*un homme du monde*' were not translated as 'layman', some adjustment would have to be made in the discussion that follows. It would not, however, affect the main thrust of my criticism of Bernard's reasoning.
17. Bernard, *Introduction*, p.40. I have followed Bernard in the use of commas in the first sentence. The punctuation is important: the commas mean that the relative pronoun 'who' ('*qui*') refers to the *whole* class of 'laymen' ('*les gens du monde*'), not to a subclass. In other words, Bernard is saying that *all* laymen, not just *some*, are moved by ideas totally different from those that animate the physiologist, and therefore judge vivisection differently.
18. Ibid., p.41. The passage that begins 'The physiologist is not a layman' follows immediately in the text.
19. Ibid., pp.41–2.
20. H.D. Thoreau, 'Walking', in Harding (ed.), *Selected Works of Thoreau*, p.685.

CHAPTER TWENTY

The Kangaroo's Grasp

Revised version of a talk given at Mansfield College, Oxford, June 1995.

THE MOST NATURAL THING

This being a meeting of the Oxford Society for the Ethical Understanding of Animals, I assume that all of us take the following question seriously: How should we – we human beings – treat our fellow creatures?[1] I imagine also that we share the view that, on the whole, we do not treat them well. Many of us will feel that this is putting it mildly. We are moved to stand up for animals: to speak out about the wrongs that are done to them and to advocate on their behalf. Furthermore, we look around at how human beings treat each other and what do we see? All too often, prejudice and discrimination aimed against this group or that. But (we say to ourselves), whereas society recognizes these wrongs, it does not seem to recognize the wrong – or the extent of the wrong – done to animals as a group. And it's the most natural thing in the world to want to say, 'Look, what we do to animals can be just as bad as what we do to each other. In fact, it comes down to the same thing. Just as there is prejudice and discrimination against certain groups – Blacks, Jews, women and others – so there is against animals.'

This, essentially, is how the word 'speciesism' came to be coined: by way of analogy with racism (and antisemitism) and sexism.[2] At first, the idea seems compelling. The term captures our sense that the question of how we treat animals is a serious moral issue. It seems to take it out of the realm of sentimentality and into the domain of justice. So, it is not surprising that it has caught on among campaigners for animals. I believe, however, that the concept, though well intended, is misbegotten. It is misbegotten not only because the analogy on which it is based is too weak to sustain it, but also because it tends to diminish the very creatures on whose behalf it was introduced, thereby doing them an injustice.

The argument I shall make is not complete. Moreover, it is almost entirely negative or sceptical; it does not put forward a coherent alternative to the approach it criticizes, let alone a systematic moral theory. I am not sure that the urge to systematize in ethics does not tend to distort the issues or at least prevent them from coming to light. Be that as it may, speaking as someone who has been active in the animal rights movement, all too often I feel, in the face of the facts, as dumb an animal as any on earth.[3] I would like to be able to speak with confidence and clarity about every controversial question concerning the treatment of animals, but I cannot. At the same time, there is something to be said for casting about for words. Sometimes the very terms we use get in the way of thinking; and in order to find the right words we must first clear the ground of the wrong. Such is my limited aim here. Thus, to the extent that it succeeds, my argument does not exactly represent a gain in understanding; unless clearing away an obstacle to thinking constitutes a gain.

I wish I could do more. If I could, it would be by way of taking up the hint dropped in my opening sentence: the idea of animals as fellow creatures. This idea is at the heart of an essay by Cora Diamond, 'Eating Meat and Eating People', which she wrote precisely as a 'response' to the kind of approach 'encapsulated in the word "speciesism" ', and which is seminal for my own thinking on the subject.[4] If I have nothing to add to the idea I can at least illustrate it; and towards the end of my talk I shall let one fellow creature speak for itself: a kangaroo that I met early one morning on the coast of north-eastern Australia, an animal that did not need an advocate and which had a firm grip on what it wanted: me.

THE CONCEPT OF SPECIESISM

'Speciesism' is a specious word. It is certainly an 'awkward' one, as Richard Ryder, the psychologist who might deserve the credit for coining it, acknowledges.[5] Even Peter Singer, the moral philosopher who has helped popularize the term (and who got it from Ryder), acknowledges that 'the word is not an attractive one'.[6] Certainly, it does not trip off the tongue lightly. But this is not why I flinch every time I hear it, nor is it why I think it rings hollow. The fact that it is new is not a strike against it exactly but it does make a difference. When a word has been around for a while it tends to sink in, as it were, and mesh with the rest of the language; to acquire twists of meaning depending on context; to become, if not attractive, at least alive. It is true that 'speciesism' has made its way into the dictionary, including

the 1989 edition of the *Oxford English Dictionary*. But being in the
dictionary is not the same as being alive. 'Speciesism' is a manufactured word and whatever life it possesses it borrows from the words on
which it has been consciously patterned.[7] The question is whether this
patterning works or not, a question that invites us to reflect as much
on the imitated words as on the imitating.

Here is how Ryder justifies the term: 'I use the word "speciesism" to
describe the widespread discrimination that is practised by man against
other species, and to draw a parallel with racism. Speciesism and racism
are both forms of prejudice that are based upon appearances – if the
other individual looks different then he is rated as being beyond the
moral pale.'[8] Similarly, he says, with sexism, though he mainly draws on
racism to make his point. He asks, rhetorically, 'When did those with
black hair have a moral right to mistreat those with red hair – or even
those with blue or purple hair?' Predictably, he adds: 'Of course Hitler
thought this. Those with blond hair had a moral right – not to say a
moral *duty* – to mistreat those with alleged Semitic features.'[9]

I say 'predictably' because Hitler seems be the gold standard for
anyone who wants to portray a particular view or practice as wrong;
and it appears to be the fate of almost any moral controversy that,
sooner or later, people on opposing sides call each other Nazis. This
is, perhaps, a symptom of the temptation in ethics to assimilate all evils
to one big evil. Be that as it may, the 'parallel' Ryder draws oversim-
plifies the nature of racism and distorts it.

Prejudice against people with red hair is certainly reprehensible, but
it is not *racist*. First, redheaded people do not compose a group – or a
group of the right sort. They do not, for example, constitute a distinct
population with common ancestors from whom they have inherited
a set of distinguishing physical characteristics; nor do they form a
separate community. Second, racial prejudice is not 'based upon
appearances' merely. Ryder has missed more than the finer points of
Nazi racial ideology if he thinks otherwise. Looks, in the Nazi scheme
of things, were only telltale signs; and even then they were not decisive.
Under the Nazis your hair could be blond, your eyes blue, but you still
might be classified as Jewish. This is because racial identity was based
not on appearances but on extraction. Hence the terms of the Blood
Protection Law, one of the 1935 Nuremberg Laws, which defined a
person as a 'full Jew' or less than a 'full Jew' depending on how many
of their grandparents were Jewish – not depending on observable or
visible physical traits.[10] The Nazis did not exclude Jewish people
because they *looked* different; it was on the inside, so to speak, in their

genes (and ultimately in their character, dispositions and mental capacities), where the real difference was supposed to lie.

There are, of course, other versions of racism; and nowadays the word is loosely used to refer to discrimination on the grounds of ethnicity or nationality or even culture, not just biology or heredity. But, while the word 'racism' might possess a range of meanings, there are outer limits; and bias against people with red hair does not qualify. It is, so to speak, skin deep; whereas racism always goes deeper – even if it is triggered by the fact that someone's skin is dark or their eyes narrow or their nose crooked.[11]

By the same token, certain views are *clearly* racist. With this in mind, I would like to conduct an experiment. Ryder makes the following claim about speciesism and racism: 'The illogicality in both forms of prejudice is of an identical sort.'[12] Let us put this to the test. Consider the following sentence: 'Because one species is more clever than another, does it give it the right to imprison or to torture the less clever species?'[13] The sentence is one of Ryder's and, once again, the question is clearly rhetorical. I take it that there are two implications. First, anyone who answers in the affirmative is a speciesist. Second, a non-speciesist (such as Ryder himself) would say, 'No, just because we human beings are more clever than other species, that does not give us the right to imprison them or torture them.' If the logic of speciesism and racism are indeed identical, we ought to obtain the equivalent result when we pose the corresponding question, substituting 'race' for 'species'. Let us try it and see: 'Because one race is more clever than another, does it give it the right to imprison or to torture the less clever race?' No doubt a good Nazi would say it does. But suppose someone says, 'I disagree: just because we whites are more clever than other races, that doesn't give us the right to imprison them or torture them.' What would we call such a person – if not a racist?

Similarly, Ryder's line of reasoning does not exactly bolster the analogy with sexism. He argues: 'Surely, a superior understanding entails greater responsibility rather than the opposite; just as an adult recognizes a degree of responsibility towards an infant, so also should he towards animals.'[14] Think how a feminist would react to a man who argued that men, owing to their superior understanding, have a greater responsibility towards women, as they do to children – and animals. This is not a way of renouncing male chauvinism; it *is* male chauvinism. (Again, the parallel idea, that racial superiority implies a special moral responsibility towards members of inferior races, is not a disavowal of racism but one of the forms it can take.)

The thrust of my argument is not that Ryder is guilty of prejudice against animals. But there is something problematic about the phrase 'superior understanding'. What does it mean? Or rather, when does it mean something and when does it not? There is no denying that different species have different capacities and propensities which, so to speak, go with the territory. Cats have better night vision than dogs; dogs can hear sounds that to us are inaudible; and we, for that matter, are fleeter of foot than tortoises. But do we possess 'superior understanding'? Or rather, what exactly does it mean to say that we do or that an animal's understanding is not as good as ours? I know what it means to say that I do not have as good a grasp of the theory of relativity as Stephen Hawking does. (In fact I do not have any grasp of it at all.) But what would it mean to say this: 'Toffee the tortoise does not grasp the theory either'? Or this: 'Toffee and I do not understand relativity.' Suppose he did – but there's the rub: how are we supposed to suppose such a thing? Then again, I know how to test my speed against Toffee. But my understanding? It is not as if he and I can submit ourselves to an IQ test. And why not? Because Toffee is not even intelligent enough to have his intelligence tested? Or is it because the very idea of such a contest is absurd – precisely because a tortoise is a tortoise and *specifically* not a human being? Not being human, it does not come within the ambit of a tortoise to have any kind of grasp of the theory of relativity. Nor a lack of grasp – and that is the point.

This is not to say that the word 'understand' cannot be applied to animals. We can, for example, say of Rusty the dog, 'She understands the game of fetch.' But we cannot, in the same way, say, 'She does not understand the game of chess.' For *of course* she cannot play chess – not because she has not been taught the game, nor because she is too thick to learn it, but simply because she is a dog. Strictly speaking, it makes no sense to say that she *cannot* play chess; for it could not make sense to say that she *can*. (That the point is conceptual is shown by the fact that to say 'Rusty is good at fetch but she's hopeless at chess' is to make a joke, where the joke lies in saying two logically incongruous things in the same logical breath.) In general, the sense of the word 'understand' undergoes a degree of change when it is applied to animals rather than human beings. So, it is not as if we can simply aggregate the things animals are said to understand, and aggregate the things human beings are said to understand, and thereby determine whose understanding is superior. And so, again: What does it mean to say, absolutely, that we possess 'superior understanding'?

To speak in terms of our 'superior understanding' seems to imply that it is possible to make a linear comparison between ourselves and animals, measuring them against our capacity for, say, abstract thought or logical reasoning or self-reflection. The effect of this is to turn animals into deficient human beings (or small children). If Ryder is guilty of anything, it is not prejudice against animals but a false comparison with ourselves that tends (as I said in my introduction) to diminish them. I shall develop this point later.

THE PRINCIPLE OF EQUALITY

Animal Liberation, the book by Peter Singer that has been described as 'the bible of the animal liberation movement', was published in 1975.[15] The argumentative portions of the text are substantially the same in the second (1990) edition, from which I now reproduce this explanation of what it means to be a speciesist:

> Racists violate the principle of equality by giving greater weight to the interests of members of their own race when there is a clash between their interests and the interests of those of another race. Sexists violate the principle of equality by favoring the interests of their own sex. Similarly, speciesists allow the interests of their own species to override the greater interests of members of other species. The pattern is identical in each case.[16]

Now, it is true that this version of the argument does not contain the error Ryder makes in representing racism and sexism as 'based upon appearances' merely. But the net result is much the same. For the effect of the pattern that Singer calls identical is to flatten racism and sexism and to reduce them to the *level* of a prejudice based on looks – or based on anything else, for that matter, however idiosyncratic. For not only is the pattern identical it is also indefinitely repeatable at the mention of a feature – any feature whatsoever. In effect, Singer himself makes this point when he writes, 'Why pick on race? Why not on whether a person was born in a leap year? Or whether there is more than one vowel in her surname?'[17] If racists and sexists 'violate the principle of equality' by favouring members of their own race and sex respectively, 'yearists' would discriminate on the basis of year of birth, 'vowelists' would go according to the spelling of a person's name, and so on, for every other imaginable moral fetish. The list of offending 'ists' is open-ended and, on this account, it is all the same, logically and morally speaking.

But, in reality, racism and sexism are not reducible to mere arbitrariness. They are far more complex than Singer's account suggests; nor are they as symmetrical. I shall make just a few, rough observations in this connection, commenting in turn on the nature of racism and sexism, and then turning to speciesism.

What is racism? Singer (see above) depicts racists as 'giving greater weight to the interests of members of their own race when there is a clash between their interests and the interests of those of another race'. To begin with, this account strikes me as stilted and, to say the least, somewhat limp. It is as if racism were merely a matter of leaning more this way than that, of preferring to benefit one person over another where a choice must be made. As an account of nepotism, or of favouritism in general, this might do. But it lacks a crucial ingredient: aversion, contempt, a sense of superiority, or something of the sort – the sort of thing that leads some ethnocentric individuals, especially the younger male variety who wear big boots, not to *wait* for 'a clash between their interests and the interests of those of another race' but to go out at night and *create* one.

There is a second respect in which Singer's formulation seems altogether to miss the racism in racism; the expression 'their own race'. Put it this way: if someone said, 'I am fair-minded: I do not put the interests of my own race before the interests of another race', I would need persuading that this person was not a racist. Conceivably, they are speaking in an acceptable idiom; but, in order to be in a position to judge, I would need to know more about them and the circumstances of their utterance. On the face of it, the very terms of their utterance – belonging to a race or having a race that is 'my own' – are redolent of racism. (This is one point where the parallel with sexism breaks down. For, although there might be a question about what it means to be a man or a woman, it is not problematic – or not in the same way – to say 'my sex' or 'my gender'.)

This leads to the third point: What if the interests of different so-called races could be catered for equally – but separately? What, in a word, about the principle of apartheid, of 'separate but equal' development? In practice, of course, the social system that used to exist in South Africa was not remotely equitable. But suppose it had been: suppose the nation's total resources had indeed been shared equally, on a per capita basis, among the entire population, but without relaxing the laws that determined, along racial lines, where people could live and work and with whom they could consort? On the face of it, such a segregated society would not, by Singer's account, be racist. If I am right, then this is a reductio ad absurdum of his argument.

As regards sexism, Singer's formulation is, in a sense, too even-handed. He speaks of sexists as 'favoring the interests of their own sex', as if it made no difference whether the gender of the offending party were male or female. But, first, the word 'sexism' was not coined in a vacuum; it comes out of feminism and reflects a certain state of affairs, one in which relations between the sexes are configured in specific ways, embodied in social structures and institutions, and so on. This is the world, or the state of the world, to which the word refers; it is, so to speak, its natural home. That is to say, all of this is implicit in the criticism that the word was invented to register: a criticism of men or of a culture or society that puts women down. (So, Maggie Humm, the feminist writer, defines sexism as a 'sexual relationship in which males denigrate females'.[18]) It does not cut both ways – or not evenly. Consider a standard example of a sexist practice: the male dining club that does not admit women (except on 'ladies' nights'). What about a women's dining club that excludes men (except on 'gentlemen's nights')? Would such a thing be 'sexist'? Singer would say it is as sexist as the first example. But this entails a substantial drop in the meaning of the word, leaving over only the formal or abstract idea of inequity or bias.

Moreover, the word 'sexism' does not refer simply to a state of affairs in which men's interests prevail over those of women. It refers to a certain conception of what those interests consist in; for example, in the idea that a woman is better off being at home, minding the baby and the kitchen, rather than pursuing a career independently of her family. In a similar vein, feminists will cite certain forms of preferential treatment of women (perhaps exemption from combat duty in the armed forces) or behaviour that used to be called gallant (such as a man paying the bill for dinner) as sexist. Indeed, a man might put the interests of a woman, *because* she is a woman, first – and *for that very reason* be convicted of sexism. It would require some work to make Singer's account of the matter square with this sort of case.

So, speciesism cannot fit the pattern for racism and sexism – a breach of the principle of equality – for the simple reason that there is no such pattern. Furthermore, there is something rather precious about speaking of speciesists in the abstract, seeing as we – we human beings – are the only species against whom the charge of speciesism can conceivably be brought. Or is it speciesist to think this? I would not ask were it not for an intriguing entry in the second (1987) edition of the Random House *Dictionary of the English Language*. Here is how speciesism is defined: 'discrimination in favor of one's species, usually the human species, over another, esp. in the exploitation or mistreatment of animals by humans'. The qualifying phrase 'usually the human species' is what I find intriguing. How usual is usual? Have other species on occasion committed the offence? Against whom? Are we ourselves sometimes on the sharp end of the stick, discriminated against by our fellow creatures? Do the Random House editors think that *Jaws* was about a shark that was prejudiced against people? Or is this an object lesson in the use of dictionaries: that they should never be consulted without a sense of humour?

Random House notwithstanding, no one I have read on this subject denies that, apart from some hypothetical extra-terrestrials, bigotry is the sole prerogative of the human race (although we did have a dog in my growing-up home who – embarrassingly – barked furiously at dark-skinned passers-by on the street).[19] Not that other denizens of our planet necessarily treat each other well. Violence among species is a fact of life in the wild, and Singer, who is no romantic, is resigned to the fact. 'We may regret that this is the way the world is', he says, 'but it makes no sense to hold nonhuman animals morally responsible or culpable for what they do.' Therein lies a contrast with us: 'Every reader of this book, on the other hand, is capable of making a moral choice on this matter.'[20]

THE ARGUMENT FROM MARGINAL CASES

At this point, Singer anticipates an objection. He imagines someone seizing on his words and using them as evidence against him: 'Now, someone is sure to say, I have admitted that there is a significant difference between humans and other animals, and thus I have revealed the flaw in my case for the equality of all animals.'[21] Singer's reply takes the form of an argument that is a commonplace, if not a cliché, among advocates for animals:

> I have never made the absurd claim that there are no significant differences between normal adult humans and other animals. My point is not that animals are capable of acting morally, but that the moral principle of equal consideration of interests applies to them as it applies to Humans. That it is often right to include within the sphere of equal consideration beings who are not themselves capable of making moral choices is implied by our treatment of young children and other humans who, for one reason or another, do not have the mental capacity to understand the nature of moral choice.[22]

To put it another way: if we give 'equal consideration' to those members of our own species who are not 'normal adult humans', we ought to do likewise with members of other species who are on the same mental footing. To do otherwise is sheer speciesism: discrimination on the basis of species.

In the philosophical literature on animal and ethics this line of reasoning is known as 'the argument from marginal cases'. Jan Narveson, a critic of the argument and the man who gave it its name, points out that it 'looms very large' in the writings of such thinkers as Singer and Tom Regan.[23] Regan himself has said that it is 'the most common type' of argument advanced in support of the view that animals (or some animals) have rights.[24] The 'marginal cases' in question are members of our own species who are not 'normal adult humans' but whom we do not treat as though of no account in their own right. Regan calls such people 'marginal humans'.[25]

Scouring the literature and drawing on a number of different authors, I have compiled a list of the 'marginal humans' in our midst: young children, babies, infant human beings, the mentally enfeebled, the severely mentally enfeebled, intellectual cabbages, people who are profoundly and permanently disabled intellectually, mentally defective humans, human beings with severe and irreparable brain damage, the severely retarded and hopelessly senile, human idiots, morons, young morons, very young morons, people with congenital dysfunctions, lunatics, imbeciles and (an ambiguous category) intellectual incompetents. If all these 'marginal humans' have rights (so the argument roughly goes), so too should animals – or at least *some* animals, namely, those whose mental life is on at least as high a level. As Ryder succinctly puts it, 'We have no more right to exploit an ape than we have a mentally retarded child.'[26]

The trouble with this argument is that if it succeeds, it fails. For, as John Rodman has pointed out in 'the Liberation of Nature?', the argument (which he calls 'The Method of Argument from Human Analogy and Anomaly') requires us to think of animals as, in effect, 'inferior human beings'. Seen this way, animals are 'degraded'.[27] This is not, of course, the intention of anyone who subscribes to the idea that animals are the victims of prejudice and discrimination. But it is inherent in an approach that, as Rodman observes, applies to animals 'the moral/legal paradigm of entities, rights, and obligations'.[28] At the heart of this approach is the figure of the individual, the bearer of rights in the modern liberal tradition: human, adult, normal.

Among the moral philosophers who share this approach, Regan and

Singer are the chief representatives of the two main schools of thought. Regan's moral theory, set out in *The Case For Animal Rights*, can be understood as an amendment to Kant. In place of Kant's 'kingdom of ends', embracing all rational beings, Regan introduces the 'moral community' of those beings that have 'inherent value' (a value 'logically independent of their utility for others'). A being has inherent value, in Regan's theory, if it is the 'subject-of-a-life'. Those beings that satisfy this criterion come under two headings: 'moral agents' and 'moral patients'. The former denotes 'normal adult humans'. The latter is a mixed bag of 'infants, young children, and the mentally deranged or enfeebled of all ages', along with 'mentally normal mammals of a year or more'. All members of the moral community have rights as individuals.[29] Singer's position in *Animal Liberation* is based on Bentham. It is a form of utilitarianism, the theory that an action is right to the extent that it tends to maximize overall pleasure and minimize overall pain. Singer writes, 'the conclusions that are argued for in this book flow from the principle of minimizing suffering alone'.[30] As a utilitarian, Singer does not credit the concept of rights; though, like his mentor Bentham, he sometimes stoops to using the word.[31]

Much printer's ink has been spilt over the issue of rights versus utility. But under the skin Regan and Singer are brothers. 'Each to count for one and none for more than one', the Benthamite formula that Singer reproduces with approval and which 'the principle of equality' is meant to encapsulate, is a classic expression of the liberal individualism that, in their different ways, they share.

There is, in Singer's case, a complication that comes from his dividing beings with consciousness into two kinds: individuals (persons) and 'receptacles for experiences'. He draws the line this way: 'Rational, self-conscious beings are individuals, leading lives of their own, not mere receptacles for containing a certain quantity of happiness. Beings that are conscious, but not self-conscious, on the other hand, can properly be regarded as receptacles for experiences of pleasure and pain, rather than as individuals leading lives of their own.'[32] By this criterion, Singer thinks that many of the animals that suffer at our hands qualify as individuals. He thinks this is clearly the case with apes, dolphins and whales, and might apply also with monkeys, dogs, cats, pigs, and various other species.[33] As for the rest of sentient nature, it is hard to know just what to make of his concept of a 'receptacle for experiences'. He thinks chickens might be a case in point. But even as he contemplates this possibility, he speaks of 'the pleasures of chickens': *of* them, not *in* them.[34] In the same vein, he says that every sentient being 'has an interest in experiencing as much pleasure and as little pain as possible'.[35] What can it possibly mean to speak of a *receptacle* having an *interest* in what goes on inside it? In any event, on account of this interest, all sentient beings come within 'the sphere of equal consideration of interests'.[36] Bentham's slogan 'Each to count for one' applies to the lot. In short, Singer's concept of a 'receptacle for experiences', if it is not simply incoherent, is the liberal individual in an attenuated form.

It is here, at the heart of the approach, where Singer and Regan and the rest seem to me to go wrong. In mounting this criticism I do not mean to be attacking the liberal tradition itself. As it happens, I believe it represents a real human achievement to conceive of one another, friend and stranger alike, as entitled to equitable treatment, each of us in our own right. But individualism is not a cure-all. It will do no good where the warp in human relations consists in something other than a violation of the principle of equality. This is obvious in the context of our private relationships, our friendships and partnerships, our dealings with one another within families and groups. It is also true of the twists or knots that occur in the fabric of a society – as with racism and sexism. And, as we have seen, when the liberal model of the individual is imposed on animals, inevitably it diminishes them. It diminishes them because to qualify for rights, or for equal consideration, animals must be thought of as littler individuals or proximate persons, like infants and imbeciles; moral homunculi pursuing their limited interests – limited, that is, when the model of comparison is the life led by us 'normal adult humans'.

But animals are not variations on the theme of Homo sapiens or stunted versions of ourselves. They are not lobotomized people, nor are they infants who will never grow up. (An ape is not a mentally retarded child.) There is something badly flawed about an argument that requires us to think of animals this way; and something wrong with us if we *need* to think of them this way in order to rectify our conduct towards them.

So limited are the interests that animals pursue, according to Singer, that their lives, as a rule, are not as 'valuable' as ours. 'It is not arbitrary', he writes, 'to hold that the life of a self-aware being, capable of abstract thought, of planning for the future, of complex acts of communication, and so on, is more valuable than the life of a being without these capacities.'[37] Whatever 'more valuable' might mean, the concept has lethal implications: 'Normally this will mean that if we have to choose between the life of a human being and the life of another animal we should choose to save the life of the human'.[38] (But not necessarily: the animal might have priority if 'the human being in question does not have the capacities of a normal human being'.[39])

Regan agrees that, all other things being equal, the life of a human being comes first. He asks us to imagine a 'lifeboat' scenario: 'There are five survivors, four normal adult human beings and a dog. The boat will support only four. All will perish if one is not sacrificed.' The question is this: 'Which one ought to be cast overboard?' Regan thinks that the dog should draw the short straw; indeed a million dogs should be cast overboard 'if that is necessary to save the four normal humans'.[40] Why? Because 'no reasonable person would deny that the death of any of the four humans would be a greater prima facie loss, and thus a greater prima facie harm, than would be true in the case of the dog'.[41] In other words, compared to each of the 'normal adult human beings', the dog has less to lose.

Perhaps it is not surprising that Singer and Regan, being normal adult human beings themselves, hold such opinions. But, whatever you make of these views, they sound distinctly odd as the expression of an argument made on behalf of the oppressed animals of the world in the name of their liberation and their rights. Moreover, if this is what the campaigners *against* speciesism say, the analogy with racism and sexism seems even less compelling.

A JOLT TO THE SYSTEM

I come, at last, to my encounter with the kangaroo, to which I alluded at the beginning of the paper: a case of a creature that knew, in its bones, to stand up for itself. We (my human companion and I) were at a place called Cape Hillsborough on the Queensland coast, a long way from civilization, and serious about seeing marsupials. Someone in a neighbouring cabin told us that if we went down to the beach at sunrise there should be lots of kangaroos for us to feast our eyes on – but to be sure to bring something for them to feast on too. So, we bestirred ourselves at dawn and betook ourselves to the beach, each carrying a paper bag of breadcrumbs and bits of breakfast cereal. We emerged from the forest fringing the bay; and there they were, maybe half a dozen giant rat-like creatures, staking out the shoreline, at least a quarter of a mile away (the tide was out). We were quite content to stand and stare. But not they, not after one of their number spotted us. Suddenly they all did an about-face and came leaping across the sand in our direction. It is hard to convey the odd mixture of exquisite pleasure and mounting terror that we felt as they approached, bouncing along as if there were springs attached to the soles of those oversized feet. They pulled up sharp when they reached us, like a delegation, and waited. Somehow you expected one of them to say, 'We have come from the planet Mars. Take us to your leader.' That they did not speak made it all the more uncanny. For there they stood, upright, and almost as tall as a full-grown normal adult human being. As they grouped around us we doled out the grub as equitably as we could. They were all most polite and patient; with one exception. The roo in question, practically tall enough to look me straight in the eyes, reached out one long slender forearm and grasped me. I say 'grasped' but 'impaled' might be more accurate, for it detained me with long thin talons rather than with fingers or digits. My jacket being new, I went with the flow, leaning forward into this warm but alien chest, while out of the corner of my eye I could see a snout delving into the bag of titbits I was holding.

You could say that this creature had a claim on me; it certainly felt that way. But what sort of claim? Let's say a claim on my humanity. I don't mind calling this a claim on my sympathies. But as soon as I use a word like 'sympathies' I lay myself open to attack. The attempt to apply the language of prejudice and discrimination, of liberation and rights, to our treatment of animals, reflects a reaction against another kind of language, one that sentimentalizes the issues. Words like 'kindness' and 'cruelty', 'love' and 'pity' have (you will say) been done to death. I do not altogether disagree. But, on the one hand, to talk in terms of sympathy is not in itself, or not necessarily, sentimental. On the other hand, sentimentality can appear in other guises. 'The welfare of animal-citizens', says Ryder, 'is as much our concern as is that of humans.'[42] But animals are not citizens; and in its own way, it is just as sentimental to think of them as disadvantaged members of society as it is to dress poodles up to look like people and get them to stagger about on their hind legs, admiring them for their cuteness.

The idea that animals are a victimized group has a powerful appeal to those of us who are looking for a way of articulating our sense that they are wronged and mistreated. It is simple; it is inclusive; and it appears to elevate the issues, making them into a matter of social justice. But it is possible to think that what we do to animals can be just as bad as what we do to each other without folding the one question into the other. It is a mistake to try to carry over the language of 'prejudice' and 'discrimination' from the realm of human affairs, within which it developed with all its complexity, into the somewhat different, somewhat similar, arena of our dealings with animals. Somewhat similar:

certainly there are parallels and there is a degree of overlap. But, in order to come to an understanding about this, it is necessary to take the long way round – the way of meticulous description – rather than opt for the quick fix of a catchword, like 'speciesism'.

There are various ways of forgetting our fellow creatures, various means for burying them – or rather ourselves – alive. Dust settles and so do words. Perhaps what we need are writers who will give us the equivalent of what that roo gave me: a jolt to the system – to the system of our ideas. The writers I have been criticizing do not jolt or change our minds. They see their ideas as challenging; but, fundamentally, what they are challenging us to do is to persist in existing habits of mind. Their 'radical' proposal is to enlarge the citizen roll: to extend the frontiers of civil society so as to include animals within the liberal dispensation (although, like children and the insane, as non-voting members). But when that roo took me in hand, as it were, it was not like a fellow citizen apprehending me in the street. It was more like a creature from another world; or rather, from this one: a reminder that there is more to this world than our cities and our politics; more to us as well: more to our humanity. This 'more' is what I miss in the writings I have criticized: the element of telling surprise. If the prod I received from that kangaroo did not make me jump out of my skin exactly, it did take me out of myself for a moment, the kind of moment that lingers on. That biped left its mark: not as fellow citizen but as fellow creature.[43]

We began with the question 'How should we – we human beings – treat our fellow creatures?' This, I grant, remains the question. Except that it is not a question that can be granted, simply, or taken for granted, but one that must always be worked for, working always against the sludge of words, new as well as overused, that kill thinking and numb our sensibilities. Against this slew of words, we need the *shock* of words.

POSTSCRIPT

Throughout this argument I treat the words 'racism' and 'sexism' as though we know where we stand with them. But I am not sure that I do. It is not so much that I am uncertain what account to give of their meaning. That is true; but, more to the point, I am unsure about what I am doing when I use them; or whether I want to be doing with them what they seem of their own accord to do. Both words are polemical: they serve to deliver a punch to people you oppose. That is not the only way they are used, but even when they are not being used that way they seem to radiate heat. They are like the word 'fascism' in this regard. And, as with 'fascism', the attitudes and the practices they denote are unquestionably pernicious. The trouble is that the use of these words can itself be pernicious – and all too often is. They behave, in a secular and liberal society, the way words like 'heretic' and 'infidel' do in a religious society; that is to say, they are subject to similar vicissitudes. It is an odd and telling fact about us that words that express our moral outrage are prone to being used in ways that are themselves morally outrageous. (This is the starting point for an enquiry into a realm of our language.)

NOTES

1. This chapter is adapted from a talk, of which I gave different versions (under various headings) in the early to mid-1990s at Hebrew University (Jerusalem), Saint Xavier University (Chicago), York University (Toronto) and The University of Chicago. The text here is based on the final version, given at Mansfield College, Oxford, June 1995, under the title 'The Concept of Speciesism'. It is heavily edited.

2. The analogy tends to treat antisemitism as merely a form of racism. This is problematic in itself, but for the purposes of this chapter I let the point go.

3. Being active in the movement that went by this name does not mean endorsing the name by which it went – which I never did. In any case, my activism petered out in the 1990s.

4. Cora Diamond, 'Eating Meat and Eating People', in her *The Realistic Spirit: Wittgenstein, Philosophy and the Mind* (Cambridge, MIT Press, 1991), p.319. The essay was originally published in *Philosophy*, 53 (1978).

5. Ryder says he 'promulgated the awkward word *speciesism*' in his pamphlet 'Speciesism', published in 1970. See his 'The Struggle against Speciesism', in David Paterson and Richard D. Ryder (eds), *Animals' Rights – A Symposium* (Fontwell: Centaur Press, 1979), pp.4; 219, n.8. It would not be surprising if others coined the word independently and on the same basis. I, for one, plead guilty; in a way, I am arguing now against a confusion I fell into, or a temptation I fell for, at one time.

6. Peter Singer, *Animal Liberation* (New York: New York Review of Books, 1990), pp.269 (n.4), 6.

7. It might be objected that 'sexism' is no less 'manufactured' than 'speciesism'. No doubt. I have nothing against neologisms. But they do not always take. The question is whether *this* one will take.

8. Richard D. Ryder, *Victims of Science: The Use of Animals in Research* (London: National Anti-Vivisection Society, 1983), p.5. The whole paragraph from which this extract is taken is in italics.

9. Richard D. Ryder, *Speciesism: The Ethics of Animal Abuse* (Horsham: Royal Society for the Prevention of Cruelty to Animals, 1979) (eight-page pamphlet, unpaginated).

10. See Robert N. Proctor, *Racial Hygiene: Medicine Under the Nazis* (Cambridge, MA: Harvard University Press, 1988) p.132.

11. Tony Kushner has pointed out to me (in conversation) that there is more to the prejudice against people with red hair than just aversion to the colour. There is a 'redhead' stereotype; so it is a trifle hyperbolic to describe such a prejudice as 'skin deep'. Nonetheless, for the reasons given, it is not *racist*.

12. Richard Ryder, 'Experiments on Animals', in Stanley Godlovitch, Roslind Godlovitch and John

Harris (eds), *Animals, Men and Morals: An Enquiry into the Maltreatment of Non-Humans* (New York: Taplinger, 1972), p.81.

13. Ryder, *Speciesism*.
14. Ryder, *Victims of Science*, p.3.
15. Singer quotes the tag line in the preface to the 1990 edition of the book (*Animal Liberation*, p.viii). He says he finds it 'flattering' but adds modestly, 'I don't believe in bibles: no book has a monopoly on truth.'
16. Ibid., p.9. Singer also speaks of 'equality of consideration', 'equal consideration of interests' and 'equal consideration of pain or pleasure'. It seems that these are meant to be alternative ways of formulating the same principle, which he calls 'basic' (p.2).
17. Peter Singer, *Practical Ethics* (Cambridge: Cambridge University Press, 1979), p.20.
18. Maggie Humm, *The Dictionary of Feminist Theory* (Columbus, OH: Ohio State University Press, 1990), p.202.
19. Whenever an extra-terrestrial is brought into the argument, it is never a triffid or a similarly vegetal monster; invariably it is like us. Ryder, for instance, poses the rhetorical question: 'If some creatures from outer space invaded Earth and proved to be stronger or vastly more intelligent than ourselves, would they be justified in ordering us to be vivisected?' (*Victims of Science*, p.3). But what sort of being can *give orders*, if not a human being or one that is human-like? Ryder goes on to speculate how they (the space invaders) might 'explain to us' that they 'naturally regretted' having to perform experiments on us. He even imagines 'one of their scientists' trying to 'justify himself', saying: ' "Please don't think I am a sadist. As a matter of fact I am very fond of humans and keep several as pets." ' The more Ryder fills out the picture, the less alien these aliens sound. In fact they turn out to be just like you and me – only bigger and cleverer. (They are like characters in a fairy tale or children's story: non-human on the outside, human on the inside.) And if the family resemblance were not so close, what sense would it make to ask whether their behaviour can be *justified*?
20. Singer, *Animal Liberation*, p.224.
21. Ibid., p.225.
22. Ibid., p.25.
23. Jan Narveson, 'Animal rights', *Canadian Journal of Philosophy*, 7 (1977), pp.161–78.
24. Tom Regan, 'An Examination and Defense of One Argument Concerning Animal Rights', in his *All That Dwell Therein: Animal Rights and Environmental Ethics* (Berkeley, CA: University of California Press, 1982), p.116.
25. Ibid., p.116.
26. Ryder, *Speciesism*.
27. John Rodman, 'The Liberation of Nature?', *Inquiry*, 20 (1977), p.94.
28. Ibid., p.85. I am conscious of the debt I owe Rodman, whose essay opened my eyes to the depth of the problem with the approach that I am criticizing. I do not, however, follow him when he develops his thesis that liberation movements 'are ultimately all allies' on the grounds that 'the same principles are at stake in every sphere' (p.117).
29. Tom Regan, *The Case for Animal Rights* (Berkeley, CA: University of California Press, 1983). For the moral community, moral agents and moral patients, see pp.152–3. For inherent value and subject-of-a-life, see p.243. For mentally normal mammals, see p.78. Just because an animal does not qualify as a 'moral patient', it does not follow, according to Regan, that we can do with it as we please: see p.391. He leaves open the (purely theoretical) possibility that a being, such as a tree, or a collection of beings, such as a forest, might possess inherent value even though not the subject of a life: see pp.245–6, 362–3 and 395–6.
30. Singer, *Animal Liberation*, p.21.
31. 'My very sparing talk of "rights" in *Animal Liberation* occurs mostly in the context of *ad hominem* arguments. Elsewhere when I talk of rights, I do it, as I have said, as a concession to popular rhetoric.' Peter Singer, 'Utilitarianism and Vegetarianism', *Philosophy and Public Affairs*, 9 (1980), p.327.
32. Singer, *Practical Ethics*, p.102.
33. Ibid., p.103.
34. Ibid., p.104.
35. Ibid., p.102.
36. Ibid.

37. Singer, *Animal Liberation*, p.20.
38. Ibid., p.21.
39. Ibid.
40. Regan, *Case for Animal Rights*, p.351; see also pp.324–5.
41. Ibid., p.324.
42. Ryder, *Speciesism*.
43. On seeing animals as fellow creatures, see also Chapter 19, 'In the Shadow of Dr Moreau'.

CHAPTER TWENTY-ONE

Science and the Image of God

A NEW VISION OF WHO WE ARE

Peter Singer is a distinguished social mammal. Professor of Bioethics in the University Center for Human Values at Princeton, author of numerous books and innumerable articles on ethics and editor of Blackwell's *A Companion to Ethics*, he is one of the most ubiquitous moral philosophers of our time.[1]

In *Rethinking Life and Death*, published in 1994, he made a startling announcement about the place of humankind in the scheme of things.

> Our isolation is over. Science has helped us to understand our evolutionary history, as well as our own nature and the nature of other animals. Freed from the constraints of religious conformity, we now have a new vision of who we are, to whom we are related, the limited nature of the differences between us and other species, and the more or less accidental manner in which the boundary between 'us' and 'them' has been formed.[2]

The whole of this 'new vision' can be condensed into 'the essential Darwinian insight that we are animals too'; or, more precisely, like 'our nearest relatives' the great apes, 'we too are social mammals'.[3] (Hence the quip in my opening sentence.) Singer believes, moreover, that a new ethic flows from this new vision, an ethic that no longer privileges human beings – since the distinction between 'human being' and 'animal' can no longer be sustained.[4]

To avoid misunderstanding, let us be clear that Singer does not deny that there are differences between humans and non-humans. His point is that these differences do not add up to a distinction between humans and animals; that they are merely differences between *one* species of animal, the *human* animal or homo sapiens, and *other* species of animal. You could put it this way: Singer has no objection to distinguishing between humans and non-humans if this is like distinguishing between, say, dogs and non-dogs, cats and non-cats, horses and non-horses. In other words, we can, if we want, divide all animals into two groups, placing animals of one sort in the one group and lumping all other types of animals together in the other group. Thus, if we want, we can divide animals into humans and non-humans. What Singer denies is this: distinguishing humans from non-humans is distinguishing non-animals from animals.

In this chapter I shall try to take stock of Singer's new vision of who we are. Although I shall focus on Singer's work, he is not alone in championing the set of ideas contained in the 'new vision' passage. Go to any bookstore, browse in the popular science section, and you will find an abundance of books expounding one version or another of the idea that we now know that we are nothing more than animals; for example, *Darwin's Dangerous Idea* by philosopher Daniel Dennett and *The Blind Watchmaker* by zoologist Richard Dawkins. They might not agree with each other about ethics, but Singer, Dennett and Dawkins all share one fundamental belief: Darwin was right, Moses was wrong; the *Origin* supersedes Genesis.

Seeing as these writers champion *science*, there is an oddly romantic cast to their language. But that's just it: they *champion* science, entering the lists against myth and superstition – in a word, religion. When Dennett calls Darwin's idea 'dangerous', he does not mean harmful; he means exciting, provocative, daring. It is harmful only to outmoded views that are vulnerable to the truth it contains. The idea in question, of course, is the theory of evolution by natural selection. This is Darwin's 'great idea', and here are some things Dennett says about it. 'I have found not just lay people and religious thinkers, but secular philosophers, psychologists, physicists, and even biologists who would prefer, it seems, that Darwin were wrong.' (Notice that they would *prefer* this. The next quotation, I think, explains why.) 'Darwin's dangerous idea cuts much deeper into the fabric of our most fundamental beliefs than many of its sophisticated apologists have yet admitted, even to themselves.' (Even to *themselves*, as if the truth that Darwin tells is hard to face and calls for moral courage.) The 'basic Darwinian idea ... really does have far-reaching implications for our vision of what the meaning of life is or could be'. (Our *vision* of the *meaning* of life, not just a *theory* of its *origins*, as if Darwin were not merely a biologist but a prophet or sage.) 'In a single stroke, the idea of evolution by natural selection unifies the realm of life, meaning, and purpose with the realm of space and time, cause and effect, mechanism and physical law. But it is not just a wonderful scientific idea. It is a dangerous idea.'[5] I agree with Dennett: Darwin's theory *is* a wonderful idea;

but not a wonder*working* one, which it would be if it could really unify these realms. I agree also that it is dangerous: it must be to cause a rational philosopher to produce such intoxicated prose.

Singer's prose is no less heady. It has the same romantic cast, proclaiming a new and great discovery, one that threatens the outmoded beliefs to which we cling but which promises something even better if only we can overcome our resistance and summon up the courage to embrace it. Some of this shows up in the 'new vision' passage, on which I shall now comment, sentence by sentence, starting with that startling announcement:

> Our isolation is over.

We do not need to know what this means to know it means something momentous. We know this because it is pithy. Even if we do not know what it means we know it augurs well because something that sounds like a punishment or deprivation – isolation – is at an end. 'At last', we sigh, and we still do not know what it means. Who is the 'we' that 'our' refers to? What isolation? If it is over, when did it start? Part of the answer lies in the eerie-sounding pronouncement that comes six sentences before the 'new vision' passage: 'There are other persons on this planet.'[6] This is not directed at a solipsistic individual, someone who believes that she or he is the only person in the world. Singer is addressing, as it were, the solipsism of the species. He is saying that there are other species on earth whose members are persons. Specifically, he means the great apes: chimpanzees, gorillas and orang-utans. But in time, he thinks, it might turn out that persons appear in the guise of other species too; he mentions whales, dolphins, elephants, monkeys, dogs, pigs 'and other animals'.[7] He is being pedantic, rather than romantic, applying a strict concept of person (which looks back to Locke): 'a being with awareness of her or his own existence over time, and the capacity to have wants and plans for the future'.[8] So, if there are more persons than we realized, there are also fewer: 'Not all members of the species *Homo sapiens* are persons, and not all persons are members of the species *Homo sapiens*.'[9] So pedantic (if this is the right word) is he that he argues that '*we* are not, and never were, infants, fetuses, or embryos'. He continues: 'Our lives as *persons* ... did not begin until some time after birth when we ceased to be beings with momentary interests and became "continuing selves".'[10] Never an infant, fetus, or embryo? I think he should speak for himself, for I am positive that I, a human being, was all three. *My* life is from dust to dust. My life as a person did not begin, as Singer thinks his did, 'some time after birth'. *I* was *born*.[11] Be that as it may, there is more to our isolation being over. It is not only a matter of there being 'other persons' but of our being on all fours with all other critters. Our isolation is over because we are no longer the odd one out, which is what Genesis says we are when it says we – and we alone – are made in God's image (Gen. 1:26–7).[12] Now we know better, as the next sentence in the 'new vision' passage states:

> Science has helped us to understand our evolutionary history, as well as our own nature and the nature of other animals.

Think about the components of this sentence and the way they are put together. *Science* has helped us; and somehow as I read this I feel that that capital S would be in place even if the word did not come at the beginning of the sentence; that it suits the standing of science as Singer writes about it. Science has *helped* us, like a benevolent uncle or good Samaritan. It has given us a helping hand, as though there we were, groping in the dark, trying in vain to understand our evolutionary history, when along came Science; and thus we were able to reach the goal of our enquiry. (As if it were possible to make sense of the enquiry *except as* scientific.) It (Science) has also helped us understand 'our own nature'; our *nature*, not just our origins. I am not sure what this means but, borrowing language from Dennett, the implication is that biology cuts deep 'into the fabric of our most fundamental beliefs'. For surely our beliefs about human nature must count among the most fundamental; and when Singer says Science he is referring to biology: to findings in evolutionary theory, ethology and genetics.[13] (As I say, I am not sure what he means, but, on the face of it, for an understanding of human nature it seems sensible to turn to those disciplines called 'humanities'. We might do worse than read Thucydides or *King Lear* or *Crime and Punishment*. Or we might examine the shenanigans in a canvass by Breughel. Or perhaps, for a plunge into the depths of 'human nature', listen to Milosevic exonerate himself.) The sentence goes on to say that Science, which has helped us understand 'our own nature', has helped us understand (in the same breath with just a copula between the two phrases) 'the nature of other animals'. The word 'other', slipped in quietly in front of 'animals', signifying that we are animals too, casually delivers the coup de grâce, cutting us down to size.

However, this comedown, though humbling, is both liberating and enlightening, as the third and final sentence in the passage declares:

> Freed from the constraints of religious conformity, we now have a new vision of who we are, to whom we are related, the limited nature of the differences between us and other species, and the more or less accidental manner in which the boundary between "us" and "them" has been formed.

It is curious that Singer says religious *conformity*, rather than teachings or doctrines. The word suggests that we have been hemmed in by something that has not only constrained our thoughts but our very lives, thus enhancing the joy of being *freed*. The main point, of course, is that what has constrained us is religion, while what has freed us is Science, or the understanding Science has helped us to gain. Moreover, the understanding we have gained with the help of Science is more than scientific: it is a *vision*, a *new* one, of 'who we are' and 'to whom we are related'. *Who* we *are*, not just how humans evolved; to *whom* we are related, not to *what*, as if we were talking about a family tree rather than a taxonomy. These personal pronouns colour the remainder of the sentence, which thus conveys the idea that, thanks to Science, the Berlin Wall of 'the boundary between "us" and "them" ', humans and animals, has come tumbling down. Our isolation is over.

The 'new vision' passage is so rife with confusion that, to quote Dr Abbott in an episode of *Fawlty Towers*: 'There's enough material there for an entire conference.'[14] But, before tackling (some of) the confusion, I first want to examine the effect that this vision has on ethics, bearing in mind that Singer is a moral philosopher and that he derives a new ethic from the new vision. Specifically, what happens when we take the moral question 'How should we treat animals?' and plug in the new vision of who 'we' are? We get an explosion. Putting it more prosaically, I shall argue that if we abandon the distinction between a human being and an animal, the question 'How should we treat animals?', along with all other moral questions, disappears; for morality cannot be a branch of biology.

PIGS, PIGGONS AND PIGGLES

Applying the new vision of ourselves, the question expressed by (a) 'How should we treat animals?' could also be expressed by (b) 'How should we human animals treat non-human animals?'[15] That is to say, in the light of the new vision, (a) and (b) ought to be two different ways of formulating the same question. Seen this way, (a) is merely an abbreviated version of (b). It might be handy to have the abbreviated version, but (b) appears to have a twofold merit. First, it is more explicit, spelling out who the parties are: human and non-human. Second, it clarifies that they have a certain commonality, namely, animality. For it reformulates the question as a question about how one group of animals – human ones – should treat another group – non-human ones. This makes the terms 'human' and 'non-human' mere modifiers of the substantive 'animal,' as if under the skin we and they, humans and non-humans, are substantially the same, and the differences merely, as Singer puts it, 'differences of degree, not of kind'.[16]

So we have, apparently, two different sentences that ask the same question. However, I do not think these two sentences come to the same thing at all. Notice that (b) amends (a) in two places: the phrase 'human animals' is inserted in the subject place (we *human animals* ...) and the qualifier 'non-human' is inserted in the object place (... *non-human* animals). The effect of these amendments is to alter the sense of the question. One way of putting this is to say that the words that are added, taken together, make a statement. The statement they make can be broken down into two parts and is in this vein: 'We human beings are a species of animal' (first part) 'and the question of how we should treat animals is a question about how one species of animal should treat other species' (second part). The first part of this statement reflects Singer's new vision of who we are. The second part is a corollary of the first. I shall call the complete statement the New Vision Claim. Later I shall argue that the first part of the New Vision Claim, though not false, is misleading. But, taking the second part first, it seems to me that what it says *cannot* be true. The question of how we should treat animals *cannot* be a question about how one species of animal should treat other species because, in the relevant sense of the word 'should', it makes no sense to speak about how animals should or should not behave.

Now, there is one sense in which we *can* talk about how an animal 'should' behave, where what we mean is something like this: this is what a healthy individual of its kind would normally do in the circumstances. So, for example, you might say that when the wolf knocks at their door, the three little pigs should run away. That is to say, this is what *should* happen if they are normal, healthy pigs. So, if one of them doesn't scram, there must be something wrong with it. But to say there is something wrong with the pig is not the same as saying that the pig has done something wrong. You could say it has acted strangely; but not badly. And there's the rub. In the relevant sense of 'should', to say that you or I should behave a certain way – for example that we should not be cruel to animals – is to say that if we do then we have acted badly. It is certainly not to say that we have acted *strangely*, for there is nothing strange about human beings acting badly.

But, someone might object: Surely there is a perfectly familiar sense in which we can talk, and do talk, about animals being bad or being good. 'Good dog, Rusty' does not mean 'I am pleased with you because you have behaved like a normal, healthy canine should.' It might mean (and often did mean) the opposite: 'I am pleased with you because you did not run into the road and chase that squirrel when I said "Stay!", even though that went against your nature.[17] You did what you should do. Good dog.' True. And the fact that certain animals are so far inside the circle of our lives that we not only speak *about* them this way but also *to* them deserves closer attention. Be that as it may, to say that Rusty behaves as she should is not to say that she has an answer to the question 'What should I do?' She *could* not have an answer, for there is, for her, no question. The question does not arise for her; it *cannot* arise for her, for she is a dog. But ethics is the raising of this question. And when I say that it makes no sense to speak about how animals should or should not behave, I mean it makes no sense to speak about their having the question 'What should I do?'

I am saying, to recap, that the question 'How should we treat animals?' cannot be reformulated as the question 'How should we human animals treat non-human animals?' If this is not immediately apparent it might be because of the influence of the word 'we'. A question about how *we* should behave seems like a paradigm of a moral question. So, let us take the word 'we' out of question (b). Now it reads: 'How should human animals treat non-human animals?' If this still seems to be a viable question it might be because the word 'human' carries over the everyday meaning it has when it is not used in zoology as a term for a species of animal. So let us take a species other than the human and try asking the corresponding question. Instead of the question 'How should human animals treat non-human animals?', we shall ask 'How should pigs treat non-pigs?' That the question is absurd is obvious. But less obvious is why. It is tempting, but mistaken, to think that the question is absurd in the way in which it is absurd to ask 'How do pigs fly?' But the question 'How do pigs fly?' is absurd only because pigs, as it happens, do not fly. If the facts were otherwise, if they sprouted wings and took to the air, it would not be absurd to ask how they do it. But they do not have wings; they cannot fly; and for this reason the question 'How do pigs fly?' is absurd. It is, so to speak, *contingently* absurd; that is to say, it would not be absurd if the facts

were otherwise. However, the question 'How should pigs treat
non-pigs?' is absurd in a different way or for a different reason. It is
logically absurd; that is to say, the absurdity lies not with facts but with
concepts: with what it means to think of something as an animal and
with the relevant sense of 'should'. The question is absurd because to
think of something as an animal is to think of it as something about
which such questions as 'How should it treat others?' make no sense.
And if it cannot make sense to ask such questions of *any* species of
animal, then, a fortiori, it does not make sense to ask such questions
of the *human* species (the human animal). In short, the question 'How
should human animals treat non-human animals?' does not make
sense.

One possible objection to this line of argument is that I am making
too much of the point that there is a difference between two kinds of
absurdity: the kind involved in 'How do pigs fly?' and the kind
involved in 'How should pigs treat non-pigs?' For, in the first place, it
is not clear that the two questions *are* absurd in different ways. And,
in the second place, whether they are or not does not have the significance I think it has. Here is how the objection might proceed. Suppose
one day a perfectly sober naturalist on a walk in the woods were to
glance up at the sky and catch sight of a beast that in all respects
resembles the animal we now call a pig, complete with short legs,
cloven hoofs, bristly hair and prominent snout – except that the animal has wings on its flanks. This could be described in one of two
ways: either as the discovery of a variety of pig with wings or as the
discovery of a new (pig-like) species that is able to fly: call it a piggon.
(Not to be confused with a pigeon.) It all depends on the definition
of 'pig'. If a pig, by definition, is an animal without wings, then the
creature is piggon not pig. Otherwise it is pig. If pig, then the question
'How do pigs fly?' ceases to be absurd; it was absurd on account of
the facts merely. If piggon, it remains absurd in virtue of the concept
of pig. But whether pig or piggon, piggon or pig, is immaterial. For,
either way, it is conceivable that such an animal would exist; and were
it to exist it would not be absurd to ask how it flies.

Likewise (the objection continues), granted that the question 'How
should pigs treat non-pigs?' is absurd as things stand, it could be said
to be absurd in one of two ways. Either it is absurd on account of the
fact that pigs, as it happens, lack the relevant capacity. Or it is absurd
in virtue of the concept of pig. Either way, it is conceivable that our
sober naturalist would come across a type of animal that, resembling
in all respects the animal we now call a pig, has the capacity to reflect

on its behaviour. It matters little whether the definition of pig is such that we would call this animal a pig or coin a new name for it, say, piggle. The point is this: it is conceivable for such an animal to exist; and were it to exist, whether pig or piggle, it would not be absurd to ask how it should treat other animals.

So (the objection concludes) it is not true that such questions – questions about how one species of animal should treat other species – cannot make sense. Consequently, given that we human beings do have the relevant capacity, given that we can reflect on our behaviour, the question 'How should we human animals treat non-human animals?' makes perfect sense.

In replying to this objection I wish first to say that I have no opinion, one way or the other, on the subject of pigs and wings. Or rather, while I am inclined to regard the having of wings as a logical possibility for a pig, I have no investment in this view. Let naturalists and zoologists argue the toss. Whatever they decide is fine with me. And if they say that a pig with wings is no pig, then I would agree that the question 'How do pigs fly?' is not absurd on account of the fact that they happen not to possess wings but rather in virtue of the concept of pig. I accept, moreover, that a piggon is a conceivable (if improbable) flying animal, so that if such a creature were to exist it would make sense to ask how it flies. But this point does not have the significance my interlocutor thinks it has. For it does not follow that, given that we human beings have the capacity to reflect on our behaviour, it makes sense to ask 'How should we human animals treat non-human animals?' This is because there is a world of difference between a piggon and a piggle.

A way of pointing the difference is to say that the difference between a pig and a piggon is a different kind of difference from the difference between a piggon and a piggle. That is to say, having or not having wings is not like having or not having the capacity to reflect on your behaviour and to ask yourself 'What should I do?' The former is a matter of physiology, the latter pertains to a form of life. This makes the concept of a piggle more complex than the concept of either a piggon or a pig. It makes it complex in something like the way the concept of a human being is complex; and this complexity undermines the argument made in the objection. That argument, you recall, is as follows: It is conceivable for such an animal as a piggle to exist; were piggles to exist it would not be absurd to ask how they should treat animals that belong to other species; therefore it is not the case that such questions – questions that ask how one species of animal should treat other species – cannot make sense. Granting both of the premises, the conclusion does not follow. It begs the question. It assumes that to speak about how piggles *as such* should behave and to speak about how piggles *as animals* should behave are equivalent. But given what piggles are, this is to assume what is at issue.

Given what they are, this is how the matter, as I see it, lies. Suppose one day a piggle were to come across a piggon that has got into a pickle; possibly it has broken its wing and is grounded. The piggle sees the piggon's plight and, being a conscientious piggle, wonders what would be the right thing to do: whether to help the piggon, perhaps to carry it home and nurse it back to health, or whether to walk on by and refrain from interfering in the natural order. Certainly the piggon is an animal; certainly the piggle is too; but the question of how to behave towards the piggon arises for the piggle, and applies to the piggle, not as an animal, not qua member of the piggle species, but as a piggle *as such*: as a *piggle being*, so to speak. We human beings are like piggle beings in this respect.

Recall the New Vision Claim: 'We human beings are a species of animal' (first part) 'and the question of how we should treat animals is a question about how one species of animal should treat other species' (second part). Turning now to the first part (having taken the second part first): the claim that we are a species of animal is not so much false as misleading. It is not false to say that we are animals, since we are: we are hominids, in the order of primates, placental mammals, vertebrates in the phylum Chordata. And, yes, we are *social* mammals. That is to say, we can be classified as such in a taxonomy. But in the context of ethics it is misleading to describe ourselves this way because it tends to give rise to a fallacy. Consider the following parallel: If it is true that we are animals of a certain species, it is also true that we are physical objects of a certain type. That is to say, we occupy space within typical parameters of size, shape and build. So do animals. So, on the face of it, we can make the following claim along similar lines to the New Vision Claim: 'We human beings are a type of physical object' (first part), 'and the question of how we should treat animals is a question of how one type of physical object should treat other types of physical objects' (second part). This claim, like the New Vision Claim, involves an inference from a (true) statement about what we *are* to an analysis of the question 'How should we treat animals?' But this is a non sequitur. From the fact that we are corporeal beings and that animals are too it does not follow that the question of how we should treat them is a question in physics. Likewise, from the fact that we are one species of animal among others it does not follow that the question of how we should treat other species is a question in ethology.

Not only does it not follow, but posing the question in these terms is to lose it. Cora Diamond observes, 'it is not members of one among species of animals that have moral obligations to anything'.[18] In a way, the whole of what I have been saying in this section is just an elaboration of her remark. Singer says something that superficially is similar but is crucially different: 'it makes no sense to hold nonhuman animals morally responsible or culpable for what they do'.[19] But the point applies to animals generally; restricting the point to *non-human* animals is unnecessary and carries a misleading implication. It makes no sense to hold animals, *as such*, morally responsible for what they do. Hence to see ourselves *as* animals – human animals – is to cease to see ourselves as beings for whom it makes sense to raise precisely those issues that Singer the moral philosopher insists upon, issues that can be expressed by the question 'How should we treat animals?'

DISTINGUISHING VISION FROM FACT

So far I have argued that Singer cannot have it both ways: he must give up either his new vision or his new ethic, for the former subverts the very possibility of the latter. It is time to scrutinize the new vision itself. In this section I shall examine its status: What does it mean to call it a 'vision' and does the *Origin* supersede Genesis? In the next (and final) section I shall consider its content: If we look at the world through Singer's eyes, can we see ourselves as human?

Singer insists we are just another species of animal. He asserts this simultaneously as both a scientific fact and as the content of a new vision. But it cannot be both at the same time: either it is a statement of fact or it is a new way of seeing things. If a fact, then it is not exactly news; it would not have been news to Aristotle, an exponent of biology or natural history. If, on the other hand, it constitutes a new *Weltanschauung*, a different view of our place in the scheme of things, then it is not something we can learn from science. Science can teach us many things. But it cannot teach us how to *take* the things it teaches, how to fit them into the larger picture; it cannot *give* us that larger picture. That is not in the gift of science – of *any* science. What Singer is trying to do, it seems to me, is to pull a vision out of a fact; and his rhetoric is so much sleight of hand. This is not to say that we cannot be struck by facts, including scientific facts, such that we come to see the world differently. But our new vision, if we attain to one, is not buried inside the facts as the kernel of truth they contain. A fact, however complex or recondite, is what it is, no more and no less. It bears its truth on its face. It is frank with us. But on the subject of its ultimate significance, it is absolutely dumb. Take the vastness of the universe: its size is a fact. But what does it signify? The absence of God or the greatness of God? It – the fact – does not vouchsafe a reply.

Whenever we try to turn a scientific theory into a thoroughgoing worldview, we leave the province of science behind and enter the realm that philosopher Stephen Toulmin calls 'scientific myth'.[20] Toulmin does not mean a myth that is scientifically sound. He means a myth formed by extending scientific terms 'beyond their original scope'.[21] An image might help explain what he means. Imagine a cloak that fits you perfectly. Now try to imagine spreading the cloak so that it wraps itself around the globe. It would be a stretch, to say the least. One example that he gives is 'Evolution with a capital E'.[22] Take, for example, what Richard Dawkins says in his preface to *The Blind Watchmaker*: he wants to persuade the reader 'not just that the Darwinian world-view *happens* to be true, but that it is the only known theory that *could*, in principle, solve the mystery of our existence'.[23] God knows what he means by mystery. But, putting that to one side, the sentence is at odds with itself. Darwin's *theory* – of evolution by natural selection – is one thing; a Darwinian *world view* quite another. The latter, in Toulmin's terms, is a 'scientific myth'.

Against all such attempts, all grand schemes that purport to be wrought out of the raw material of scientific theory and fact, Toulmin offers the following caution:

> When we begin to look to the scientist for a tidy, a simple, and especially an all-purpose picture of the world; when we treat his tentative and carefully-qualified conclusions as universal certainties; or when we inflate some discovery having a definite, bounded scope into the Mainspring of the Universe, and try to read in the scientist's palm the solutions of difficult problems in other fields – ethics, aesthetics, politics or philosophy; then we are asking of him things he is in no position to give, and converting his conceptions into myths.[24]

This is precisely what I see Singer doing – converting science into myth – when he comes to us from the frontline of evolutionary biology, like Moses or Zarathustra descending from the mountain, proclaiming a new vision and announcing the end of our isolation.

Our isolation, on Singer's account, has been with us for thousands of years. It began in the beginning, with 'the Hebrew view of creation' in Genesis, chapter 1. This is where he locates the 'origins' of the 'distinctive western view' that human life – and only human life – is sacred.[25] Here is a short extract from an interview with Bob Abernethy for the programme 'Religion and Ethics Newsweekly', broadcast on US television in September 1999:

> Abernethy: Some of your critics have accused you ... of abandoning the entire Judeo-Christian tradition regarding the value of human life. What do you say to that?
>
> Singer: I accept the accusation. I think that the Judeo-Christian tradition has an unjustifiable bias in favor of human beings *qua* human beings; to that extent it needs far-reaching revision. If you look at the book of Genesis, you see there the idea that humans are special, that God created humans in his own image and gave them dominion over the other animals.[26]

Singer adds at once, 'Since Darwin, at least, we've known that that's factually false.' 'Factually false': those are his actual words. It is factually true that he said them. Nor is this just a slip of the tongue in front of the camera. He has made similar claims in print elsewhere. In *A Darwinian Left*, for example, he says that the 'view' that there was 'an original Adam' to whom God gave dominion over animals is 'thoroughly *refuted* by the theory of evolution'.[27] In *Rethinking Life and Death* he says, 'With the *disproof* of the Hebrew myth of creation, the belief that human beings were specially created by God, in his own image, was ... undermined. So too was the story of God's grant of dominion over the other animals.'[28] So, Singer means what he says when he describes Genesis as 'factually false'.

There again, what *is* he saying exactly? When he speaks of the *myth* of creation, he *could* be using it as synonymous with 'factually false' (as in 'the myth that everyone in England takes tea at four o'clock', or 'the myth that all professors of moral philosophy are wise'). It is more likely, however, that by myth he means a pre-scientific theory, since he treats the biblical account of creation as something that Darwin *refutes* and *disproves*.

Now, to construe Genesis this way is to treat it as a work – a defective work – of natural history or natural science. You could call this 'a genre mistake'. In a scientific text like the *Origin of Species*, nature is seen as a physical system. Thinking of nature this way, the scientist tries to give a true account of what the world is made of and how it works. In Genesis, the natural world is seen as part of the larger scheme of things within which we lead our lives, rather than as the object that in science we study. It is seen as *creation*: as something that contains or expresses the vision of its *creator*. Thinking of the world *this* way, the reader tries to derive a true understanding of what matters in life. It is an entirely different exercise. The biblical account of creation is not a theory that is false, any more than chalk is inedible cheese. It houses a vision. You could call it a 'myth', but it is neither a fiction nor a pre-scientific hypothesis: it is a 'deep narrative', a story that indicates the underlying significance of things and the larger context of our lives. Myths in this sense of the word cannot be disproved. They are not theses supported by empirical evidence or refuted by the lack thereof. They live and they die; they can be remembered and forgotten; they can fall into disuse or they can be recovered and restored, like the reinstating of the book of the law in the days of Josiah (2 Kings, 23:1–3).

At the same time, there is no denying that people have treated the creation story in Genesis as though it were in competition with secular accounts of the natural world; and they still do. Now, the era matters: there is a world of difference between present-day proponents of 'creation science' and, say, the eight authors of the Bridgewater Treatises, works in natural theology intended to illustrate 'the Power, Wisdom and Goodness of God in the Works of Creation', published in the 1830s, more than two decades before Darwin's *Origin* appeared in 1859.[29] In *our* day and age, the very expression 'creation science' is an oxymoron. So-called 'creation scientists' are guilty of making the same genre mistake that I have attributed to Singer. Singer represents Genesis as outmoded. But it is only a certain understanding of it that is outmoded: his own and theirs.

Singer, Dennett and Dawkins, all of whom speak as if the theory of evolution subverts Genesis, sit at the same table as the creationists, but on opposite sides. Both sides agree that Darwin and Moses are at logger-heads; it's just that they disagree about who is right. From where I am standing, I would not weep if Moses were to visit a plague on both their houses.

SEEING OURSELVES AS HUMAN

'What, in the end, is so special about the fact that a life is human?'[30] If the question has a familiar ring, it is because it is reminiscent of one that is as old as the Hebrew scripture: 'What is man, that thou art mindful of him?' (Psalms 8:4). Singer and the psalmist are, of course, coming at this from opposite ends of the spectrum. The psalmist goes on to note that God has made us 'a little lower than the angels'. Singer holds that we are no higher than the animals. How *could* we be, since we *are* animals? It is a simple matter of logic: nothing can be higher than itself. What he is really asking is this: Why do human animals think – imagine – that they are inherently superior to other animals?

Speaking for myself, I do not. When I watch a rook on the wing in a swirling wind, maintaining its position as it sways above the trees, I marvel at its skill and I do not feel superior. It is not merely that I recognize that I could not perform that manoeuvre. For, equally, watching the downhill events in the Winter Olympics, I recognize that I could not emulate the agility of the athletes. I mean something about the rook that does not apply to the skiers. With the skiers, what I marvel at is the sight of exceptional human beings capable of performing such phenomenal feats. With the rook it is the reverse: its skill comes so naturally: it could be any rook; that is what I marvel at.

Animals impress me with their completeness. They are completely themselves; and they do not need a vision of who they are. I know myself better than to think I can match them in *this*. But *this* is not just a particular faculty or ability; *this* is everything. I can match them and beat them in certain respects, but not in *this*; which is all the more reason to wonder with the psalmist what we are. The answer, according to the same Hebrew scripture, is that we are creatures made in the image of God. So, if God is mindful of us, then we must be mindful too; except that we are not, or not sufficiently. So, this is what we are: beings that are not completely themselves, creatures that fall short of the mark. Our incompleteness means that our humanity is unfinished business. A dog cannot be an undog, a rook not an unrook, but a human being can be inhuman. What does this signify? It means we see ourselves as held to a standard, as if to a covenant. Seeing ourselves this way, we see ourselves precisely as *human*: as human beings and *not* animals. Better and worse, right and wrong, are in our bones on *this* vision of humanity – an old one that I find in Genesis. That is my answer to Singer's question, What is so special about the fact that a life is human?

If we put on our scientific spectacles and peer at ourselves through the lens of biology, what we see is one species of animal among others: the *human* animal. Looked at this way, *of course* there is nothing 'special' about us: something *specific* but nothing *special*. But we do not go through life with these spectacles on. And when we take them off, what do we see? What *I* see is a world populated with people, on the one hand, and animals, on the other. I *live* my life in this world. I wonder what it is like to conduct your everyday business – outside the laboratory – with those scientific spectacles on. I wonder if it is humanly possible.

Seeing ourselves as *not* animals is not like seeing ourselves as not pebbles or not trees. We are not in danger of confusing ourselves with trees or pebbles; there is no need to insist upon the difference. So, paradoxically, the emphatic 'not' in 'we are *not* animals' testifies to our affinity with them. You could call this kinship; and in this sense of kinship lies the basis for a sensibility that could lead us to treat animals differently, seeing them as *with* us, alongside us in creation, rather than merely as resources at our disposal or as obstacles in our path.[31] I hope it does; though I fear this might not happen until pigs have wings and piggle beings walk the earth.

POSTSCRIPT

Singer's view of personhood leads him to put infants on a par with fish: both can feel pain and pleasure but neither has a right to life. 'Since neither a newborn human infant nor a fish is a person, the wrongness of killing such beings is not as great as the wrongness of killing a person.'[32] In rebuttal of a view in which infants have the same moral status as fish, I offer the following anecdote. Faron was born in Lutheran General Hospital, Chicago, on 27 December 1993. Her mother Lenore tells me that she smiled on the second day of her life and laughed on the tenth. I shall let Lenore take over the narrative for a while: 'She was so round and strong and robust that when I'd go to the grocery store people would guess she was six months old when she was only three weeks. They were astounded because she was so aware and responsive and enjoyed things. We called her a little Buddha because she was so round and just liked being held in a seated position and she was so composed and she'd look around and seem to be taking it all in ... Her eyes were so dark and intense everyone assumed they were black until she looked at them with her intense gaze and then they'd suddenly see that her eyes were a very deep blue with curling lashes.'[33] Faron was less than three weeks old when the four of us went out for dinner on my birthday: Lenore, Phillip (her husband and Faron's father), myself and Faron, who occupied the chair opposite me in the restaurant. We drank to the future. One morning, soon after, Lenore went into Faron's room and lifted her up. She was 'dry and light like a husk'. We buried her in Westlawn, a Jewish cemetery on the west side of Chicago. It was early February and the snow lay deep. As I recited the mourners' Kaddish over her grave I thought of those dark eyes and their intense gaze. I grieved over all the experiences – the challenges and tribulations, pleasures and pains – that would never be hers even though they were her birthright: her *human* birthright in her passage from dust to dust.

NOTES

1. This chapter is an amalgamation of two substantially different versions of the same talk given (under various headings) at the Oxford Centre for the Environment, Ethics and Society (Mansfield College, Oxford), Saint Xavier University (Chicago), Council of Christians and Jews (Oxford) and Ampleforth College (Yorkshire) between 1999 and 2003.
2. Peter Singer, *Rethinking Life and Death: The Collapse of Our Traditional Ethics* (New York: St Martin's Griffin, 1994), pp.182–3.
3. Ibid., p.176.
4. Though he makes a vigorous case for this new ethic, he acknowledges that a different – but new – ethic could be derived by abandoning the 'assumptions'; f the old: see ibid., pp.220–2.
5. Daniel Dennett, *Darwin's Dangerous Idea* (New York: Touchstone, 1996), pp.11, 18, 19, 21.
6. Singer, *Rethinking Life and Death*, p.182.
7. Ibid., p.182.
8. Ibid., p.218.
9. Ibid., p.206.
10. Ibid., p.241.
11. This disagreement over the relationship between 'person', 'human' and (indirectly) 'I', shows, as much as anything else, the difference – the chasm – that separates my own approach to life, death and everything in between, from Singer's. I devoted more space to the topic of personhood in one version of the talks on which this chapter is based, looking at the implications he draws for infants, whose moral status he equates with that of fish (ibid., p.220). But this does not fit the flow of the current argument. But see the postscript.
12. Singer quotes verses 26–8 in full (but inaccurately) on pp.165–6 of *Rethinking Life and Death*.
13. Singer, *Rethinking Life and Death*, pp.174–82.
14. 'The Psychiatrist', first broadcast on BBC Television on 26 February 1979.
15. This section of the chapter goes back to my article 'How Do Pigs Fly?', *Oxford Magazine*, 120 (1995), pp.15–17.
16. Singer, *Rethinking Life and Death*, p.171.
17. 'often did mean': Rusty was a real live red setter who lived with us when I was growing up.
18. Cora Diamond, 'Eating Meat and Eating People', in her *The Realistic Spirit: Wittgenstein, Philosophy and the Mind* (Cambridge, MA: MIT Press, 1991), p.333.
19. Peter Singer, *Animal Liberation* (New York: New York Review of Books, 1990), p.224.
20. Stephen Toulmin, *The Return to Cosmology* (Berkeley, CA: University of California Press, 1982). See especially 'Scientific Mythology', pp.19–85.
21. Ibid., p.8.
22. Ibid., p.22.
23. Richard Dawkins, *The Blind Watchmaker* (New York: Norton, 1996) p.xiv.
24. Toulmin, *Return to Cosmology*, p.82.
25. Singer, *Rethinking Life and Death*, p.165.
26. 'An Interview', in Peter Singer, *Writings on an Ethical Life* (New York: Ecco, 2002), p.320.
27. Peter Singer, *A Darwinian Left* (London: Weidenfeld & Nicolson, 1999), p.16 (emphasis added).

28. Singer, *Rethinking Life and Death*, p.171 (emphasis added).
29. Peter J. Bowler, *Evolution: The History of an Idea* (Berkeley, CA: University of California Press, 1983), p.123. They were published between 1833 and 1836. An early example of the genre is John Ray, *The Wisdom of God Manifested in the Works of Creation* (1691).
30. Singer, *Rethinking Life and Death*, p.105.
31. It will be said that this departs from the view in Genesis concerning human 'dominion' over animals: see, for example, Genesis 1:26. But (as a vast literature on the topic demonstrates) the meaning of 'dominion' is open to wide interpretation.
32. Ibid., p.220.
33. The quotes are from an email, 6 February 2002. I am grateful to Lenore and Phillip for their permission to remember Faron in this way.

CHAPTER TWENTY-TWO

Next Year in Neverland

THE CONCEPT OF THE CHILD

When we speak of the rights of the child, of whom are we speaking?[1] The answer, of course, is any child and all children. But what do we mean by 'child'? In one sense of the word, anyone who is somebody's daughter or son – a first generation descendant – is a child; and as Wendy says to 'the lost boys' when she begins her bedtime story, 'Almost everything is a descendant.'[2] But this is not the sense of the word that is appropriate. When we speak of the rights of the child, we mean 'child' as distinct from 'adult', not 'parent' (although we might speak of children's rights vis-à-vis their parents). So, the question is: How do we distinguish a child from an adult? One answer is, by age, a child being a minor, a person under full legal age. On the face of it, this is the answer contained in the United Nations Convention on the Rights of the Child (UNCRC). Article 1 stipulates that for the purposes of the Convention, 'a child means every human being below the age of eighteen years unless, under the law applicable to the child, majority is attained earlier'. But how much earlier? Though it might be hard to specify, there must be a lower limit. Suppose, *ad absurdum*, a nation were to lower the age of majority to 5. This would make the provisions of the UNCRC inapplicable to human beings over the age of 4. There is nothing in Article 1 to prevent this, but it would go against the whole spirit and intention of the Convention. This shows that formal legal status – being a minor – is not at the heart of the UNCRC's definition of the child. There is a substantive concept that lies in the background of Article 1. This is the concept of the child that I wish to explore.

A child, we are saying, is not an adult. Then what is an adult? Not a child. We can play this game till pigs can fly or Peter Pan grows up, but it will not get us any nearer to distinguishing the one from the other. Let us begin with the obvious: the fact emphasized by René Descartes, the seventeenth-century French philosopher, who points out that 'we were all children before being adults'. He emphasizes this fact because it has, he thinks, profound human significance. As adults, he says, 'our judgments' are not as 'pure or solid as they would have been had we the full use of our reason from the moment of our birth and had we never been led by anything but our reason'.[3] We do not need to follow him further than this, nor even so far. If we set aside his exclusive focus on reason and judgement and if we take his observations quite generally, they seem to hint at something like the following concept of childhood: a period in life that precedes adulthood, in the course of which we develop certain faculties, the full possession of which constitutes an adult's estate. Or, more succinctly, a child is someone growing up.[4] This is the concept of the child encapsulated in the UNCRC, with its focus on the child's 'development', its emphasis on 'the evolving capacities of the child', and the principle that the rights of the child should correspond to those evolving capacities.[5] It is a broad concept, covering everything from infancy to adolescence.[6] 'A child', concludes historian Anna Davin, 'is someone at a certain stage in the life cycle.'[7] If this 'stage' is understood to subsume several successive stages, and if it is understood that the next stop is adulthood, then we seem to have a working answer to our question.

Or do we? I remember, as a child, wincing when grown-ups used the word 'stage' to talk about children's feelings, interests, and experiences. This was because it sounded patronizing; as if 'stage' came with 'mere' clinging to it; as if the things that mattered to me and my friends were trivial; as if we were going through a phase out of which we would grow, and childhood were just a preliminary to the real thing: being grown-up. Of course, I have grown out of that stage now. I no longer mind if childhood is called a stage. (It does not bother me in the least.) However, there is something in my juvenile reaction to the word that I think is true and which I wish to carry forward into this chapter. If childhood is a step in the direction of adulthood, it is not merely a means towards the end of growing up; it is also a state in its own right. When we speak of children having rights, we think of childhood as an end in itself.[8]

At the same time, a child is not a completely different form of life from that of an adult human being. Consider, in contrast, the caterpillar. A caterpillar is a stage in the life cycle of a butterfly or moth. But tell that to the caterpillar, which thinks it is a worm with legs and not a member of the lepidopteran family. If it senses the life it harbours within, if it feels those six insect feet kicking in its belly, or the brush of wings against the inside of its skin, it probably thinks an alien creature has invaded its body. Munching its way across green leafy pastures, what does it know about life on the wing? To all intents and purposes, when the butterfly hatches, the caterpillar dies. It does not grow up. Children, in contrast, grow up. (All except one, of course, but we shall get to him soon.) They do not incubate the adult within; they develop in the direction of adulthood over time.

So, let us by all means think of the child as someone at a certain stage in life. But we must be clear that there are two sides to this concept. On the one hand, a child is someone evolving into an adult. On the other hand, there is more to being a child than potentially being a man or woman: there is the actual thing itself, today, now, for its own sake, and not for the sake of a future grown-up state. These two elements are in tension, and it is easy to forget one when insisting upon the other. Yet, if we are to hold on to our concept of the child, they should fit together, like two sides of a coin, or a thing and its shadow. How can we unite them in our minds?

In this chapter, I take my cue from Wendy. When she discovered Peter foolishly trying to stick his shadow on with soap, she resorted sensibly to needle and thread.[9] I shall imitate her example, after a fashion, by trying to sew the two sides of our concept together; only the thread I shall use is imaginary. Specifically, I shall try to imagine, side by side, the two central figures in J.M. Barrie's story. Other characters will come into the picture, but the focus will be on Wendy and Peter. This is partly because Barrie himself emphasizes their relationship, and partly because, on my reading, they reflect the two sides of our concept of the child.[10] Consequently, I shall ignore vast tracts of the narrative and drama. I say 'narrative and drama' because the story I refer to is told in two places: the novel *Peter and Wendy* and the play *Peter Pan*.[11] I shall draw on both sources freely, ignoring differences between them, taking what I want and neglecting to point out what does not suit my purpose. Some might call this cheating, but it isn't. I am playing by the rules, the ones I have made up for the occasion. (Peter would approve.) For the aim of the game is not really to arrive at an adequate reading of the story. The aim is to use the story to bring our concept of the child to the imagination: to imagine the idea of growing up. (Peter would scowl.) Keeping this image – the image of the child – in mind, I shall conclude by arguing that when we speak about children's rights, we are not speaking simply about human rights for young people. It makes a world of difference that it is the *child* of whom we speak.

THE WORLD OF THE CHILD

Peter Pan

If we conceive of the child as someone at a certain stage in life, a young person who is growing up, then nothing and no one seems as antithetical as Peter Pan, 'The Boy Who Would Not Grow Up'.[12] This singular fact is his defining difference: 'All children, except one, grow up.'[13] So, does Peter Pan represent another concept of the child, a viable alternative to the one I am exploring in this chapter? If so, and if he were to write his own Convention on the Rights of the Child, or if one were to be written for the likes of him (except that he has no peer), it would have to be a substantially different document, based on the principle of the *non*-evolving capacities of the child. I imagine him (or his lawyers) erasing the word 'development' every time it occurs in the UNCRC. Article 29, for example, states that the education of the child shall be directed to the 'development of the child's personality'. *That* would have to go, for a start. In fact, the whole of this article, as well as the previous one, would be anathema to Peter Pan, especially the bit about making 'primary education compulsory' (article 28 (a)).[14] In place of the present articles 28 and 29, with their several subclauses and sub-subclauses about the right to education, there would be a terse statement along these lines: 'States Parties recognize the right of the child not to go to school.' I suppose the supreme right in Peter Pan's Convention would be this: 'Every child has the right not to grow up.' All other rights would spell out the ramifications of this basic right. In the light of this, it is worth asking the question, Could Peter Pan conceivably exist?

The question can be put this way: Is Peter Pan a real boy? In the story, he is certainly called a boy by the narrator, by other characters, and by himself. 'Boy' is the first word Wendy uses when she is woken by his sobs in her nursery and sees him for the first time. She addresses him thus: 'Boy, why are you crying?' Crying is certainly something boys do; so is denying they cry, which Peter does a minute later. Wendy thinks he is crying because (as he has just told her) he does not have a mother. ' "I wasn't crying about mothers", he said rather indignantly. "I was crying because I can't get my shadow to stick on. Besides, I wasn't crying." ' The logic of this retort does rather tend to reinforce the impression that Peter is a veritable child. He loves to play, like a child, and can 'never resist a game'. He is 'greedy' for stories, especially if they are about him.[15] He is cocky and conceited, cunning and naive, selfish, generous, heartless, kind. He is mischievous. He has a strong sense of fair play and wants to kill pirates. (He also wants to *be* one.) So far, so real.

He could still be a real boy when he tells Wendy that he does not want to grow up. ' "I don't want ever to be a man", he said with passion. "I want always to be a little boy and to have fun." '[16] Any boy might say this with passion. But, given the sort of boy Peter is, does it mean the same when *he* says it? Let us consider the implications of the difference – the defining difference – between Peter and other children. All children, except Peter, grow up. To begin with, this does not mean that *in fact* all other children grow up. The facts of life are sadly different. The point, I take it, is that *in principle* they grow up; they grow up, all other things being equal. (Hence the special poignancy of the death of a child: the sense that they have lost a future into which they were still growing.[17]) So, when other children say 'I don't want to grow up', they are, as it were, defying nature (like an apple on a tree saying 'I don't want to fall down'). But when Peter says it, what does it mean? For he is in the opposite case. Not growing up is not just a contingent fact about him, something that happens to be true; it is written into his very nature. He *sounds* like a real child when he says, 'I don't want ever to be a man. I want always to be a little boy and to have fun.' It *sounds* like a protest against fate. But it cannot be one, not *really*, since it precisely *is* his fate to be the boy who never grows up. So, how exactly should we hear his plaint?

While we are pondering this, let us turn to the question of Peter's parentage. If he is a real child, whose child is he? He tells Wendy that he does not have a mother, and that he has not 'the slightest desire to have one'. This does not mean that he *never* had one. Indeed, he goes on to tell Wendy that he ran away from home when he 'heard father and mother talking of what I was to be when I became a man'. However, it is difficult to accept this story at face value, partly because he says, almost in the same breath, 'I ran away the day I was born'. Either he was unbelievably precocious as a newborn infant, or he is confused, or this is a piece of honest make-believe. (For Peter, 'make-believe and true were exactly the same thing'; as far as I am aware, he never lies.) And then there is the story he tells about the day he flew home, only to find 'the window was barred, for mother had forgotten all about me, and there was another little boy sleeping in my bed'. The narrator remarks, 'I am not sure that this was true, but Peter thought it was true'. So, even if *Peter* thinks his account of his origins is true, *we* might not be so sure. In the final analysis, we cannot be certain that he was born at all. For the narrator says, 'Now, if Peter had ever quite had a mother, he no longer missed her.'[18] If Peter were a real boy, this 'if' and 'quite' would be unthinkable. Real children come from the womb; there are no ifs and quites about it.[19]

Furthermore, real children have a determinate age that changes with the years. They have birthdays. But not Peter.[20] Not only does he never grow up, he never grows older. When Wendy asks him how old he is, he replies, 'I don't know, but quite young'.[21] 'Quite young' is quite broad. But based on his behaviour and appearance, we can surely set some outer limits. He is not a toddler. And although his pranks are adolescent, there are clear indications that he is pre-pubescent. (His horror of beards suggests that he thinks puberty is beyond the pale.[22]) He strikes me as somewhere in the region of 8 or 9 or 10 years old. And yet, he still has 'all his first teeth'.[23] He still has them, moreover, at the end of the tale, after the years have come and gone and 'rolled on again', and Wendy is married with a daughter named Jane, and the nursery window blows open of a sudden, and Peter drops on the floor. 'He was exactly the same as ever, and Wendy saw at once that he still had all his first teeth.'[24] He, however, does not yet realize that she has changed and become a grown-up woman. She tries to prepare him for the shock: 'Peter! Peter, do you know how long it is since you were here before?' 'It was yesterday.' Now, it is one thing to say, as Wendy tells her daughter just before Peter drops in, that he has 'no sense of time' and that 'all the past was just yesterday' for him. He would not be the first child, nor the last, to live in the moment. It is another thing to say that *time*, as it were, has no sense of *him*. This makes him timeless. Which makes him different not just from other children but from all humankind. As Jane observes, 'Everybody grows up and dies except Peter, doesn't they?'[25] All children, except one, grow up. All people, except one, are mortal. Peter is that one. Then who or what is Peter?

This question rings a bell. In their 'final bout' aboard the pirate ship the *Jolly Roger*, Captain James Hook and Peter Pan are locked in combat. The children are watching, spellbound. To the brigand, Peter 'is less like a boy than a mote of dust dancing in the sun'. The elusive Pan pirouettes and lunges, and the captain's cutlass goes clattering to the deck. Hook appears undone! But instead of pressing home the advantage, Peter picks up the weapon by its blade, and 'presents the hilt' to his foe. ''Tis some fiend fighting me!' exclaims the perplexed Hook. 'Pan, who and what art thou?' Peter's reply hangs in the air, poised like the sword of Damocles. 'The children listen eagerly for the answer, none quite so eagerly as Wendy.' Then Peter's spirit strikes. 'I'm youth, I'm joy, I'm a little bird that has broken out of the egg.'[26]

Handing Hook back his sword, Peter is keeping the fight – the game – alive. He is perpetuating the moment. This is what drives him; or rather, he *is* that drive. He is youth: not *a* youth, not an individual child, but youth itself. Refusing to grow up, he is not an actual boy protesting against fate; he is the spirit of that protest. If from start to finish he is 'a strange boy', it is not because he is unlike other real children, but because, unlike other children, he is not real. Wounded by Hook and stranded on Marooners' Rock in the mermaids' lagoon, the waters rising inexorably, Peter revels in the unfamiliar feeling of fear: he feels it as 'a drum beating in his breast *as if* he were a real boy at last' (emphasis added). He exclaims, 'To die will be an awfully big adventure.' But his exhilaration is pathetic, for he is *not* a real boy. When Tinker Bell is fading away after drinking from the poisoned chalice, Peter 'rises and throws out his arms he knows not to whom, perhaps to the boys and girls *of whom he is not one*' (emphasis added).[27] He is not one of them because he cannot age and he cannot die – because he does not live. And yet uniquely, he can reach them. 'There were no children there, and it was night-time; but he addressed all who might be dreaming of the Neverland, and who were therefore nearer to him than you think; boys and girls in their nighties, and naked papooses in their baskets hung from trees.'[28] He is 'nearer than you think' to children in the world, nearer than anyone could possibly be, because he is no distance at all from them; he is *part* of them, but not *one* of them. (Which is why, despite the fact that he is joy, he is 'tragic'.[29])

This, as I read it, is 'the riddle of his being' of which he can never 'quite get the hang'.[30] Nor can we, because he does not quite hang together: he keeps having adventures without time ever lapsing. If he *seems* viable as a person, it is because his exploits and experiences appear to make up a segment of a human life.[31] But actually, they don't, for Peter Pan only ever occupies the present moment; he does not exist on either side of it. The story creates the illusion of a real boy by making that moment last longer than an instant – which perforce it must, for otherwise there would *be* no story. However, when the fairy dust has settled, the fiction does not fly: Peter Pan could not be a real person. And yet, what he personifies *is* real, or a real part of what it means to be a child. If we try to imagine childhood as purely a state in its own right, wholly an end in itself, something that exists for its own sake only and not at all in relation to the future adult that the child becomes – we imagine Peter Pan. And if Peter Pan is ultimately unimaginable – if he could not conceivably exist – then this image of childhood is incoherent too. Or incomplete: it is only half the story. Turning to Wendy, we meet Peter's other half. More accurately, we meet a girl who represents the other element in our concept of the child: the emerging adult.[32]

Wendy

In the young Wendy, the emphasis on the future adult is so pronounced that she is in danger of ceasing to be a child altogether. She is 'every inch a woman, though there were not very many inches'.[33] She is so closely identified with her mother, who she pretends to be at the beginning of the story, and whose style of life she leads at the end, that she is practically a miniature Mrs Darling.[34] In the Neverland, the boys go down on their knees outside the house they have built for her, begging her to be herself: 'O Wendy lady, be our mother.' For a moment she demurs (or pretends to), protesting that she is 'only a little girl' and has 'no real experience'. But Peter explains that what they need 'is just a nice motherly person'. 'Oh dear', she sighs, 'you see I feel that is exactly what I am'. As if to prove the point, she promptly chides them, 'Come inside at once, you naughty children; I am sure your feet are damp.'[35] They call her 'Mummy', and she plays the part by frequently saying, 'Oh dear'.[36] She is a 'housewife'. In their home under the ground, she makes the rules, cooks the meals, does the washing, darns the clothes, tells them stories, and tucks them up in bed at night. She loves to give them their medicine, 'and undoubtedly gave them too much'. She is such a nice motherly person, and her hands are so full with 'those rampagious boys of hers', that there are 'whole weeks' when she is 'never above ground'. In fact, the prospect of looking after them was the main attraction by which Peter had lured her to fly away with him to the Neverland in the first place. '"Wendy", he said, the sly one, "you could tuck us in at night." "Oo." "None of us has ever been tucked in at night." "Oo", and her arms went out to him. "And you could darn our clothes, and make pockets for us. None of us has any pockets." How could she resist?' Even when the children have their great adventure with the pirate ship, her point of view is strictly grown-up. 'No words of mine can tell you how Wendy despised those pirates. To the boys there was at least some glamour in the pirate calling, but all that she saw was that the ship had not been scrubbed for years.' It is exactly what Mrs Darling would have noticed; both of them liked everything to be shipshape and 'just so'.[37]

So, Wendy is 'Mother Wendy'.[38] But there is also Wendy the would-be girlfriend or mate. For, while her feelings for Peter are partly maternal, they are also romantic. In the frame of this story, such feelings are not in the repertoire of a child; they are distinctly adult. Tinker

Bell and Tiger Lily, who are attracted to Peter in the same way, are both portrayed as young women rather than as little girls. (Tinker Bell, of course, is a fairy, but love conquers the species divide.[39]) Wendy understands that they are her rivals in love. She feels pangs of sexual jealousy when Peter mentions their names. (Tinker Bell feels the same way, only more so: she 'hated' Wendy 'with the fierce hatred of a very woman'.[40]) All of this, naturally, goes over Peter's head. Finally, Wendy forces the issue. It is the dramatic climax of their relationship:

> WENDY: (knowing she ought not to probe but driven to it by something within) What are your exact feelings for me, Peter?
> PETER: (in the class-room) Those of a devoted son, Wendy.
> WENDY: (turning away) I thought so.[41]

Wendy knows she ought not to inquire into his feelings about her. But why shouldn't she? Perhaps she feels it is intrusive, or unbecoming, or unwise. But fundamentally, it is inappropriate. For there is nothing within Peter that answers to the 'something within' Wendy that is driving her. Peter is 'in the class-room'; that is to say, he is being a good little boy, behaving himself, giving 'Miss' what he thinks is the right answer, the one she wants to hear. But his answer could not be more wrong. There could not be a deeper gulf between them than the one that opens up at this moment. It is the gap between her grown-up emotion and his youthful naivety. It is a woman falling for a boy as if he were a man. The faux pas is too great. She turns away.

Ironically, it is precisely Peter's boyish insouciance that saves Wendy. In the story, he rescues her from the pirates. In this reading of the story, he saves her from a fate worse than Hook: growing up too soon. He saves her, that is, from being possessed by the future adult, the 'something within' that is driving her. 'She was one of the kind that likes to grow up. In the end she grew up of her own free will a day quicker than other girls.'[42] So, if Peter is The Boy Who Would Not Grow Up, Wendy is The Girl Who Could Not Wait To Grow Up. Both, in their opposite ways, are unlike other children: he is the exception to the rule that all children grow up, she is its exceptional illustration, its clearest exponent. In Wendy, the future adult presses so hard that you wonder: Why only a day? Why doesn't she grow up a week ahead of other girls, a month, a year, five years; or even an entire childhood? Who or what keeps the woman in Wendy at bay? It is Peter, oblivious to her amorous advances. For, as I shall try to elucidate, if Wendy would have got her man, she would have lost her portion in the Neverland – to where we now must turn.

The Neverland

How do you approach the Neverland?[43] It is a baffling question, whether you mean the place or the topic. Peter Pan's directions for going there are: 'Second to the right and then straight on till morning.'[44] But what sort of directions are these? Surely, they lead no place. But in that case, they point the way, since 'no place' is just what 'Neverland' means – which is a good way of approaching the topic. For this no place is an island, like another land that never was: More's Utopia, whose name means the same.[45] The story of Peter Pan and Wendy, in other words, belongs to utopian literature. The Neverland is an island paradise for children.[46]

Being for children, this no place is like no other no place on earth. The categories are different. I do not mean the creatures, though there are numerous unearthly or fabulous beings, including mermaids, fairies, and Never birds. I mean the fabric of reality: space and time do not behave themselves here, or do not behave the way they do in an adult (no) place. Time is not unreal, it's just unruly: 'It is quite impossible to say how time does wear on in the Neverland, where it is calculated by moons and suns, and there are ever so many more of them than on the mainland.' The seasons do not take their proper turns: 'It is summer time on the trees and on the lagoon but winter on the river, which is not remarkable on Peter's island where all the four seasons may pass while you are filling a jug at the well.' And space expands like a toy balloon, so that all ten children can tramp into Wendy's house at the same time, even though it has been built to fit her snugly: 'In they went; I don't know how there was room for them, but you can squeeze very tight in the Neverland.' The whole island seems squeezed very tight, given its geography of mountains, forest, river, and lagoon. This is because its scale is proportioned to the fun it sustains: it is 'very compact, not large and sprawly with tedious distances between one adventure and another, but nicely crammed'.[47] In short, the island is a whole world, a *child's* world where even time and space play up.

It is a *world*, not a *place*, not a location on the globe, not even an imaginary one. It is no use trying to find it on a map, because only mainland shows up on maps. You can only get there by flying, which means being a child, for when you grow up you forget how to fly. It took the children 'many moons' to get there, 'and, what is more, they had been going pretty straight all the time'. But which moons are being counted here? The one that revolves round the earth once a month, or the plethora that appear in the Neverland sky? (After all, the children are already high on fairy dust.) Furthermore, the Neverland is so perilously close that 'in the two minutes before you go to sleep it becomes very nearly real'; hence the need for night-lights. A mere 'film' separates it from the mainland – which Peter (and Tinker Bell) break through at the beginning, startling Mrs Darling as she dozes in the nursery. Summing up, we can say with some assurance that there is no way to make sense of these facts. Then what is the nature of the gap that separates island from mainland?[48]

Is it fantasy? Is the island mere make-believe? It is, if you approach it with the point of view of someone in 'the grown-up world', someone like Mr Darling in the city, 'where he sits on a stool all day, as fixed as a postage stamp'.[49] If that is your approach, the island will forever recede and be a land you never find: a Neverland.[50] To put it another way, in an adult accounting of 'the real world', the world of a child exists purely as make-believe; it has no standing other than as fantasy. But when Wendy, John and Michael approach the Neverland for the first time and are fired upon by Long Tom, the pirates' big gun, whose thunderous boom fills them with terror, the children 'learn the difference between an island of make-believe and the same island come true'.[51] So, it is *not* make-believe; it is real. But what does this mean? What would Mr Darling say it means? He would scoff at the very notion. He would say (I presume), 'The idea of a make-believe island that comes true is itself make-believe', and file it under Stuff and Nonsense. In a way, he would be right. For what does it mean to say that the island has 'come true'? It does not mean that what was once make-believe has now become real by the normal criterion of reality, the one used on the mainland; it means the *criterion* has changed. The *perspective* has shifted from adult's to child's.

Thus, on the island, the children still distinguish between make-believe and true – but on their own terms.[52] Sometimes, their distinction corresponds to the one made on the mainland. For example, the children know, in a perfectly straightforward sense, the difference between real and pretend dinners.[53] But at other times, the distinction seems to cut across the usual one. So much so, that it is hard to say that there is a *criterion* of reality on the Neverland: a hard and fast basis for telling the difference between true and pretend. When the boys construct Wendy's house, they really do gather branches, and lay a mossy green roof on top of its red walls. There are windows with yellow blinds, and a door that actually opens. The sole of Tootles's shoe makes 'an excellent knocker', while John's hat, with its top pushed out, furnishes a chimney. The moment it is perched upon the roof, the chimney starts to smoke. Is the smoke as real as the rest? Perhaps so, on the principle that function follows form, as if this were a law of children's nature. Or is the smoke just pretend, like the roses 'peeping in' at the window, which, on Peter's stern command, 'they made-believe to grow'?[54] It is hard to say, and wrong to try. For the point is this: the smoking chimney *makes sense* in this world. There is, in short, a *world* of difference between Mr. Darling's office and Peter's island. Going from the one to the other, from the mainland to the island, is a sea-change.[55]

For the children, it is a homecoming:

> Wendy and John and Michael stood on tiptoe in the air to get their first sight of the island. Strange to say, they all recognized it at once, and until fear fell upon them they hailed it, not as something long dreamt of and seen at last, but as a familiar friend to whom they were returning home for the holidays.

They can even pick out, from their crow's-nest in the sky, features of the island beneath them – features that in a sense belong to them. ' "I say, John, I see *your* flamingo with the broken leg." "Look Michael, there's *your* cave." "John, what's that in the brushwood?" "It's a wolf with her whelps. Wendy, I do believe that's *your* little whelp" ' (emphasis added). They have never visited the island before, but it is theirs. So much so, that 'the island was looking out for them. It is only thus that anyone may sight those magic shores.'[56] In other words, the Neverland comes naturally to the children. They feel like they are coming home (or that home is coming to them) because they *are* at home here. Here everything is on *their* terms, not on terms set by adults.

Now, to speak of 'their' terms is to speak of the terms set by Peter. For the Neverland is not just his place of abode, it is his domain, his dominion. The island is animated by his spirit and subject to his will. 'Feeling that Peter was on his way back, the Neverland had again woke into life.' This is how it pays homage to Peter. The wild beasts go on the prowl, greeting him 'in the way they think he would like them to greet him'. The mermaids 'for the same reason' commence combing their hair. The pirates 'for the same reason' slink ashore in their longboat. 'The whole island, in short, which has been having such a slack time in Peter's absence, is now in a ferment because the tidings has leaked out that he is on his way back; and everybody and everything know that they will catch it from him if they don't give satisfaction.' Peter lords it here; even the sun is 'another of his servants'. His chief antagonist understands this boy's sway. ' "So, Pan", said Hook at last, "this is all your doing." "Aye, James Hook", came the stern answer, "it is all my doing."'[57]

In other words, the entire Neverland serves the purpose of this youth – who is the spirit of youth. It is *his* island, where children can be children; this is its very raison d'être. And it is Wendy's reason for being there, whether she knows it or not. It is true that Peter lures her to his island by appealing to her maternal longings. But he has already won her 'intense admiration' because he is acquainted with fairies. Moreover, he uses mermaids as bait as well. ' "And Wendy, there are mermaids." "Mermaids! With tails?" "Such long tails." "Oh", cried Wendy, "to see a mermaid!" ' Fundamentally, Peter addresses her as a child, and his island is a child's safe haven. Among the marauding beasts, predatory pirates, and other Neverlandish hazards, Wendy is perfectly safe. She is safe, as a child, from the encroachments of the adult within. Here on the island she can indulge her sense of responsibility to her heart's content. She can darn umpteen pairs of socks, dish out bucketfuls of bitter-tasting medicine, tuck up lost boys in bed all night, mutter 'Oh dear' every other minute; and still be a child. For she *really* does these things; but she does them in a child's world. So, there is no danger that she will grow up overnight. On Peter Pan's island, growing up is 'against the rules'.[58] I think this means against its concept: growing up is *inconceivable* on the Neverland, the land of never growing up.

Even after the children return to the mainland, Wendy receives visits from Peter.[59] She accompanies him back to the Neverland the following year 'to do his spring-cleaning'; and again two years later, for the same purpose.[60] The deeper point being this: taking her to his island, he brings her back to the present, against the tenacious pull of the future adult. Thus, when the woman in Wendy woos Peter, her very childhood is at stake. For Pan, the universal spirit of youth, is the soul of the Neverland. If Peter ceased to be Pan, the Neverland would vanish. And if Wendy were to win Peter's hand, he would cease to be Pan: he would be a man. No Pan, no Neverland. No Neverland, no childhood. So, when Wendy courts Peter and risks losing Pan, she risks all.[61] Not that she knows it. And not that there is the slightest chance of the gallant Peter being her beau; for he is nature's own gentleman.

In sum, Peter, the spirit of youth, is not a real boy. Wendy is a flesh-and-blood human being; but take Peter away from Wendy, and she reverts prematurely to being a little woman. Put them together, and a real child comes into being. A real child, according to the concept under discussion in this essay, is someone at a certain stage in life, a young person growing up. A real child is evolving into an adult – but concomitantly has the experience of not being one. This experience –

of not being grown-up – is precisely what the Neverland provides for. Put it this way: In the story's accounting of 'the real world', childhood is not just a preliminary to the real thing: the things that matter to a child are just as real as the bills the Darlings have to pay or their dinner party at number 27.[62] In effect, the Neverland is a representation of make-believe on the mainland, representing it as real; this is 'the difference between an island of make-believe and the same island come true'. Within its 'magic shores', the world of the child is real – as real in its own right as the grown-up world.

Thus, through the alchemy of the Neverland, our concept of the child is transmuted into an abiding image that floats before our mind's eye: Wendy and Peter Pan side by side in flight.

THE RIGHTS OF THE CHILD

If we can manage to keep this image in mind, perhaps we shall not lose sight of whom we are speaking when we speak of the rights of the child.[63] Wendy, as a little girl, needs to be given the chance to take responsibility for matters that will concern her as a grown woman. But she is *not* a grown woman; and to treat her as such would be, as it were, to adulterate her youth. One way of talking about this is to say that a vein of play must run through all her work; otherwise she will become a drudge, even if a contented one (for she wants to do the work). She is entitled to that vein; and equally to the process that leads it to wane over time. Peter grants her the first right, though he would deny her the second.[64] But she is entitled to both because both belong to a child's estate. She is, in short, entitled to her childhood.

The right to childhood is not mentioned in the UNCRC, but it is proclaimed by the convention as a whole; it is the sum of its parts.[65] If we forget the sum, we are liable to mistake or misapply the specific rights the Convention enumerates. The Preamble, citing the Charter of the United Nations, recognizes 'the inherent dignity and ... the equal and inalienable rights of all members of the human family'. It is an apt metaphor: if *children* do not belong to the human *family*, then no one does. But if they belong to it *as* children, and if this is what the UNCRC intends, we must remember of whom the Convention speaks. A child is not just a young human being. A child, according to the concept that informs the Convention, is someone at a certain stage in a human life. The rights of a child, therefore, are not simply human rights for the young; they are specifically rights for a child: for a child to *be* a child.

Without Peter, Wendy is not a child: she is a grown-up woman in the body of a little girl. And whereas Peter without Wendy could not conceivably exist, variations on the theme of Wendy are unhappily commonplace. Children, in all sorts of ways, in all kinds of circumstances, have adulthood thrust upon them before they have had the chance to be children. It would certainly be ironic if, in the name of their rights, children were denied the very thing to which they are most entitled. Thus, we must continually try to keep the child in view as we explore the rights of children laid down in such instruments as the UNCRC.

After the children return home, Wendy looks out the window and sees Peter playing a prank: he is 'hovering in the air, knocking off tall hats with his feet'. *Wendy* sees him, but the grown-up victims of his playfulness do not; they are 'too old'. 'You can't see Peter if you are old.' Uniquely, it seems, Wendy, the grown woman, now mother of Jane, can. Perhaps this is because, despite her maturity, Wendy wishes she could fly back to the Neverland with him: ' "If only I could go with you", Wendy sighed.' Once upon a time, something within her drove her towards growing up. Now the inner voice is different: 'Something inside her was crying, "Woman, woman, let go of me." ' [66]

Don't let go of him, Wendy. Wendy, don't let go. If once you let Peter give you the slip then you might as well balance your accounts and write your will and be done with it. We live in hope – don't you remember hearing the grown-ups say this when you were young? But what did they know of hope? Hope is the spirit of youth, spurring us on. And the spirit of youth – you know this better than anyone – is Pan the prankster. He is youth, he is joy: you heard him say so yourself when he played havoc with Hook, keeping the fight – the game – alive, living to fight another day; and another and another, for ever and ever amen. That, funnily enough, is what 'never' means in Pan-speak: never ending. The essence of Pan is never-ending. So, don't let him slip through your fingers, not as long as you have the breath to utter, 'If only I could go with you.' If only we, we normal adult humans, wherever we live on the mainland, whether Hackney or Chicago, Timbuktu or Tel Aviv, Harrow-on-the-Hill or Jerusalem: if only we could go with you too. And, as I type these names, casting my mind back across the places and spaces of this book, I find myself craning my neck to see beyond the text, facing forwards, facing east. A childish phrase enters my head and I feel like saying, softly, along with the woman Wendy: 'Next year in Neverland'.

L'shonoh habo'oh!

NOTES

1. This chapter is adapted from 'Wendy and Peter Pan: Exploring the Concept of the Child', in Kathleen Alaimo and Brian Klug (eds), *Children as Equals: Exploring the Rights of the Child* (Lanham, MD: University Press of America, 2002). The final paragraph has been rewritten with the present book in mind. An appendix to *Children as Equals* contains the full text of the 1989 United Nations Convention on the Rights of the Child (UNCRC), from which I quote below.

2. J.M. Barrie, *Peter Pan*, in his *Peter Pan and Other Plays* (Oxford: Oxford University Press, 1995), edited by Peter Hollindale, p.131 (Act 4, Scene 1). The play *Peter Pan* was first performed (in London) in 1904. It underwent several revisions, and was not published until 1928. On 22 February 1908, a new scene was added near the end of the play. This scene, which was not performed again in Barrie's lifetime (he died in 1937), was first published in 1957 as *When Wendy Grew Up: An Afterthought*. It corresponds closely to the final chapter – also called 'When Wendy Grew Up' – of the novel. The novel was published in 1911 under the title *Peter and Wendy* (see note 9). In the 1921 edition, the title was expanded to *Peter Pan and Wendy*. In more recent editions, the title has been contracted to *Peter Pan*. In this chapter, I draw upon all three sources: the play as published, the added scene as published, and the novel. For the purposes of the discussion, I treat the added scene as part of the play (though I cite it separately). I quote from Barrie's ample stage directions without distinguishing them from the script, treating them as integral to the work. For the lost boys, see note 35.

3. René Descartes, *Discourse on Method*, in his *Discourse on Method and Meditations on First Philosophy* (Indianapolis, IN: Hackett, 1993), p.8. The *Discourse* was published in 1637. Part 4 contains his famous first principle, 'I think, therefore I am' (p.19). The (implicit) foundation of Peter Pan's metaphysics is slightly different: 'I pretend, therefore it is.'

4. Hence the expression 'grown-up' as a synonym for 'adult'. The word 'adult' seems to contain within itself the germ of this concept. The word derives from the Latin *adultus*, the past participle of *adolescere*, to grow up. *Adolescens* is the present participle. It is as if 'adults' have accomplished what 'adolescents' are still in the process of doing.

5. The 'development' of the child is mentioned twice in the Preamble. It comes up again in Article 7, and recurs in several later articles, where it is sometimes analysed; e.g. Article 27 specifies 'physical, mental, spiritual, moral and social development'. The notion of 'the evolving capacities of the child' is introduced in Article 5. Note also the importance attached to *preparing* the child for later life; according to Article 29, one of the aims of education is to prepare the child 'for responsible life in a free society'.

6. Perhaps it is even broader than that. The Preamble to the United Nations Declaration of the Rights of the Child (1959) notes that the child needs special safeguards and care 'before as well as after birth': see P.R. Ghandhi (ed.), *Blackstone's International Human Rights Documents* (London: Blackstone Press, 2000), p.51. This phrase is cited in the Preamble to the UNCRC. At the other end of the spectrum, adolescence shades into adulthood; it does not end at midnight when a person turns 18. The discussion in this chapter does not apply straightforwardly, if at all, to the concept at its margins – at either end of the spectrum. It concerns the broad middle range. As for 'second childhood', that is, of course, a different idea altogether: it is derivative from the concept under discussion in this chapter, rather than being part of it. The UNCRC is not a charter for the senile.

7. Anna Davin, 'What is a Child?', in Anthony Fletcher and Stephen Hussey (eds), *Childhood in Question: Children, Parents and the State* (Manchester: Manchester University Press, 1999), p.33.

8. The phrase 'end in itself' is borrowed from Kant's moral philosophy. However, I am not suggesting for one moment that Kant himself sees childhood as an end in itself.

9. J.M. Barrie, *Peter and Wendy*, in his *Peter Pan in Kensington Gardens and Peter and Wendy* (Oxford: Oxford University Press, 1999), edited by Peter Hollindale, pp.89–90.

10. Barrie's emphasis is reflected in the title of his novel, *Peter and Wendy*. Their closeness is underscored from the start. Wendy's mind is 'scrawled all over' with Peter, even before she has met him, whereas he is only 'here and there' in the minds of her brothers, John and Michael. When her mother asks her about Peter, she says confidently 'he is just my size'. The narrator tells us, 'She meant that he was her size in both mind and body; she didn't know how she knew it, she just knew it' (*Peter and Wendy*, pp.74, 75).

11. See note 2.

12. This is the subtitle of the play *Peter Pan*.

13. *Peter and Wendy*, p.69. This is the opening sentence of the novel.

14. '"I don't want to go to school and learn solemn things", he told her passionately' (ibid., p.217).

15. *Peter Pan*, p.98 (Act 1, Scene 1); *Peter and Wendy*, pp.90, 148, 96, 226. See also *Peter Pan*, p.153 (Act 5, Scene 2).
16. *Peter and Wendy*, p.92. I do not mean that Peter represents what it *means* to be a boy, as if, for example, every boy wants to kill a pirate. Nor, for that matter, do I mean to imply that no girl ever harbours this hope. The story reflects the Edwardian era in which it was written, including ideas about children and gender that were current at the time. But this is beside the point. The point here is simply that these elements in Peter's personality are consistent with his being a real boy, albeit a boy of a certain sort. Likewise, I do not mean that every child wants to remain a child, nor that this is something that a given child wants always. All I mean is that such a wish is characteristic of children, and the sort of wish a real child might express. It is also characteristic of children to want to play at being grown up. Peter is a typical child in this respect too.
17. James Barrie was 6 years old when his 13-year-old brother David died. According to Hollindale, 'David's death was undoubtedly the origin of Peter Pan' (Introduction to *Peter Pan*, p.xxiii). The death of a child also lies in the background of Wendy, whose name Barrie coined, adapting it from the sobriquet given him by Margaret Henley, who died at the age of 5. 'She had tried to say James was her friend, but it came out "fwend" and then "fwendy" in her infant pronunciation. James made the change from fwendy to Wendy, and he had the name he wanted for his heroine.' Susan Bivin Aller, *J.M. Barrie: The Magic Behind Peter Pan* (Minneapolis, MN: Lerner Publications, 1994), pp.81–2. This adds poignancy to the final event in the narrative: Peter Pan flies off to the Neverland with a little girl named Margaret, daughter of Jane, daughter of Wendy, so she can be his mother (*Peter and Wendy*, p.226). 'Margaret' was also Barrie's mother's name.
18. *Peter and Wendy*, p.90; *Peter Pan*, p.99 (Act 1, Scene 1); *Peter and Wendy*, pp.128, 167, 170.
19. I am speaking of a world prior to the advent of cloning, test tubes, and incubators.
20. Here I am cheating slightly, but even so. That Peter does not have birthdays is implied by the fact that he does not age at all. But I am also thinking of Peter Pan in an earlier incarnation. In *Peter Pan in Kensington Gardens* (1906), we are told, 'Peter is ever so old, but he is really always the same age, so that does not matter in the least. His age is one week, and though he was born so long ago *he has never had a birthday*, nor is there the slightest chance of his ever having one' (emphasis added) (*Peter Pan in Kensington Gardens*, in *Peter Pan in Kensington Gardens and Peter and Wendy*, p.12.). This children's book consists of six chapters previously published as part of *The Little White Bird* (1902), which was thus the first published text containing a character called Peter Pan. The story is quite different, and there is no Wendy, but there are strong family resemblances between the earlier and later versions of Peter. The earlier Peter, however, seems to be a younger child than the later one. The earlier one is recalled when 'our' Peter (the one who knows Wendy) says that when he left home, he 'ran away to Kensington Gardens and lived a long time among the fairies' (*Peter and Wendy*, p.92). Moreover, several elements in the earlier story are imported into the later, including the tale about Peter returning home and finding another boy in his stead, with the window to his room barred. According to the map at the Marlborough Gate entrance of Kensington Gardens, London, the famous Peter Pan statue sculpted by Sir George Frampton is 'taken largely' from *The Little White Bird*. However, we could just as easily be looking at 'our' Peter as we gaze at the juvenile piper standing astride a tree trunk swarming with life, both animal and fairy, while a Wendy-like figure clambers over the top, apparently attempting to join him. A small metal plaque on the ground in front of this tableau says, 'Children: Please do not climb on this beautiful statue – you will harm it.' As I stood there and read the inscription, I wondered, 'What would Peter do if he were in my shoes now?'
21. *Peter Pan*, p.99 (Act 1, Scene 1).
22. 'I don't want to be a man. O Wendy's mother, if I was to wake up and feel there was a beard!'. *Peter and Wendy*, p.217.
23. Ibid., p.77. He also retains his 'first laugh' (p.94).
24. Ibid., pp.220, 223.
25. *When Wendy Grew Up*, in *Peter Pan and Other Plays*, pp.161, 159 (Act 1, Scene 1). Peter not only telescopes the past into a single day, 'yesterday', he is also exceedingly forgetful. For example, within a year, much to Wendy's dismay, he completely forgets their adventures in the Neverland. ' "Who is Captain Hook?" he asked with interest when she spoke of the arch enemy' (*Peter and Wendy*, p.219). Peter's forgetfulness goes hand in hand with his not growing up: he has neither future nor past.

26. *Peter Pan*, p.145 (Act 5, Scene 1). 'I'm a little bird that has broken out of the egg.' This harks back to the earlier Peter Pan story (see note 20), in which babies are said to be birds before they are born as human beings. Peter himself was initially a bird. After he flies the coop (his parents' home) at the age of one week, he ends up on the island that comes to be known by his name (which is where all the birds that turn into boys and girls are hatched). The wise old Solomon Caw tells Peter that henceforth he is 'a Betwixt-and-Between', meaning that he is part human, part bird (*Peter Pan in Kensington Gardens*, pp.10, 13, 14, 17). He retains his kinship with birds in the later story. When he re-enters the Darling house to bar the window against Wendy's return, he 'flutters about the room joyously like a bird'. Just before the curtain falls at the end of the play, 'the Never birds and the fairies gather closer' (*Peter and Wendy*, pp.149, 154 (Act 5, Scene 2). See also *Peter and Wendy*, p.139: 'Or suppose we tell of the birds that were Peter's friends'.

27. *Peter and Wendy*, pp.77, 214; *Peter Pan*, p.125 (Act 3, Scene 1); pp.136–7 (Act 4, Scene 1). See also p.118, where he warns Wendy against the mermaids: 'They are such cruel creatures, Wendy, that they try to pull boys and girls *like you* into the water and drown them' (emphasis added). The next stage direction says that Wendy is 'too guarded by this time to ask what he means precisely by "like you", though she is very desirous of knowing.' By 'like you', I take him to mean 'of whom you are one' rather than 'of your sort'. In other words, he is saying, 'They try to drown all boys and girls; so, you are at risk, and I am not.'

28. *Peter and Wendy*, p.185.

29. He is 'the tragic boy' (*Peter and Wendy*, p.224). Some will say that Peter's tragedy is that he is without a loving home. Others might say it is the fact that the world changes – that Wendy grows up and becomes a woman, and so on. I think these things are sad or painful, perhaps, but what is tragic is his exclusion from humankind. He stares in at the window 'at the one joy from which he must be for ever barred' (p.214): a human life.

30. *Peter Pan*, p.153 (Act 5, Scene 2).

31. He does not, however, appear to have a human body made of flesh and blood. He can float on air; he 'is no weight at all'; and, at least until Wendy does the cooking, all his meals are 'pretend'. Captain Hook gives the order, 'Cleave him to the brisket', but suspects he does not have one: *Peter and Wendy*, p.103; *Peter Pan*, p.124 (Act 3, Scene 1); p.127 (Act 4, Scene 1); p.144 (Act 5, Scene 1). He has a detachable shadow. He cannot be touched – except by fairies: *Peter Pan*, p.98 (Act 1, Scene 1); p.117 (Act 2, Scene 1). In short, to the extent that he is an individual being at all, Peter Pan is more spirit than matter, more elfin than human, less waif than will-o'-the wisp.

32. Wendy, in contrast to Peter, is a real human being. It would miss the point to object that since both are merely characters in a work of fiction she is no more real than he is. She is real, as are the other children in the story, in the sense that she is a *conceivable* person. (She is a real *possibility*.) Wendy is a real person in the 'world' of the story, just as Juliet is in Shakespeare's play or Anna Karenina in Tolstoy's novel. Peter is not. Not that he is not a real element in the story; of course he is. But he is not a real *person*. (How can I say this, when his personality is so vivid and his predicament so touching?)

33. *Peter and Wendy*, p.91.

34. Their houses are closely identified too. In the stage directions for the opening scene of Act 1, the family home is called 'the Darling house'. When Wendy wakes up in the house that Peter and the boys have made for her in the Neverland, she strokes it and calls it a 'darling house'. Moreover, the real house 'wanders about London looking for anybody in need of it, like the little house in the Never Land': *Peter Pan*, p.87 (Act 1, Scene 1); p.116 (Act 2, Scene 1).

35. *Peter and Wendy*, pp.131–2. The boys comprise Peter, the lost boys, and Wendy's brothers, John and Michael. The lost boys 'are the children who fall out of their prams when the nurse is looking the other way. If they are not claimed in seven days they are sent far away to the Never Land': *Peter Pan*, p.101 (Act 1, Scene 1). Their number varies from time to time. When the Darling children visit the Neverland, there are six. So, counting John and Michael, Wendy has eight children in her care. Peter, arguably, makes nine, but she prefers to think of him as the father of the household (*Peter and Wendy*, pp.160–1).

36. *Peter and Wendy*, pp.158, 159, 161, 164, 165.

37. Ibid., pp.157, 132–5, 170, 135, 97, 192, 71, 183. No doubt, the idea of womanhood represented by Wendy and her mother is very narrow; it is relative to a particular period, culture and class, and it is part of a larger script about gender that pervades the story. But all this is beside the point for the purposes of my argument in this essay. The point is that Mrs Darling embodies a version of what it means to be an adult, and that in Wendy the emphasis

falls on the future adult. A whole essay could be written about Wendy and Peter based on their different gender roles. This would be to view the story through the lens of a different topic. I write what I see through mine. (See also note 16.)

38. *Peter and Wendy*, p.151.
39. That Tinker Bell is physically mature is made clear by the description of her attire when she accompanies Peter Pan on his quest to retrieve his shadow: she is 'exquisitely gowned in a skeleton leaf, cut low and square, through which her figure could be seen to the best advantage' (*Peter and Wendy*, p.88). She wears a negligee, not a child's robe or nightgown (p.169). She is, incidentally, 'slightly inclined to *embonpoint*' or plumpness, unlike the fairy with the hourglass figure in Walt Disney's animated film (p.88).
40. *Peter and Wendy*, pp.162, 111.
41. *Peter Pan*, p.130 (Act 4, Scene 1). See also p.135.
42. *Peter and Wendy*, p.220.
43. In his Explanatory Notes, Hollindale says it is the Neverland in the novel, the Never Land in the play as published, and the Never Never Land in the play as performed (*Peter and Wendy*, p.232; *Peter Pan*, p.311). It is also the Never Never Land in the published text of *When Wendy Grew Up*. Hollindale mentions that in the first draft of the play it was the Never, Never, Never Land. But never mind whether there is a 'never' more or less, for it is the same non-existent place nevertheless.
44. *Peter Pan*, p.98 (Act 1, Scene 1). In the novel, the narrator, noting that these directions are useless, offers a disarming explanation for why Peter gives them: 'Peter, you see, just said anything that came into his head' (*Peter and Wendy*, p.102).
45. Thomas More, *Utopia*, 1516. The name 'Utopia' combines the two Greek words *ou* and *topos*, 'no' and 'place'. In pointing out this parallel, I am not offering an explanation for why Barrie called the island the Neverland (or the Never Land or the Never Never Land: see note 43). In his Explanatory Notes, Hollindale says, 'there was an actual district in Australia called the Never, Never, Land' (*Peter and Wendy*, p.232). Perhaps this suggested the name to Barrie. In any event, my speculations linking the Neverland and Utopia are strictly interpretive and not in the least historical. I certainly see no reason whatsoever to mention, even in passing, that More's work is prefaced by a letter addressed to a certain 'Peter' (Peter Giles).
46. By 'paradise' I do not mean to imply perfect bliss, but more like perfect fit: corresponding to a child's idea of an ideal form of life. I do not mean that the Neverland is *every* child's idea of paradise, only that being a child's paradise is, so to speak, the *principle* of the island. The specifics, as with other aspects of the story, belong to the author (though I do not think they are entirely idiosyncratic) and his period (though by no means are they all passé). (See also note 16.)
47. *Peter and Wendy*, p.136; *Peter Pan*, pp.105–6 (Act 2, Scene 1); *Peter and Wendy*, p.132; *Peter Pan*, p.105 (Act 2, Scene 1).
48. *Peter and Wendy*, pp.221, 105, 74, 77.
49. Ibid., p.98; *Peter Pan*, p.90 (Act 1, Scene 1). Trying to tackle the metaphysics of the Neverland is tricky. Even trickier is trying to work out the precise relationship between the island, the mainland, and the grown-up world. The latter two are not, I think, quite identical; but I tend to slip into treating them as if they were, and this will have to do.
50. Or a land you lose: 'We too have been there; we can still hear the sound of the surf, though we shall land no more' (*Peter and Wendy*, p.74).
51. Ibid., p.110.
52. All except Peter, for whom 'make-believe and true were exactly the same thing' (ibid., p.128. See also p.135). They *would* be, since the distinction does not apply to him: he is neither one nor the other. It is tempting to think that, if not real, he must be pretend. But that is a misconception. It is more accurate to say that we must pretend to pretend that he exists. Even more accurately, I can no longer tell whether I am saying something intelligible or just pretending to do so – such is the spell cast by Peter Pan.
53. Again, except for Peter: 'Make-believe was so real to him that during a meal of it you could see him getting rounder' (ibid., p.135).
54. Ibid., pp.130–1; *Peter Pan*, pp.115–16 (Act 2, Scene 1).
55. The allusion is to Ariel's song: 'Full fathom five thy father lies; / Of his bones are coral made; / Those are pearls that were his eyes; / Nothing of him that doth fade / But doth suffer a sea-change / Into something rich and strange' (*The Tempest*, Act I, Scene 2). It does not seem wrong to hear echoes of this song – nor of Prospero's magical island and 'brave new world' – when speaking of the Neverland. Moreover, the aerial Peter has several of Ariel's attributes. (He has some of Prospero's too, as will soon emerge.)

56. *Peter and Wendy*, p.105. Young children often have to stretch their bodies and crane their necks when they want to see something novel and interesting; hence the description of the children standing 'on tiptoe in the air' when in fact they have a clear view of the island beneath them. Flamingos are given to standing on one leg, the other leg being withdrawn into their bodies; hence Michael's flamingo with the broken leg. These descriptions illustrate Barrie's ability to subtly convey a child's-eye view of things.

57. Ibid., p.112; *Peter Pan*, p.105 (Act 2, Scene 1); *Peter and Wendy*, p.202. As Hook discerns, Peter is Pan. Pan was a Greek god of woods and pastures, player of pipes and practical jokes, playmate of nymphs, son of Hermes – the fleet-footed winged god and travellers' guide. The traces of Peter's pedigree are everywhere in the story. He is Peter Pan, son of Pan, grandson of Hermes.

58. *Peter and Wendy*, pp.93, 97, 112.

59. Note that the lost boys also return to the mainland, where they are adopted by Mr and Mrs Darling, and, like Wendy, John and Michael, grow up, turning into respectable citizens and losing their ability to fly. Tootles becomes a judge, Slightly becomes a lord (ibid., pp.215–16, 220). Only Peter remains on the Neverland, together with his cast of characters.

60. Ibid., p.218.

61. This line of reasoning might make it seem as if Wendy 'risks all' for children everywhere, not just for herself; for surely, *all* children stand to lose their childhood if Peter is no longer Pan. However, Neverland logic does not necessarily work along straight lines. So far, I have been speaking of the Neverland in the singular, as a unique island or world. This is how the story, for the most part, has it too. But initially, the novel refers to 'the Neverlands' in the plural: 'Of course the Neverlands vary a good deal' (ibid., p.74). The text indicates that there is a different Neverland for every child; 'but on the whole the Neverlands have a family resemblance'. You would think, however, that the Neverlands must do more than *resemble* each other; they must be one and the same island. If there is more than one, which is the home of Peter Pan? Or does each have its own Peter Pan? Assuming the Darling children fly to the same island, whose Neverland is it and which Peter takes them there? How could *all* the children recognize the island when they see it for the first time? And, stranger still perhaps, how could each of them pick out features from *each other's* Neverland (ibid., pp.105–6)? The obvious solution to these conundrums is this: There is just one Neverland and it has a family resemblance to itself. This solution to the quantitative problem affords a basis for arguing that Wendy 'risks all' for herself only, not for the children of the world. Using Neverland logic, we can reason as follows: If Wendy were to win Peter's hand, Peter would no longer be Pan; if Peter were no longer Pan, the Neverland would cease to exist; but the Neverland resembles itself; therefore, it itself would continue to exist; but it itself cannot exist unless Peter is Pan; therefore, Peter would continue to be Pan, and children would continue to be children. QED.

62. Ibid., pp.70–1, 99.

63. Keeping the image in mind is not enough; we have to apply it in a given case. This – the application of the double-sided concept of the child – is problematic and will vary from case to case according to such variables as the age and maturity of the child, the circumstances, and so on. This chapter does not aim to provide any help with applying the image; it only aims to provide the image.

64. Jane Rubenstein (in conversation) has emphasized to me the second of these two points – that Peter would keep Wendy from *ever* growing up; hence her need to leave the Neverland eventually. This sheds light, I think, on the fact that she is resolved to return to the mainland, in defiance of Peter's will, and that her resolve prevails (ibid., pp.167–71).

65. The Preamble to the UNCRC does, however, note that according to the United Nations Universal Declaration of Human Rights (1948), 'childhood is entitled to special care and attention'. The United Nations Declaration of the Rights of the Child (1959) goes further in proclaiming 'a happy childhood' as part of the 'end' which its provisions serve (Ghandhi, *Blackstone's*, p.51).

66. *Peter Pan*, p.151 (Act 5, Scene 2); *Peter and Wendy*, pp.225, 223.

Epilogue:
Being Jewish and Doing Justice
(Or, The Blast of the Shofar)

Revised version of a lecture given at the symposium 'Higher roads to Peace', Carbondale, Illinois, Pesach 2010.

'To accept the Torah is to accept the norms of a universal justice'.
(Emmanuel Levinas, *Nine Talmudic Readings*)

The subject of this symposium – 'higher roads to peace' for Arabs and Jews – is of great public interest. It is also of deep personal moment to me. For, as someone who is Jewish, I find myself situated on the inside of the subject. Were this not the case, I am not sure that I would have anything to say about it; or, if I did, it would not be the lecture I am about to give.[1]

If there is animosity between Arabs and Jews today, it is largely on account of a single issue: the Israeli–Palestinian conflict, the roots of which go back over a hundred years. What does it mean, in the context of this conflict, to speak of peace? There are those on either side who seek to thrust peace down the throat of the other side. On this view, peace is a cessation of hostilities that results from crushing the will of the enemy. I am not sure that this option, if available at all to either party, is equally available to both. For the conflict today is primarily between the State of Israel and the stateless Palestinians who live in the territories occupied by Israel since the end of the 1967 June War; and between a state and the stateless, between occupier and occupied, there is no equal contest.[2] Be that as it may, a peace in which the will of one side has been crushed by the other is like the peace of the dead. It is not, I take it, the kind of peace that is the subject of this symposium. No higher road can lead there.

The kind of peace to which a higher road can lead is not an external place that could be reached by some other route. It is something internal to the road, a result that the road produces of itself. It is more like the yield of a harvest than a destination.

What kind of peace is joined to what road in this manner? On this question, a certain wise Palestinian from antiquity, Rabbi Shimon ben Gamliel, who died in the same year that the temple in Jerusalem was destroyed by the Romans (70 CE), has something to say that has a bearing: 'The world rests on three things: justice, truth and peace'.[3] Some time later, Rav Muna, commenting on this comment (as rabbis are wont to do), observed, 'The three are one, because if justice is done, truth has been effected and peace brought about'.[4] In other words, peace depends on justice, and justice on truth. Without truth no justice, without justice no peace.

It is no easy thing to follow this bearing. But if what we are looking for is a dignified way out of the current impasse and a higher path to the future for Palestinians and Israelis – a path that elevates those who travel it – then this is the direction to take. The question I wish to raise is this: At its heart, does Judaism itself – by which I mean the broad human tradition which bears this name and not the religion alone – point out this direction?[5]

There is a true story that my sister tells that provides a perspective on this question. Some years ago, Francesca worked for the London Borough of Hackney, which includes Stamford Hill, an area with a large population of strictly observant Orthodox and Ultra-Orthodox (Haredi) Jews. Hackney Council is controlled by the Labour Party – and probably has been since the creation of the world over 5,000 years ago. When my sister was an employee, one of the Labour councillors was a rabbi from Stamford Hill. One day, curious about his left-wing leanings, Francesca approached him with a question. 'Rabbi', she said, 'Tell me: Where do you get your socialism from?' 'From the Torah', came the instant reply. Then after a pause he added, 'Mind you, you can find almost anything you want in the Torah!'

Was he joking or was he serious? Like the challah over which a blessing is made on Shabbos and festivals, the rabbi's words should be taken with a pinch of salt. I can almost see the twinkle in his eye as he said 'almost'; the word is dripping with irony. But, as so often with rabbis his quip made a profound point. On the one hand, what you find in the Torah depends on what you bring to it. On the other hand, you cannot simply impose your will upon it. Reading the Torah is a matter of give and take: the text is a given but how we take it is down to us; ultimately, to each of us, even if we come together to form a denomination or a school of interpretation. Judaism is a configured space; it is an arena of argument, not a body of doctrine. No one speaks for Judaism – except for every Jew. And to the question that I have posed – whether Judaism points us in the direction of a higher road to peace – Jews give more than one answer.

One answer was given by rabbis in the Israel Defence Forces (IDF) during Operation Cast Lead, Israel's twenty-two day military offensive in the Gaza Strip in December 2008 and January 2009. The rabbis set out to educate Israeli soldiers. Their aim, in the words of Brigadier General Rabbi Avichai Rontzki, the chief army rabbi, was 'to fill them with yiddishkeit and a fighting spirit'. *Yiddishkeit* in this context means, roughly, Jewish values or a Jewish way of doing things. So, what values are Jewish according to Rabbi Rontzki? His office sent Israeli soldiers a publication entitled 'Daily Torah Studies for the soldier and the commander in Operation Cast Lead'. The text told them that there is 'a biblical ban on surrendering a single millimeter of it [the Land of Israel] to gentiles'. It went on to avow, 'We will not abandon it to the hands of another nation, not a finger, not a nail of it.' Since 'it' includes the West Bank and the Gaza Strip, there is not much respect here for Palestinian rights. Regarding appropriate conduct in the field, the IDF rabbinate cautioned soldiers thus: 'When you show mercy to a cruel enemy, you are being cruel to pure and honest soldiers. This is terribly immoral.'[6]

Some religious groups went even further. One flyer, attributed to 'the pupils of Rabbi Yitzchak Ginsburg', called on Israeli soldiers 'to spare your lives and the lives of your friends and not to show concern for a population that surrounds us and harms us'. In case the point needed clarifying, the flyer added: 'As for the population, it is not innocent.'[7] So much for the distinction in international humanitarian law between combatant and civilian!

Judged by the standards set by *these* religious authorities, the IDF acquitted itself rather well. A joint report by Physicians for Human Rights–Israel and the Palestinian Medical Relief Society said: 'The underlying meaning of the attack on the Gaza Strip, or at least its final consequence, appears to be one of creating terror without mercy to anyone.'[8] 'Terror without mercy' seems not a million miles away from the morality that Rabbi Rontzki and others uphold. This casts a new light on something that Defence Minister Ehud Barak said in March 2009: 'I have no doubt in my heart that the IDF is the most moral army in the world.'[9] Well, if 'moral' means what the IDF rabbinate says it means, he might have a point.

However, if Barak had taken his moral cue from Rabbis for Human Rights, his verdict on the IDF might have been different. The group, which was founded in 1988, is 'the only Israeli rabbinical organization comprised of Reform, Orthodox, Conservative, Reconstructionist and Renewal rabbis and students'. It calls itself 'the rabbinic voice of conscience in Israel'.[10] It describes itself as Zionist; but its idea of appropriate conduct is rather different from that of the IDF rabbinate.[11] Rabbi Arik Ascherman, the executive director, 'has been at the forefront of resistance to the construction of what Israel calls its "security barrier" penning in and carving up West Bank villages'; he has held up the destruction of 'illegally built Arab homes in East Jerusalem by standing in front of the bulldozers'; and he 'has spent years planting himself atop doomed Palestinian homes, reading extracts of international law to Israeli forces as they demolish the buildings beneath his feet'.[12]

The name of Rabbi Ascherman's group is apposite, for when I speak of justice in this lecture I mean a dispensation in which human rights – basic rights that accrue to each and every one of us purely and simply in virtue of being human – are a fundamental element. For many of us who are Jewish, whether secular or religious or neither (or not-exactly-either), the connection between our Jewish identity and human rights runs deep.[13] There are, broadly, two reasons for this. Partly, it is a matter of collective experience and collective memory. The Universal Declaration of Human Rights (UDHR), adopted by the General Assembly of the United Nations on 10 December 1948, was not created in a void. The nations of the world were recoiling from the horrors of the Second World War, as the Preamble indicates when it notes that 'disregard and contempt for human rights have resulted in barbarous acts which have outraged the conscience of mankind'.[14] Barbarous acts were committed on all sides. But this clause alludes, above all, to the Nazi Holocaust. Along with others, six million Jews – two-thirds of the Jewish population of Europe – were murdered by the Nazi German state. Deprived of their liberty, robbed of their belongings, pressed into forced labour, Jews lost every right that makes life worth living before losing the right to life itself. All this took place within living memory – if not our own then that of our parents or grandparents.

War is full of horrors. But what made the Nazi Holocaust especially horrifying is that it went beyond warfare. The so-called Final Solution of the so-called Jewish Question was not a move in a wider military strategy, a means to the end of victory over the Allies; it was an end in itself. At the core of the 'barbarous acts' committed by the Nazis against the Jews was the doctrine of *lebensunwertes Leben*, 'life unworthy of living'. The same is true of the murderous Nazi campaigns against the Roma and Sinti ('Gypsies'), disabled, homosexuals and certain other groups. The aim in each case was to wipe out people who, according to Hitler, belong to groups that are so inherently contemptible that they deserve to die.

The repugnance felt at this Nazi doctrine lies at the heart of the UDHR. The preamble opens with words that repudiate it utterly: 'Recognition of the inherent dignity and of the equal and inalienable rights of all members of the human family is the foundation of freedom, justice and peace in the world'. The inherent dignity of all: this axiom is the antithesis of the Nazi doctrine of the inherent contemptibility of some. And since the idea of inherent dignity is fleshed out in the language of human rights, this language has a special resonance for those groups, such as Jews, who were targeted by the Nazi doctrine.

Furthermore, while the calamity (Shoah) of the Nazi period was on an unprecedented scale, Jews, especially in Europe, were for centuries a vulnerable minority who did not enjoy equal status with non-Jews (or specifically Christians) and were frequently subject to oppression, exclusion and persecution. This collective experience has been handed down, from one generation to the next, in collective memory; which, to repeat, is one reason why many of us, as Jews, feel a commitment to human rights.

The other reason – the second part of the answer – goes deeper, in a way, into our Jewish identity: it is not just a reaction to the treatment meted out by others or by fate. For, when the language of human rights is spoken, many of us hear the voices of those Hebrew prophets, rabbis and other Jewish figures down the centuries for whom Judaism means nothing if it does not mean social justice and, in particular, protecting those who are vulnerable. We think, for example, of the reiterated concern for 'the stranger, the orphan and the widow' (Deut. 14:29 and passim) and of Amos denouncing 'those who devour the needy, annihilating the poor of the land' (Am. 8:4). We recall the passage in the Mishna that says that 'Adam was created alone to teach you that if anyone destroys one life, Scripture reckons it as if he had destroyed a whole world.'[15] The strength of this admonition reminds us of the right to life.

But are we being anachronistic? Are we reading a modern concept – human rights – into the thought of another era when the concept did not exist? This is a complex question, but the answer, on the whole, is: no, we are not. Let us look briefly at both sides of the argument.

On the one hand, it could be argued that when the Torah enjoins us, say, to care for 'the stranger, the orphan and the widow' it is saying that we have a responsibility for their wellbeing, rather than saying that they have a right to our care, let alone a *human* right in the modern sense. Michael Berger and Deborah Lipstadt maintain that there is 'a fundamental theoretical difference between Jewish law and modern notions of human rights'.[16] And the Jewish political theorist Milton Konvitz observes, 'There is no word or phrase for "human rights" in the Hebrew scriptures or in other ancient Jewish texts.'[17]

On the other hand, as Konvitz goes on to say, the absence of the word or phrase does not necessarily mean that 'the ideas and values' that we associate with human rights in the modern sense did not exist; he thinks they *did* exist.[18] Perhaps the committee of Jewish scholars who translated the *Tanakh* for the Jewish Publication Society, published in 1985, agreed with him. For, if you consult their widely-respected translation, you will find that Deuteronomy says as follows: 'You shall not subvert the *rights* of the stranger or the fatherless'; 'Cursed be he who subverts the *rights* of the stranger, the fatherless, and the widow' (Deut. 24:17; 27:19). Similarly, Isaiah says, 'Uphold the *rights* of the orphan' (Is. 1:17). And when Jeremiah rebukes King Shallum (Jehoahaz), he contrasts him with his father Josiah who 'upheld the *rights* of the poor and needy' (Jer. 22:16).[19] I assume that the translators chose the word 'rights' because they wanted to find a contemporary idiom that would convey 'the ideas and values' expressed in the Hebrew text.

Besides, what exactly *are* human rights in the modern sense? Berger and Lipstadt follow a well-established path when they go back to the Enlightenment for what they call the 'philosophical basis of modern human rights'.[20] Roughly, they think that this basis lies in the view that each of us (or each adult human being) is an autonomous individual who, in seeking his or her own interest, comes into conflict with other individuals. Our human rights, on this basis, are the claims that each of us is entitled to make – against each other and the state – in order to promote our own interest and protect our own individual liberty.

This might be the basis for the concept of human rights in the American Declaration of Independence or the American Bill of Rights. But is it the basis for the UDHR (which is the source for subsequent human rights declarations, conventions and covenants)? Is this the view of human beings and the vision of human life that it contains? It is not. Recall the opening of the preamble, which refers to 'all members of the human family'. In the same vein, Article 1 says that all human beings 'should act towards one another in a spirit of brotherhood'. The sense of this is that we ought to matter *to each other* and not only to ourselves. The implication of Article 1 is that this is a principle that is as fundamental as the principle of equality (that no one matters less than anyone else). Similarly, as Norman Solomon points out, Rabbi Akiva, nearly two thousand years ago, 'reduced' the Torah to the biblical commandment that 'you shall love your neighbour as yourself' (Lev. 19:18).[21]

In short, the UDHR model of the human *family* is strikingly different from the model of universal *competition* that Berger and Lipstadt (rightly or wrongly) associate with the modern idea of human rights. (Arguably, it is closer to Kant's concept of a kingdom of ends, a rather different model that also goes back to the Enlightenment; but this is beside the point.) The 'spirit of brotherhood' that the UDHR invokes is closer to the spirit of *cooperation* or at least of mutual concern. Family means kinship; kinship suggests ties; ties imply that we are responsible for each other. (You could say that the 'R' in 'UDHR' stands for Responsibilities as well as Rights.) With this in mind, Francesca Klug, one of the prime movers behind the UK Human Rights Act of 1998 (and, yes, the sister who used to work for Hackney Council), has argued that the UDHR represents a 'second wave' of human rights, the emphasis shifting from *liberty* to *community*.[22] This shift has affected the whole sense of the language of human rights today.

Now, just as the UDHR begins with 'the human family', so does the human story in the opening chapter of Genesis. Eve and Adam are not just the *original* couple, they are the *originating* couple: they are *grandma* Eve and *grandpa* Adam, ancestors of us all. Thus, in both texts (the UDHR and Genesis), we are neither a mere collection of individuals, nor are we a set of essentially different kinds (as with any model based on a division of humankind into biological races). In both texts, *essentially* we are members of a single – universal – extended human family.

Furthermore, in the Genesis account, Adam and Eve are distinguished from all other beings that have the breath of life by a singular point concerning their creation: they are made *b'tzelem elohim*, in the image of God (Gen. 1:27). From this feature the rabbis in the Talmud derive the principle of *kevod habriyos* ('honour of the created') or *kevod haodom* (honour of humanity') or, in idiomatic English, human dignity. This inference assumes that the same quality imparted to Adam and Eve – the image of God – is passed on to all their descendants; that is to say, it is *inherited*. In other words, human dignity, according to the Talmud, is inherent – which is precisely what the UDHR asserts with its opening words and which grounds the whole of its system of universal human rights.

So, when I, along with many fellow Jews, hear ancient voices from Hebrew scripture and rabbinic literature in the modern language of human rights, are we wrong? I do not think so. This is not to say that the old ideas and values are *identical* with human rights in the modern sense; they are not. Nor is it to suggest that these are the only voices in the Jewish tradition. Certainly, they are not the loudest. Collectively, they seem to distil into a still, small voice, whose answer to the question that I posed – whether Judaism points us in the direction of a higher road to peace – is a simple 'Yes': yes, in a word, to justice, justice at the beating heart of Judaism.

And there's the rub. For the position with Judaism today is this: there are two suitors seeking to win its heart. One is the principle of unconditional support for Israel, the other is the principle of unconditional commitment to justice. Judaism cannot have both these principles at its heart, any more than the Israelites could have more than one God (or a God who is not one) and still retain the identity they acquired when, speaking in unison (for once and once only), they signed on the dotted line at Sinai to become 'the people of God' (Ex. 19:8, 24:3; Deut. 27:9).

So sharp is the clash between these two principles that there comes a point where the conversation over Israel breaks down and the arena of argument turns into a battlefield. At stake in this battle is the very idea of the Jewish people, of belonging to the House of Jacob, of being a Jew. Several years ago, when Israel carried out Operation Defensive Shield in the West Bank, someone close to me wrote as follows: 'I would go so far [*sic*] to say – speaking entirely for myself – that it is getting hard to hold on to any Jewish identity at all when it bears no relation whatsoever to the mindless nationalism one is forced to listen to from Jews round the world every day.' Though speaking for herself, her words spoke for many others who felt (as another friend put it at the time) 'the untenable position of being Jewish today'.[23] Similar feelings resurfaced last year during Operation Cast Lead in Gaza. One friend wondered out loud if she could 'resign' from being Jewish. She was not alone. In the same week, the rabbi of a large and prominent North London congregation devoted his weekly message to 'those who said to me, "I wish I could resign from being Jewish" '. He added, 'These were not people who come from the fringe but people with a sore heart.'[24]

The clash of principles vying for the heart of Judaism has become sharper with the passage of time. Never has it been sharper than at the time of writing. Operation Cast Lead, like a powerful earthquake, continues to produce aftershocks – not only on the ground in Gaza and the region but also in the Jewish world. One such aftershock was the Goldstone Report and its reception. The UN Fact Finding Mission on the Gaza Conflict, headed by Judge Richard Goldstone, published its report in September 2009. The mission investigated the conduct of the war in Gaza and concluded that 'actions amounting to war crimes and possibly, in some respects, crimes against humanity, were committed by the Israel Defense Forces (IDF)'.[25] It also found that the firing of mortars from Gaza into Israel 'would constitute war crimes and may amount to crimes against humanity'.[26] But this did not soften the blow for Israel in the report. Nor did it diminish the blows that rained down upon Goldstone's head for the crime of suggesting that a crime had been committed by Israel. Michael Oren, Israel's ambassador to the United States, said the report 'goes further than Ahmadinejad and the Holocaust deniers' and that 'it portrays the Jews ... as Nazis'.[27] Alan Dershowitz described the report as 'a defamation written by an evil, evil man' and called its author 'a traitor to the Jewish people'.[28] Testifying before the UN Human Rights Council in Geneva, Anne Bayefsky, a senior fellow of the Hudson Institute, compared the report with the notorious *Protocols of the Elders of Zion* and accused Goldstone of using his Jewishness 'to jeopardize the safety and security of the people of Israel'.[29]

That he is a member of the Board of Governors of the Hebrew University, Jerusalem (from whom he has received an honorary doctorate) and that he has spoken of his 'love for Israel': these are seen more as aggravating than mitigating factors by those who vilify Goldstone. Goldstone, for his part, told CNN that, as a Jew, he has 'an even bigger duty to investigate war crimes'. The author of *For Humanity: Reflections of a War Crimes Investigator* (2001) observed, 'I probed war crimes in other countries ... so why should Israel be different?'[30] Speaking precisely as a Jew, he was asserting the principle of unconditional commitment to justice as against the principle of unconditional support for Israel.

For this very reason – because he put justice first – others of us have spoken up in his defence, speaking out against the vilifiers.[31] There is a battle of voices within the Jewish world, which ultimately affects the outcome of the conflicts between Arabs and Jews, Israelis and Palestinians. For you cannot gain access to a higher road to peace by leaving your own identity behind, as though in order to reach the plane of the universal you must give up the place of the particular. And those who say they wish to *resign* from being Jewish, heard slightly differently (which is how I hear them), mean almost the opposite: what they want is to *re-sign*: to sign on again, to reclaim the deeds to the title 'Jewish' and to their joint tenancy in the House of Jacob.

The timing of this symposium is auspicious. It is taking place during the festival of Pesach, which, for Jews, is the festival of freedom – but not only for Jews, as the late Rabbi John Rayner, former President of Liberal Judaism in the UK, once remarked in his Passover sermon to his London congregation. He said, 'If the Exodus from Egypt is a liberation paradigm for *us*, it can also serve that purpose for other peoples, and it has done so. Almost every national liberation movement in Europe, America and Africa has invoked the Exodus, drawn inspiration from it, and used its slogans, as in the spiritual, "Let My people go".' Quoting the nineteenth-century German Romantic poet, he added: 'As Heinrich Heine famously said, "Since the Exodus, Freedom has always spoken with a Hebrew accent." ' But Rabbi Rayner was conscious of the irony of this remark in the circumstances of our times. Pointing out that the Palestinians 'are still awaiting their national liberation', he commented acidly: 'To their ears freedom speaks with anything *but* a Hebrew tongue.'[32]

In the end, the accent that matters is not the way we pronounce our words but where we place the emphasis when we speak. No Jew consulting the diversity of sources within the broad Jewish tradition, no rabbi delivering a sermon, can escape the necessity of deciding what to accentuate. And if you regard the text you are reading as authoritative, as many Jews see the Torah, then the burden of responsibility that falls on your shoulders is this: how to take what is given. So, in what direction does Judaism point? Here is the answer that Rabbi Elizabeth Tikvah Sarah gave last Tuesday (the first day of Pesach) to her Brighton congregation on the south coast of England. By a stroke of good fortune (which my grandmother would have called *b'sheht*, meaning it is not a stroke of good fortune at all but an act of divine providence), her sermon landed in my email inbox three days ago. Remembering that we were 'strangers in the land of Egypt', she points out, is what this festival is all about. 'But why? Why do we need to remember?' That is the question she poses and this, in a nutshell, is her answer: Once an oppressed group, such as the Jews, are no longer oppressed, but, on the contrary, in a position of dominating others, 'there is the danger of becoming forgetful'. Perhaps we could add the danger that is the other side of the same coin: remembering so narrowly that our memories are only for ourselves and our suffering. Calling to mind those ancient Hebrew voices that some of us hear when the language of human rights is spoken today, she places the emphasis, clearly and boldly, on a Judaism of justice:

So, what would Isaiah and Jeremiah and Micah and Amos be

saying to the government of Israel today? What would they say about the forty-two year occupation of the West Bank and the continuing domination of another people against their will? What would they say about house demolitions in East Jerusalem and the destruction of Palestinian neighbourhoods to make room for the ever-expanding Jewish settlements? Would they not call the government to account and rail against injustice?[33]

When Rabbi Arik Ascherman sits on the roofs of Palestinian homes in the teeth of the bulldozers sent in by the IDF, it is as if he were simultaneously protecting the House of Jacob from demolishing itself. And when Jews around the world speak out about Israel, condemning its breaches of human rights and denouncing policies that are inimical to peace, peace based on the principle of *kevod habriyos* and not on superiority of arms or the crushing weight of oppression, we are not turning *against* our Jewish identity: we are turning *towards* it. We are seeking to mend its breaking heart by affirming a Judaism of justice. Being Jewish, we are heeding the directive that Moses gave to *am Yisroel*, the people of Israel, who, standing at Sinai, suspended between the house of bondage and the Promised Land, heard the words pointing out a higher road to life, 'Justice, justice shall you pursue' (Deut. 16:20): words that resound down the centuries and, like the blast of the shofar, remind the people who they are.

NOTES

1. This Epilogue is adapted from the talk, 'Being Jewish, Doing Justice and the Israeli–Palestinian Conflict', given as the Wayne Leys Memorial Lecture at a symposium, 'Higher Roads to Peace: The Role of Ethics in Resolving Conflicts between Arabs and Jews', Southern Illinois University, Carbondale, Illinois, 5 April 2010. As with the Prologue, I have retained the original frame of the talk but made substantial alterations to the text.
2. I say 'primarily' because there is, as it were, a second front within Israel proper: the tense relations between Jewish and Palestinian citizens of the state.
3. Bab. Tal., *Avot* 1:18, in N. Solomon (ed.), *The Talmud: A Selection* (London: Penguin, 2009), p.555.
4. Tractate *Derech Eretz Zuta*, Perek Hashalom, 2, in A. Cohen (ed.), *The Minor Tractates of the Talmud*, vol. 2 (London: Soncino Press, 1971), pp.597–8.
5. On Judaism as not (just) the religion, see Chapter 7, and my book *Offence: The Jewish Case* (London: Seagull Books, 2009), Chapter 1.
6. Amos Harel, 'IDF Rabbinate Publication during Gaza War: We will show no mercy on the cruel', *Haaretz*, 26 January 2009, http://www.haaretz.com/hasen/spages/1058758.html.
7. Ibid.
8. Rory McCarthy, 'Israel Created "terror without mercy" in Gaza', *Guardian*, 7 April 2009, http://www.guardian.co.uk/world/2009/apr/07/israel-gaza-human-rights-report.
9. 'Barak: No doubt IDF is most moral army in the world', YNet, 25 March 2009. http://www.ynetnews.com/articles/0,7340,L-3692383,00.html.
10. See website of Rabbis for Human Rights: http://www.rhr.org.il/page.php?name=about&language=en.
11. 'Rabbis for Human Rights gives voice to a Jewish and Zionist tradition of concern for Human Rights', website of Rabbis for Human Rights: http://www.rhr.org.il/index.php?language=en.
12. Chris McGreal, 'The Rabbi who Pricks Israel's Conscience', *Guardian*, 25 March 2005,

http://www.guardian.co.uk/world/2005/mar/25/israel.

13. The next portion of the original lecture – on the reasons why human rights matter to many Jews as Jews – was adapted from the essay 'Jewish Identity and Human Rights', which appeared in Alan Brown and Mary Hayward (eds), *World Religions in Education, Vol. 27: Human Rights and Responsibilities*, published by the Shap Working Party on Education in Religion (London, 2006–07).

14. See the text of the UDHR. Available on the UN website: http://www.un.org/Overview/rights.html.

15. Bab. Tal., *Sanhedrin* 37a. In a footnote to the phrase 'one life', Solomon points out: 'The words "of Israel" appear in some copies, but manuscript evidence as well as the sense of the passage suggest that this is a very late interpolation.' Solomon (ed.), *The Talmud*, p.503.

16. Michael S. Berger and Deborah E. Lipstadt, 'Women in Judaism from the Perspective of Human Rights', in Michael J. Broyde and John Witte, Jr (eds), *Human Rights in Judaism* (Northvale, NJ: Jason Aronson, 1998), pp.80–1.

17. Milton R. Konvitz (ed.), *Judaism and Human Rights* (New Brunswick, NJ: Transaction Publishers, 2001), p.13.

18. Ibid.

19. Emphasis added in all cases.

20. Berger and Lipstadt, 'Women in Judaism', p.82. They think that the origins of the Enlightenment view can be traced back to the ancient Greek Sophists.

21. Solomon, *The Talmud*, p.522. There is a debate within rabbinical Judaism about who the word 'neighbour' applies to. Rabbi John Rayner discusses this in 'The Golden Rule' in his *Signposts to the Messianic Age* (London and Portland, OR: Vallentine Mitchell, 2006), pp.7–10. He argues that aside from 'technical legal considerations', the injunction in Leviticus 19:18 'was always understood in Judaism as applying to Jews and non-Jews alike' (p.9).

22. She believes a 'third wave' is now emerging which has to do with a change in the *place* of human rights in society, rather than a change in the *concept*. See Francesca Klug, *Values for A Godless Age: The Story of the United Kingdom's New Bill of Rights* (London: Penguin, 2000), Introduction, especially pp.9–12. I owe my present understanding of human rights to her work.

23. Private email correspondence, 16 April 2002 and 23 July 2002.

24. Rabbi Jonathan Wittenberg, New North London Synagogue, email to congregation, 16 January 2009.

25. 'UN Mission Finds Evidence of War Crimes by Both Sides in Gaza Conflict', UN News Centre, 15 September 2009 (based on a press briefing), http://www.un.org/apps/news/story.asp?NewsID=32057.

26. Ibid.

27. Michael Oren, 'Deep Denial, *New Republic*, 6 October 2009, http://www.tnr.com/article/world/deep-denial.

28. 'Dershowitz: Goldstone is a Traitor to the Jewish People', *Haaretz*, 7 February 2010, http://www.haaretz.com/hasen/spages/1146392.html.

29. Tovah Lazaroff, 'UN Report a 21st Century Blood Libel, Scholar Says in Geneva', *Jerusalem Post*, 30 September 2009, http://www.jpost.com/Home/Article.aspx?id=156240.

30. Biography of Richard Goldstone on website of the Constitutional Court of South Africa: http://www.constitutionalcourt.org.za/site/judges/justicerichardgoldstone/index1.html; 'Goldstone: As Jew, It's My Duty to Probe War Crimes', YNet News, 4 October 2009, http://www.ynetnews.com/articles/0,7340,L-3785344,00.html.

31. So, for example, under the headline 'British Jews do not speak with one voice', several UK Jewish groups placed a full-page advertisement in *The Times* – an open letter to Prime Minister Gordon Brown with over 500 signatures – condemning 'the vilification of Richard Goldstone' (1 December 2009).

32. Rayner, 'The Big Issue', *Signposts to the Messianic Age*, pp.60, 63. The sermon was given on the first day of Pesach, 8 April 2001. He went on to say that this is 'the big issue' [block capitals in the original] today. 'I believe that our relationship with the Palestinians is the greatest moral test we Jews have faced in modern times, and, to put it mildly, we have not acquitted ourselves well' (p.63).

33. Extract from Passover Sermon by Rabbi Elizabeth Tikvah Sarah, Brighton and Hove Progressive Synagogue, 30 March 2010 (typescript).

Glossary of Hebrew and Yiddish Terms

aleph	first letter in the *aleph bais* (Hebrew alphabet)
aliyah	ascent; immigrating as a Jew to the State of Israel
am hasefer	people of the book
am Yisroel	the people of Israel
apikoros	a non-believer or heretic
Ashkenazi	pertaining to Central and East European Jews
Bab. Tal.	Babylonian Talmud
bais	second letter in the *aleph bais* (Hebrew alphabet)
bar mitzvah	ceremony at which boys aged 13 are initiated into adulthood
behemoth	beast
bentsh	recite grace after meals
bimah	podium
bissel shikker	a little tipsy, drunk
broyges	offended
bubbe	grandmother
bubbemeises	lies, nonsense
challah	a loaf of plaited bread used for ceremonial purposes
chalutzim	pioneers
chamsin	hot wind in Israel from the Negev (the south)
chasan	groom
chaverim	friends
chazan	cantor
chochmoh	wisdom
chutzpah	cheek, audacity
davaning	praying
Dayan	judge (office)
derech eretz	courtesy

drashah	sermon
erev	eve
Eretz Yisroel	Land of Israel
frum	pious, devout, observant
Gan Aden	Garden of Eden
gimmel	third letter in the *aleph bais* (Hebrew alphabet)
goldene medina	America
Gush Emunim	'bloc of the faithful', religious group supporting Jewish settlements
Haggadah	book containing the service for the Passover meal
Halacha	religious law
Hamotzi	blessing over bread
Haredi	Ultra-Orthodox Judaism
Har HaZeitim	Mount of Olives
hora	a Jewish folk dance
Kaddish	a prayer (in Aramaic) recited by mourners
kallah	bride
kevod habriyos	honour (or dignity) of the created (specifically human beings)
kevod haodom	honour (or dignity) of humanity
kiddush	blessing over wine to sanctify the Sabbath or a festival
kinder	children
kipah	skullcap
Koheles	Ecclesiastes
kop	head
lockshen pudding	a dessert made with fine noodles, dried fruit and cream
l'shonoh habo'oh!	to next year!
madreigah	plane or level
matzo	unleavened bread
Megillah	lit. 'scroll'; 'the five Megillahs' are a group of books in the *Tanakh*
mensch	a worthy human being
Menschlichkeit	humanity
minyan	a quorum of ten required for a communal religious service
mishpochoh	(extended) family
Mishna	the core of the Talmud
mitzvah	commanded act, good deed
neshumah	soul

nudnik	an annoyingly obtuse person
Ostjuden	Jews from Eastern Europe
oyevim	enemies
Pesach	Passover
Protestrabbiner	Herzl's terms for the German rabbis who opposed him in 1897
rebbe	a rabbi regarded by someone as their special mentor or guide
Rosh	head, principal
schlep	a long and arduous trek
Seder	Passover meal
Sefer Torah	scroll containing the Five Books of Moses
Shabbos	Sabbath
Shavuoth	Pentecost
shechita	slaughter of animals for food in accordance with Halacha
shmata	rag
shochet	Jewish slaughterer qualified according to Halacha
shofar	ram's horn, blown at Rosh Hashanah (the New Year)
shrei	scream
shtetl (*stetl*)	mainly Jewish village or small town in Eastern Europe
shtiebel	room or small hall for prayer and study
shtum	silent
shul	synagogue (shulgoer: a person who regularly attends services)
siddur	prayer book
simcha	party, joyous occasion
tallis	prayer shawl
talmud chacham	a person versed in the Talmud, a distinguished scholar
talmudai chachamim	plural of *talmud chacham*
Tanakh	the bible or 'Old Testament'
tsuris	troubles
Tzion	Zion
vav	sixth letter in the *aleph bais* (Hebrew alphabet)
vi a loch in kop	like a hole in the head
Yiddishkeit	Jewishness, a way of life of Ashkenazi Jews
Yidl	Jew

Yom Ha'atzmaut	Israel's Independence Day
Yom Kippur	Day of Atonement
zemiros	hymns
zeyda	grandfather

Index